Multimedia and Megachange: New Roles for Educational Computing

Multimedia and Megachange: New Roles for Educational Computing

W. Michael Reed
John K. Burton
Min Liu
Editors

CRC Press
Taylor & Francis Group
Boca Raton London New York

CRC Press is an imprint of the
Taylor & Francis Group, an informa business

Multimedia and Megachange: New Roles for Educational Computing has also been published as *Computers in the Schools*, Volume 10, Numbers 1/2 and 3/4, 1994.

Reprinted 2009 by CRC Press

Library of Congress Cataloging-in-Publication Data

Multimedia and megachange : new roles for educational computing / W. Michael Reed, John K. Burton, Min Liu, editors.
p. cm.
"Has also been published as Computers in the schools, volume 10, numbers 1/2 and 3/4, 1994"–T.p. verso.
Includes bibliographical references.
ISBN 1-56024-693-6 (acid-free paper)
1. Computer-assisted instruction. 2. Interactive multimedia. I. Reed, W. Michael. II. Burton, John K. III. Liu, Min.
LB1028.5.M84 1994
371.3'34–dc20 94-40532
CIP

Multimedia and Megachange: New Roles for Educational Computing

Contents

ABOUT THE EDITORS

W. Michael Reed, PhD, is Professor of Instructional Computing and English Education at West Virginia University, where he also directs the College of Human Resources and Education Microcomputer Lab and heads up Master's and doctoral specializations in instructional technology. His primary research interests center on hypermedia environments, linear versus nonlinear pathways while using hypermedia environments, and the theoretical frameworks of hypermedia environments.

John K. Burton, PhD, is Professor of Educational Psychology and Instructional Technology at Virginia Tech, where he has been on the faculty since 1977. Over the past 5 years, he has published research focusing on the uses and underlying theory of hypermedia.

Min Liu, EdD, is Assistant Professor of Instructional Technology at the University of Texas at Austin. Her current research interests center on the impact of interactive multimedia and hypermedia technology on learning and higher-level thinking skills, the design and development of hypermedia environments, and the use of the technology in second language learning.

INTRODUCTION

D. LaMont Johnson

Multimedia and Megachange

Seymour Papert, in his latest book *The Children's Machine* (1993), speaks of megachange. He points out that megachange has occurred in nearly every field of human endeavor, with one notable exception–education. Papert's major premise is that megachange will also come to education as we move into the next century. He believes that technology will play a key role in bringing about and shaping this megachange.

Of all the technological developments that have come along in the past two decades, multimedia has the most promise for bringing about megachange in education. Most educational innovations over the past 50 years have involved little more than a flirting around the edges of what has become the traditional teaching and learning process. This traditional teaching and learning process is basically limited to three steps: (a) the teacher presents information, (b) the students attempt to absorb the information, and (c) the teacher tests the students to see how well they have absorbed the information. Information is nearly always presented in the same fashion in this traditional process. The information is presented either by lecture or by text, both of which, by their nature, are linear. When multimedia is used interactively, it has the potential to strike at the very heart of this traditional teaching and learning process. It has the potential to change the way we think about the whole process of teaching and learning. It has the potential to turn learning into a nonlinear process. John Hirschbuhl (1992) has provided a succinct insight into this potential:

[Haworth co-indexing entry note]: "Multimedia and Megachange." Johnson, D. LaMont. Co-published simultaneously in *Computers in the Schools* (The Haworth Press, Inc.) Vol. 10, No. 1/2, 1994, pp. 1-2; and: *Multimedia and Megachange: New Roles for Educational Computing* (eds: W. Michael Reed, John K. Burton, and Min Liu) The Haworth Press, Inc., 1994, pp. 1-2. Multiple copies of this article/chapter may be purchased from The Haworth Document Delivery Center [1-800-3-HAWORTH; 9:00 a.m. - 5:00 p.m. (EST)].

> Today we are using multimedia as a tool for helping learners master thinking skills for assimilating massive quantities of information. In order to make full use of technology, multimedia must be used as an engine to enable learners to transform information into knowledge by means of inquiry based on higher-order thinking. (p. 321)

The vision the interactive multimedia enthusiasts have of learners navigating their way through vast databases of text, sound, graphics, and video is exciting. While there is plenty of room for skepticism and while it is easy to point to the need to move slowly, this whole movement definitely suggests that technology may well provide us with the tools that can help us gain new insights into teaching and learning processes.

Multimedia has the potential to help us incorporate some of the educational innovations that have long been advocated but only sparsely assimilated into American education. Innovations such as active learning, critical thinking, and discovery learning are natural elements of a teaching and learning process that involves interactive multimedia.

Once we begin to change the way we think about the teaching and learning process, we will see megachange occur in education. Such change will result in spin-off changes such as classroom management, sources of information, evaluation, and grading. I, for one, am eager to see such change begin. I believe that this volume of *Computers in the Schools* will become a landmark publication on the topic of multimedia in education. The issues and trends described and analyzed in the many works included in this volume should set a research and development agenda for educators for the near future. It is my hope that when we look back and ask ourselves when megachange really began, we will note that the serious exploration of multimedia as a means of changing the teaching and learning process was an important shift in emphasis, and that the publication of this volume was a landmark event.

REFERENCES

Hirschbuhl, J. J. (1992). Multimedia: Why invest? *Interactive Learning International, 8*(4), 321-323.

Papert, S. (1993). *The children's machine: Rethinking school in the age of the computer.* New York: Basic Books.

THEORETICAL/CONCEPTUAL

David M. Moore

The Parable of the Expensive Ballpoint Pen (Revisited): Implications for Hypermedia

Several years ago when computers were rapidly being integrated into schools, a colleague sadly noted that many of the then present uses and functions of the computer and corresponding software could be done with a reliable ballpoint pen (Moore, Bedient, & Scholes, 1986). Indeed, the appearance of relegating the potential educational advantages of the computer to only drill-and-practice exercises associated with old teaching machines was of great concern to many innovative computer users. Since then, of course, computers and their applications have improved. Hypermedia has arrived, and my observant colleague's concerns about the use of computers in schools are no longer valid. Or are they?

The concept of hypermedia has been present in academic circles for a

DAVID M. MOORE is Professor of Education, Virginia Tech University, Blacksburg, VA 24061-0341.

[Haworth co-indexing entry note]: "The Parable of the Expensive Ballpoint Pen (Revisited): Implications for Hypermedia." Moore, David M. Co-published simultaneously in *Computers in the Schools* (The Haworth Press, Inc.) Vol. 10, No. 1/2, 1994, pp. 3-7; and: *Multimedia and Megachange: New Roles for Educational Computing* (eds: W. Michael Reed, John K. Burton, and Min Liu) The Haworth Press, Inc., 1994, pp. 3-7. Multiple copies of this article/chapter may be purchased from The Haworth Document Delivery Center [1-800-3-HAWORTH; 9:00 a.m. - 5:00 p.m. (EST)].

long time. For example, Bush (1945) discussed the concept immediately after World War II. The advance of the technology of current computers and their corresponding software has made this concept not only possible but practical.

The terms *hypertext* and *hypermedia* are interchangeable as used in many publications. Hypermedia is the prolongation of hypertext by means of technology. Marchionini (1988) defined hypertext as "the electronic representation of text that takes advantage of the random access capabilities of computers to overcome the strictly sequential medium of print on paper" (p. 8). Hypermedia (computers interacting with video, laser disc, etc.) extends the random access ability to include visual materials, sound, and graphics. There is also the added dimension of almost unlimited data available to the user with the addition of compact discs to the hypermedia mix.

Only a few years ago, in books and journal articles, we read almost daily how computers would change our life styles, our work and leisure habits, and, of course, our education and learning strategies. Today, we are bombarded with similar views and predictions concerning the potential of hypermedia.

Educators for years stressed the need for student-directed education in which learning would be enhanced over the teacher-directed instruction models (e.g., Merrill, 1975). The technology is now present for the student to easily interact with a varied and complex electronics environment. Many hypermedia users feel that with the various authoring languages available such as *Hypertalk,*™ students themselves can now develop their own effective learning environments. Computer companies, such as Apple, state in their promotional materials such things as "with *Hypercard* you can . . . collect, explore and organize information just as you do in your mind–by association . . . and a lot of people . . . the eager, and the innovative will now have a medium for sharing their knowledge, their findings, their particular thread of thought" (Apple Computer Inc., 1987, p. 2). The implications being, of course, by using this authoring package, knowledge can be organized in the appropriate manner in which people learn (Morariu, 1988). Learners can look and listen to material on a particular subject in a variety of "suggested traits . . . or they can create new pathways for themselves and others to follow by forging new links and even by extending the material . . . blurring the distinction between author, editor and reader" (Megarry, 1988). Trotter (1989) indicates that hypermedia employs a strategy that is advantageous to students in that (a) the learner is in charge and (b) the learner can use a variety of media to approach the subject. "Having choices and variety lessens the likelihood of boredom: and using a variety of media enhances learning, because text, graphics, and sound reinforce one another" (p. 35).

The potential of hypermedia noted above, is similar to the ideas mentioned in Papert's (1980) book *Mindstorms, children, computers and powerful ideas* in which he described the potential of students creating their own learning environments (by means of the microcomputer language LOGO). Papert described how students could truly become not only active participants but developers of their own instruction. Papert (1980) stressed that it is possible to design computer programs in which "children can learn to use computers in a masterful way, and that learning to use computers can change the way they learn everything else" (p. 8). Professional journals have published everything from major articles to entire issues devoted to the concept of hypermedia. One only has to look at the impact of Apple's *Hypercard*™ to realize that hypermedia is the hottest thing to happen to education since the arrival of the microcomputer. In fact, as I write this article, another new journal devoted entirely to the use and development of hypermedia–*Journal of Educational Multimedia and Hypermedia*–was introduced through BITNET. The bandwagon appears to be moving and even the dreaded "panacea" word has cropped up in some quarters. No doubt the potential for educational use of hypermedia is enormous. Many publications and promotions note the advantages of using hypermedia. These advantages include the addition of combining sound and picture, the interactive opportunities for the learner, the ability to structure one's learning approach, the ability of the system to "remember," the ability to pursue cross-references and, of course, improving the learner control over the subject matter.

However, Merrill (1988) suggests that, for every innovative hypermedia program on the market, many more are called innovative only because they happen to use the computer as its base of operation. Most hypermedia programs lack even "the fundamentals of effective educational design" (p. 37). Hypermedia programmers need to be aware and deal with the complex dynamics of the student, the content, and the complex interactive pedagogy that are based upon "cognitively oriented design theories" (Dale & Swagger, 1988). Awareness of other design problems such as managing an electronic environment and ability to evaluate students who have been given the opportunity to manage their own instruction via hypermedia are essential.

Marchionini (1988) in an excellent overview of potential drawbacks to the utilization of hypermedia included the following points: (a) disorientation by the user because of inexperience of both the user and teacher, (b) user distraction due to the large amount of information and the wide variety of operations necessary, (c) engineering and human factor concerns, and (d) "the classic tension between empowering learners with great freedom to direct their own learning and assuring society that all students learn a common body of skills, concepts and principles" (p. 11). My observant but sad colleague noted earlier that many of the instructional uses of the computer were neither creative nor thought provoking and their use was only equivalent to an expensive, however fancy ballpoint pen. Alas, the same view may be true concerning the use of hypermedia technology. Hypermedia has the potential to become an educational tool of enormous magnitude. However, teachers must know its limitations as well as its advantages. Nowhere is the concept of instructional design more important than in the development of hypermedia programs because of the complexity of the equipment and the sometimes complicated organizational nature of the content. Teachers also need to be able to orchestrate these varieties of content and media.

Computers and their innovative uses (such as hypermedia) are not always the answer to improve instruction, but solid instructional design may be the closest solution possible. In spite of advertisements to the contrary, most teachers will *not* become hypermedia authors or developers. More likely, teachers will become consumers of commercially developed packages. The old analogy of teachers being users rather than producers of educational films is probably also accurate for the future of the use of hypermedia. It is more realistic that teachers need to acquire the skill to select and use commercial applications and programs rather than design and program their own hypermedia (Moore et al. 1986).

Few teachers will have the direct opportunity to make design inputs and content recommendations on commercially produced hypermedia. To be honest, few teachers will have the time, the expertise, or the disposition to develop their own hypermedia instructional packages. It will be important, therefore, for teachers to have ready access to knowledgeable people who can work with them to develop skills in judging and evaluating hypermedia. Teachers can learn by working with existing hypermedia programs and getting assistance from local experts. Unfortunately, in difficult economic times, media and computer support (both personnel and facilities) are the first casualties. If these local experts, such as a school media specialist, are not available, this support role may fall to other knowledgeable teachers. These other teachers, who have this knowledge of the concept of hypermedia systems, can act as a buffer between the user and the zealous salesman or flashy advertisements. It may be true that many past technology "fads" prevalent in education might have been omitted if there had been closer cooperation between the teacher and the designer of the materials. Thus, while most teachers cannot directly affect the development of these materials, with assistance they can learn to select the most useful materials that will fit the exact need of the particular subject, lesson, or unit.

Many teacher education institutions provide a required course in the selection and utilization of educational media. However, many of these courses are able to do no more than allow teachers the opportunity to learn how to operate a computer with minimal skill. These colleges have not equipped teachers in their training to deal with selecting or even using the current technologies much less the ability to design appropriate but complex technologies such as hypermedia. It will become necessary, therefore, for teachers to spend time on their own to become knowledgeable (not necessarily experts) on the technology of hypermedia with the purpose not to design materials but to be able to select and integrate the technology into their own classes.

Current use and design of hypermedia materials have highlighted concerns, some of which have been noted herein. Until these are addressed, my colleague's earlier lament about the computer and the fancy ballpoint pen may be just as valid in today's hypermedia world.

REFERENCES

Bush, V. (1945). As we may think. *Atlantic Monthly, 176*, 101-108.

Dale, C. & Swagger, K. (1988). The evolution of instructional design principles for intelligent computer-assisted instruction, *Journal of Instructional Development, 11*(1), 15-22.

Hypercard: Freedom to associate. (1987). Cupertino, CA: Apple Computer Inc.

Marchionini, G. (1988). Hypermedia and learning: Freedom and chaos, *Educational Technology*, 8-12.

Megarry, J. (1988). Hypertext and compact discs: The challenge of multi-media learning, *British Journal of Educational Technology, 19*(3), 172-183.

Merrill, M.D. (1975). Learner control beyond aptitude-treatment interaction, *AV Communication Review, 23*, 217-226.

Merrill, M.D. (1988). Don't bother me with instructional design–I'm busy programming, *Computers in Human Behavior, 4*(1), 37-52.

Moore, D.M., Bedient, D.O. and Scholes, G.W. (1986). An expensive ballpoint pen? *IAECT Journal*, 23-25.

Morariu, J. (1988). Hypermedia in instruction and training: The power and the promise, *Educational Technology*, 17-20.

Papert, S. (1980). *Mindstorms, Children, Computers and Powerful Ideas,* New York: Basic Books, Inc.

Trotter, A. (1989). Schools gear up for "hypermedia"–a quantum leap in electronics learning, *The American School Board Journal*, 35-37.

Robert J. Myers
John K. Burton

The Foundations of Hypermedia: Concepts and History

INTRODUCTION

Hypermedia has become the "buzzword" in education in the early 90s. Yet there is much confusion as to what it means, where it comes from, and how it may be (and has been) used. The purpose here is to provide a foundation for the chapters to follow–to provide a historical context and a conceptual base as well as to describe some of the recent systems and issues that have emerged. As such, it is appropriate to begin by defining key terms.

While definitions vary, Ted Nelson (1987) who coined the term *hypertext*, defines it as non-sequential writing. Obviously, a system which permits nonsequential writing could permit nonsequential reading. In Nelson's view, hypertext is free from the constraints of sequence imposed by books. He saw authors writing novels as they conceived them, rather than in a sequence forced upon them by linear text. Similarly, readers could freely attack the novel by symbol, character, theme, chronology, etc., creating their own flashbacks and "fast forwards" at will.

ROBERT J. MYERS, Research Associate, NASA Classroom of the Future, Wheeling Jesuit College, Wheeling, WV.
JOHN K. BURTON is Professor of Education, Virginia Tech, Blacksburg, VA 24061-0313.

[Haworth co-indexing entry note]: "The Foundations of Hypermedia: Concepts and History." Myers, Robert J. and John K. Burton. Co-published simultaneously in *Computers in the Schools* (The Haworth Press, Inc.) Vol. 10, No. 1/2, 1994, pp. 9-20; and: *Multimedia and Megachange: New Roles for Educational Computing* (eds: W. Michael Reed, John K. Burton, and Min Liu) The Haworth Press, Inc., 1994, pp. 9-20. Multiple copies of this article/chapter may be purchased from The Haworth Document Delivery Center [1-800-3-HAWORTH; 9:00 a.m. - 5:00 p.m. (EST)].

Nelson also proposed the term *compound hypertext* to refer to non-sequential writing by multiple authors *at the same time*. Thus, several authors could read, add to, or annotate the same growing corpus in any order they chose. From an author's perspective, hypertext is probably best conceived as a multidimensional word processor (Frase, 1990). From the reader's viewpoint, Frase (1990) presents the metaphor of a "transescalator," permitting movement in all directions through the *hyperspace* of novels or databases. Yet an escalator, even a transescalator which moves sideways, moves in a sequence. For the reader, hypertext is perhaps closer to *Star Trek*'s transporter, allowing the user to "beam" to any coordinates in a given hyperspace of information. *Hypermedia* is an extension of hypertext that goes beyond the traditional text and graphics of books to include sound, animation, and video (via, e.g., CD-ROM).

Conklin foresaw a problem in confronting users with an infinite (or at least very large) number of choices from an infinite (or again very large) number of possible points in a given hyperspace. This problem, of course, implies some sort of user aids, "planned presentations" or "lines of structure" (Nelson, 1988). This solution implies still another problem: that inherent in choosing planned presentations or lines of structure. Suffice it to say that hypertext (or hypermedia) means only that the author (or authors) is (are) "absolutely free" to make choices. A filmmaker who presents a single non-sequential time of structure via a flashback or foreshadowing would probably qualify as a hypermedia author if (as they are) a film is shot in one sequence and presented in another, or during editing, the end is moved to the beginning to provide a flashback or interspersed throughout to provide foreshadowing.

ADDITIONAL TERMINOLOGY

In any database's hyperspace are *nodes* or single units of information (e.g., a document, "film clip," speech, song, etc.). Experts often disagree on the definition of a "unit" of information, but Shneiderman and Kearsley's (1989) notion of a node as a single concept or topic (though admittedly vague) probably suffices as well as any. The key is that whatever we call a node must be self-contained in that it stands alone. A single node does not require that a reader has viewed any other nodes.

A *link* connects nodes. Taken together, links form a *path* through the database. The author provides the ability to link from one node to others. Available means include index searches or filters which provide restrictions or other options. Large databases may use hierarchical or relational structures. Many hypertext systems maintain a *path history* or *knowledge trail* so readers can retrace links or *backtrack*. This process of moving and retracing through a database is called *navigation*. Many systems provide *bookmarks* to allow the reader to "dog ear" nodes for later ballistic linking without retracing an entire path. Using *windows* permits more than one node to be active at the same time.

Having defined common terms used in hypertext and hypermedia, we now jump to where these notions came from and the people responsible for the ideas behind them. The search is nonsequential and the filters are hypertext and history. We now link to . . .

HISTORY

Bush

In 1945, Vannevar Bush, the director of the Office of Scientific Research and Development, opined that instruments were at hand that would extend the power of the mind. In Bush's words, "The summation of human experience is being expanded at a prodigious rate, and the means we use for threading through the consequent maze to the momentarily important item is the same as was used in the days of square-rigged ships" (p. 102). He proposed a powerful mechanical aid to assist with repetitive thoughts common to the extraction of material from existing records. He called his device "memex."

Bush believed that the human mind operated by association. His memex, a desk-like device, contained viewing screens, buttons, levers, and a keyboard. The proposed memex could store almost anything, including books, pictures, periodicals, and newspapers. It could also digest longhand notes, photographs, sketches, and memoranda. The essence of memex was associative indexing. The selection of any item could allow the immediate selection of another. By forming associations at will, the user could build a custom-made trail through the material. Bush wrote, "It is exactly as though the physical items had been gathered . . . from widely separated sources and bound together to form a new book. It is more than this, for any item can be joined into numerous trails" (p. 107).

Memex offered several advantages. It could store trails for future reference, and it allowed users to add marginal notes and comments. Bush wrote that new forms of encyclopedias would appear: " . . . with a ready-made mesh of associative trails running through them, ready to be dropped into the memex and there amplified" (p. 108). Although the technology of 1945 could not support memex, Bush's perception of human information processing and vision of technology to come were revolutionary. Not until the computer and associated software matured could some of Bush's concepts be put into practice.

Engelbart

Douglas Engelbart is another pioneer whose work has contributed significantly to hypermedia. Engelbart is credited with many inventions which, in his words, "augment" the human intellect. Among his inventions are the mouse, multiple windows, and electronic mail. One of his major contributions is a theory about augmentation frameworks.

Engelbart (Engelbart & Hooper, 1988) says that an augmentation system has two components. The first is the human system. It includes contributions from culture, such as language and customs. The second component is a tool system. Contributions to the tool system allow us to perform tasks such as communicating, retrieving, or manipulating. He suggests it is necessary to develop a new augmentation discipline. This new discipline would explore and develop methodologies and skills required for the tool system. We can already see his ideas' impact in direct manipulation interfaces provided by the mouse and windows.

Two systems built by Engelbart at the Stanford Research Institute incorporated many of his ideas. The first, "NLS" (oN Line System), included electronic mail, computer conferencing, multiple windows, and a mouse. The second, "Augment," contained cross-referenced links within and between documents. Augment was noteworthy for providing the ability to expand or contract displayed information according to the user's needs. Filters further customized detail of available information. These efforts fell under an umbrella that he termed *Knowledge Workshop*.

Engelbart designed the Knowledge Workshop based on his augmentation theory to increase a person's capability in tackling complex situations, gaining comprehension, and deriving solutions. Users could solve problems faster, obtain better answers, and find solutions to previously insolvable problems. Extensions of these processes to an academic or learning environment are appropriate.

Nelson

A third researcher who had profound impact upon the conceptual underpinning of hypertext and hypermedia is Theodore Nelson. As stated earlier, it was Nelson who coined the term *hypertext* in the 60s to describe a system of nonsequential writing. His major hypertext project is Xanadu. Megarry (1988) describes Xanadu succinctly, "Project Xanadu [is] a system with the modest goal of linking, online, and in real time, just about all the knowledge in the world, adding new knowledge as it became available, and allowing anyone to locate information through an indexing system that searched for ideas (however they were expressed) rather than for specific words or strings" (p. 175). As with memex, Xanadu would allow the creation of knowledge trails and user annotation. While Xanadu has not been fully implemented, there has been a proliferation of other packages with hypermedia characteristics.

Weyer

A good example of a system that helped span the gap between vision and the coming widespread use of hypermedia is the Electronic Encyclopedia. In 1984, Weyer and Borning presented a prototype that allowed a user to browse existing encyclopedias. Browsing may be likened to flipping through a magazine in search of interesting items, then following paths of interest by use of associations or references. Using the Electronic Encyclopedia, users made selections from an alphabetical list of topics, then followed a number of references or cross-references. The latter consisted of textual, video, and pictural nodes. The system amplified some searches by simulations. For example, an excellent simulation followed viewing films of the Tacoma Narrows Bridge collapse. Follow-up information included a discussion of damping and harmonic motion. Users could experiment with effects of various loads on bridges, some of which would result in a simulated collapse.

The Electronic Encyclopedia was primarily textual in orientation. The authors envisioned a future version that encompassed more simulations and video images. They also foresaw the capability of forming associations by use of better knowledge representation structures. A closer look at their vision will help define some terms and point to advances in hypermedia.

Weyer and Borning's (1984) vision of hypermedia's potential moves "beyond browsing" (p. 65). They suggested four additional system features: models, tours, filters, and guides. Models help form knowledge representations. The goal is to represent knowledge to users according to their needs, interests, background, or previous system interactions. Tours take a user on a pre-packaged path to view selected topics. A tour of hypermedia's evolution, or the changed face of Eastern Europe, are examples. While tours offer little user choice, the program tailors them to the user's interests. Filters (analogous to camera lens filters) keep out unnecessary information or add detail. Filters can also put together information from several related areas. Last, a humanlike guide serves as the user's personal agent in assisting with system usage. The guide personalizes the search by learning users' preferences, then using them to help tailor searches. The guide in Apple's Knowledge Navigator is a prime example (Sculley, 1989).

Weyer (1988) expands on the concept of the guide by proposing that hypermedia systems act as intelligent tutors–becoming a "partner" with the learner. This partner becomes an active participant in searching for, interpreting, and creating knowledge. Weyer suggests that the system act as a coach, tutor, or guide–one that encourages the learner to " . . . question, conjecture, create, and experiment" (p. 91). By guiding, Weyer means that the system should be capable of guessing the learner's current level of understanding. Last, the system should have some idea of the learner's immediate needs, making suggestions about appropriate courses of action.

HYPERTEXT/HYPERMEDIA SYSTEMS

Hardware

Advances in hardware have helped bring hypermedia systems to everyday use. One of the most common is the laser disc. A laser disc, often referred to as a video disc or optical disc, can store up to 54,000 individual pictures or 30 minutes of full motion video. Although laser discs have been available for nearly a decade, their proliferation was slow until the recent advances in computer power, software, and display capabilities. Another storage medium that has helped hypermedia is the Compact Disc-Read Only Memory (CD-ROM). This disc, the size of an audio compact disc, can store 270,000 typed pages. It can also store audio, video, and animated sequences. A popular use of CD-ROM is the storage of complete encyclopedias.

Systems

The *Voyage of the MIMI*, developed at the Bank Street College of Education (Gibbon, 1988), was an early project designed to link television, video disc, and microcomputer software. Dramatic episodes about a ship named the "MIMI" allowed learners to engage in interdisciplinary studies. Students followed the MIMI as its crew studied East Coast marine biology. In addition to situations encountered by the crew, students had access to 13 laser disc documentaries involving visits to various scientific sites. There were also microcomputer programs providing additional depth in scientific experiments.

The second Bank Street project, *Voyage of the MIMI II*, also takes a multi-disciplinary approach toward discovery-based learning experiences

(Wilson, 1990). Instead of marine biology, the designers base this program on anthropology. Its aim is to evoke student curiosity for the subject matter while being fun and easy to use for 8 to 14 year-old students. One unique aspect of MIMI II is the surrogate travel feature; it allows the student to tour an ancient Mayan site in Mexico. Capabilities include climbing in and around the temple, zooming in for close looks, listening to an archaeologist, or hearing the sounds of the local rain forest. Students can create a scrapbook of pictures from the site. These provide the ability to put together presentations about the subject matter.

The package having the largest popular impact may be *HyperCard*. Introduced by Apple in 1987, this software allows everyday users to create their own hypermedia products. No longer must the user have access to a mini or main-frame computer with exotic artificial intelligence or database software to turn out hypermedia. *HyperCard* programs running on the Macintosh and similar programs on other personal computers control external resources such as sound, laser disc, and CD-ROM players. With software like *HyperCard* as a tool, teachers have the option of authoring their own hypermedia products, or taking advantage of the thousands of commercial and public domain programs in existence.

Hypermedia or multimedia packages are now proliferating. National Geographic's *Mammals: A Multimedia Encyclopedia* contains still pictures, full motion video, text, and vocalizations of over 100 animals (Applications, 1991, p. 6). Another new application designed to "turn kids on" is *Columbus: Encounter, Discovery, and Beyond* from Synapse Technologies and IBM. This multi-disciplinary program allows students to link from one topic to another while exploring the Renaissance and the Age of Discovery. Disciplines include math, science, art, and philosophy (p. 11). Scholastic's *Point of View* allows students to link documents, speeches, sound, still pictures, and drawings to a textual timeline of U.S. History. A new addition in the series focuses on the American Civil War. While hypermedia is reaching into every discipline, questions continue to be asked about how, when, and under what circumstances to employ hypermedia.

DESIGN AND IMPLEMENTATION ISSUES AND CONSIDERATIONS

The educational community is witnessing the harnessing of instructional media that was previously impractical. But, as Hooper (1988) questions: "What happens when you combine the traditions of movie making, graphic design, computer education, encyclopedia development, text publication, public television, computer workstation design, classroom teaching, library organization, entertainment, and psychology?" (p. 329). The designer's challenge is to contend with a variety of issues regarding the content, structure, and navigational aids in an instructional hypermedia environment.

One commonly finds articles that tout the ability of hypermedia to "excite or turn on" a learner in a discovery environment. Heller (1990) defines discovery learning as a *learner* activity that results in new understandings from following available alternatives. While the optimism about hypermedia and discovery learning is appealing, several questions about the efficacy of this approach must be answered. For example, do these methods improve retention and comprehension? Will every student be "turned on" by this medium, or only those possessing certain traits? Last, what keeps learners involved or engaged in the task?

Most will agree that learning requires engagement. Engagement might be defined as an active absorption in the task at hand. How does a program achieve and maintain this engagement? Present technology provides the capability of searching vast arrays of information, but the types of nodes encountered by the learner play a large role in learners' degree of engagement. A node could merely present factual data to learners. Many will argue, however, that engagement is not likely to come from linking a series of factual nodes. Possible answers may be found in greater usage of the affective domain in hypermedia presentations (Koethe, 1990). The effective use of meaningful stories and surprises may also enhance engagement (Hooper, 1988). Hooper suggests that affective domain usage is the very essence of serious presentations. The *Voyage of the MIMI* project presented above makes extensive use of drama and emotion–especially in a ship wreck and survival episode.

Another important issue is the design of the hypermedia interface. An *interface* consists of those visual and audio cues that allow us to use the system. Menus, beeps, maps, buttons, and icons are some of the items that make up an interface. This area is particularly important in that it has direct effect upon many of the questions posed above. It is also a particularly lucrative area for those searching for research topics. Unfortunately, much of the literature about this subject offers only heuristics about design. One will commonly find such statements as: use white space, avoid scrolling, and maintain consistency. Perhaps more germane are questions posed by Meyrowitz (1988): what is the best way to organize links, symbolize links, or visually represent the network of links?

Discussion of representing links may evoke the image of menus and other forms of navigation. Learners range from first-time users, who are unfamiliar with the system as well as the content, to those who have used the system frequently. Navigational options may have to change based on users' experience level. Another issue concerns the number of trails available to users. Conklin (1987) cites a trail-rich environment as a potential place for cognitive overload. He states that a good navigational system must tell learners where they are located, and how to get to the desired place. Other good navigational aids tell learners where they have been–so that backtracking is possible.

The amount of learner control the system provides is a very important consideration. One often hears the word *interactivity* in the same breath as *hypermedia*. Unfortunately, studies in computer-based instruction show that allowing users a great deal of control results in less learning, that students lack metacognitive skills, and that they use inappropriate learning strategies (Steinberg, 1989). Of course these observations do not apply to all learners. There is usually an interaction between achievement and learner traits, e.g., low versus high achievers. Tennyson and Buttrey (1980) found that learner control works when advisement (e.g., progress updates, and study suggestions) is provided. To provide the best degree of learner control, systems may have to determine the learner's profile, then guide, or advise accordingly.

HYPERMEDIA IN EDUCATION

The hype about hypermedia itself carries some risk. Bosco (1989) warns that hypermedia can easily be used in trivial or ineffective ways, and it is too easy to get wrapped up in the technology. The penalty for this enthusiasm could do a number of things. It could lead to promises that are not delivered (a frequent experience with technology in education). It could also cause a failure to take a critical look at the technology. That is, does hypermedia have, or will it have, the ability to affect the learning process in a positive way? If hypermedia positively affects learning, then why don't more schools use it?

Costs may dissuade schools from using hypermedia–time, for example. For all the advances in software, it still takes a considerable amount of time to become adept at using developmental packages. In addition, few people have the combination of skills required to develop excellent hypermedia packages. The lack of funds has to rank high on the list of reasons as well. Often, a hypermedia system requires two monitors, special interface cards, and an assortment of cables, players, and software. Until systems become cost efficient, and requirements narrow to a single unit (as the current trend indicates), many schools may stay on the sidelines.

There will arise many situations in which a group of students clusters around a workstation in pursuit of some learning objective. Most of the questions posed above remain, but now research concerning cooperative learning and its usage in a hypermedia environment come into play. If cooperative learning and hypermedia do go hand and hand, should we think about changing the structure of the school from its traditional "one teacher and many students" orientation? One might picture the teacher as more of a mentor, guide, or fellow traveler in the realm of hypermedia. If hypermedia and cooperative learning provide positive results, won't there be a significant resistance to change–especially from the established order?

One frequently hears a call "back to the basics" or an emphasis on the three Rs. It is likely that the suggestion of building a curriculum around hypermedia could convey threatening overtones to these advocates. Another issue is that the use of hypermedia may not contribute directly to standardized test scores. We certainly witness national figures calling for standardized tests to measure educational progress across the country. The challenge may be for designers of educational hypermedia to create incentives to move to new instructional models by producing clearly superior products.

The authority figure, the teacher, may feel some unease about his or her role in all of this. Will there be a loss of identity if the teacher is not viewed as the subject matter expert? (Gibbon, 1988). Will teachers be comfortable with the noise and confusion sometimes found when groups of students gather around workstations? In addition, teachers have sometimes charged that they are merely the delivery person of prepackaged curricula, and that they don't have ownership over the topic or the content of their instruction (Wolk, 1991). Yes, there is risk, but many proponents of hypermedia contend that the rich contextual content, and textural environment has the power to take the teacher's role into new and exciting areas.

Hypermedia also holds out a promise to contribute significantly to adult education. National leaders have been calling for continuing adult education at least as far back as Thoreau (1845). The ability to continue learning is particularly important now that industrial countries are headed toward (if not well into) the information era. This implies a changing work force; one that needs to be flexible and adaptable to the changing needs and skills required for employment (Sculley, 1989). Hypermedia, with its ability to provide course materials in a variety of formats such as CD-ROM and laser disc, can play a large role in this continuing education. This situation is almost like having one's own university on call in support of a lifetime of learning.

Our purpose has been to introduce the reader to some of the background and issues, as well as present and potential uses of hypermedia. We have the opportunity to present to a learner, or other users, a vast array of media. Yes, it is exciting, but there is a need to carefully evaluate this technology's impact on learning processes. Issues raised here and elsewhere affect nearly every facet of instruction–including design strategies, educational psychology, and effective use of technology. Researchers need to determine how, when, and under what circumstances learners profit from hypermedia. Answers to these issues will help the community keep the hype out of hypermedia and contribute to the effective usage of promising technology.

REFERENCES

Applications, Encyclopedias and Archives. (1991, September). *Supplement to T.H.E. Journal*, pp. 6-11.

Bosco, J. (1989). Interactive Video: Educational Tool or Toy. *Interactive Video, The Educational Technology Anthology Series*, (pp. 3-9). Englewood Cliffs, NJ: Educational Technology Publications.

Bush, V. (1945). As We May Think. *Atlantic Monthly, 176*(1), 101-108.

Conklin, J. (1987). Hypertext: An introduction and survey. *IEEE Computer, 2*(9), 17-41.

Engelbart, D. & Hooper K. (1988). The Augmentation System Framework. In: S. Ambron & K. Hooper (Eds.), *Interactive Multimedia*, (pp. 19-32). Redmond WA: Microsoft Press.

Fraase, M. (1990). *Macintosh Hypermedia.* Glenview, IL: Scott, Foresman and Company.

Gibbon, Y.G. (1988). The Voyage of the MIMI. In: S. Ambron & K. Hooper (Eds.), *Interactive Multimedia* (pp. 181-192). Redmond WA: Microsoft Press.

Heller, R. (1990). The Role of Hypermedia in Education: A Look at the Research Issues. *Journal of Research on Computing in Education*, Summer, 431-441.

Hooper, K. (1988). Multimedia in Education. In: S. Ambron & K. Hooper (Eds.), *Interactive Multimedia* (pp. 317-329). Redmond WA: Microsoft Press.

Koetke, W. (1990). A Multimedia Interface. In: S. Ambron & K. Hooper (Eds.), *Learning with Interactive Multimedia* (pp. 349-356). Redmond WA: Microsoft Press.

Megarry, J. (1988). Hypertext and compact discs: The challenge of multi-media learning. *British Journal of Educational Technology, 19*(3), 172-183.

Meyrowitz, N. (1988). Issues in Designing a Hypermedia Document System. In: Ambron S. & Hooper K. (Eds.), *Interactive Multimedia* (pp. 33-86). Redmond WA: Microsoft Press.

Nelson, T. (1987). *Dream Machines.* (rev. ed.) Redmond, Washington: Tempus Books of Microsoft Press.

Nelson, T. (1988). Managing immense storage: Project Xanadu provides a model for the possible future of mass storage. *Byte, 13*(1), 228-238.

Sculley, J. (1989). The Relationship Between Business and Higher Education: a Perspective on the 21st Century. *Communications of the ACM, 32*(9), 1056-1061.

Shneiderman, B. & Kearsley, G. (1989). *Hypertext Hands-on.* New York: Addison-Wesley.

Steinberg, E.R. (1989) Cognition and learner control: a literature review, 1977-1988. *Journal of Computer-Based Instruction, 16*, 117-121.

Tennyson, R. & Buttrey, T. (1980). Advisement and management strategies as design variables in computer-assisted instruction. *Educational Communications and Technology Journal, 28*, 169-176.

Thoreau, H. (1854). *Walden.* Signet Classics, New York, New York.

Weyer, S. (1988). As We May Learn. In: S. Ambron & K. Hooper (Eds.), *Interactive Multimedia* (pp. 87-104). Redmond WA: Microsoft Press.

Weyer, S. & Borning, A. (1984). A Prototype Electronic Encyclopedia. *ACM Transactions on Office Information Systems, 3*(1), 63-68.

Wilson, K. (1990, Spring) The Palanque Prototype: A Multimedia Design Example. *Multimedia Review*, 34-38.

Wolk, R. (1991). Teaching, Learning, and Technology. *Teacher Magazine.*

RESEARCH

Cleborne D. Maddux

Multimedia, Hypermedia, and the Culture of Schooling

Computer education has had more than its share of trendy, fashionable applications. Most of these have failed to live up to the unreasonable expectations set up by well-meaning advocates who indulged in extravagant claims concerning benefits to be derived.

I have repeatedly suggested that this cycle of unrealistic claims followed by unrealized expectations has fueled the backlash against the use of computers in education. In fact, at one time, I felt the situation was serious enough that the entire future of educational computing was at risk. Indeed, I feared that we might one day see computers, like the learning machines of the 1960s, gathering dust in school storage rooms or classroom closets across the nation.

I no longer fear the complete demise of educational computing. While I

CLEBORNE D. MADDUX is Associate Editor-Research, Professor of Education, and Chairman, Department of Curriculum and Instruction, College of Education, University of Nevada, Reno, Reno, NV 89557-0023.

[Haworth co-indexing entry note]: "Multimedia, Hypermedia, and the Culture of Schooling." Maddux, Cleborne D. Co-published simultaneously in *Computers in the Schools* (The Haworth Press, Inc.) Vol. 10, No. 1/2, 1994, pp. 21-26; and: *Multimedia and Megachange: New Roles for Educational Computing* (eds: W. Michael Reed, John K. Burton, and Min Liu) The Haworth Press, Inc., 1994, pp. 21-26. Multiple copies of this article/chapter may be purchased from The Haworth Document Delivery Center [1-800-3-HAWORTH; 9:00 a.m. - 5:00 p.m. (EST)].

was worrying about the effects of extravagant and unrealized claims by advocates, computers were quietly becoming indispensable in every walk of modern life in the U.S. I can't remember the last time I was in an office of any kind, in which every phase of work activity did not revolve around one or more computers. From business, to government, and finally and belatedly to schools, computers have become ubiquitous.

Because computers are everywhere, and because they occupy a central position in so many human activities, they are no longer at risk of disappearing from public school classrooms. In fact, they have acquired so much cultural momentum that we could probably not stop their continued and increasing presence in schools even if we tried! Like the automobile in the culture at large, the computer in American society occupies a place that includes, but transcends its value as a tool. The automobile and the computer are means that have become, at least to some extent, ends in themselves.

A less exotic example of this cultural phenomenon within the subculture of schooling, is the *chalkboard.* The chalkboard has acquired such subcultural momentum that no one asks principals or teachers whether or not they need one. When schools are built, they are included without debate–seemingly without thought. When technical improvements such as boards for use with dry-erase markers become available, there may be debate about whether to adopt the innovation, but the assumption that some variation of a chalkboard is needed goes largely or completely unchallenged.

Computers may have not yet achieved this degree of momentum in schools or in the culture at large. However, they continue to gain cultural momentum daily, and I suspect that many office managers assume that computers will be needed in the same way that many educational policy makers assume that chalkboards will be needed in schools. It seems inevitable that in the near future, computers will occupy an analogous place in the subculture of schooling.

Be that as it may, the point is that although computers are here to stay, we should strive to avoid the destructive cycle of unrealistic promises followed by disappointment and disillusionment. This phenomenon slows the intelligent integration of computers into the curriculum, and makes teachers and others cynical about innovations of any kind.

This volume deals with the use of multimedia in education. Although I am cautiously optimistic about the potential of multimedia, I think there are a number of related issues and problems that must be resolved, but that are not being widely discussed. Unless they are discussed and resolved, I believe that multimedia may simply be another example of a promising application that will eventually be discarded when it fails to live up to the advance notices of radical advocates.

In the first place, there is considerable confusion about terms and what they mean. The terms *multimedia, interactive multimedia,* and *hypermedia* are used with little consistency and great diversity of meaning.

The term *multimedia* merely implies that more than one media is involved. One of these may or may not include a computer, a laser-disk player, or some other audio-visual aid. In a recent book, we used an IBM package called *Exploring Chemistry* as an illustration of multimedia: "Designed for use in college-level general chemistry classes, the program combines expository text displayed on the computer's screen with video clips from a laser disk" (Maddux, Johnson, & Willis, 1992, p. 318). Although *Exploring Chemistry* is also interactive, not all multimedia includes this characteristic:

> Exploring Chemistry is interactive because it involves students directly in the action of the lesson. The decisions a student makes determine what happens next in the lesson. It involves multimedia because students work with several media including computer text, computer graphics, and video from the laser disk. (p. 319)

Exploring Chemistry is not *hypermedia,* however, because the material is presented in a linear fashion. Spiro and Jehng (1990) suggest that hypermedia makes use of *hypertext,* which is:

> Computer-based texts that are read in a nonlinear fashion and that are organized on multiple dimensions . . . The same material (which can be any kind of randomly accessible medium, e.g., text, video, audio) is capable of being explored in different ways, with the different exploration paths producing what are essentially *multiple texts* for the same topic. (p. 166)

With these distinctions in mind, there are a number of issues that should be explored. First, it seems apparent to me that the future of all these applications is tied closely to our ideas about what activities constitute legitimate teaching and learning. It also seems apparent that even though we have been giving lip service for decades to the importance of individualization of instruction, most teaching in most classrooms is total group at worst, small group at best.

What has this to do with the topic at hand? It seems to me that when considering the practicality of multimedia, interactive multimedia, or hypermedia, *only multimedia lends itself to small or large group instruction, while interactive multimedia or hypermedia requires use by individuals.* After all, interactive multimedia requires the response of an individual to determine what happens next, and hypermedia requires individual decisions in the creation of multiple texts or paths. Thus, the future of interactive multimedia or hypermedia looks relatively bleak, given the point above about the predominance of whole group instruction in U.S. schools. Furthermore, I see no indication whatever that teachers, principals, or parents are ready to move toward true, meaningful individualized instruction.

Even the use of multimedia creates many problems. For years I have been amused when I have attended conferences or school district opening day orientations for which the organizers employed a consulting firm to make a multimedia presentation to the group. Typically, hordes of technicians swarmed over the conference site setting up special screens, stereo sound equipment and speakers, multiple slide projectors, a maze of cables, and a host of other exotic equipment. I used to chuckle at the thought that anyone might think that even a greatly simplified version of multimedia would appeal to a busy classroom teacher.

Of course, the use of computers, CD-ROM, laser disks, etc., have greatly simplified the equipment setup required for many multimedia, interactive multimedia, or hypermedia presentations. Nevertheless, setup is still complicated, and configuring a computer for use with specific multimedia software and other hardware can be extremely difficult and time-consuming. It is true that setup and configuration is improving steadily. However, lack of compatibility and lack of standardization remain difficult problems. Then too, the extensive use of multimedia, interactive multimedia, or hypermedia cannot take place until there is a large, excellent base of software packages to draw from. We are far from that point. At present, even if teachers are willing to invest the time, effort, and expense needed to acquire and use a multimedia presentation, they will be unable to locate suitable software for anything more than an occasional topic in an occasional subject.

Hardware is another difficult problem. Most multimedia, interactive multimedia, or hypermedia presentations run only on relatively sophisticated hardware. In general, the schools do not have such equipment, and still rely heavily on first generation computers. Ely (1993) suggests that:

> Apple II operating system computers are found in 61% of the schools; MS-DOS in 24% of the schools; Radio Shack in 4%; and Commodore in 4%. Macintosh operating systems are found in 4% of the schools. (p. 53)

Sometimes I read articles suggesting that the future of multimedia, interactive multimedia, or hypermedia is for teachers to create their own lessons, rather than purchasing commercial ones. I am as skeptical of this suggestion as I was a few years ago when I read suggestions that teachers should use Basic, Logo, or Pilot to construct their own educational software. While it is true that multimedia authoring systems are also improving rapidly, I suspect they will always be complicated and time-consuming, and while a few teachers will undoubtedly enjoy the time and effort required to master them, most will not.

Additional problems for interactive multimedia and hypermedia involve the numbers of computers in schools. Even though most schools do have some computers, there are nowhere near the number that would be needed for large numbers of teachers to make even limited use of computers for individual instruction. In fact, Ely (1993) reports that one third of schools in the U.S. still have only one computer for each 45 students, while only 10% have one computer for nine students. Although schools are spending more money on computers, this problem continues to plague us because many older computers are breaking down or are obsolete. Therefore, in many cases, additional funds are only replacing existing machines, rather than further reducing the ratio of students to computers.

Another problem with all of the above applications is the lack of research evidence for their efficacy. It is commonly asserted that the non-linear nature of hypermedia is similar to the way individuals think and learn things in the natural world. Such an assertion is intellectually appealing, but the idea that the world was flat was intellectually appealing to many people for generations.

I addressed the lack of research evidence on the efficacy of hypermedia in a recent publication:

> Is this really more consistent with the way children think and learn? Is there evidence that such is the case? If children really do learn more efficiently in non-linear fashion, we strongly suspect that there are many critical learner and teacher variables that must be taken into consideration. For example, it may be that beginning learners learn more efficiently in a linear fashion, while advanced learners profit more from hypermedia approaches. In any case, the state of the art in research on this topic is in its infancy, and we should not jump to the conclusion that non-linear learning is best for everyone, in every subject, at every age. (Maddux, Johnson, & Harlow, in press)

One bright spot in the area of research is the recent publication of *Cognition, Education, and Multimedia,* edited by Don Nix and Rand Spiro

(1990). This volume does an excellent job of exploring seminal research on thinking, and relating the results of this research to the use of multimedia, interactive multimedia, and hypermedia. There is far too little of this sort of research that is finding its way into educational computing research.

I would like to emphasize that the Nix and Spiro (1990) book relates research *on thinking and learning* to computing. What is definitely NOT needed is a series of studies that compares the effects of teaching some subject through the use of multimedia, interactive multimedia, or hypermedia, to the effects of teaching the same material traditionally (whatever that is). Instead, research should focus on finding effective ways to use this promising hardware and software to teach specific knowledge or skills to specific kinds of learners at specific ages. Research on ways to avoid the problems outlined above is also needed.

This brings me to the point of this article. I would like to invite the submission of manuscripts that can help resolve any or all of the above problems for consideration of publication in this section of *Computers in the Schools*. This volume represents a step in the direction of finding ways to eliminate the barriers to the use of multimedia, interactive multimedia, and hypermedia in the classroom. It is only through research that I believe we can avoid having this promising set of applications become simply another educational computing disappointment, and one that leads yet again to throwing out the baby with the bath water.

REFERENCES

Ely, D. P. (1993). Computers in schools and universities in the United States of America. *Educational Technology, 33*(9), 53-57.

Maddux, C. D., Johnson, D., & Harlow, S. (in press). Educational computing: Avoiding the Everest Syndrome in the 21st century. In: Willis, J. (Ed.), *Proceedings of the 1994 international conference of the Society for Technology and Teacher Education*. Charlottesville, VA: Association for the Advancement of Computing in Education.

Maddux, C. D. Johnson, D. L., & Willis, J. W. (1992). *Educational computing: Learning with tomorrow's technologies*. Boston, MA: Allyn and Bacon.

Nix, D. & Spiro, R. (Eds.) (1990). *Cognition, education, and multimedia: Exploring ideas in high technology*. Hillsdale, NJ: Lawrence Erlbaum.

Spiro, R. J. & Jehng, J. (1990). Cognitive flexibility and hypertext: Theory and technology for the nonlinear and multidimensional traversal of complex subject matter. In: D. Nix & R. Spiro (Eds.), *Cognition, education, and multimedia: Exploring ideas in high technology*, pp. 163-205. Hillsdale, NJ: Lawrence Erlbaum.

W. Michael Reed
Min Liu

The Comparative Effects of BASIC Programming versus *HyperCard* Programming on Problem Solving, Computer Anxiety, and Performance

RESEARCH FRAMEWORK

One of the most common research focuses in instructional computing during the last decade has been the learning of programming languages for the development of problem-solving skills (Clements, 1986; Dalbey & Linn, 1985; Reed & Palumbo, 1992). Although findings have been somewhat inconclusive, there have been consistent trends in later and lengthier studies that learning such languages will enhance problem-solving skills (Burton & Magliaro, 1987/1988). Although a plethora of studies on programming languages has emerged, very little research on authoring languages such as *HyperCard* has been conducted.

W. MICHAEL REED is Professor of Instructional Computing and English Education, West Virginia University, Morgantown, WV 26506.
MIN LIU is Assistant Professor of Instructional Technology, Department of Curriculum and Instruction, University of Texas at Austin, Austin, TX 78712.

[Haworth co-indexing entry note]: "The Comparative Effects of BASIC Programming versus *HyperCard* Programming on Problem Solving, Computer Anxiety, and Performance." Reed, W. Michael and Min Liu. Co-published simultaneously in *Computers in the Schools* (The Haworth Press, Inc.) Vol. 10, No. 1/2, 1994, pp. 27-46; and: *Multimedia and Megachange: New Roles for Educational Computing* (eds: W. Michael Reed, John K. Burton, and Min Liu) The Haworth Press, Inc., 1994, pp. 27-46. Multiple copies of this article/chapter may be purchased from The Haworth Document Delivery Center [1-800-3-HAWORTH; 9:00 a.m. - 5:00 p.m. (EST)].

Even though a search of ERIC documents dated January 1982 to September 1991 resulted in identifying 99 articles specifically about *HyperCard*, about 90% of them were on the educational applications of *HyperCard*: (a) personal experiences of using *HyperCard* or developing *HyperCard*-based courseware (Bowers & Chia, 1990; Hopper, 1990; Percival 1990); (b) discussions on how to use *HyperCard* (Duhrkopf, 1988; Harris & Cady, 1988; Vacarro, 1988); (c) explorations of the potential of *HyperCard* (Camp & Cogan, 1988; Campbell, 1989; May, 1990; McDowell, 1989) and (d) comparisons between *HyperCard* and other authoring tools (Brader, 1990; Harris & Cady, 1988).

The different content-areas in which *HyperCard* has been applied include (a) language and learning (Campbell, 1989; DiPardo & DiPardo, 1990; May, 1990); (b) history (Crane & Mylonas, 1988); (c) science (Barba & Merchant, 1990; Hall, Thorgood, Hutchings, & Carr, 1989; Miller & Radziemski, 1988); (d) second language learning (Ashworth & Stelovsky, 1989; Underwood, 1989); (e) library science (Bourne, 1990; Holleman, 1990; Neuman, 1991); (f) theatrical performance (Friedlander, 1989); (g) computer science (Gustafson & Reeves, 1990; Percival, 1990); and (h) social studies (Horton, Boone, & Lovitt, 1990). Categories other than content area were: (a) multimedia and hypermedia (Ashworth & Stelovsky, 1989; Campbell, 1989; Jonassen, 1989; Lanza & Roselli, 1991; Tripp & Roby, 1990) and (b) learning disabilities (Horton, Boone, & Lovitt, 1990).

HyperCard has been found to be an excellent tool for creating prototypes of some more complicated and comprehensive projects (Boyle & Snell, 1990; Duhrkopf, 1988; Harris & Cady, 1988; Jonassen, 1989, 1990; Monk, 1990). Also, it has been used in training and teaching and has received positive reactions (Dufresne, Jolin, & Senteni, 1990; Tucker & Dempsey, 1990). Likewise, it has been used extensively and effectively in illustrating instructional design principles and multimedia and hypermedia theories and concepts (Boyle & Snell; Gustafson & Reeves, 1990; McKnight, Dillon, & Richardson, 1990).

But, none of these works has addressed the problem-solving potential of learning authoring languages such as *HyperCard*, a computer use that has been dominating computer-related research line for years. Despite the proven importance of programming languages' role in developing problem-solving skills, the creation of authoring languages such as *HyperCard* has led some computer educators to question the teaching of such languages as BASIC. Most computer educators would concur that using BASIC to create any complex software is unwise–certainly when comparing it to the easier and multi-featured authoring language such as *HyperCard*. Choosing *HyperCard* over BASIC, however, when the purpose of the instruction is to promote problem-solving skills, may not be a sound decision. That is, if the purpose of teaching a language is to enhance problem-solving skills, choosing a more flexible authoring language may not promote the development of problem-solving skills. A programming language requires the developer to work with each command, rather than with *HyperCard* objects that simplify the construction of programs.

The few *HyperCard*-based studies that exist focus on using already-developed software, rather than programming in *HyperCard.* For example, Lanza and Roselli (1991) investigated the effects of a structured approach versus a hypertextual approach for teaching Pascal. The study, with Information Science undergraduates, involved comparing the effect of a *HyperCard*-based, non-linear and less structured program versus a linear and more structured CAI program on the learning of Pascal. Although there were no significant performance differences, 63% of the CAI group considered the structured program to be boring; 76% of the *HyperCard* group considered the hypertextual approach to be stimulating.

Tripp and Roby (1990) investigated a less structured versus a more structured hypertext environment using *HyperCard* in terms of the relative effects on the learning of Japanese by graduate and undergraduate students. More structured involved a visual that suggested the structure of the database, whereas less structured involved a graphical background that did not reflect the structure of the database. More structured also involved advance organizers describing the structure of the lexicon, whereas less structured involved presenting a paragraph on the Japanese language. There were no significant main effects, but there was a significant interaction between visual metaphor and advance organizer with those students receiving only one structured device performing better than those receiving two.

In another study, Horton, Boone, and Lovitt (1990) used *HyperCard*-based hypertext software to increase textbook comprehension and compared it to when the students simply read the textbook. The computer treatment was significantly more effective. A fourth study, one by Colloum and Cockerton-Turner (1990), found that pairs versus individuals performed better when attempting a computer-presented physics problem.

There is obviously little research on *HyperCard* to-date, and the few studies briefly described above do not represent any consistent focus. A critical area not represented by any of the research is the effect of *HyperCard* on developing problem-solving skills, an area that has been valued and heavily researched during the last decade.

PURPOSE OF STUDY AND RESEARCH QUESTIONS

The purpose of this study was to compare the effectiveness of the BASIC programming language versus the *HyperCard* authoring language on promoting problem-solving skills and the reduction of computer anxiety. It also determined the relationships between (a) problem solving and computer anxiety, (b) problem solving and programming, (c) problem solving and debugging, (d) computer anxiety and programming, and (e) computer anxiety and debugging.

Here are the research questions: (a) What are the comparative effects of BASIC versus *HyperCard* on problem solving and computer anxiety? (b) What effect does language have on language competency measures (debugging and programming)? (c) What is the relationship between problem solving and (1) computer anxiety and (2) language competency as measured via programming and debugging exercises? and (d) What is the relationship between computer anxiety and language competency as measured via programming and debugging exercises?

DESIGN OF THE STUDY

Sample

Two groups of students participated in this study. One group (N = 13) received instruction on the BASIC programming language. The second group (N = 8) received instruction on the *HyperCard* authoring language. The instruction for each language lasted six weeks with two weekly meetings of approximately 90 minutes each. Outside-class assignments required an average of over three hours for each class meeting. Therefore, minimal exposure to each language was approximately 54 hours over a six-week period.

Independent Variable

The independent variable in this study was computer language–either BASIC or *HyperCard*. BASIC instruction centered on (a) immediate versus delayed BASIC commands; (b) DOS versus Applesoft BASIC commands; (c) static and animated graphics; (d) 10-resolution and hi-resolution graphics; (e) TEXT commands; (f) numeric versus string variables; (g) modularity (subroutines); (h) iteration (FOR/NEXT); and (i) logical constructs (IF/THEN). The *HyperCard* instruction centered on (a) the browsing environment of *HyperCard* via the navigation tools; (b) the painting tools; (c) the authoring environment of *HyperCard* (its five objects: stack, card, background, field, and button); (d) animation; (e) the programming environment of *HyperCard* including such commands as go, put, visual effects, show and hide, domenu, repeat, and if/then; and (f) the multimedia capabilities of *HyperCard*.

Dependent Measures

Problem Solving. The problem-solving instrument was comprised of 61 items taken from the Deduction and Interpretation sections of the Watson-Glaser Thinking Appraisal instrument and from the Analysis of Relevant and Irrelevant Information and the Analysis of Attributes sections of the Ross Test of Higher Cognitive Processes instrument. The instrument has proved to be valid and highly reliable (Reed & Palumbo, 1987/1988, 1992).

Computer Anxiety. The 20-item computer anxiety instrument was based on a modified version of the Spielberger Self-Evaluation Questionnaire. The instrument has proved to be valid and highly reliable (Reed & Palumbo, 1987/1988, 1992).

Programming. As part of the BASIC test, the assignment was to write a program that (a) asked the user for two numbers; (b) asked the user which mathematical operation–addition, subtraction, multiplication, or division–he or she would like to perform using the two numbers; (c) required an error trap for division by zero; (d) presented the result of the operation; and (e) then gave the user the option to repeat the sequence with two different numbers. The range was 0 points to 35 points. (See Appendix A for the BASIC programming assignment.)

As part of the *HyperCard* test, the assignment was to create a stack that consisted of at least four cards. The first card was the title card with one background; the remaining cards had another background. Pictures representing four different objects were to be on the second card. Each object was to be labeled by information in a field. A click on an object would take the user to a description of the object, presented on a card or a field. The program had to have an option to exit at any point, and the instructions for the user were to be clear. The movements between cards were to be accompanied by visual effects. The range was 0 points to 30 points. (See Appendix B for the *HyperCard* programming assignment.)

Because the programming measure for the BASIC group had a different range (0 to 35) than the measure for the *HyperCard* group (0 to 30), scores were changed to percentages, giving a range from 0 to 100.

Debugging. As part of the BASIC test, the students were assigned to debug a program, presented in paper-form, that had 10 errors. They were to identify the 10 errors, explain why each was an error or what would happen if the program were executed without correcting it, and then correct it. The errors ranged from incorrect syntax, missing commands, excessive numeric variable values, and illogical sequence of commands. The range was 0 points to 30 points. (See Appendix C for the BASIC debugging assignment.)

As part of the *HyperCard* test, the students were required to debug a HyperTalk script, presented in paper-form with 10 errors. They were to engage in the same debugging steps–explain why each was an error or what would happen if the program were executed without correcting it, and then correct it. The errors ranged from incorrect syntax to missing commands to illogical commands. The range was also 0 points to 30 points. (See Appendix D for the *HyperCard* debugging assignment.)

Procedures

During the first class meeting, students in both classes responded to the 61-item problem-solving instrument and the 20-item computer anxiety instrument. During the 12th meeting they responded to the same instruments. During the second through the ninth meetings, they received instruction in either BASIC or *HyperCard*–as explained above under the Independent Variable section. During the 10th meeting, they took either the BASIC or the *HyperCard* test. During the 11th meeting, the evaluated tests were returned and correct and incorrect answers were explained.

Analysis of the Data

Research Question: What are the comparative effects of BASIC versus *HyperCard* on problem solving and computer anxiety? Two 2 × 2 analyses of variance (Course: BASIC versus *HyperCard*; and Data Collection: pretest versus posttest) with a repeated measure on one factor (Data Collection: pretest versus posttest) were conducted with problem solving as the dependent measure in one and computer anxiety as the dependent measure in the other.

Research Question: What effect does language have on language competency measures (debugging and programming)? Two unpaired *t*-tests were conducted comparing the debugging scores of the *HyperCard* group versus those of the BASIC group in one procedure. Comparisons were then made with the programming scores of the *HyperCard* group versus those of the BASIC group in the other procedure.

Multiple regressions were conducted on the following research questions: What is the relationship between problem-solving and (a) computer anxiety and (b) language competency as measured via programming and debugging exercises? Also, what is the relationship between computer anxiety and language competency as measured via programming and debugging exercises?

RESULTS

Problem Solving

There was a significant main effect of Data Collection on problem solving: $F(1,19) = 8.167$, $p = .01$. That is, the study-participants' problem solving increased from pre-treatment to post-treatment ($X_{pre} = 45.81$; $X_{post} = 48.00$). There was not, however, a significant main effect of Course on problem solving: $F(1,19) = .175$, $p = .68$. There was also not a significant two-way interaction: $F(1,19) = 2.173$, $p = .157$. There was a significant increase in problem solving for the BASIC group: $t(12) = -3.309$, $p = .006$ ($X_{pre} = 44.923$; $X_{post} = 48.00$). There was not, however, a significant change in problem solving for the *HyperCard* group: $t(7) = -.563$, $p = .591$ ($X_{pre} = 47.25$; $X_{post} = 48.00$). Although there was not a significant main effect of Course on problem solving, the pre-treatment to post-treatment (Data Collection) significant increase was due to the increase for the BASIC group. (Table 1.)

Computer Anxiety

There was a significant main effect of Data Collection on computer anxiety: $F(1,19) = 54.893$, $p < .0001$. That is, the study-participants' computer anxiety decreased from pre-treatment to post-treatment ($X_{pre} = 47.714$; $X_{post} = 35.476$). There was not, however, a significant main effect of Course on computer anxiety: $F(1,19) = .478$, $p = .498$. There was also not a significant two-way interaction: $F(1,19) = 2.219$, $p = .153$. There was a significant decrease in computer anxiety for the BASIC group: $t(12) = 5.06$, $p = .0003$ ($X_{pre} = 48.077$; $X_{post} = 37.769$). There was also a significant decrease in computer anxiety for the *HyperCard* group: $t(7) = 5.486$, $p = .0009$ ($X_{pre} = 47.125$; $X_{post} = 31.75$). These results indicate that the respective treatments were equally effective at significantly reducing the study-participants' computer anxiety. (Table 1.)

TABLE 1. Means and Standard Deviations of *HyperCard* and BASIC Groups' Pre-Treatment and Post-Treatment Scores for Computer Anxiety, Problem Solving, Debugging, and Programming

	HyperCard n = 8		BASIC n = 13		Both n = 21	
	Pre	Post	Pre	Post	Pre	Post
Computer Anxiety[1]	47.125 (8.643)	31.75 (10.553)	48.077 (14.192)	37.769 (11.577)	47.714 (12.133)	35.476 (11.33)
Problem Solving[2]	47.25 (9.192)	48.00 (7.251)	44.923 (5.235)	48.00 (4.865)	45.81 (6.882)	48.00 (5.71)
Debugging[3]		28.375 (2.722)		18.077 (4.192)		22.00 (6.277)
Programming[4]		92.5 (9.754)		82.077 (11.243)		86.762 (11.832)

1 = significant pre-treatment to post-treatment decrease for the *HyperCard* group, the BASIC group, and both groups combined
2 = significant pre-treatment to post-treatment increase for the BASIC group and both groups combined
3 = significant difference between the *HyperCard* group and the BASIC group
4 = significant difference between the *HyperCard* group and the BASIC group

Performance Measures

Programming. The *HyperCard* group performed better on the programming exercise than did the BASIC group: $t(19) = -2.213$, $p = .039$. The mean for the *HyperCard* group was 92.75; for the BASIC group, 82.077. (Table 1.)

Debugging. The *HyperCard* group also performed better on the debugging exercise than did the BASIC group: $t(19) = -6.612$, $p < .0001$. The mean for the *HyperCard* group was 28.375; for the BASIC group, 18.077. (Table 1.)

Correlations

Both Groups Combined. There were significant, high correlations between post-treatment computer anxiety and debugging when factoring in Course: $r = .893$, $p < .0001$. Course had a positive relationship with debugging: $t(20) = 6.531$, $p = .0001$, *beta* = 9.043, *beta weight* = .717. Because the BASIC group was coded as 1 in the regression and the *HyperCard* group as 2, this finding indicates that the *HyperCard* group scored higher on the debugging exercise. An unpaired *t*-test comparing the groups' means, as explained above in the Debugging section, supports this finding. Post-treatment computer anxiety, however, had a negative relationship with debugging: $t(20) = 3.43$, $p = .003$, *beta* = −.209, *beta weight* = −.376. That is, those with relatively lower computer anxiety generally performed better on the debugging exercise, regardless of course grouping. Based on the *beta weights*, course grouping had a stronger relationship with debugging than did computer anxiety. (Table 1.)

There were no other significant correlations when factoring in Course.

HyperCard Group. There was a significant, high, negative correlation between problem-solving and computer anxiety: $r = -.709$, $t(7) = 2.466$, $p = .049$. That is, for the *HyperCard* group, those study-participants who had relatively lower computer anxiety generally had relatively higher problem-solving scores.

There were no other significant correlations.

BASIC Group. There was a significant, medium, negative correlation between programming and computer anxiety: $r = -.566$, $t(12) = 2.28$, $p = .044$. That is, for the BASIC group, those study-participants who had relatively lower computer anxiety generally had relatively higher programming scores. There was a significant, medium, negative correlation between debugging and computer anxiety: $r = -.649$, $t(12) = 2.826$, $p = .017$. That is, for the BASIC group, those study-participants who had relatively lower computer anxiety generally had relatively higher debugging scores.

There were no other significant correlations.

DISCUSSION

Problem-Solving Skills

The problem-solving skills of the BASIC group improved from the beginning of the treatment to the end, whereas the problem solving skills of the *HyperCard* group did not. This finding supports our earlier notion that *HyperCard* may simplify programming so much due to its authoring features that thinking processes critical to enhancing problem-solving skills may not occur.

Although BASIC and *HyperCard* are similar in certain ways, a profound difference is ease in use. *HyperCard* shares certain similar features with BASIC. Each of the five objects in *HyperCard* (stack, card, background, field, and button) can be compared to the subroutines in BASIC. Each of them has its own characteristics and performs certain functions. Fields are used to store information much like the arrays in BASIC. Like BASIC, HyperTalk (the scripting language for *HyperCard*) has its control statements, time/date functions, math functions, math operation capability, and file handling capability. However, unlike BASIC, programming in *HyperCard* is nonlinear in nature, although BASIC can be taught in a nonlinear fashion. Each of the five objects has its own separate scripts and is independent of one another. Because the objects in *HyperCard* can be linked in different ways, there are no strict beginning and ending points. But, despite similarities, a fundamental difference is that *HyperCard* simplifies software construction (see Henry & Southerly, this volume, for a detailed comparison of the two languages).

That the BASIC group improved in problem solving is not especially surprising. A large amount of research to date has supported this finding. Although many studies exist, a few are virtually identical in design: Reed and Palumbo, 1987/1988; Reed, Palumbo and Stolar, 1987/1988; and Reed and Palumbo, 1992. In each of these studies, the BASIC participants' problem-solving scores increased significantly over the course of nine weeks. One essential difference, between this study and the three cited, is that this study occurred over a six-week, rather than a nine-week, period. In another study–Palumbo and Reed (1987/1988)–problem-solving scores were collected at the four-week point to attempt to determine at what point measurable changes in problem solving might occur. There was not a significant increase from the onset of the study to the four-week mark, indicating that changes in problem solving occurred between the five-week and nine-week points. The sample in this study was comparable to those in the other four. A fairly safe inference is that it takes between five and six weeks–45 to 54 hours–for problem-solving skills to be measurably affected.

Computer Anxiety

For both groups, computer anxiety decreased. This is not surprising because many studies have shown that computer anxiety can be significantly decreased even after very brief exposures to computer instruction. For example, Overbaugh and Reed (in press) found that computer anxiety was significantly reduced after three weeks, two hours per week, of instruction–only six hours. Studies involving BASIC (Reed & Palumbo, 1987/1988; Reed & Palumbo, 1992) cite four weeks of instruction as being effective at reducing computer anxiety. This study found that, after six weeks of instruction, computer anxiety was significantly reduced regardless of language. One interesting note is that the BASIC group reduced their anxiety by 10.308 points, whereas the *HyperCard* group reduced theirs by 15.375–not significantly different, but nonetheless different. The point that *HyperCard* is "easier" than BASIC, as speculated earlier, is supported to some extent by the *HyperCard* group's greater reduction in computer anxiety, especially if we ascribe to the notion that a reduction in computer anxiety reflects some degree of success at using the language. Such success might be influenced by the ease of the language. It is supported to a much greater extent when comparing the two groups' performance measures, as explained next.

Performance Measures

The *HyperCard* group outperformed the BASIC group on both the programming and debugging exercises. The BASIC group improved their problem-solving skills and the *HyperCard* group did not. A logical interpretation is that *HyperCard* has simplified programming so much that *HyperCard* programmers can be more successful at using the language than those using BASIC–but, at the expense of "bypassing" critical thinking skills that promote the enhancement of problem-solving skills.

The *HyperCard* group had significantly higher performance scores, but did not develop problem-solving skills. This suggested that *HyperCard* was easier. Another interpretation is that *HyperCard* programmers were more successful at using that language than were those using BASIC–and apparently *HyperCard* was so much easier that it did not result in the programmers improving their problem-solving skills.

The relatively lower BASIC performance scores are consistent with two studies by Reed and Palumbo (1987/1988, 1992) which used identical BASIC performance measures. In the 1992 study the research participants scored 81.07 on the programming task; this study, 82.08. For the debugging measure, the 1987/1988 participants scored 18.91; this study, 18.08. In all three studies, the samples were very similar and the instruments, where administered, were identical.

The Correlations

The two significant, negative correlations for the BASIC group provide even more evidence of BASIC's relatively greater difficulty. The correlations were (a) between debugging and computer anxiety and (b) between programming and computer anxiety. Based on these correlations, it is clear that greater computer anxiety was associated with poorer debugging and programming performances. Although the negative relationship between computer anxiety and debugging emerged when including all the participants regardless of language grouping, the absence of a relationship for the *HyperCard* group, when looking at each group separately, limits the relationship just to the BASIC group. That is, computer anxiety had a significant, negative relationship with debugging in the multiple regression–when Course was held at its mean. When simple regressions were conducted to determine significant relationships within each group, the relationship between computer anxiety and debugging emerged–when dealing with only the BASIC group. This occurrence within the BASIC group provides evidence that BASIC is more difficult because differing performance scores on language-related tasks were related to different levels of computer anxiety, as reflected by this negative relationship. The performance scores on the language-related tasks by the *HyperCard* group, however, were not related to different levels of computer anxiety, indicating that the performance tasks were not as difficult. A possible related example for illustrative purposes is that differing levels of mathematics anxiety may not distinguish performance when the math problem is adding 2 plus 2. Most likely, people, regardless of their anxiety, could perform that calculation. However, if the math problems were more difficult–finding the square root of 27 times eight–varying levels of mathematics anxiety would distinguish performance. Our point is that the greater difficulty of BASIC, relative to *HyperCard*, is at least partly reflected by the negative, distinguishing relationships between computer anxiety and the two performance measures. There is, very likely, other evidence that indicates BASIC is more difficult, but it is not apparent in this study.

IMPLICATIONS

The results of this study support our earlier suspicion that, while *HyperCard* is superior to BASIC for software construction, BASIC appears to be the language of choice when the purpose is to develop problem-solving skills. As we have stated, *HyperCard* is easier than BASIC, as reflected by the higher performance scores and greater reduction in computer anxiety. This point of greater ease for *HyperCard* is especially germane to pre-service and in-service instruction when prospective and practicing teachers are expected to work with a computer language–for example, as part of a computer literacy course. It may also be preferred over programming languages when students are to use a language to develop projects such as the one described by Lehrer, Erikson, Love, and Connell (this volume). In this case, the purpose of the instruction was to develop software or to construct knowledge structures, rather than develop problem-solving skills. The absence of an increase in problem-solving scores indicates that *HyperCard* should not be used if that is the purpose of instruction. BASIC apparently enhances problem-solving skills partly because it is more difficult and requires more detailed thought.

A possible design change for further research might involve comparing BASIC commands with only HyperTalk scripting commands. In our study, the *HyperCard* instruction involved seven sessions on authoring features and only three sessions on scripting commands. It must be noted, however, that many of the authoring features were facilitated by script-like aids, such as the navigation commands. Another consideration in this proposed study is whether HyperTalk might be taught without the foundational instruction on the authoring features. Given the probable need of this foundation, a research concern then would be time on task. That is, would more time for this information need to be built into *HyperCard* instruction? Would the resulting differences or similarities be due to the parallel features of the two languages or would it simply be that the *HyperCard* group spent more time? Because time would be difficult to dispute, the instruction for the BASIC group would probably need to be rethought to lengthen the exposure to BASIC so that the length of treatment for both groups would be similar. Perhaps the more "authoring" features of BASIC could be the central instruction early in the treatment.

If this lengthier *HyperCard* treatment were implemented, a repeated measure design might be used so that the mid-treatment data point would be the same as the post-treatment data in this study. This would allow us to compare the pre-treatment/post-treatment scores of this study to the pre-treatment/mid-treatment scores of the future study. Similar findings would confirm or contradict the results in the *HyperCard* portion of this study.

Despite the changes we might make in our subsequent studies, it is clear via the ERIC search that there is a virtual vacuum of hypermedia/multimedia research. Probably almost any line of research would contribute. Fortunately, unlike some of the past research directions of instructional computing, there is body of research–related both to CAI and programming languages–that can help formulate the research questions and guide the designs.

REFERENCES

Ashworth, D. & Stelovsky, J. (1989). Kanji City. An exploration of Hypermedia applications for CALL. *CALICO Journal*, *6*(4), 27-39.

Barba, R. H. & Merchant, L. J. (1990). The effects of embedding generative cognitive strategies in science software. *Journal of Computers in Mathematics and Science Teaching*, *10*(1), 59-65.

Bourne, D. E. (1990). Computer-assisted instruction, learning theory, and hypermedia: An associative linkage. *Research Strategies, 8*(4), 160-171.

Bowers, D. & Chia, T. (1990). HyperCard in educational research: An introduction and case study. *Educational Technology, 30*(2), 19-24.

Boyle, C. C. & Snell, J. R. (1990). Intelligent navigation for semistructured hypertext documents. In: R. McAleese & C. Green (Eds.), *Hypertext: State of the art* (pp. 29-42). Oxford, England: Intellect.

Brader, L. L. (1990). Tools of the courseware trade: A comparison of toolbook 1.0 and HyperCard 2.0. *Tech Trends, 35*(5), 10-17.

Burton, J. K. & Magliaro, S. (1987/1988). Computer programming and generalized problem-solving skills: In search of direction. *Computers in the Schools, 43*(4), 63-90.

Camp, J. & Cogan, M. (1988). HyperCard: A milestone in educational computing. *Electronic Learning*, (7), 46-47.

Campbell, R. (1989). (I learned it) through the Grapevine: Hypermedia at work in the classroom. *American Libraries, 20*(3), 200-202, 204-205.

Clements, D. H. (1986). Effects of Logo and CAI environments on cognition and creativity. *Journal of Educational Psychology, 76*, 1051-1058.

Colloum, C. J. & Cockerton-Turner, T. (1990). Using hypertext for educational "help" facilities. In: R. McAleese & C. Green (Eds.), *Hypertext: State of the art* (pp. 105-113). Intellect: Oxford, England.

Crane, G. & Mylonas, E. (1988). The perseus project: An interactive curriculum on classical Greek civilization. *Educational Technology, 28*(11), 25-32.

Dalbey, J. & Linn, M. C. (1985). The demands and requirements of computer programming: A review of the literature. *Journal of Educational Computing Research, 1*, 253-274.

DiPardo, A. & DiPardo, M. (1990). Towards the metapersonal essay: Exploring the potential of hypertext in composition class. *Computers and Composition, 7*(3), 7-22.

Dufresne, A., Jolin, N., & Senteni, A. (1990). Hypertext documents for the learning of procedures. In: R. McAleese & C. Green (Eds.), *Hypertext: State of the art* (pp. 97-104). Oxford, England: Intellect.

Duhrkopf, R. (1988). HyperCard as a tool for educational software development. *The American Biology Teacher, 50*(2), 121-122.

Friedlander, L. (1989). Moving images into the classroom: Multimedia in higher education. *Laserdisk Professional, 2*(4), 33-38.

Gustafson K. L. & Reeves, T. C. (1990). IDioM: A platform for a course development expert system. *Educational Technology, 30*(3), 19-25.

Hall, W., Thorogood, P. , Hutchings, G., & Carr, L. (1989). Using HyperCard and interactive video in education: An application in cell biology. *Educational & Training Technology International, 26*(3), 207-214.

Harris, M. & Cady, M. (1988). The dynamic process of creating hypertext literature. *Educational Technology, 28*(11), 33-40.

Holleman, P. (1990). Macintosh HyperCard library instruction program. *Community & Junior College Libraries, 7*(1), 59-75.

Hopper, J. (1990). Student-directed learning using HyperCard. *Computers in the Schools, 7*(4), 83-98.

Horton, S.V., Boone, R. A., & Lovitt, T. C. (1990). Teaching social studies to learning disabled high school students: Effects of a hypertext study guide. *British Journal of Educational Technology, 21*(2), 118-131.

Jonassen, D. H. (1989). *Hypertext/Hypermedia.* Englewood Cliffs, NJ: Educational Technology Publications.

Jonassen, D. H. (1990). Semantic network elicitation: Tools for structuring hypertext. In: R. McAleese & C. Green (Eds.), *Hypertext: State of the art* (pp. 142-154). Oxford, England: Intellect.

Lanza, A. & Roselli, T. (1991). Effects of the Hypertextual approach versus the structured approach on students' achievement. *Journal of Computer-Based Instruction, 18*(2), 48-50.

May, C. (1990). *The American Short Story: From Poe to O. Henry. A HyperCard application.* California State University, Long Beach, English Department. (ERIC Document Reproduction Service ED 330 315)

McDowell, E. E. (1989). The development of an instructional program on employment interviewing. Paper presented at the 75th Annual Meeting of the Speech Communication Association, (San Francisco, CA, November 18-21). (ERIC Document Reproduction Service ED 312 726)

McKnight, C., Dillon, A., & Richardson, J. (1990). A comparison of linear and hypertext formats in information retrieval. In: R. McAleese & C. Green (Eds.), *Hypertext: State of the art* (pp. 11-19). Oxford, England: Intellect.

Miller, A. & Radziemski, C. (1988). Software reviews. *School Science and Mathematics, 88*(6), 528-530.

Monk, A. F. (1990). Getting to known locations in a hypertext. In: R. McAleese & C. Green (Eds.), *Hypertext: State of the art* (pp. 21-27). Oxford, England: Intellect.

Neuman, D. (1991). Designing library instruction for undergraduates: Combining instructional systems design and naturalistic inquiry. *College and Research Libraries, 52*(2), 165-176.

Overbaugh, R. C. & Reed, W. (in press). The effects of prior experience and instructional format on teacher education students' computer anxiety and performance. *Computers in the Schools.*

Palumbo, D. B. & Reed, W. M. (1987/1988). Intensity of treatment and its relationship to programming languages/problem-solving research. *Computers in the Schools, 4*(3/4), 113-121.

Percival, J. M. (1990). Graphic interfaces and online information, *Online Review, 14*(1), 15-20.

Reed, W. M. Palumbo, D. B., & Stolar, A. L. (1987/88). The comparative effects of BASIC and Logo instruction on problem-solving skills. *Computers in the Schools, 4*(3/4), 99-111.

Reed, W. M. & Palumbo, D. B. (1987/88). The effect of BASIC programming on problem solving and computer anxiety. *Computers in the Schools, 4*(3/4), 85-97.

Reed, W. M. & Palumbo, D. B. (1992). The effect of BASIC instruction on problem solving skills over an extended period of time. *Journal of Educational Computing Research, 8*(3).

Tripp, S. D. & Roby, W. (1990). Orientation and disorientation in a Hypertext lexicon. *Journal of Computer-Based Instruction, 17*(4), 120-124.

Tucker, S. A. & Dempsey, J. V. (1990). Photo-interviewing as a tool of inquiry. Paper presented at the National Consortium for Instruction and Cognition, Boston, MA, April 16-20. (ERIC Document Reproduction Service ED 318800).

Underwood, J. (1989). HyperCard and interactive video. *CALICO Journal, 6*(3), 7-20.

Vaccaro, B. (1988). HyperCard applications. *Small computers in Libraries*, (8), 30-35.

Appendix A

Programming Portion of BASIC Test

Write a program that---

asks the user his or her name
once the name is given, the screen should then clear
after clearing, the computer should address the user by name with a friendly message that is FLASHing
after a five-second delay, the program should ask the user for two numbers; the first question should appear halfway down the screen, and the other should appear a few lines above the bottom of the screen
after the two numbers are given by the user, the screen should clear and ask which mathematical operation he or she would like to perform on the two numbers—addition, subtraction, division, or multiplication
once the operation is selected, the screen should then clear and the "product" of the operation should appear (that is, if the user inputs 5 and 7 and chooses multiplication, then the "product" appearing on the screen would be 35)
after the "product" appears on the screen, the computer should then ask if the user would like to enter two new numbers; if so, you should have programmed in lines that would allow him to do that (the option to turn off the machine and run the program again is not acceptable!); if not, then the program should end

SAVE this program under your last name.

SOME POINTERS:

1. *Consider each part of the assignment separately; that is, break the task down into smaller subtasks.*
2. *For the division option, you need to include an error trap that does not allow 0 as the second number; simply put, you cannot divide by zero.*
3. *Error trap where you want the user to make a selection from a set of specific response choices.*
4. *Use REMs when you go from one section of the program to another.*

In this program you are using INPUT and GET commands, string and numeric variables, conditionals, iteration, some form of modularity, and various TEXT-related commands. You might want to check your program for this.

Appendix B

Programming Portion of HyperCard Test

Create a HyperCard stack using your name that---

consists of 4 cards with the first card as the title card
has at least two backgrounds with the title card having one background and the second card having another background;
contains pictures representing four different kinds of objects on the SECOND card (They can be from Art ideas or hand-drawn)
labels each object with a field or a tool.
has four transparent buttons on top of each of the objects. A click on a picture will display a description of the object. The description should be simple, one or two lines for example. The description of TWO objects will be displayed on CARDS and the description of the other two objects will be displayed on POP-UP FIELDS. There should be a return button on the description cards in order to go back. The return button can be on background if these two cards have a different background from the ɪest of cards (i.e., your stack has three backgrounds or on foreground if they share the same background with the rest your stack has two backgrounds). The pop-up fields will appear for 2 seconds, and then disappear.

Things to consider:

1. *The program should have an exit at any point.*
2. *The directions for the users as to what to do should be clear.*
3. *The movements between cards should be accompanied by visual effects.*
4. *Concentrate on the main part and keep a simple design for the backgrounds.*
5. *Make sure your stack works.*

Appendix C

Exercise for BASIC Debugging

Ten programming errors exist in the following ***high-res*** program. The errors range from incorrect sequence of commands to incorrect commands for a given mode to absent commands to unnecessary commands. These errors will result in an improperly executed program.

You need to do the following three steps:

1. identify the error
2. explain what would happen or not happen if the error were executed
3. give the correction.

```
10 HOME
20 GR
25 REM ******** BACKGROUND *******
30 HCOLOR = 1
40 FOR A = 0 TO 159
50 HPLOT 0, B TO 279, B
60 NEXT A
70 HCOLOR = 3
75 REM ******** ANIMATION *******
80 FOR PLANE = 0 TO 200 STEP -2
90 GOTO 1000
100 HCOLOR = 1
110 GOSUB 2000
120 HCOLOR = 0
130 GOSUB 1000
140 GOSUB 2000
150 NEXT PLAIN
1000 REM ********* FIRST PART OF OBJECT **************
1010 HPLOT PL, 0 TO PL + 20, 0 TO PL + 50, 10 TO PL + 20, 20 TO PL, 20 TO PL, 0
2000 REM ********* SECOND PART OF OBJECT *************
2010 HLIN PL, 21 TO PL + 80, 21 TO PL + 80, 31 TO PL, 21
2020 RETURN
```

Appendix D

Exercise for HyperCard Debugging

This stack has two cards. On the first card, there are a card field called "one" and a card button called "debug." On the second card there is a card field called "two," and a background field called "BK field." The debug button on card one has the script listed below. This script contains 10 errors.

You are to (a) identify the 10 errors; (b) explain why each is an error or what would happen if the program were executed without correcting it; and (c) correct them.

```
on mouseUp
    repeat 5
        hide field "one"
        visual barn door open very slow
        visual iris
        go next
        put "It is sunny." to card field "two"
        put 10 into holder
        put 20 into card field "BK field"
        add field "BK field"  holder
        put holder in msg
        go
        show card field "one"
        show card button "Show me"
    end
    do menu "Quit HyperCard"
end mouseUp
```

Gail E. Fitzgerald

Hypermedia in Teacher Education: Development of Course Support Materials

While computer-based activities have been used extensively in corporate training programs and specialized professional schools, their use by faculty in teacher education has a short history. Teacher educators have taught about technology rather than with technology. Computer-based instruction at the post-secondary level has been poorly developed. Most instructor-designed courseware used in higher education have been created as isolated products on a piecemeal basis by individual faculty with specialized interests. What exists is fragmented, unfocused, uneven in quality, and rarely disseminated (Hannafin & Mitzel, 1990).

With the recent development of easy-to-use hypermedia authoring programs, interest in creating course support materials is increasing among teacher educators. Much of this popularity grows from the promise of programs such as *Hypercard* and *Authorware Professional* for the Macintosh and *Linkway* and *ToolBook* for MS-DOS platforms. These high-powered authoring programs allow a developer to create stacks composed of computer screens which are linked together by buttons. Graphics, video, and audio can easily be integrated into these hypermedia stacks, creating flexible, interactive learning experiences for students. These stacks can be used to assemble lecture materials, compile related instructional materials for students to peruse, or create structured interactive learning activities.

Just because authoring tools are readily available, effective instruction-

GAIL E. FITZGERALD is Associate Professor, Department of Special Education, West Virginia University, Morgantown, WV 26506-6122.

[Haworth co-indexing entry note]: "Hypermedia in Teacher Education: Development of Course Support Materials." Fitzgerald, Gail E. Co-published simultaneously in *Computers in the Schools* (The Haworth Press, Inc.) Vol. 10, No. 1/2, 1994, pp. 47-68; and: *Multimedia and Megachange: New Roles for Educational Computing* (eds: W. Michael Reed, John K. Burton, and Min Liu) The Haworth Press, Inc., 1994, pp. 47-68. Multiple copies of this article/chapter may be purchased from The Haworth Document Delivery Center [1-800-3-HAWORTH; 9:00 a.m. - 5:00 p.m. (EST)].

al design is not ensured. According to Hannafin and Mitzel (1990), "It is now comparatively easy to create *something* via the computer, but as demanding as ever to create *something instructionally worthwhile*" (p. 198). As teacher educators begin developing courseware, design guidelines are needed for matching hypermedia activities to instructional goals.

The purpose of this article is to briefly examine a design model for hypermedia materials and to give recommendations for developing course support materials in teacher education. The model links the design of computer-based activities to instructional goals organized by stages of learning. Examples of hypermedia courseware used in special education are included to guide similar applications by faculty in higher education.

THE STAGES OF LEARNING MODEL APPLIED TO HYPERMEDIA DESIGN

A developer of computer-based materials needs to consider the instructional goals for the materials. Computer-assisted instruction (CAI) is typically categorized as drill-and-practice, tutorial, problem solving, simulation, or database. Each type of CAI activity has unique characteristics and is used for different educational purposes. Effective instruction requires a match between CAI design and learner outcomes (Gagne, Wager, & Rojas, 1981; Bell, 1985; Hagler, 1987; Roblyer, 1988).

The stages of learning model is useful for depicting these relationships. It is based on original work of Gagne (1974) and further described by Criswell (1989). In this model, learning is viewed as developing systematically through the stages of acquisition, fluency, maintenance, generalization, and application. By considering the stage of learning needed to meet a learning objective, a decision can be made as to the type of computer-based activity which will be most effective.

These two dimensions, e.g., stage of learning and type of CAI material, can be organized into a matrix to guide the design of hypermedia materials. These relationships are shown in Table 1. The matrix displays the following relationships: Tutorial approaches are most effective for presenting new information; drill-and-practice approaches are needed for building speed and accuracy; drill-and-practice and databases are effective for recall and rehearsal; and problem-solving and simulation programs are useful for generalization and application purposes. As teacher educators become developers of hypermedia materials, this design matrix provides a helpful framework for selecting and designing effective courseware.

Teacher training involves the development of knowledge, skills, and

TABLE 1. Matching Hypermedia Materials to Instructional Stages

Stage \ Type	Drill and Practice	Tutorial	Problem Solving or Simulation	Database
Acquisition		X		
Fluency	X			
Maintenance	X			X
Generalization			X	
Application			X	

applications. The weakest link in preservice teacher education is the translation of knowledge and skills taught in methods classes to performance skills in the classroom (Rule & Salzberg, 1988). Computer-based training activities afford an intermediary step by providing practice in applying skills to classroom-anchored scenarios.

The hypermedia materials described in this article consist of a series of computer-based learning activities developed to supplement instruction in behavior management skills for special education teachers. Their content includes instruction on behavioral terminology, effective classroom management procedures, behavioral observation and data interpretation skills, and strategies for designing behavior change interventions.

These materials were pilot tested in a behavior management course in special education in which practicing teachers employed on a "temporary permit license" were enrolled for graduate credit. The materials were entirely supplemental. No part of the course grade was based on computer activity scores. Each class day consisted of approximately 45 minutes of computer lab work in which the activities correlated with the daily lecture topics. As seen in Table 2, these materials were highly valued by students as an effective method of instruction.

Most teachers in this course had minimal computer-using skills. 55% of the teachers listed the computer learning station activities as one of the three strengths of the course, with comments such as "computer time increased fluency," "the computer activities were great for working on concepts and major points," and "forced me in a fun way to learn more about computer use." Only one negative evaluation comment about the computer activities was recorded. This particular teacher reported that the multiple choice computer quizzes were very difficult, as her "personal learning style is more conducive to essay type questions."

TABLE 2. Ratings of Instructional Approaches in Behavior Management Course

Instructional Method	Sample Size	Mean Rating	Standard Deviation
Structured in-class activities	24	5.92	.282
Examples of applied interventions	24	5.83	.381
Instructor lectures	24	5.75	.442
Computer-based learning activities	24	5.67	.702
Independent project time during class	24	5.63	.576
Textbook	24	5.46	.658
Pre-course self-study readings	24	5.25	.847
Case study discussion groups	24	5.17	.816

Note: 6-point scale ranging from 1 (not helpful) to 6 (very helpful)

In the remainder of this article, the materials, their design, and course integration will be described. The relationship between the courseware being described and the matrix model is shown in Table 3.

DEVELOPMENT OF THE HYPERMEDIA INSTRUCTIONAL MATERIALS

The materials were created using the *Authorware Professional* authoring system, Macintosh version (Macromedia, 1992). This authoring program offers a powerful array of features for creating hypermedia materials, including text, graphics, animation, sound, and video. With this program, very complex, high-quality applications can be developed. Lessons are created by moving design option icons onto a flowline, similar to a flowchart; opening them up and entering content; and designing alternative branches through the activity.

Authorware Professional is very well-suited for instructional courseware where the developer chooses to control the instructional interaction. User responses can be judged by the number of trials, a text response, click/touch area, a keypress, pushbutton, location of a movable object on screen, or as a timed response. Branching capabilities as well as perpetually active buttons are available. By defining system variables, learner data can be collected and written to data files for instructor review. In addition to controlled lesson interactions, hypermedia materials can be assembled that allow the user to navigate independently through the materials.

TABLE 3. Course Support Materials Used in Behavior Management Course

Type / Goal	Drill and Practice	Tutorial	Problem Solving or Simulation	Database
Acquisition	Interactive Quizzes	Graphing Progress Lines		
Fluency	Terminology & Coding Flashcards			
Maintenance				Strategies Hyperbase
Generalization			Videodisc Coding Practice	
Application			Schedules of Reinforcement	

HYPERMEDIA FOR ACQUISITION GOALS

Tutorials. The goal of instruction at the acquisition level is for the learner to acquire new knowledge or skills. Tutorials are the appropriate form of computer-based instruction for teaching new information. The model for developing tutorial software that is most widely used is the events of instruction model (Petry, Mouton, & Reigeluth, 1987; Gagne, Briggs, & Wager, 1988; Ranker & Doucet, 1990). The tutorial lesson should model what a good "tutor" does. The steps include (a) gaining the learner's attention, (b) informing the learner of the objective of instruction, (c) recalling prerequisite knowledge, (d) presenting new material, (e) guiding learning, (f) providing opportunities to demonstrate learning, (g) giving performance-based feedback, (h) evaluating performance, and (i) enhancing retention through relevance.

A computer-based tutorial should be designed for stand-alone use. The learner must be able to acquire and practice the lesson's content independent of supplemental instruction. Thus, tutorial designs are extremely complex to design. Only small amounts of information can be presented at any one time. Chunking and sequencing the content are critical. Sufficient practice must allow for discrimination of examples and non-examples and ellucidate their critical features (Criswell, 1989). Effective design utilizes the demonstrate-practice-feedback format. Feedback to the learner must be immediate and corrective. Further, the tutorial must teach the structure of the content itself and provide mnemonic assistance for retaining new information and skills (Hannum, 1988).

In the application *Graphing Progress Lines*, a tutorial approach is used to teach a six-step procedure for computing a line of progress for evaluating behavioral data (Alberto & Troutman, 1990). The user learns the steps of this procedure by moving objects on the screen with the mouse from one location to another. In this sequence, the learner places vertical lines at the mid-session points on the left and right halves of the graph (Figure 1), places horizontal lines at the mid-performance points on each half, and then connects them by dragging a line through the point intersections. Following the tutorial portion of the program, new data graphs are presented for the learner to practice the technique. For any errors made in identifying the correct intersects, detailed corrective feedback is provided. The last stage of the tutorial utilizes actual data from clinical case studies discussed in the course (Figure 2).

In the field testing of this tutorial, students independently progressed through the tutorial three times. Pre-to-post accuracy scores only improved from 48% to 62% (n = 24). It was determined that the tutorial had a major weakness in not providing a mnemonic structure to aid learners in remembering the steps of the procedure during practice (Hannum, 1988). Thus, a perpetually active "*help*" option has been added that allows the student to access assistance as desired within the tutorial.

Interactive Quizzes. Computer-based tests are frequently used to assess mastery. Tests can also be used as advance organizers for class material. To guide acquisition, tests taken prior to instruction direct the student's attention to important content and motivate the student to retain that information. The same interactive tests can then be used following instruction to assess learning and provide informative feedback on errors. Recordkeeping features in computer programs provide learners as well as the instructor important information regarding errors, progress, and mastery.

In the application *Interactive Quizzes*, a series of multiple choice quizzes are used to assess knowledge of lecture content and assigned readings. Each quiz includes ten items. In the pre-test version, the learner receives feedback stating whether the response was correct or incorrect and what topic to pay attention to in class activities. In the post-test version, the leaner's initial response is scored and remedial feedback pro-

FIGURE 1. Screen from application *Graphing Progress Lines* showing tutorial step

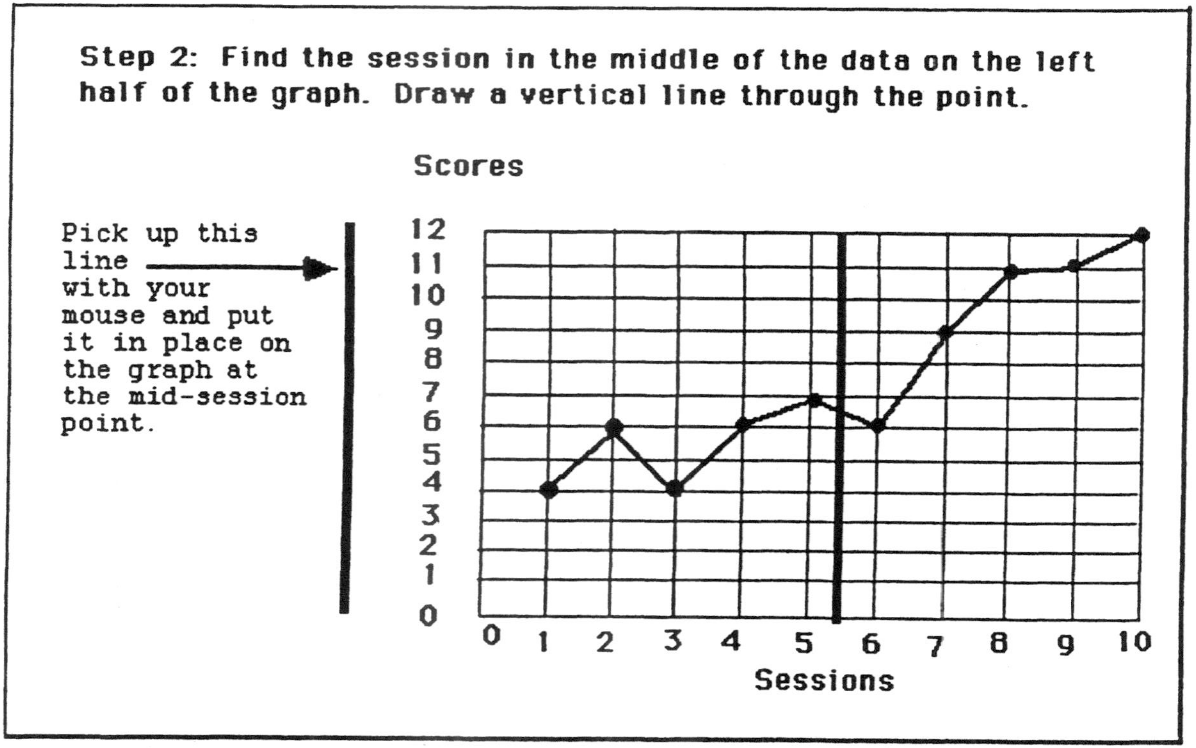

FIGURE 2. Screen from application *Graphing Progress Lines* for data interpretation

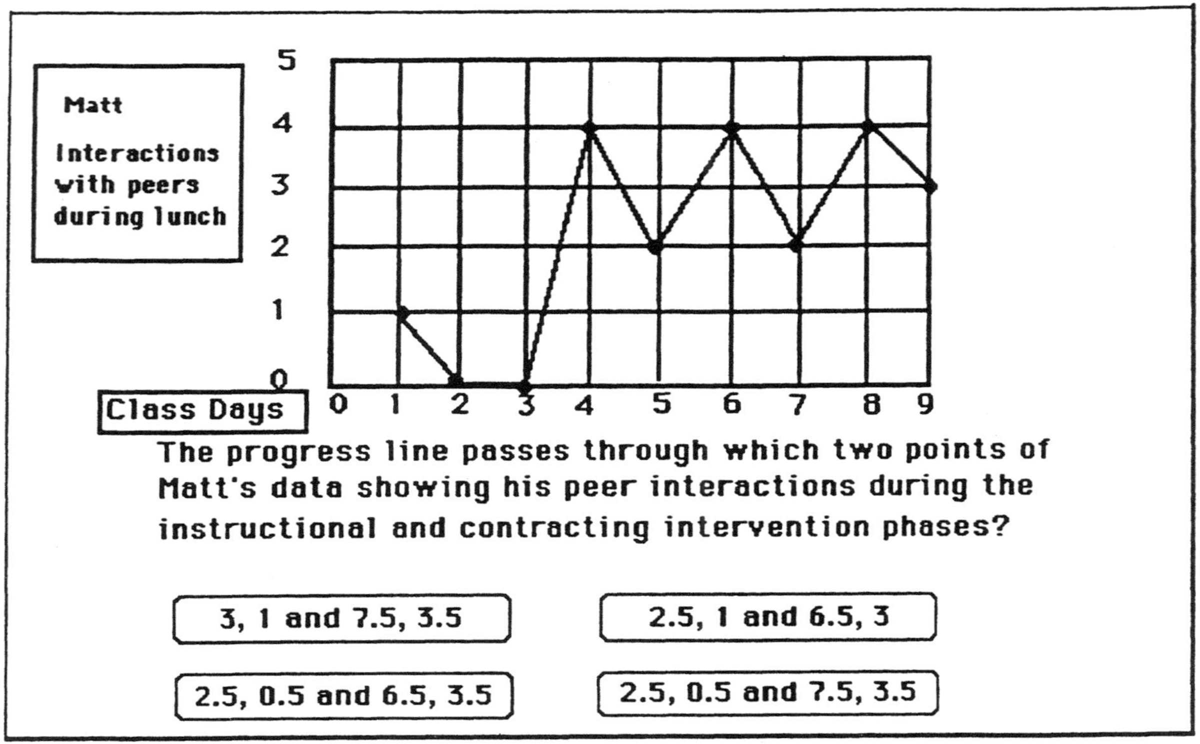

vided. The learner is allowed to continue trying response foils until the correct one is located. When the correct response is selected, brief explanatory feedback is provided (Figure 3).

In the field testing of five interactive quizzes, the mean scores of the learners improved from 45.6% (pre) to 80.2% (post), (n = 24 on five different quizzes). The findings indicated that the pre-quizzes served as effective advance organizers to guide students in their independent study and class participation.

Hypermedia for Fluency Goals

Drill-and-Practice. Following acquisition, the goal of instruction is to enable the learner to rapidly access new knowledge or use new skills in a fluent manner. The focus is for the learner to demonstrate both speed and accuracy in utilizing the acquired information. It is important that skills become automatic so that the learner can use and apply the skills without undue cognitive processing. The most effective type of computer-based instructional approach for building fluency is drill and practice.

Material in drill-and-practice programs is typically simple and repetitive. Directions for using the program must be clear so the learner can practice the skill without continual program prompting. Feedback should provide immediate knowledge of the accuracy of the response and brief corrective information should be provided for incorrect responses (Criswell, 1989). To increase motivation, the program should allow user control over the practice strategy (Keller & Suzuki, 1988).

Two vocabulary drills, *Terminology I and II*, were developed using a timed drill-and-practice format (Figure 4). In these drills, a definition is presented on screen and the learner must locate the correct term and click on it. The response is timed for 12 seconds. Each response is followed by simple feedback of "correct" or "try another word" if the initial response is incorrect. If the allowable response time elapses, the correct word is highlighted and the program continues. Only the learner's first response is scored for recordkeeping purposes.

In the field testing of these two vocabulary drills, learners were instructed to utilize the drill for three practice sessions or until reaching 80% correct. Under these conditions, the mean scores of the learners increased from 35% (pre) to 78% (post), (n = 18 on two different drills). It was found that repeated practice using the drills over three trials each was effective in helping students build speed and accuracy with behavioral terminology.

Another drill-and-practice application, *Coding Flashcards*, provides practice in coding children's classroom behavior. Prior to using this program, students are taught a behavior observation code for observing and

FIGURE 3. Screen from application *Interactive Quizzes* showing response feedback

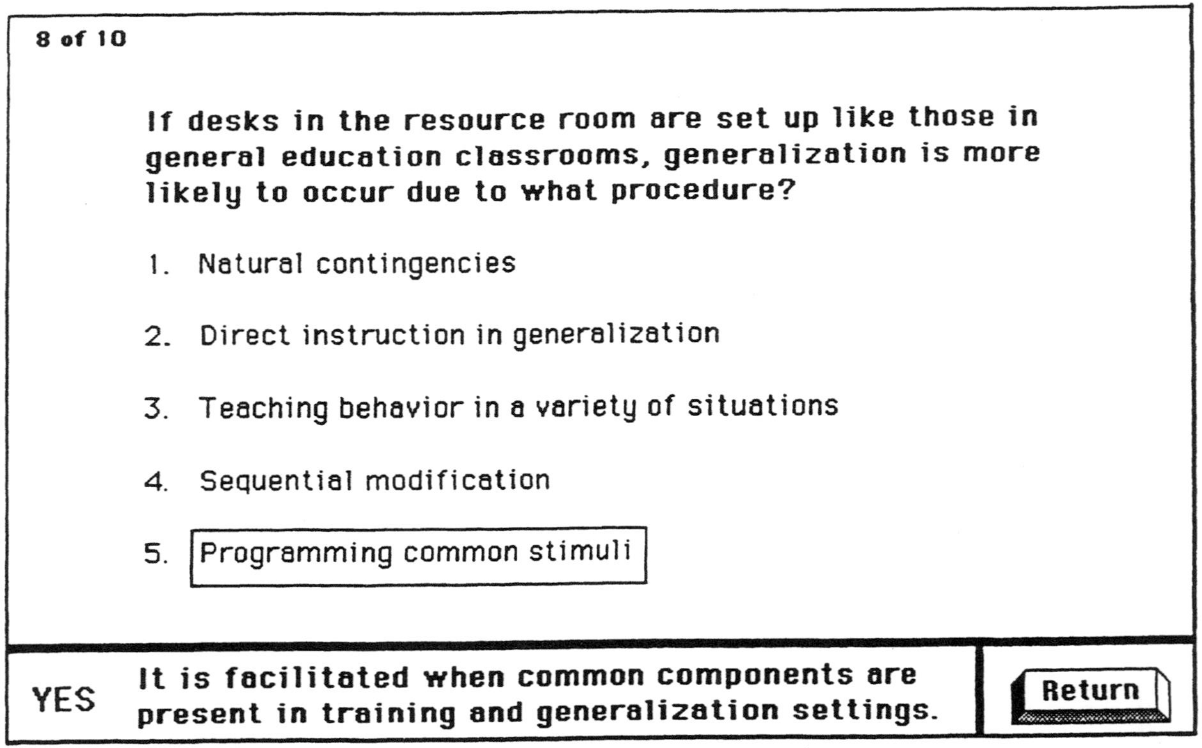

FIGURE 4. Screen from application *Terminology II* showing timed drill format

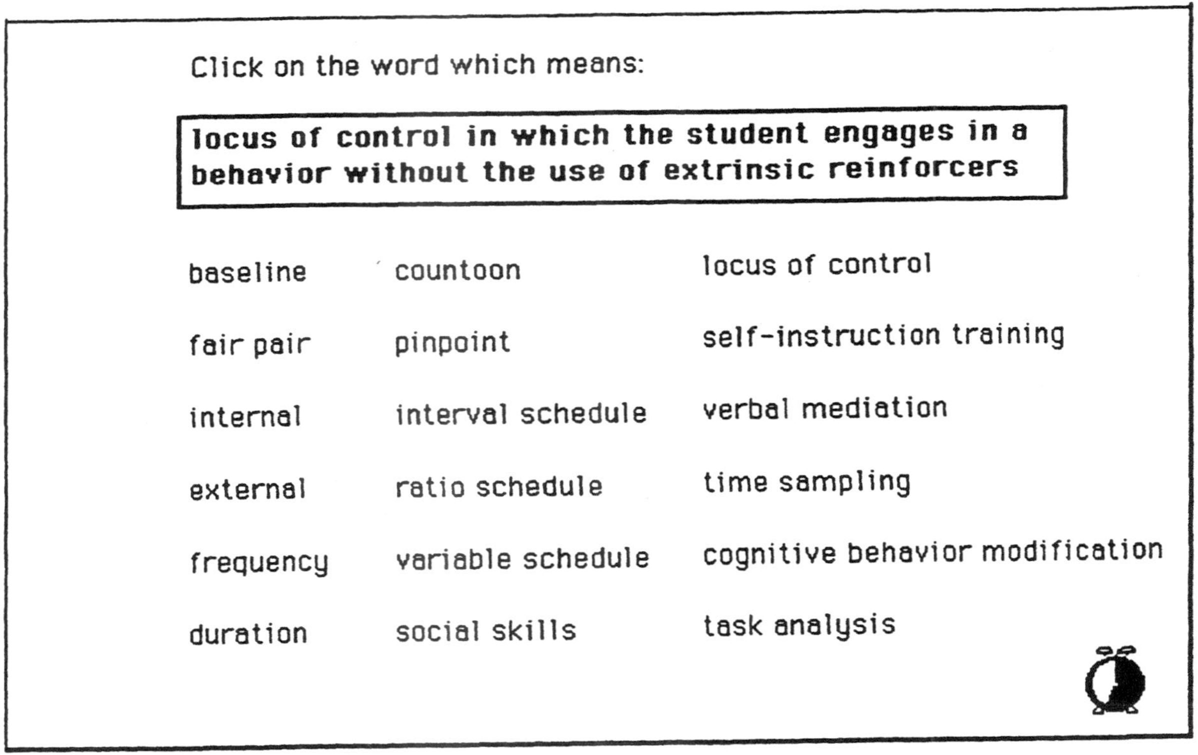

classifying children's classroom behavior into discrete categories. The codes are memorized and practiced with paper-pencil memory aids. Following acquisition, learners use the computerized flashcard drill program to build speed and accuracy. In this application, brief behavioral descriptions are provided on screen and the learner must enter the behavioral code within a specified response time (Figure 5). The behavior vignettes are selected on a randomization basis from a pool of items representing all behavior codes in the procedure. Learners select their practice speed for each trial; each flashcard appears for 12 seconds at "learner speed," 8 seconds at "practice speed," and 6 seconds at "observer speed." When mastered, the learners apply the observation coding procedure in classrooms using a 6-second time sampling unit.

Data have been gathered from student practice logs to evaluate the effectiveness of the coding drill program. As graduate students utilized the drill to build fluency, data were compiled on the number of trials, practice speed, and coding accuracy. They used the program at their own discretion for practice; no requirements were set for frequency or duration of practice sessions. The directions in the program suggest that users achieve the following proficiencies: 80% at "learner speed," 85% at "practice speed," and 90% at "observer speed." These recommendations are based on acceptable levels of observer reliability in coding accuracy.

Although practice patterns varied across individuals, 25% of the practice time overall was spent acquiring initial fluency at the "learner speed," 19% of the practice time was spent building moderate fluency at the "practice speed," and 56% of the practice time was spent reaching and maintaining fast fluency at the "observer speed." Based on an average of 18 practice sessions for each of the five students using this drill, the mean fluency scores increased from a baseline of 61% to an average high score of 88% at "learner speed," 91% at "practice speed," and 95% at "observer speed." The drills were clearly effective in building acceptable levels of observer proficiency. This progress was documented across repeated practice sessions.

Hypermedia for Maintenance Goals

Programs which are developed for the goal of maintenance need to ensure that learning persists over time. For some skills, additional drill and practice may be necessary to maintain prior levels of learning or proficiency. For this purpose, drills may be used on a periodic basis, or intermittent drills may be inserted into related instructional materials.

Information Database. Another strategy for enhancing maintenance is

FIGURE 5. Screen from application *Coding Flashcards* showing corrective response

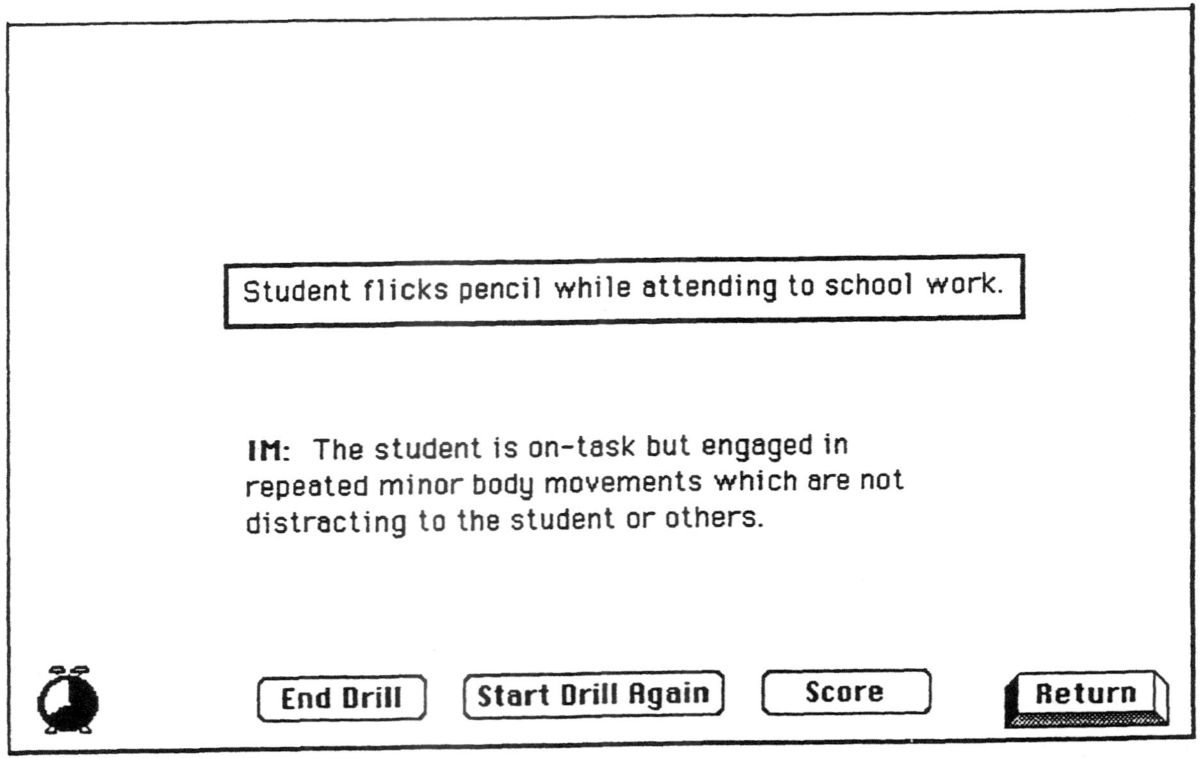

the use of an organizational structure of the knowledge that is meaningful for the learner. After knowledge or skills are mastered, they can be organized into a computer information base to allow easy retrieval (Mackay, 1988). Using newer hypermedia approaches, learners can access this information in a non-sequential manner, thereby searching and reviewing information in an individual way (Jonassen, 1988). In organizing the framework for the information base, identical categories and features presented during acquisition should be utilized. This assists learners in readily locating and remembering the information.

The application *Strategies Hyperbase* includes information on a variety of behavior intervention strategies. The behavior change strategies are matched to those taught in the behavior management course. Information for each strategy in the hyperbase includes a definition, example, suggestions for defining behaviors and consequences, implementation guidelines, and recommended recordkeeping procedures (Figure 6). The strategies in the hyperbase include point card systems, contracting procedures, classroom time-out, behavioral counseling approaches, written mediation essays, self-monitoring procedures, self-instruction training, token reinforcement systems, and generalization procedures. The hyperbase is linked by buttons and users are able to locate specific information very quickly.

Information in the hyperbase is made meaningful in a number of ways. First of all, during the acquisition stage, students are required to develop their own descriptions, examples, and criteria for each strategy. Second, students utilize the criteria during clinical case study discussion groups. Following the behavior management course, students are provided personal copies of the program to use during student teaching as a guide for implementing behavior change interventions in the classroom. The hyperbase remains a resource over time that teachers can refer back to for refreshers and share with others in collaborative consultation efforts.

Hypermedia for Generalization Goals

At the generalization stage, learners must utilize knowledge or skills in a variety of situations that are different from the instructional setting. Practice for generalization can be provided by mixed drill-and-practice activities or by using simulations. Stimulus materials used for generalization should be similar to those used during instruction and include mixed practice with different situations (Criswell, 1989).

It is important to create divergent practice opportunities when designing computer-based simulations (Reigeluth & Schwartz, 1989). Transfer at higher application levels is enhanced by variation. When introducing the

FIGURE 6. Screen from application *Strategies Hyperbase* showing the example

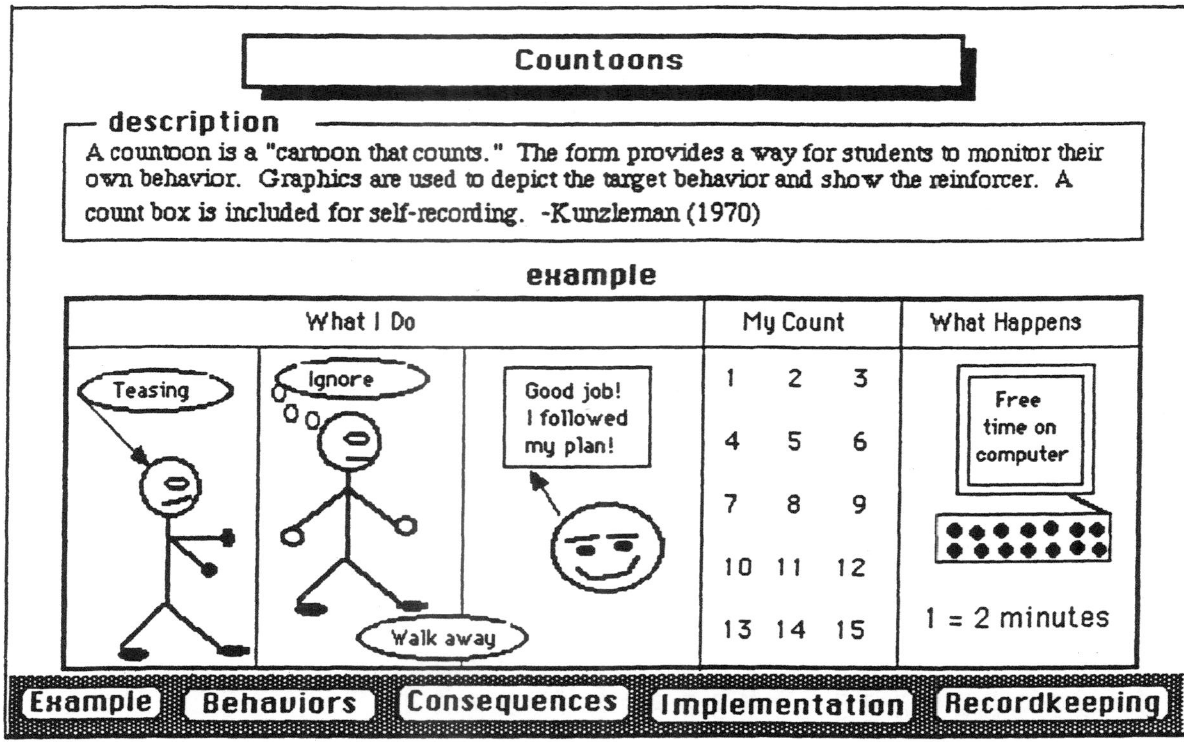

simulation, fidelity should be kept low so that the user attends to the essential features in the situation. By allowing the learner to select among a variety of practice applications, the skills become more relevant and useful to the individual (Keller & Suzuki, 1988). Complexity in generalization increases as the simulation becomes more realistic (Alessi, 1988).

Even though users have considerable freedom during simulations to select actions, feedback is critical for helping the user assess the success of the approach during the application exercise. By allowing the user to explore alternative actions and replay the simulation, feedback becomes an important element of instruction. However, it should be given in such a manner that it is not intrusive. The process of problem solving in the simulation should not be continuously interrupted (Munro, Fehling, & Towne, 1985).

Realtime Simulation. In the application *Videodisc Coding Practice*, learners practice observation coding with a variety of classroom scenes contained on a videodisc. For each practice scene, instructions are given on the computer screen through animation to demonstrate the sequence for coding the behavior of the target student and peers (Figure 7). When the video practice scene starts, a digital beeper sound emitted through the computer signals the user at six-second intervals. At the sound of the beeps, the user enters a behavior code into the keyboard.

The video scenes are controlled by the computer which starts and stops the video in one-minute segments. When the minute ends, the learner's entries are displayed on the computer screen side-by-side to those of the "master" coder (Figure 8). The learner is allowed to repeat the minute as many times as desired for practice-to-mastery or to continue forward to the next segment.

These videodisc observation coding materials have been prepared for future use in observation training. The current training sequence includes class instruction (acquisition), coding flashcards (fluency building), and guided practice with videotapes. Following this sequence, students' accuracy scores for reliability ranged from 33% to 63% with a mean of 49% (n = 16). it is hoped that extended practice with these interactive materials will enable learners to reach the minimal coding reliability level of 80% prior to actual classroom usage. It is clear that instruction through lectures, flashcards, and videotapes has not been adequate for reaching the necessary reliability standards within the existing time frame.

Hypermedia for Application Goals

At the application stage, learners must utilize knowledge or skills in new ways. This may involve modifying or combining knowledge or skills

FIGURE 7. Screen from application *Videodisc Coding Practice* giving directions

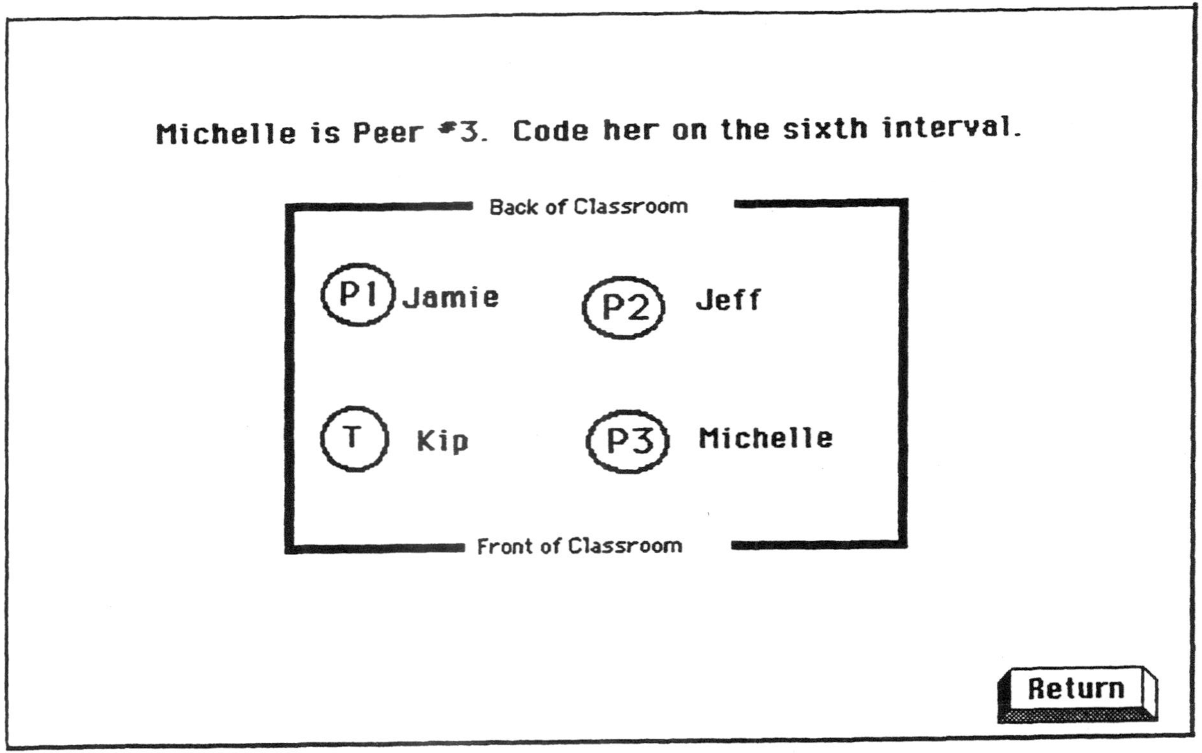

FIGURE 8. Screen from application *Videodisc Coding Practice* comparing codes

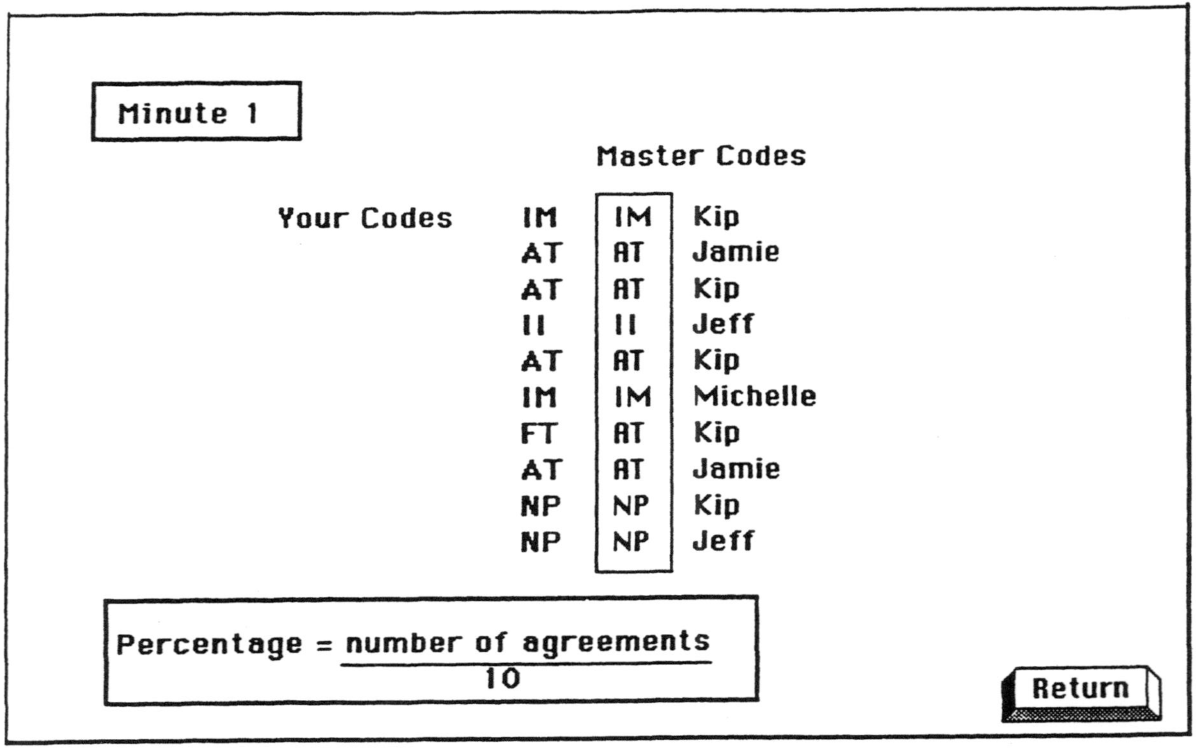

with that previously learned or applying knowledge and skills to new situations. Some simulations are quite specifically focused on problem-solving activities requiring information to be adapted or applied (Wood, Combs, & Swan, 1985; Cruickshank, 1988). Other simulations are completely self-paced, non-linear, and provide information through multimedia options. These simulations offer a case study scenario and require the user to investigate for information, formulate hypotheses, and evaluate outcomes (Falk & Carlson, 1988).

Typically, the development of multimedia simulations goes beyond the time and resources available to individual faculty members. Two approaches successfully used in large-scale authoring projects are to assemble a faculty development team with shared resources or to join a consortium group with other universities. One realistic option for small projects is to create computer-based problem-solving activities that are integrated with case studies used in a course. This approach provides a bridge between real world examples used in instruction and independent practice in problem solving through computer-simulation activities.

Analogue Simulation. In the application Schedules of Reinforcement, students make instructional decisions for providing reinforcement based on scenario data. The scenarios are matched to behavior interventions taught in the behavior management course. Using the movable object response mode, the learner moves a reinforcer symbol to the performance trial where reinforcement should be provided according to the specified schedule (Figure 9). Other practice items require the learner to examine instructional data and determine the reinforcement schedule utilized in the simulation. Corrective feedback is provided for each response.

In the field testing of this simulation, students were directed to practice with the program three times or until an 80% accuracy score was achieved. Pre-to-post accuracy scores improved from 49% to 81% ($n = 24$). Although a simple simulation program, the practice activities were successful in providing an intermediary step between learning about schedules of reinforcement and applying this knowledge to instructional decisionmaking.

SUMMARY

With new, easy-to-use hypermedia-authoring tools, faculty in higher education are showing more interest in creating their own course support materials. In teacher education, there is a need for courseware that provides a bridge between preservice instruction and the applied role of teachers as decision makers in the classroom. Computer-based learning activities can be developed to support all levels of instruction from knowledge acquisition to skills application.

FIGURE 9. Screen from application *Schedules of Reinforcement*

Fixed Ratio FR2

Place the (R+) symbol on the next trial where the teacher would reinforce Josh when he places his game piece independently on the board.

CODE FOR SCORING TRIALS:
+ = PERFORMED BEHAVIOR INDEPENDENTLY
C = PERFORMED BEHAVIOR UPON CUEING
- = DID NOT PERFORM BEHAVIOR APPROPRIATELY
® = REINFORCEMENT PROVIDED

(R+)

	TRIALS									
	1	2	3	4	5	6	7	8	9	10
ASK FOR GAME CARD	C	C	+	+	+	+	C	+	+	+
PLACE GAME PIECE	-	-	C	C	+	+ (R+)	C	+	+	+
RETURN GAME CARD	-	-	C	C	C	+	+	-	C	+
HANDS OFF BOARD	—	-	-	C	C	C	C	-	-	C

The use of hypermedia in instruction does not escape the concern raised by Hannafin and Mitzel (1990) toward computers in instruction. To paraphrase their concern in terms of hypermedia, it is now comparatively easy to create hypermedia materials but as demanding as ever to create something instructionally worthwhile. The matrix model illustrated in this article can be helpful in guiding the design of effective hypermedia materials. To create something worthwhile requires that the type of activity be matched to desired outcomes of instruction and based on good instructional design principles.

A variety of hypermedia courseware materials implemented in a graduate-level behavior management course were described in relation to this design model. Because the use of hypermedia in education is a relatively new application, field testing is important to evaluate the materials as well as to monitor learning. Initial findings indicated that students had positive responses to this instructional approach and demonstrated improvements across all stages of learning. Refinement was necessary in the materials as well as course integration procedures. More field-based research is needed to determine the factors critical to successful integration of hypermedia in teacher education.

REFERENCES

Alberto, P. & Troutman, A. (1990). *Applied behavior analysis for teachers.* Columbus, OH: Merrill Publishing.

Alessi, S. (1988). Fidelity in the design of instructional simulations. *Journal of Computer-Based Instruction*, 15(2), 40-47.

Authorware Professional. (1992). San Francisco, CA: Macromedia.

Bell, M. (1985). The role of instructional theories in the evaluation of microcomputer courseware. *Educational Technology*, March, pp. 36-40.

Criswell, E. (1989). *The design of computer-based instruction.* New York: Macmillan.

Cruickshank, D. (1988). The uses of simulations in teacher preparation. *Simulation and Games*, 19(2), 133-156.

Falk, D. & Carlson, H. (1988). Using interactive videodiscs to increase sensitivity to human diversity. In: Society for Applied Learning Technology, *Proceedings of the Sixth Annual Conference on Interactive Instruction Delivery*, (pp. 150-154), Orlando, FL.

Gagne, R. (1974). *Essentials of learning for instruction.* Hinsdale, IL: The Dryden Press.

Gagne, R., Briggs, L., & Wager, W. (1988). *Principles of instructional design (3rd ed.).* New York: Holt, Rinehart, & Winston.

Gagne, R., Wager, W., & Rojas, A. (1981). Planning and authoring computer-assisted instruction lessons. *Educational Technology*, September, pp. 17-21.

Hagler, P. & Knowlton, J. (1987). Invalid implicit assumption in CBI comparison research. *Journal of Computer-Based Instruction, 14*(3), 84-88.

Hannafin, K. & Mitzel, H. (1990). CB authoring tools in postsecondary institutions: A review and critical examination. *Computers in Education, 14*(3), 197-204.

Hannum, W. (1988). Designing courseware to fit subject matter structure. In: D. H. Jonassen (Ed.), *Instructional Designs for Microcomputer Courseware* (pp. 275-305). Hillsdale, NJ: Lawrence Erlbaum Associates.

Jonassen, D. (1988). Integrating learning strategies into courseware to facilitate deeper processing. In: D. H. Jonassen (Ed.), *Instructional Designs for Microcomputer Courseware* (pp.151-182). Hillsdale, NJ: Lawrence Erlbaum Associates.

Keller, J. & Suzuki, K. (1988). Use of the ARCS motivation model in courseware design. In: D. H. Jonassen (Ed.), *Instructional Designs for Microcomputer Courseware* (pp. 401-434). Hillsdale, NJ: Lawrence Erlbaum Associates.

Mackay, W. (1988). Tutoring, information databases, and iterative design. In: D. H. Jonassen (Ed.), *Instructional Designs for Microcomputer Courseware* (pp. 327-345). Hillsdale, NJ: Lawrence Erlbaum Associates.

Munro, A., Fehling, M., & Towne, D. (1985). Instructional intrusiveness in dynamic simulation training. *Journal of Computer-Based Instruction, 12*(2), 50-53.

Petry, B., Mouton, H., & Reigeluth, C. (1987): A lesson based on the Gagne-Briggs theory of instruction. In: C. M. Reigeluth (Ed.), *Instructional Theories in Action.* Hillsdale, NJ: Lawrence Erlbaum Associates.

Ranker, R. & Doucet, R. (1990). SOCRATES: A computer-based lesson development advisor. *Educational Technology*, March, pp. 46-50.

Reigeluth, C. & Schwartz, E. (1989). An instructional theory for the design of computer-based simulations. *Journal of Computer-Based Instruction, 16*(1), 1-10.

Roblyer, M. (1988). Fundamental problems and principles of designing effective courseware. In: D. H. Jonassen (Ed.), *Instructional Designs for Microcomputer Courseware* (pp. 7-34). Hillsdale, NJ: Lawrence Erlbaum Associates.

Rule, S. & Salzberg, C. (1988). The role of videodiscs in special education methods courses. *Journal of Special Education Technology, 10*(2), 80-85.

Wood, M., Combs, C., & Swan, W. (1985-86). Computer simulations: Field testing effectiveness and efficiency for inservice and preservice teacher preparation. *Journal of Educational Technology Systems, 14*(1), 61-74.

Leah P. McCoy

Decisions in Inferential Statistics with *HyperCard*: Design and Field Test

Nearly every graduate student in education has faced the big question: Which statistical procedure is appropriate for my study? Often students are deep into their thesis or dissertation topics and only casually interested in the actual statistical analysis. They have passed the required research and statistics courses, but the "mystery of statistics" is just that, a mystery. They know isolated bits of information, such as "a 2 × 3 ANOVA examines the effects of two levels of one independent variable and three levels of another independent variable." But what they are lacking is the "big picture." They are unable to integrate all their knowledge about statistical analysis into a coherent overview; in short, they are unable to apply it. At this point, they usually approach a faculty member or advanced graduate student in statistics and humbly beg, "Please tell me what to do."

While there will always be a need for faculty members and others to advise and react to research design ideas, there is a great need for some method of helping students to begin thinking about the application of various statistical procedures to their specific problems. While most students will probably not be able to independently complete the design of the statistical analysis for their research, they need some assistance in beginning to focus on an appropriate procedure. This project involved

LEAH P. MCCOY is Associate Professor of Education, Wake Forest University, Winston-Salem, NC 27109.

[Haworth co-indexing entry note]: "Decisions in Inferential Statistics with *HyperCard*: Design and Field Test." McCoy, Leah P. Co-published simultaneously in *Computers in the Schools* (The Haworth Press, Inc.) Vol. 10, No. 1/2, 1994, pp. 69-77; and: *Multimedia and Megachange: New Roles for Educational Computing* (ed$: W. Michael Reed, John K. Burton, and Min Liu) The Haworth Press, Inc., 1994, pp. 69-77. Multiple copies of this article/chapter may be purchased from The Haworth Document Delivery Center [1-800-3-HAWORTH; 9:00 a.m. - 5:00 p.m. (EST)].

design and testing of a hypermedia tool for this purpose–*Decisions in Inferential Statistics with HyperCard (DISH)*.

DESIGN

The design and testing of this project roughly followed four steps. First, from the author's extensive experience in instructing and counseling students regarding choice of statistical procedure, an informal assessment of many graduate students in education revealed their need for a statistical decision tool. The knowledge structure of many of these students was surprisingly similar; they had many statistical skills and concepts but were unable to apply them in practical contexts. There was a need for a tool that would help them to match their own statistical requirements with appropriate procedures.

The second consideration involved examination of the related research. Only two recent studies investigating similar problems were located. Olsen and Bozeman (1988) designed a "decision aid" for assisting students in choosing an appropriate statistical procedure. Given short descriptions of typical educational research situations, participants were asked to choose a statistical procedure. Three treatment groups were defined by the type of decision aid available during the test: (1) the course text only (control group), (2) a paper flow chart that decomposed the decision of choice of a procedure into a series of smaller decisions, or (3) a computer program that used a series of questions to simulate the flow chart. Results showed that the computer *and* the flow chart groups performed significantly better on the test than the textbook group. There was no difference between the computer and flow chart groups. While these results support the use of a logic-based tool for assistance in decision making, there is no indication that the computer tool was different from the paper version.

A study by Varnhagen and Zumbo (1990) investigated the effect of supplemental computer-assisted-instruction (CAI) lab instruction in statistics. Three groups used either no supplementary instruction, a flat "page-turning" CAI program, or an interactive, branching CAI tutor. They found no effect of the type of lab on achievement, but several significant differences in affective measures of the three groups. Using path analysis, they further analyzed these relationships and concluded that the lab format also had a significant indirect effect on achievement.

The results of these two studies suggest that a statistical computer supplement is desirable. The programs used in these studies were not described in detail, but both suggest a branching, interactive format. Olsen and Bozeman described their program as a series of questions that simulate a flow chart. Varnhagen and Zumbo actually compared a branching program to a sequential (flat) organization and found positive effects on both cognitive and affective measures. While both of these studies concluded that a statistics tool was useful, they left unanswered many questions about the specifics of the tool.

The next step was the overall design of the computer tool. One primary consideration was that the program should have the capability of branching to various specific procedures based on different criteria. For example, some students may know (or guess at) the name of the procedure they want to examine, and others may be able to describe the study in various ways. *HyperCard* was selected as an appropriate and accessible format for the program (Beekman, 1992; Hibino & Brade, 1991; Kaehler, 1988). This hypermedia format allowed a logical organization that incorporated a complex branching capability with a simple user interface, thus maximizing utility while minimizing operational difficulties. Content of several educational statistics texts (Runyon & Haber, 1991) was examined, and statistical procedures were evaluated by their simplicity, frequency of use, and coverage of various common situations. Six procedures were chosen for inclusion in the program: (a) Chi-square test of independence, (b) T-test for independent samples, (c) one-way analysis of variance, (d) factorial analysis of variance, (e) correlation, and (f) multiple regression analysis.

A structure for organizing this information into a clear, logical "big picture" was planned and diagrammed (Figure 1). After a short introduction/review of inferential terms, a main menu guided the user to his or her choice of three specific menus: statistical procedure menu, research question menu, or groups and data menu (Figure 2). Each of these three submenus branched to the six procedures listed above, but enabled the user to select by either procedure name, form of research question, or nature of the groups and data.

Each of the six specific procedures was explained by three screens that described the procedure in detail with examples of questions and conclusions. At any point in the program, the user could select MORE ABOUT THIS, RETURN TO DEFINITIONS, RETURN TO MAIN MENU, or END. It should be noted that commercial programs are available that roughly fit this purpose, but the decision was made that design of a specific hypermedia tool that *exactly* matched the background and needs of students in educational statistics would be more powerful and useful.

The fourth step was evaluation of the program. Periodically, as the program was being developed, formative evaluation was conducted informally by having selected students (who were not participating in the

FIGURE 1. Structure of DISH program

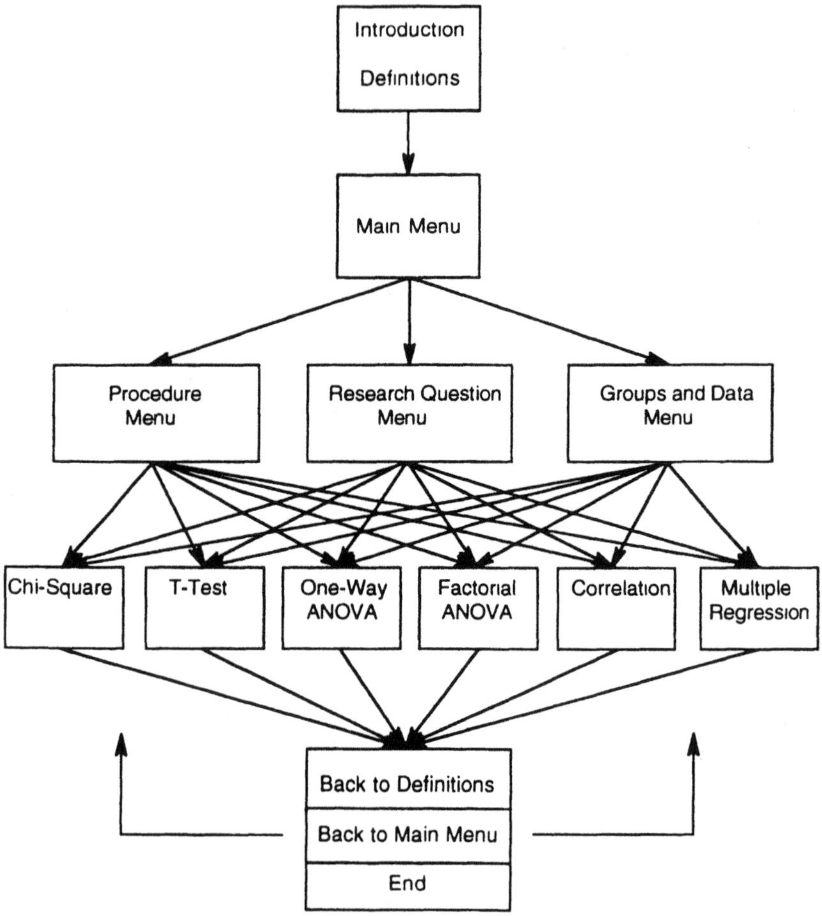

later study) use and comment on the program. The basic structure and content of the program were not questioned, and changes that occurred from this procedure were largely in presentation of the text. Unclear or confusing statements were rewritten, and additional examples were added. A summative evaluation study was then conducted to assess the efficacy of the program when used with a larger group of students in a practical situation.

FIGURE 2. DISH Research Questions Menu

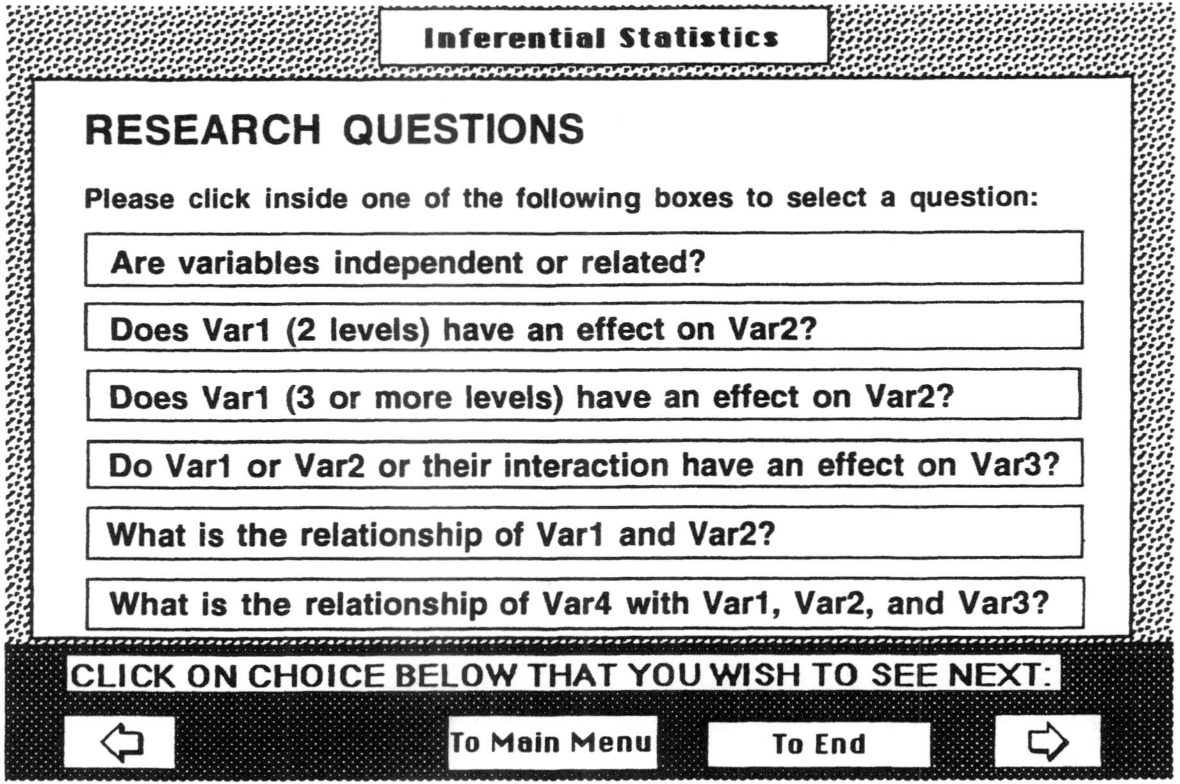

METHODS

Participants in the study were 31 graduate students in education. All students were enrolled in an introductory statistics course, and had previously used Macintosh computers. Participants were randomly assigned to either the computer or the paper materials group. Each student was given an overview of the project and an individual introduction to the materials. They were instructed to become familiar with the materials, and then to use them as a reference while they were answering the questions.

The material for the experimental (computer) group was the DISH (Decisions in Inferential Statistics with *HyperCard*) program described above. The control group used a printed version of the program. It contained exactly the same text, but was sequential and did not have menus for branching and cross reference. After a brief introduction, participants worked individually either in a computer lab or in a classroom. There was no time limit, but times were recorded and compared in the analysis.

Data was collected on a Record Sheet which had two parts. First was a description of ten research situations where students were encouraged to use the assigned "materials" in making decisions about which statistical procedure would be appropriate for each. Second were a series of five affective questions to which they responded on a scale of one to ten to indicate their assessment of the ease of use of the materials, helpfulness of the materials, contribution to their understanding of statistics, and improvement of their confidence on the present exercise and in future use.

Data analysis involved a series of independent *t*-tests to determine the effect of the different materials (computer or paper) on the following dependent variables:

1. Score on the decisions
2. Time to complete the decisions
3. Ease of use of materials
4. Helpfulness of materials in decision-making
5. Improvement in understanding of statistics
6. Confidence in completing immediate decisions
7. Confidence in ability to make future decisions

RESULTS

Means, standard deviations, and *t*-test comparisons of groups are presented in Table 1. Separate variances *t*-tests were used because of unequal group sizes.

There were no differences in the two groups in either score or time

TABLE 1. Comparison of Computer and Paper Groups for All Variables

Variable	Group[a]	Mean	*S D*	*T*	Probability
Score	Computer	7.00	2.19		
	Paper	8.00	1.64	1.44	.161
Time	Computer	22.94 (minutes)	7.94		
	Paper	19.00 (minutes)	6.13	1.55	.132
Easy	Computer	9.00	1.16		
	Paper	7.73	1.98	2.16	.042*
Helpful	Computer	9.00	1.10		
	Paper	8.47	1.85	0.97	.343
Understanding	Computer	6.88	1.59		
	Paper	6.33	1.59	0.95	.351
Confidence Now	Computer	7.88	1.46		
	Paper	7.67	2.69	0.27	.793
Confidence Later	Computer	8.69	1.20		
	Paper	7.47	2.77	1.57	.133

Notes: [a]Computer $n = 16$, Paper $n = 15$, * $p < .05$

needed to complete the exercise. Similarly, there were no significant differences in participants' perception of helpfulness of the materials, aid in improving understanding of statistics, or improvement in confidence in either immediate or future decisions. There was a significant difference, however, in participants' perception of ease of use of the materials ($t(22) = 2.16$, $p < .05$). The computer group reported that their materials were easier to use than the paper group.

CONCLUSIONS

The DISH computer tool was found to be as equally effective as a paper version of the same basic text in assisting students to make decisions about which statistical procedure to use in a given situation. The time required to complete the exercise was not different for the two groups.

Responses to the questions about helpfulness and present and future confidence in making statistical decisions were not significantly different for the two groups. The means for both groups were uniformly high on these three questions, ranging from 7.47 to 9.00 on a ten-point scale. A control group which used neither material was not included in this study, so it is not possible to clearly attribute these high scores to the use of the decision materials.

The students in the DISH computer group judged their materials easier to use than did the paper group. It is likely that this was due to the branching organization of the computer program, and the interactive format that immediately moved to the procedure chosen either by name, by research question, or by description of the groups and data. This is the obvious benefit of using a hypermedia format; the organization of the program was able to approximate the nonlinear nature of the content. Use of *HyperCard* facilitated the organization of the six parallel statistical procedures in a way that assisted the user in accessing any procedure directly and in a variety of ways. Because of this logical organization of the material, the students found the material easier to use.

While there was not a difference between the hypermedia and paper materials on most variables, this study involved a small group, a limited topic, and a short time. Also, the dependent variable was scored on a fairly simple test involving application of the information, rather than higher level tasks. It is possible that a lengthier experiment would find more significant results.

These results have important implications for instructional design. When information is not naturally linear, the typical page-after-page design of instructional materials (whether in a textbook or on a computer) is not the easiest format for students to use. A logical organization that is interactive and allows branching is a much clearer model of many topics. Further development and testing of logically organized materials for many different contents and topics are recommended.

REFERENCES

Beekman, G. (1992). *HyperCard 2 in a hurry*. Belmont, CA: Wadsworth.

Hibino, S. & Brade, K. (1991). A case study for developing hypermedia software. *Proceedings of the National Educational Computing Conference '91* (pp. 336-340). Eugene, OR: International Society for Technology in Education.

Kaehler. C. (1988). *HyperCard power: Techniques and scripts*. Reading, MA: Addison-Wesley.

Olsen, C.R. & Bozeman, W. C. (1988). Decision support systems: Applications in

statistics and hypothesis testing. *Journal of Research on Computing in Education*, *20*(3), 206-212.
Runyon, R. P. & Haber, A. (1991). *Fundamentals of behavioral statistics* (7th ed.). New York: McGraw-Hill.
Varnhagen, C. K. & Zumbo, B. D. (1990). CAI as an adjunct to teaching introductory statistics: Affect mediates learning. *Journal of Educational Computing Research*, *6*(1), 29-40.

Curtis J. Bonk
Padma V. Medury
Thomas H. Reynolds

Cooperative Hypermedia: The Marriage of Collaborative Writing and Mediated Environments

INTRODUCTION

After an introductory statement on the use of computer-based writing tools in the schools, this paper is split into three key sections. First, the authors present an analysis of the cognitive and social cognitive skills that may be fostered by collaborative writing and hypermedia and multimedia tools. Here, theoretical underpinnings of the use of these media tools in education are presented from Piagetian and Vygotskian perspectives. The next section of this paper begins with a discussion of the basic multimedia and hypermedia support for the proposed marriage. The balance of this section, however, compares tools and tool features presently available within collaborative writing programs, including the level and type of

CURTIS J. BONK is Assistant Professor, School of Education, Indiana University, Bloomington, IN 47405-1006.
PADMA V. MEDURY is Multimedia Consultant, Instructional Resources Support Center, West Virginia University, Morgantown, WV 26505.
THOMAS H. REYNOLDS is Assistant Professor and Director, Texas Education Collaborative, Texas A & M University, College Station, TX 77843-4222.

[Haworth co-indexing entry note]: "Cooperative Hypermedia: The Marriage of Collaborative Writing and Mediated Environments." Bonk, Curtis J., Padma V. Medury, and Thomas H. Reynolds. Co-published simultaneously in *Computers in the Schools* (The Haworth Press, Inc.) Vol. 10, No. 1/2, 1994, pp. 79-124; and: *Multimedia and Megachange: New Roles for Educational Computing* (eds: W. Michael Reed, John K. Burton, and Min Liu) The Haworth Press, Inc., 1994, pp. 79-124. Multiple copies of this article/chapter may be purchased from The Haworth Document Delivery Center [1-800-3-HAWORTH; 9:00 a.m. - 5:00 p.m. (EST)].

communication skills promoted. These packages are then clustered according to the level of collaboration and media integration. Based on trends in collaborative writing media, potential connections between collaborative writing tools, multimedia, and hypermedia are explored in the third major portion of this article. The fifth level of collaborative writing media, cooperative hypermedia, is the primary focus of this section. Because of the recency of cooperative hypermedia, tool use considerations and open research questions and issues are embedded throughout this section. In addition, opportunities and challenges made available by these innovative tools for students, teachers, and schools are discussed. Consideration of the social and cognitive principles addressed by these packages links the three sections of this paper. Finally, the conclusions section of this paper details some of the ideal and real ramifications and long-term opportunities of cooperative hypermedia tools.

INITIAL STATEMENT ON COMPUTER-BASED WRITING TOOLS

Increased use of computers has contributed to altering the role of writing in schools across all levels of education. A main problem in the integration of computers in the writing process is that software tools found in writing centers are not that much different from those found during the past two decades in the workplace. Because the computer revolution in education evolved from advances in the business community, many educators failed to appreciate and embrace the instructional potential of the computer for writing (Montague, 1990). Nevertheless, each year additional commercial software packages target educational markets, even though they may not be responsive to student writing needs. Many educators, therefore, have misguided notions of the roles and benefits of computer-based writing tools, because most commercially successful software programs are not ideal writing environments for young children or adults (Glynn, Oaks, Mattocks, & Britton, 1989; Salomon, 1993).

Had computer-based writing tools originally been created for writers struggling with their writing plans, goals, or ideas, however crude, the integration of writing tools into the curriculum would be more widespread and better researched. For instance, what would writing centers look like if initial word processors in education had successfully integrated innovations in computer-assisted planning, concept mapping, thinking skills prompting, outlining, text analyzing, idea generation, and peer editing and collaboration, as well as general word processing? Perhaps students now would find a vast repertoire of powerful knowledge-building and interconnecting tools available during composing. Unfortunately, this is not the case in all but a few prototypical writing programs.

Even though prior innovations came piecemeal and disconnected, educators are presently confronted with numerous writing tool innovations (Salomon, 1993). For instance, educators are embracing the rich instructional possibilities of systems that transmit text, music, animation, graphics, and video as well as link and extend ideas. Terms like *multimedia, hypermedia*, and *integrated media* are among the current educational buzzwords. As pointed out with prior innovations in education, these terms require a novel theoretical framework to account for how they influence learning before research on media and learning can progress (Kozma, 1991).

Industry is also being influenced by multimedia and hypermedia. But, in contrast, industry is anticipating the problems and challenges presented to employees by these new tools (Galegher & Kraut, 1990; Sarin & Greif, 1988). For instance, Galegher, Kraut, and Egido (1990) and Schrage (1990) point out that the multimedia products designed for collaborative work in industry will fail when they are inconsistent with user goals and needs. Oftentimes the social interaction and organization patterns of users are misunderstood by tool designers, thereby limiting the resulting intellectual teamwork (Hartman, Neuwirth, Kiesler, Sproull, Cochran, Palmquist, & Zubrow, 1991). Evidently, technological advances in collaborative technology must support the human relationships and teamwork involved in creating, selecting, and communicating information (Lay & Karis, 1991; Schrage, 1990).

In analyzing the current trends in multimedia, hypermedia, and collaborative writing within education, it appears that these tools need further refinement. One way to enact such improvements is to develop those tools in consideration of the models, theories, and developmental schemes that properly account for and define the social and cognitive skills impacted by their integration (Hartman et al., 1991; Salomon, 1993). This new conceptualization of integrated collaborative writing media (ICWM), hereafter referred to as *cooperative hypermedia*, points to present word processing limitations; envisioning computerized writing activities as simply an act of word processing will no longer suffice. Consequently, a major theme for this paper is that as these powerful computer-aided writing tools are developed and extended, aspects of cognitive and social cognitive skill must be evaluated.

For instance, instructional designers, researchers, and teachers need to consider the pedagogical value of *co-processing* (i.e., partners or work teams creating, reflecting, and exchanging ideas and viewpoints through interactive dialoguing, structured criticism, knowledge pooling, information sharing, and conflict resolution). In effect, co-processing involves the negotiation and reinterpretation of meaning from interaction with one or more individuals. Co-processing is the continued attempt to understand perspectives that influence written work. Hopefully, as additional collaborative writing tools are created for co-processing, writers will focus on meaning-making within written communication.

As indicated already, the theory driving computer use in the curriculum is sufficiently weak to limit computer-based writing software tool design. To avoid disappointment experienced by previous technological advancements in the schools (e.g., television and computer-assisted instruction), appropriate models and theories must first link and explain the marriage between collaborative writing and hypermedia tools. Hence, the forms of support for this marriage must include process as well as product or tool support. Some researchers argue that each of these tools–collaborative writing, hypermedia, and multimedia–is linked to major cognitive and social cognitive principles (Kozma, 1991). Although appropriate cognitive grounding detailed in the next two major sections of this paper, Process Support and Tool Support, applies to all these forms of media, the emphasis is on collaborative writing tools.

PROCESS SUPPORT

Vygotskian and Piagetian Theory

Recent investigations into the social and cognitive benefits of interactions occurring during cooperative work have found theoretical grounding in both Piagetian and Vygotskian theory (Bonk, 1991; Brown & Palincsar, 1989; Brown & Reeve, 1987; Slavin, 1987). For instance, researchers indicate that the greatest cognitive gains in writing evolve from collaborative writing (Daiute, 1986), peer response groups (DiPardo & Freedman, 1988), teacher conferencing, and other meaning-making activities (Freedman, 1987). Moreover, multistation writing opportunities provide for true "reprocessing" or reconsideration of one's thoughts as opposed to mere retranscription of someone else's ideas or simple "knowledge dumping" (i.e., word processing). There is mounting evidence to suggest that computer-based cooperative learning and other interactive environments impact positively on achievement, social cognitive ability, audience awareness, role taking, and overall cognitive and social cognitive skill (Adams, Carlson, & Hamm, 1990; Bonk, 1991; Brown, Collins, & Duguid, 1989;

DeVillar & Faltis, 1991; Scardamalia, Bereiter, McLean, Swallow, & Woodruff, 1989).

However, collaboration is a complex social and cognitive process; there are no guarantees that collaboration and interaction will trigger cognitive conflict and critical reflection of one's work (Higgins, Flower, & Petraglia, 1990), much less cognitive gain. Computer tools designed as collaborative writing partners (Salomon, 1993) may not automatically refocus the writer's attention on meaningful aspects of text. In addressing this problem, many instructional designers now account for cognitive and social-cognitive changes in computer supported collaborative environments using Vygotskian (1978, 1986) writing for their theoretical grounding as well as for practical media tools or ideas.

Vygotsky's speculations regarding learning and development provide support for many contemporary studies related to each of the following areas of research: writing, computers, cognition, and/or cooperative learning. Vygotsky argued that social interaction with adults and more capable peers is a mechanism to guide learners in reaching a developmental potential that they might not ordinarily attain (Vygotsky, 1978, 1986; Wertsch, 1985b). He used the phrase "zone of proximal development" to denote "the distance between a child's 'actual developmental level as determined by independent problem solving' and the higher level of 'potential development as determined through adult guidance' or in collaboration with more experienced peers" (Wertsch, 1985b, p. 67). Vygotsky viewed activities children could perform with the assistance of others as more indicative of their mental development than success with items they could solve on their own. For instance, two children might write at the same independent or intrapsychological level but significantly vary in the degree to which they could take advantage of adult, peer, or computerized forms of assistance (Wertsch, 1985a; Zellermayer, Salomon, Globerson, & Givon, 1991).

Important for the neo-Vygotskian operating in collaborative writing, multimedia, and hypermedia environments of the 1990s is how graduated assistance could uncover the child's potential or readiness to perform at a higher level of functioning (Brown & Ferrara, 1985; Salomon, Globerson, & Guterman, 1989; Zellermayer et al., 1991). Some students may need context-specific prompting such as replay of interactive video material, while others may need juxtaposition of graphs or charts to spur mental growth. Hypermedia linkages could display relationships among ideas as well as the changes in those relationships over time through interaction with more capable others. Cooperative writing software also might increase the avenues to social interaction by providing access to peer feedback and discussion from varying distances on a network. Through such interactions, students could gain explicit exposure to thinking skills related to writing and other interdependent domains.

For Vygotsky, a great deal of development was due to expert mediation (Brown & Palincsar, 1989). The recent increased use of the terms *cognitive apprenticeship* and *scaffolding* in educational circles (Brown et al., 1989; Schoenfeld, 1988) refers to task support and ceding of control provided by a teacher, consultant, expert, more capable peer, or computer tool for a particular behavior or skill (Tharp & Gallimore, 1988). Appropriate scaffolding commences with interaction occurring within the learner's zone of proximal development, thereby extending skills to higher levels of functioning (DiPardo & Freedman, 1988; Palincsar, 1986; Tharp & Gallimore, 1988). In effect, more capable peers on a computer network might lead the child into writing or communication tasks for which they lack complete understanding of the topic or problem situation.

Daiute and Dalton's (1988) study finds support for the viewpoint that collaborating with more capable peers on the computer increases writing performance. In this particular study, the playfulness and fun of collaboration encouraged reflection on the perspectives of others, thereby resulting in cognitive change. Daiute (1989) also notes that this playful and immature child-talk may be a critical precursor to self-regulatory strategies. In contrast, Salomon (1988) uses Vygotsky's ideas of zones of proximal development, mediated instruction, and internalization of tool-based instruction to claim that interactions with a supportive partner during composing could include a computer because this tool is vital to interpersonal processing–computers change one's relationship to the task and to the world (see also Clements & Nastasi, 1988; Higgins et al., 1990; Zellermayer et al., 1991). From this theoretical perspective, participants on a writing network eventually internalize the intelligence displayed by computerized collaborative writing partners as well as their human partners. The intent of both forms of interaction is to guide and challenge learners to new levels of growth.

Children grow socially and cognitively from opportunities to discuss, debate, and dialogue with others (Clements & Nastasi, 1988; Slavin, 1987). Providing elaborate explanations on a topic extends the cognitive understanding of all parties involved, especially those providing the assistance (Webb, 1982, 1989). According to Piaget (1963), cognitive development is contingent on an individual confronting others who hold contradictory thoughts and claims, thereby creating internal conflicts. This cognitive conflict or realization that one's thoughts or perceptions are inconsistent with new information (i.e., cognitive dissonance) pushes one toward the reconciliation of alternative viewpoints (Daiute & Dalton,

1988). Therefore, when involved in collaborative writing situations, the resolution of conflicts between one or more participants should result in higher levels of reasoning. In effect, confrontation and conflict-generated activities, such as peer interaction on a network or juxtaposition of information during a multimedia presentation, triggers cognitive dissonance or disequilibrium, causing individuals to seek additional information to resolve the conflict (Damon, 1984; Inhelder & Piaget, 1958). Stated another way, peer interaction during the composing process should be a useful aide in helping children examine multiple perspectives on a topic, or in effect, decenter from their own points of views.

The expectations for collaborative writing tools are similar to those of teacher conferences, peer response groups, and other socially mediated writing interventions; less experienced writers witness and internalize expert questioning and other mature writing behaviors (Daiute, 1986; Freedman, 1987). However, with collaborative writing tools, some anonymity is preserved and multiple participants may interact on one or more papers at the same time; the possibilities for cognitive dissonance and perspective taking are endless.

Possible outcomes of collaborative writing systems extend beyond text collaboration and include the sharing of pictures, graphics, sound, animation, and knowledge connections using multimedia and hypermedia environments. As indicated, when combining the expected decentering from collaborative writing with the multiple representations of data offered by multimedia and hypermedia systems, a plethora of cognition-enhancing opportunities are presented. Social cognitive skills develop through the opening of one's mind to multiple ways of understanding and representing information (e.g., the use of multimedia and hypermedia). At the same time, a reduction in egocentrism results from collaborative writing, especially with the higher level tools described later (i.e., cooperative hypermedia). Acceptance of multiple perspectives, therefore, becomes a critical factor in the social-cognitive growth facilitated by collaborative writing and mediated environments.

Social Cognition and Intersubjectivity

Real-time conferencing with cooperative hypermedia is the answer for those interested in promoting the simultaneous manipulation of abstract objects like word-processing documents or viewing the same data set in alternative ways (Sarin & Greif, 1988). Stated another way, shared or linked views of a computer screen foster interpersonal problem solving and an understanding of when, where, and how participants' views diverge–skills often ignored in the traditional school curriculum. Perspective-taking skills might increase conflict resolution skills, trust, self-competence, empathy, cooperativeness, responsibility, interpersonal awareness, and communication skills, while decreasing less productive social behaviors (i.e., social deviance; see Chandler, 1973). Developmental psychologists like Muuss (1988) have suggested that school curriculum be altered to provide systematic role-taking activities. Perhaps the proliferation of collaborative writing tools (especially cooperative hypermedia) may answer to this challenge. Nevertheless, few researchers have addressed the social cognitive impact of collaboratively used computer tools (Clements & Nastasi, 1988).

Selman (1971) proposed a developmental framework for social cognitive skills. According to this framework, *social cognition* is viewed as the forming of beliefs, inferences, and conceptions about the inner psychological functioning of someone else (Flavell, 1985), or, more basically, the ability to take the perspective of someone else (Selman, 1980). Not surprisingly, developmental lapses or delays in social cognitive ability could constrain one's judgment and understandings of the actions and expectations of others (Muuss, 1988). Shared experiences among participants writing on a computer network could foster interpersonal understanding and mutual knowledge, especially if they work within common zones of proximal development. Yet, since communication technologies for cooperative work make possible a variety of kinds of communication, the extent of mutual knowledge and communicative effectiveness varies widely (Krauss & Fussell, 1990). Along these same lines, the knowledge representations and points of view presented within collaborative writing networks should stimulate social cognitive development (Bonk, 1990).

Using Selman's social cognitive framework, one could conclude that students need to progress beyond their egocentric views of the world to take into account one or more differing points of view. This development might eventually lead to the highest stage in Selman's developmental scheme (i.e., societal perspective taking ability). Selman's five-stage hierarchy of interpersonal understanding could therefore be used as a framework for evaluating the effectiveness of collaborative writing (e.g., cooperative hypermedia) and other media tools. However, new assessment instruments are needed to promptly and accurately measure the social cognitive growth resulting from cooperative hypermedia environments in addition to the complex and time-consuming interviewing schemes of Selman.

Consistent interaction within cooperative hypermedia sessions extend beyond enhancing perspective-taking skills to also bind participants with increased intersubjectivity. Broadly speaking, *intersubjectivity* is an awareness of mutual understanding of common thoughts, ideas, values, or emotions of two or more individuals; that is, to know someone's reaction without verbal or nonverbal cues.

> Though an intimidating term on first exposure . . . intersubjectivity refers to the way that a group of people think and experience the world in similar basic dimensions, processes, and content. To the degree that intersubjectivity is present, that values are alike, and goals are alike, then more cooperation is possible, and thus more harmony. (Tharp, Note, & O'Donnell, 1991, p. 2)

While Tharp et al. later suggest that cultures flourish when the degree of intersubjectivity is high, so, too, the learning culture of a school or classroom may thrive with the intersubjectivity stimulated by the integration of cooperative hypermedia tools. Moreover, since culture is viewed as a set of thoughts that are shared among group members (Levine & Moreland, 1991), collaborative tools should enrich the culture of the classroom.

In summary, then, the social and cognitive ramifications of tools like collaborative writing media that support interactive dialogue and meaning-making activities are extensive. Collaborative writing should provide access to peers and cognitive coaches who foster cognitive conflict and critical reflection of one's work. In addition, during electronic writing collaboration, one's composing skills will be scaffolded to new heights. In effect, assistance from peers and teachers at the edge of one's envelope of competence is hypothesized to be internalized as independent problem-solving activity. Intersubjectivity and mutual knowledge directly influence the extent to which mediated instruction within this zone of proximal development can occur. When common zones are found, one's exposure to multiple points of view on a writing network becomes an ideal activity for enhancing societal awareness and social cognition. While perspective taking is a skill that extends to many activities besides collaborative writing, so, too, there are other forms of media that support cognitive and social cognitive ability besides collaborative writing tools (e.g., the Logo programming language; see Clements & Nastasi, 1988). The next section details the support available with multimedia and hypermedia as well as collaborative writing tools.

TOOL SUPPORT

Multimedia and Hypermedia

While addressing the social cognitive needs of the school curriculum, hypermedia and multimedia technology captures unique representations of information and makes them available to others. For the purposes of this article, *multimedia* refers to combining several media types–text, graphics, sound, animation, and video–within one computer system, while *hypermedia environments* are designed to facilitate the creation of multilayered texts and overall construction of meaning as well as the display of complex relationships and branching between ideas (Kozma, 1991). In effect, *hypermedia* is the arbitrary, but active linking of chunks of text, pictures, graphics, voice recordings, and video made available by multimedia systems (Galegher & Kraut, 1990). Because of hypermedia's concern with text structure, interrelationships, and other discourse issues that are not always available in multimedia environments, it more appropriately represents the highest level of electronic collaborative writing (see the end of this section on Process Support as well as the third major section of this paper, Wedding Plans, for an elaboration of our proposed hierarchy of collaborative writing tools).

Bolter (1991) indicates that the emergence of multimedia and hypermedia texts does not signal the death of writing but extends composition into more a flexible and interactive environment for weaving together various representations of text. "Hypermedia simply extends the principles of electronic writing into the domain of sound and images" (Bolter, 1991, p. 27). Opportunities for joint authorship and collaboration within these systems allows for many new activities and theoretical accounts of both reading and writing. According to Landow (1990), any link placed in an electronic text is a form of collaboration and sharing that heretofore could only exist in the minds of individuals originally perceiving these interrelationships. Thus, hypermedia linkages facilitate the sharing of ideas, identification of alternatives, associating ideas, and elaboration of ideas (Harasim, 1989).

Hypermedia tools also offer numerous possibilities for information sharing and intersubjectivity. Common hypertext-type features (e.g., browse and link) enable students to display relationships between terms, passages, or ideas that others have not conceived. Drawing a partner's attention to textual, graphic, and other linkages made in a hypertext document will certainly amplify the representations of meaning that are critical for mutual understanding or intersubjectivity. In terms of collaborative writing tools with hypermedia aids, student-student dialoguing not only encourages intersubjectivity through reflection, but also through browsing, cross-referencing, annotating, and representing knowledge. In effect, collaborative writing frameworks capitalize upon the capability of hypermedia environments to explore a topic in multiple ways. Assuming the relationships displayed between cooperative hypermedia participants are not buggy, the paths to increased comprehension of textual relationships should multiply with increased exposure to hypermedia devices.

Multimedia tools enable educators to present information in more than one mode, thereby facilitating at least dual coding of information (i.e., information stored verbally and visually) (Anderson, 1990; Kozma, 1991). As a result of juxtaposing ideas when using multimedia, information accessibility is strengthened, resulting in increased understanding of material and discrimination between concepts. Besides increasing memorability, multimedia tools offer opportunities to instruct within one's particular learning style strength, while also compensating for and enhancing weaknesses.

Collaborative Writing

Collaborative writing exists when groups of two or more people work in concert on a paper, research project, or other common text project, typically in an environment supportive of student idea and document sharing. The use of peers as collaborators, evaluators, and tutors is a practical tool for broadening students' sense of audience (Gebhardt, 1980) that has been extended to computer-mediated environments such as electronic mail and remote access networks (Dickinson, 1986; MacArthur, 1988). In contrast to traditional teacher-based audiences, networked peer tutors make available more varied, intimately involved, distant, and/or challenging audience experiences (Hawkins, 1980).

There are many ways to structure writing groups to increase cooperation and intersubjectivity. For instance, the use of assigned roles (e.g., executive director, reporter, author, proofreader, co-author, editor, peer reviewer, or critic) might foster positive independence and accountability of group members (Johnson & Johnson, 1987). Collaborative writing examples include students brainstorming together on the network and writing individually, students writing a first draft individually and joining products together on a network, and students brainstorming one paper from start to finish as an electronic group. As indicated earlier, the combination of peer modeling, feedback, and shared roles and responsibilities during collaborative writing extends compositions beyond initial plans and visions and changes the very nature of the writing process.

As with multimedia and hypermedia, recent advances in networking and collaborative writing tools meet a wide range of academic goals. In a general sense, "the capacity to connect with others is a significant educational goal" (Calfee & Nelson-Barber, 1991, p. 55). As Schrage (1990) notes, "Collaborative tools hold the promise of giving individuals the power to communicate and learn more effectively than they have ever imagined" (p. xxiv). Schrage further points out that the goal of collaboration is not to simply display and gain access to each other's information, but to create a shared space for idea exploration and collaboration. Hence, sharing and collaborating do not necessarily increase due to convenience, but due to the combined possibilities for fresh insights and community support.

Most collaborative writing packages (e.g., *Aspects*, *Collaborative Writer*, *Conference Writer*, CSILE, *GroupWriter*, *HyperAuthor*, *Knowledge Builder*, *LiveWriter*, and *Prose*–see Appendix B) have been developed during the past five years. As noted earlier, what is lacking in these development efforts is a unified direction or organizing framework for using these innovative composition tools. The lack of agreement as to what constitutes collaborative writing software creates difficulty in attempting to identify critical or novel tool features.

To investigate the available collaborative writing software, a questionnaire was designed and distributed to over 30 developers of these tools. This questionnaire inquired about intended audience, mode of operation, special features, and current and projected hypermedia and multimedia uses. Although the results of this survey are not directly reported in this article, categorical information obtained from software publishers, tool developers, and journal article reviews is reflected in Appendices A-D. For the purposes of this article, a *collaborative writing package* may be defined as an application that allows groups of two or more individuals to work on a common writing project in a shared environment. Collaborative writing is a specialized form of groupware: software shared by a number of network participants that may support professional office communication, but not necessarily school-based composition tasks. For example, applications like *Meeting Maker* allow groups of network participants to electronically schedule meetings by sharing a common calendar. These applications are labeled groupware, but because they fail to allow for the typing of extended text, they are not considered collaborative writing tools for the purposes of this paper. Interaction patterns that contribute to joint communication in most groupware environments are discussed next.

Collaborative Communication Features

Groupware and networking tools facilitate diverse forms of communication. However, electronic communication for collaborative purposes occurs in one of three ways:

1. *One-to-One Communication*. This basic form of communication is supported mainly by electronic mail (e-mail) systems. One-to-one communication involves sending messages or files from one person to another,

usually in a delayed response mode. *QuickMail*, reviewed later, is an example of a one-to-one type of e-mail package.

2. *One-to-Many Communication.* One-to-many communication involves real-time or delayed communication between one person (usually the teacher or conference moderator) and several other individuals (e.g., students). In terms of school settings, although communication between the teacher and a group of students is possible in this type of system, and vice versa, students do not have access to each others' documents (i.e., unless they are granted access to the teacher software application). The emphasis in this form of computer-mediated communication is on monitoring or managing student progress. *LiveWriter* (described later) is a package that supports one-to-many communication.

3. *Many-to-Many Communication.* In the most preferred form of communication, many-to-many, information flows freely among groups of individuals (e.g., teacher to groups of students, individual student to the group, student to student, student to teacher, or group to group). Many-to-many communication patterns are supported by a number of real-time brainstorming and collaborative writing packages (e.g., *Conference Writer*).

In addition to the issue of direction of communication, the efficiency and timeliness of collaborative writing are affected by the speed of communication. In other words, is the communication simultaneous/real-time (synchronous) or delayed (asynchronous)? Although asynchronous communications is not as immediate as synchronous communication, these systems are more flexible in terms of time and place-independence. Thus, asynchronous communication is the preferred mode of communication in situations necessitating personal convenience of communication. Most electronic-mail (e-mail) systems typically allow for asynchronous communication. In contrast, in synchronous or real-time communication systems, participants or workgroups can simultaneously work on the same document. *Aspects* and *LiveWriter* are two software packages that allow for synchronous communication. In some systems, participants have private spaces, scratch pads, or windows wherein they can write and edit information before mailing it to others via a shared window or chat box. The notion of private work spaces, although appealing, may create frustration when participants obtain access to the products of each other's writing, but are not directly involved in the writing process (Stefik, Foster, Bobrow, Kahn, Lanning, & Suchman, 1988).

Other Collaborative Writing Features

As with communication options, several other collaborative writing tool features offer users a variety of choices. Features to be considered for collaborative writing include the number of windows, maximum number of participants, peer feedback possibilities, networked brainstorming and dialogue, teacher coaching options, writing lessons/instruction, graphics or data import tools, networking options, notetaking and outlining tools, hardware requirements, password security and conference moderation, group products or folders, and internal tracking of comments or time stamping (hypermedia and multimedia options are discussed later). Each of these options determines the quality of perspective-taking and intersubjectivity that occurs during collaborative writing. For instance, the time-date stamping of comments on the *Conference Writer* package enables prospective team members to witness the flow of previous dialogue and idea generation activity among participants. In considering the degree of perspective-taking, the amount of available windows may be the most critical and complex consideration since the quantity and type of computer windows determine the quality and type of perspectives shared. Windows or boxes typically exist for teacher dialogue, student dialogue, student composition, other compositions, outlining tools, concept mapping tools, knowledge bases, private notes or journal entries, text publishing, and other media boxes (e.g., CD-ROM and videodisc). A window for teacher and student comments, student papers or knowledge bases, and semantic maps should promote cognitive conflict and growth as well as perspective-taking. An explanation of some of the more critical features is included in Appendix A.

With increased sharing of data and graphics between work groups, the metaphor of the computer as a lonely, depersonalized learning environment has shifted to the computer as a builder of collaborative partnerships. As indicated already, a number of software tools support active, collaborative learning and co-construction of knowledge. Presently the hierarchy in collaborative writing packages ranges from the following five levels: (1) electronic mail (e-mail) or messaging; (2) delayed/asynchronous collaboration systems; (3) brainstorming and dialoguing devices; (4) direct/real-time text collaboration; and finally (5) direct text, graphics, and other collaboration (i.e., cooperative hypermedia). This proposed hierarchy includes the three cooperative work systems described by Greif and Sarin (1988): calendar management (i.e., described here as Level 1: e-mail); asynchronous collaborative document editing (i.e., Level 2: delayed collaboration); and real-time conferencing (i.e., Level 3: brainstorming and dialoguing). Apparently, real-time collaboration on actual texts was not common until recently (i.e., Levels 4 and 5 of our hierarchy). In effect, our five-level continuum ranges from minimally collaborative tools that incorporate asynchronous communication to multiple collaboration systems with synchronous communication. The first level within this continuum, electronic mail, simply supports ongoing mental activity, while Levels 2-4 would possibly enhance it and move it in new directions. Conceivably, significant exposure to Level 5 (i.e., cooperative hypermedia) activity might elevate or change the mental activity of participants. Hence, the focus of this article is on Level 2-5 tools that enhance, elevate, or change the cognitive processes of participants. Though extensive software listings are provided in Appendices B and D, many similar tools may not be included here. Sample software categories or descriptors are as follows:

Level 1: *Electronic Mail and Messaging Tools.* E-mail systems and messaging tools allow users to send messages or files from one computer to the next. There are two types of e-mail tools: point-to-point transfers and store-and-forward exchanges. In a point-to-point transfer system, messages or files are sent directly from one computer to the other, whereas, in a store-and-forward strategy, messages or files are stored on a centralized server and users log on to this server to retrieve their messages. The store-and-forward transfer is preferred because users can log on or log off without losing messages. However, in a writing lab where students are all connected to the network at the same time, it may be more economical to purchase a point-to-point file transfer system. *DaynaMail*, *Inbox*, *Microsoft Mail*, *QuickMail*, and *cc:mail* are among the many e-mail packages that are presently available. Some of these e-mail packages have tools embedded that allow for real-time brainstorming and dialoguing, although that is not their primary function.

Level 2: *Remote Access/Delayed Collaborative Writing Tools.* This large grouping of tools (Appendix B) includes those programs that allow users to remotely access and control files on each other's computers. For security purposes, the remote computer (referred to as the host) often requires the controlling computer (the guest) to type a password for access. After password clearance, guests have access to controlling, monitoring, and file transferring operations. With the AppleTalk networking options of a Macintosh computer, packages such as *Remote Access*, *Carbon Copy*, and *Timbuktu* enable users to view host screens on a guest desktop. In addition, one can run the applications and files accessed as though they were stored on their own computer. Some remote access packages like Timbuktu allow one guest to access and control several hosts at the same time. Using this feature in the classroom, the teacher/host can access files from several student/guest computers without leaving his or her computer. In most cases, these guests can observe the single host. If Macintosh's System 7 software is an indication of trends in operating software, remote access options may soon be standard system software. As indicated earlier, delayed collaborative writing packages like *Collaborative Writer* (Duin, Jorn, & DeBower, 1991) allow multiple users to work asynchronously on the same document. In effect, although Level 2 applications are mostly asynchronous operations, they are, nevertheless, extremely sophisticated and important.

Level 3: *Real-Time Dialoguing and Idea Generation.* The previously discussed packages involve asynchronous communication between two or more networked computers, while Levels 3, 4, and 5 of collaborative writing allow for real-time synchronous communication. Here, multiple users can simultaneously brainstorm by sending messages to each other (Peyton & Bruce, 1993). Such tools are especially useful in the prewriting and postwriting phases of the collaborative writing process. Packages that fall into this category typically have a minimum of two windows: a transcript window and an edit message box/window. A transcript window is a shared screen consisting of all ongoing dialogues, while message editing boxes are private screens for creating and editing messages before sending them to the transcript window. *Conference Writer*, *GroupWriter*, and *Daedalus* are a few examples of real-time dialoguing and idea-generation software packages.

Level 4: *Real-Time Collaborative Writing (Text Only).* Some real-time collaborative tools allow a number of people to work concurrently on text-related aspects of a shared document. In this kind of a setting, WYSIWIS (what you see is what I see) occurs. A tool is WYSIWIS if all participants view exactly the same information (i.e., everyone can see where one is pointing or making changes) (Stefik et al., 1988). Unlike software in the previous category where users must press a "Send" button and "Enter" key to transfer messages to the group or team, in this category, changes to the shared document are immediately visible to all participants. In some Level 4 packages, special pointing tools allow users to draw attention to particular parts of a shared document. Private chat boxes allow for real-time dialoguing and messaging. Some packages offer the turn-taking option, a required feature for maintaining a shared focus for the group (Stefik et al., 1988). Although these packages offer synchronous, many-to-many communication, they are limited by their inability to display combinations of text, graphics, sound, video, and animation. Hence, they are single media, not hypermedia or multimedia systems.

Level 5: *Cooperative Hypermedia.* Software that falls into the final category combines Level 4, Real-Time Collaborative Writing, features with hypermedia capabilities. The shared document could include text, hypertext, graphics, video images, music, speech, animation, or electronic spreadsheets. For example, *Aspects*, a Macintosh tool, allows several people to simultaneously edit documents consisting of text and graphics. However, most software incorporating hypermedia or multimedia within a collaborative writing tool is currently available on workstations rarely found in schools (e.g., Sun Workstations). For instance, *Diamond*, a multimedia conferencing system, requires workstations costing over $20,000 each. Similarly, the CSILE package, though specifically designed for education, originally was created with costly specialized hardware (although it is undergoing conversion to a common platform). As indicated at the end of Appendix B, many cooperative hypermedia tools included here exist only in prototype form or are undergoing expansion at the time of this writing to include collaboration, networking, and/or hypermedia components.

Appendix B contains a list of software packages that fall into each category. Although the majority of tools listed in this appendix are available on personal computer systems traditionally found in schools (i.e., IBM, Apple, or Macintosh), many minicomputer and integrated learning systems also offer sophisticated tools for collaborative writing. At the time of this writing, inexpensive networking capabilities of the Macintosh line were primarily responsible for the extensive offering of collaborative writing products on this platform. While the focus here is on software affordable to schools that encourages collaborative communication, the authors realize that hardware changes in the transmission of voice, text, data, and video (i.e., wide band communication lines) will undoubtedly stimulate further collaborative communication efforts across systems at more affordable prices.

Packages in Appendix B were categorized according to information received from vendors, including brochure, journal article, videotape information, and demonstration versions of many packages. Note, however, that some packages may fall into more than one category depending upon use. The intent of this appendix is to point out the hierarchy of collaborative writing software that already exists; at the highest level are cooperative hypermedia environments. Other writing tools may incorporate sophisticated hypermedia or multimedia tools but lack networking or electronic collaboration opportunities (e.g., *HyperWriter* from NTERGAID). A few packages extend process models of writing and incorporate options meant to more accurately reflect how writers work (e.g., *Write Environment*–see Houlette, 1991), but may not contain collaboration components. Still other tools resemble brainstorming and dialogue tools but are more concerned about responding to teacher questions and open-ended probes than with composition tasks (e.g., Discourse Systems). As mentioned previously, many intriguing groupware or application sharing tools are available, but not all target writing skills (e.g., the network on *Wagon Train 1848* from MECC targets social studies knowledge and decision making). Finally, some writing tools are designed to foster brainstorming and textual analysis by an individual, not collaboration or groupwork at multiple terminals (e.g.. *Writer's Helper* from Conduit). Packages that fall within each of the five collaborative writing levels are described in Appendix C. Complete vendor names and addresses are provided at the end of this article (Appendix D).

In summary of this section, computer tools available for collaborative writing support a number of social and cognitive skills. Thinking skill support, however, will significantly vary with the type and amount of collaborative communication facilitated by the tool as well as the classroom context in which it is used. Educators concerned with addressing social cognitive needs within the school curriculum may find that Level 5 tools, "cooperative hypermedia," offer the most fruitful and intriguing avenue for these efforts.

WEDDING PLANS

Cooperative Hypermedia

As indicated, the marriage between collaborative writing and multimedia and hypermedia tools might create a new educational term (e.g., *integrated collaborative writing media* or *cooperative hypermedia*) and possibly propagate additional innovative tools. Through cooperative hypermedia tools, children may more readily realize that knowledge is socially constructed, represented, and organized in a variety of ways. Pea (1985) suggested that many writing aids such as concept mapping tools, thinking skill prompts, outliners, idea generators, hypertext devices, notecard systems, electronic books, co-authoring tools, and electronic commenting tools may increase shared or interpersonal understandings. Combinations of these tools encourage multiple forms of mental representation and offer unique opportunities for the sharing of perspectives (i.e., social cognition and intersubjectivity) heretofore lacking in many educational settings.

Educators interested in documenting the effectiveness of socially situated learning opportunities and the sharing of perspectives (Rogoff, 1990; Tharp & Gallimore, 1988) might welcome these new collaborative writing tools. As these researchers have noted (Bonk, 1991), there are a number of successful cognitive and social-cognitive interventions and techniques that share common characteristics, and have contributed to the emergence of a new paradigm within education. Accordingly, the rationale for hypermedia use is grounded in Deweyian and Vygotskian philosophies of student-centered but teacher-guided learning and development (Lehrer, 1993; see also Lehrer, Erickson, Love, & Connell, this volume).

The active engagement, open dialogue and questioning, and perspective sharing displayed within collaborative composition tasks form the heart of student-centered learning approaches. Students engage in a multitude of skill-enhancing activities during collective production of essays or papers (e.g., providing their writing colleagues with reflective questions or prompts) (Bonk & Reynolds, 1992; Scardamalia & Bereiter, 1991). Partners might paraphrase or summarize main ideas, refine interpretations, spontaneously defend and debate ideas, relate knowledge fragments to main ideas or themes, connect inert ideas to prior knowledge or common experiences, decide on the relevance or logic of new information, provide immediate feedback on concepts and ideas discussed, and, generally, share and explain knowledge (Swallow, Scardamalia, & Olivier, 1988). Of course, these cognitive activities are enhanced by how the task is perceived and contextualized, and by the common knowledge or intersubjectivity between participants.

Researchers need to discern the mutual knowledge, social cognition, and intersubjectivity addressed by existing collaborative writing software if new developmental schemes in perspective taking and cognitive ability are to be uncovered. In addition, new models and theories are needed to drive research and practice concerned with the effectiveness of collaborative writing environments. Perhaps checklists, questionnaires, and other evaluation tools that address social cognition, intersubjectivity, and other skills inherent in collaborative writing would increase our understanding of the effectiveness of these environments. Lehrer et al. (this volume) discuss more specific cognitive skills addressed by this media as well as sample assessment devices. In reviewing the first table, "Cognitive Components of Hypermedia-Based Design," of the Lehrer et al. article as well as skill summaries from Pea (1985) and Scardamalia et al. (1989), the following 10 cognitive principles of learning emerge when examining the effectiveness of cooperative hypermedia:

1. Building on existing student knowledge and experience.
2. Creating teacher-student dialogue to uncover students' interests and thought processes.
3. Making learning relevant.
4. Incorporating opportunities for product ownership.
5. Supporting student risk-taking and cooperative learning.

6. Realizing that knowledge is constructed and organized in varied ways.
7. Realizing the connectedness of knowledge.
8. Providing interactivity and immediate feedback.
9. Internalizing strategies and processes modeled by others.
10. Realizing that knowledge is not static, but grows and must be socially constructed.

From a pedagogical standpoint, appropriate use of cooperative hypermedia software provides participants with immediate feedback, modeling of alternative strategies and skills, authentic audiences, cooperative partnerships, and joint production of knowledge bases.

Some designers have explicitly sought to create software that complements the above skill needs. For instance, the CSILE project (Scardamalia & Bereiter, 1991) evolved from an attempt to design a collaborative tool based on sound cognitive principles such as supporting goal setting, knowledge building, and active or intentional learning (Scardamalia, Bereiter, McLean, Swallow, & Woodruff, 1989). While addressing most of the cognitive principles listed above, the CSILE project attempts to grant more responsibility to students for their own learning by encouraging co-construction of knowledge, perspective building, audience awareness, idea generation, deeper processing of information, and product ownership. Through knowledge-building centers and public display of student-generated work on the CSILE system, students benefit from question asking, paraphrasing, relating information to prior experiences and knowledge, generating analogies, critiquing missing information, diagnosing partner misunderstandings, and modeling solution strategies. In addition, CSILE is embedded with self-questioning prompts, private and public note features, database searching, and designated "cooperation" icons that encourage both self- and co-processing of information.

HyperAuthor (Lehrer et al., this volume), *MediaText* (Hoffman, 1991; Soloway, 1991), and *Knowledge Builder* (Freeze, 1991; Toews, 1989) are similar tools for student creation of "knowledge bases." According to Lehrer (personal communication, December, 1991), future versions of *HyperAuthor* will likely include some direct networking and collaboration tools. At the present time, students in Lehrer et al.'s (this volume) design teams orally share their hyperdocument creations to build perspective-taking and evaluation skills.

Similarly, the focus of the two *MediaText* tools is to facilitate student active or generative learning by using a common word-processing environment to access a number of rich media tools (Soloway, 1988, 1991). Like *HyperAuthor*, student-centered projects or authentic design work drives the use of *MediaText*. In essence, Soloway (1988) points out that students need activities for generating and designing original ideas and concepts as well as exposure to analysis and evaluation (for a generative-evaluative skill building framework within electronic writing, see Bonk & Reynolds, 1992). According to Soloway, the constructivistic, project-oriented learning model of *MediaText* makes evident a major transition taking place in education: a shift from students passively accessing and accepting teacher knowledge banks to students actively reflecting, sharing, and critiquing each other's learning and understanding.

When using the final cooperative hypermedia package mentioned here, *KnowledgeBuilder*, students share the work they have created on a common file server. In addition, students have access to outlining, concept mapping, draftwriting, and publishing tools. With these tools, students can request numerous reflective writing prompts that provide assistance in three main categories: the generation of ideas, composition, and revision (Freeze, 1991; Toews, 1989). Importantly, a cross-referencing of prompts to text-examples helps contextualize their active use. The thinking and writing strategy prompts of the next version of *KnowledgeBuilder* (2.0) along with projected incorporation of full motion video input/output, real-time document collaboration, and "hyper-data-links" may set a benchmark for future cooperative hypermedia.

From a more global perspective on learning and instruction, tools meeting (or evolving to meet) cooperative hypermedia standards (e.g., CSILE, *HyperAuthor*, *KnowledgeBuilder*, and *MediaText*) address communication skills, critical thinking, cooperative learning and teamwork, problem solving, creativity and flexible thinking, and academic self-concept. Of course, the authors of these four tools all point out that in order for these new tools to significantly address the above skills, the traditional roles of teachers and students must be altered (Lehrer et al., this volume; Scardamalia & Bereiter, 1991; Soloway, 1991; Toews, 1989). The critical question, therefore, is whether these tools shift classroom focus from teacher-centered, rote learning to student-centered, constructivistic foundations like knowledge construction, product ownership, active participation, self-expression, and electronic collaborative communication (Bruder, 1991). Or, as Schrage contends, "The focus of collaborative technology changes from *assigning* work to *doing* work" (p. 193). Stated another way, hypermedia tools offer students the opportunity to construct and test personal understandings of information (Wilson, 1991). The basic philosophy, therefore, is that the student is treated as someone who matters in educational reform (Fullan & Stiegelbauer, 1991). Evidently, cooperative hypermedia hold promise for the active, socially situated learning environments advocated by constructivists and progressive educators.

As these "sharing" tools increase in number and sophistication, notions of ownership and control over written documents evolve in complexity and significance. As a result, defining what "writing" is and when it occurs becomes increasingly difficult. Consider the act of linking ideas; is that considered reading or writing? And how might this linkage be enhanced with the realization of pen-based computers (Bortman, 1992)? Of course, information sharing with pen technology as well as other additions to cooperative hypermedia would more closely approximate face-to-face interaction. But, are lines, drawings, and graphic relationships underlying text even considered part of the written document? What about saved dialogue from an electronic brainstorming session that stimulated significant changes in one or more compositions? And what will happen regarding school reform efforts if collaborative writing, multimedia, and hypermedia tools persuade educators to more faintly draw the lines separating disciplines? Because many tools for enhanced perspective taking and intersubjectivity are now embedded within traditional word-processing shells (e.g., the four packages mentioned in the preceding paragraphs), it is vital that we reflect on the skills that collaborative writing software could impact before incorporating them into the classroom.

Open Issues and Questions

Many additional research-related questions about students, teachers, and schools are embedded in the two sections that follow. First of all, in working with the integration of collaborative writing and hypermedia technology, educators must ask a number of serious questions regarding the use of these tools in different educational settings. For instance:

1. What tools match ideal visions of knowledge and the learning process?
2. What kind of collaborations are preferable: one-to-one, one-to-many, or many-to-many?
3. How might rich understanding of subject matter be displayed in collaborative writing?
4. What should be sent or shared during collaborations: individual messages, text files, or multimedia documents?
5. At what stage of the writing process could one successfully use the various collaborative writing packages, especially cooperative hypermedia?
6. How anonymous should learners remain when using these tools?

7. How much control should the teacher exercise over the group writing process?
8. How informative is the tracking of time and participant suggestions?
9. How could social cognition and intersubjectivity increase as a result of using collaborative writing software? What about writing quality?
10. With a multitude of peer and teacher interactions on a network, how does one deal with issues of knowledge ownership and writing assessment?

Answers to these questions may determine the extent to which the writing process impacts on hypermedia as well as the reverse. Research on cooperative learning and group interaction indicates that cooperative dialogues about writing topics and products would encourage students to ask and record questions, explain and share findings, clarify and defend knowledge, summarize main ideas and interpretations, and refine and reformulate conclusions. In addition, the discussion of ideas should assist students in relating information to prior experiences, connecting knowledge fragments, and deciding upon informational relevance.

At the intersection of these educational innovations and challenges are groups of two or more people working in concert on a paper or project (i.e., collaborative writing), while combining several media types (i.e., multimedia) and creating multilayered texts that readily display complex relationships and linkages (i.e., hypermedia). As a result, newer forms of media are not diminishing the importance of writing, but extending it in critical directions. During the upcoming decade, opportunities for joint authorship, idea linkage and display, and interactive idea sharing and elaboration will be more obvious and important. Still, Mary-Alice White reminds us that we have reached the point where "we have all these emerging technologies coming at us so fast that we really haven't thought through how to use them, and particularly how to use them in a worthwhile way. At this stage we don't know whether multimedia helps the learning process. I think it's going to, but we just don't know" (Bruder, 1991; p. 22). Given this uncertainty, it is important to predict possible scenarios emanating from the joining of these tools.

Student Research Possibilities

In terms of the student, a number of interesting writing tool environments and corresponding research avenues are available. Assuming that cooperative hypermedia had proper organizing or orienting aids (i.e., a focus on information position/perspective as well as linkage and flow)

(Tripp & Roby, 1990; Wolfe, 1989), hypermedia navigation paths could be displayed to peers and teachers in a collaborative writing project. However, one's display of navigation paths depends on the collaborative activity (co-writers, co-publishers, co-responders, co-editors, or writer-helpers), interaction structure (cooperative, helping obligatory, or helping permitted), and assigned task (planning, composing, reviewing, and correcting) (see Saunders, 1989, for a detailed review of these different roles and responsibilities). In effect, these writing activities, tasks, and structures influence interaction patterns, dialogue, and overall learning. Or, as Hiebert and Fisher (1991) point out, the task and talk structure of reading and writing instruction significantly influences children's literacy gains. As a result, they recommend documenting shifts in the distributions of these structures to indicate the type of change occurring within a learning environment.

The recording and reproducing of relations among texts make available the reading paths and thinking patterns of more expert peers and coaches (Landow, 1990). In cooperative hypertext systems, a number of collaborations are possible, including (a) forging reading paths for others to follow; (b) providing links among documents presently on the system; (c) creating new text documents and linkages; (d) creating and linking graphic documents; and (e) providing comments and criticisms in pop-up windows or notecards (Landow, 1990). Dynamic tracing and tracking/coding of these and other collaboration linkages across media types provides researchers with explicit mappings of meaningful collaborative writing operations. The ability of the computer to maintain time-stamped log files, keystroke records, and linkage selections facilitates tracking of media effects on cognitive operations (Bonk & Reynolds, 1992; Kozma, 1991).

With cooperative hypermedia, peers could model how they queried or searched for, located, extracted, categorized, and synthesized information in a document–all vital literacy skills (Guthrie & Dreher, 1990). Picture how students might share their paths to understanding with each other through replays of their efforts. In effect, these cooperative hypermedia tools could force investigations into collective or distributed intelligence (Harasim, 1989; Pea, 1985), intellectual teamwork (Galegher et al., 1990), and intersubjectivity or intermental processing (Gallimore, Note, & O'Donnell, 1991; Tharp & Gallimore, 1988). Researchers should also investigate the forms of graphical representations of cooperative work (i.e., ways of visualizing aspects of group work) that facilitate brainstorming and other cooperative task structures within cooperative hypermedia (Lakin, 1990). In terms of these cooperative tasks, will performance be based on individually written papers, team reports, or insights and assistance provided to peers? In fact, how might the degree and type of assistance (e.g., question-asking behaviors) be measured? And how might such assistance vary by age and ability?

With improvements in idea-tracking tools, the evolution of ideas (i.e., individual and group-generated creative acts) will be available for later dissection. Imagine the interactive sharing of ownership and excitement as students are allowed to display their knowledge through words, images, movement, and sounds. As stated earlier in this paper, key educational goals in mediated environments of the 1990s include coping with multiple viewpoints, working with others, maintaining a sense of inquiry, and conflict resolution (Wilson, 1991).

There are a number of areas that research into collaborative writing and cooperative hypermedia address. Researchers could investigate the effects of collaborative writing software on perspective taking and self-concept. At the same time, attempts should be undertaken to clarify developmental patterns of social cognitive growth as a result of extensive interaction with these tools. In this regard, determining preferable types of collaborations at different points in the composing process would be helpful as well as tracking how collaborative hypermedia groups evolve and dissolve over time. Do students with opposing learning style preferences reconcile conflicting viewpoints as a result of cooperative hypermedia experiences? What mix of field dependent or field independent students might facilitate joint search, creation, and display of information nodes within a hyperdocument (Tripp & Roby, 1990)? Although there are a multitude of research avenues within cooperative hypermedia (e.g., social-cognitive and learning style benefits), researchers would, nonetheless, possess a rich tool for determining whether students reorganize their knowledge as a result of working together on a network and whether there are differential effects from available collaborative media. Of course, collaborative writing tools differ not only in student learning style and knowledge reorganization possibilities, but also in the instructional opportunities provided teachers and schools.

Teacher Research Possibilities and School Reform

Evidently, there are a number of tracks available to those interested in the marriage of collaborative writing and mediated environments, many of which broaden the student concerns discussed above to include teaching practices and school reform. As prior research questions indicate, collaborative writing may facilitate new dimensions in the traditions of teaching and learning. When using cooperative hypermedia, teachers acquire new horizons for classroom learning and beyond. At the same time, they no longer hold total control and power over student learning. Students exposed to these powerful systems, especially those incorporating multimedia and hypermedia, have opportunities to specify relationships, offer points of view, and share ways of organizing information with both their teachers and peers. Ironically, students might understand more about knowledge and its representation than many of their own teachers. In effect, student-teacher and student-student relationships may change as a result of extensive opportunities for collaborative writing.

Though the amount of control and structure may significantly decrease in collaborative writing environments, the resulting degree of structure and guidance is currently unknown (Wolfe, 1989). Possible studies include comparisons of student-centered and teacher-centered (i.e., control-oriented) instructional practices within collaborative writing software. For instance, at what point might teacher-centered methods and practices subside within collaborative writing environments to allow more student control over learning? And to what extent will teachers or students feel comfortable with the assessment of assignments written on a medium like cooperative hypermedia wherein one hears echoes of the old composition adage, "a piece of writing is never finished, just abandoned" (i.e., what follows from presuming that a task is never entirely covered or closed to changes?) (Bolter, 1991; Dyasi, 1991). Finally, do schools become more cooperative and team oriented as electronic media multiplies opportunities for social interaction (Schrage, 1990)? And, as a result, do they allow us to visualize a more social or Bakhtinian view of language that might boldly regard all writing as "essentially collaborative" (Thralls, 1992, p. 63)?

In focusing on possible teaching frameworks for collaborative writing (especially cooperative hypermedia), a number of basic pedagogical principles emerge (Scardamalia et al., 1989; Toews, 1989). One key factor is that the role of the teacher is decentralized. Though the teacher may exist as a critical node on the network, private interaction with him or her would be less threatening and embarrassing for many students than traditional instruction. In effect, teachers using cooperative writing packages are encouraged to become involved in student dialoguing, peer critiquing, and group writing activities as either a co-learner or mentor. Thus, the teacher can take part in spontaneous construction of meaning while also guiding student explorations through praise, encouragement, and constructive criticism (Scardamalia & Bereiter, 1991).

In collaborative writing, the teacher operates within a discourse community, wherein at least three types of collective production are possible: conversations, brainstorming dialogue sessions, and written correspondence about an idea or product (Rafoth, 1988; Rubin, 1988). Of course, conversations and brainstorming dialogues within collaborative writing environments are available for later individual composition efforts or joint products. Yet, a class of electronic writers, like other communities and cultures, are bound by complex, socially constructed webs of knowledge or patterns of belief (Brown, Collins, & Duguid, 1989). As students become aware of the social nature of the writing process, knowledge can be increasingly viewed as co-constructed, relevant, and interconnected, thereby instilling active student participation and idea experimentation. Importantly, the co-construction of knowledge and perceived meaningfulness results in enhanced internal access to these ideas. As ideas become less inert, students begin to view knowledge as a tool rather than useless facts (The Cognition and Instruction Group at Vanderbilt, 1990; Dewey, 1933). Perhaps, a new epistemology of learning will appear within students that will be difficult to ignore or undermine (Brown, 1990). Stated another way, the use of collaborative writing environments should foster student involvement and voice within classroom activities.

Epistemology is influenced by the fact that students of the 1990s are already more comfortable learning with visual media than previous generations. These children must also develop their interpersonal and social awareness skills deemed critical to fully participate in a global society. The extension of collaborative writing software into multimedia and hypermedia environments should enhance visual representations of information as well as interpersonal skills and social awareness and interaction skills. Perhaps visual and communication technologies like cooperative hypermedia will build on existing skills and abilities of children and extend them in important directions. Cooperative hypermedia tools could help establish linkages between people and events and perhaps assist students in discoveries that knowledge is no longer derived from competition, possession, or even personal accessibility. Instead, knowledge has evolved to issues of collaboration, co-construction, networking, and mutual access.

As indicated throughout this paper, the organizational impact of computers on the social life of the classroom is a critical research concern (Newman, 1990). For instance, do peer collaboration tools hasten the movement to recognize peers as valuable educational resources (Riel, 1990)? Does increased teacher scaffolding or guidance of student work enhance opportunities to transform the role of the teacher in the classroom? How might teachers receive scaffolding from more expert "teacher-leader" peers on the network, thereby extending Vygotsky's notion of zones of proximal development to a second tier of scaffolded assistance (Gaffney & Anderson, 1991)? Even more dramatic than teachers collaborating with each other on a network is students collaboratively writing with peers from other countries to share cultures (Riel, 1990) and enhance global understanding (Schrum, 1991). In effect, there is a blurring in the lines between teachers and students as well as a shift in the politics of reading and writing (Bolter, 1991; Landow, 1990). Though sound design features are beginning to be documented and validated in mediated environments (Kozma, 1991), systematic research should enhance our understanding of student and teacher interaction and assistance when using educational networks (Riel, 1991).

Clearly, many forms of literacy assistance are now available for both teachers and students, including new task and talk structures that transform teaching and learning (Hiebert & Fisher, 1991). According to Hiebert and Fisher, such "transformative" teaching is an opportunity for "the development of true literacy in students, that is, where students avidly use reading and writing as vehicles for thinking and living" (p. 147). In transformative educational environments, students are responsible for initiating and controlling their own learning. In addition, students extensively interact with peers since they are the primary sources for knowledge acquisition and transmission.

CONCLUSIONS

Cooperative hypermedia tools offer possibilities heretofore only realized in the minds of idealists and persistent dreamers; although Mead (1934) and Vygotsky (1978) long ago argued that social interaction "creates the mind," Bolter (1991) now contends, "writing is a way of knowing your own mind" (p. 213). Extending these statements, one might hypothesize that collaborative writing tools will reveal the minds of collaborators (i.e., by providing conversational structures to be internalized), as well as offer a tool-kit for analyzing the joint creation of mind. In effect, properly designed and used, cooperative hypermedia will be a tool that fosters "mindfulness" and constructivistic learning, instead of lapses into mindlessness surrounding other convenient word-processing tools (Salomon, Perkins, & Globerson, 1991). One must be mindful of the fact that to create a document or link in a cooperative hypermedia system is an opportunity to collaborate with all those using the tool in the past, present, or future (Landow, 1990).

Though many more lofty and dreamlike possibilities exist, the collaborative writing tool also is a pragmatic one. For instance, the wide range of cognitive and social cognitive skills promoted by these environments (e.g., perspective taking, social awareness, communication, critical thinking) are the exact skills demanded by society. Due to the wealth of recent research on cooperative learning and educational technology, there is a growing realization about the potential techniques that incorporate cooperative learning tasks and classroom situations that properly structure the use of newer technologies.

These tools not only support and enhance mental activity, but also offer hope for elevating or changing it (Lehrer, personal communication, November, 1991). At the same time, the use of these tools without consideration of the changing interaction patterns and structures they create–the channels of communication, the types of communication, the skills facilitated by new communication tools, and the patterns of classroom interaction–would certainly place a constraint on positive outcomes. Thus, a reconsideration of social and cognitive skills facilitated by various categories of cooperative hypermedia tools should enhance our understanding of human learning and development, while conceivably leading the way to discovering new skills we have yet to map and label.

What are the prenuptial agreements and understandings of the marriage of collaborative writing and hypermedia tools? Those educators and researchers rejoicing in the wedding should seriously consider the name to be used after the marriage, since there are different instructional ramifications for previously used terms, such as integrated collaborative writing media, cooperative hypermedia, multimedia composition software, and multimedia electronic information systems. Secondly, these same researchers and practitioners must ask about the cognitive and social skills inherent in this marriage. They also might ponder over questions of the fertility of the partners, the types of offspring the marriage might give birth to, the incubation period for new products, and the pedagogical design features required for enhancing life expectancy. Of course, many researchers may simply show up at the wedding or reception because they wish to make contingency plans in case of a divorce (i.e., if collaborative writing tools and hypermedia are just incompatible or research indicates a continued lack of support). These and other issues must be addressed before proper use of cooperative hypermedia can take place.

The considerable number of cooperative hypermedia tools produced during the past few years validates both Bolter's (1991) recent prophecy that we are living in "the late age of print" (p. 1), as well as Greif's (1988) statement that "all software will be groupware" (p. 12). Nevertheless, during the 1990s, research on collaborative writing and hypermedia tools must continue to focus on how to design and refine quality cooperative learning tools so that students can work together and attend the weddings of many new thoughts and ideas. As new thinking and communication tools are born, as the social life of the child is awakened, as school life becomes filled with acts of sharing and cooperation, as children are exposed to those with differing viewpoints, needs, and backgrounds, as students are empowered to construct their own meanings, so too are Dewey's and Vygotsky's progressive educational reform efforts given new birth and meaning. Unfortunately, recent texts addressing progressive education techniques offer only brief glimpses into how technology like collaborative writing tools could impact classroom activities or research (Jervis & Montag, 1991). But, if this technology is truly transformative, progressive educators may be forced to adapt a new partner in their reform efforts. At the present time, all we can hope for is that cooperative hypermedia lives long and prospers!

REFERENCES

Adams, D., Carlson, H., & Hamm, M. (1990). *Cooperative learning and educational media: Collaborating with technology and each other.* Englewood Cliffs, NJ: Educational Technology Publications.

Anderson, J. R. (1990). *Cognitive psychology and its implications.* New York: W. H. Freeman.

Bolter, J. D. (1991). *Writing space: The computer, hypertext, and the history of writing.* Hillsdale, NJ: Erlbaum.

Bonk, C. J. (1990). A synthesis of social cognition and writing research. *Written Communication, 7*(1), 136-163.

Bonk, C. J. (1991). *The emergence of cooperative reading: Analyzing components of successful programs and strategies.* Paper presented at the American Educational Research Association annual convention, Chicago, IL.

Bonk, C. J. & Reynolds, T. H. (1992). Early adolescent composing within a generative-evaluative computerized prompting framework. *Computers in Human Behavior, 8*(1), 39-62.

Bortman, H. (1992). Is there a pen in your future? *MacUser, 8*(2), 144-148.

Brown, A. L. & Ferrara, R. A. (1985). Diagnosing zones of proximal development. In: J. V. Wertsch (Ed.), *Culture, communication, and cognition: Vygotskian perspectives* (pp. 273-305). New York: Cambridge University Press.

Brown, A. L. & Palincsar, A. S. (1989). Guided, cooperative learning and individual knowledge acquisition. In: L. Resnick (Ed.), *Cognition and instruction: Issues and agendas* (pp. 391-451). Hillsdale, NJ: Erlbaum.

Brown, A. & Reeve, R. A. (1987). Bandwidths of competence: The role of supportive contexts in learning and development. In: L. S. Liben (Ed.), *Development and learning: Conflict or congruence* (pp. 173-223). Hillsdale, NJ: Erlbaum.

Brown, J. S. (1990). Toward a new epistemology for learning. In: C. Frasson & J. Gauthiar (Eds.), *Intelligent tutoring systems at the crossroad of AI and education.* Norwood, NJ: Ablex.

Brown, J. S., Collins, A., & Duguid, P. (1989). Situated cognition and the culture of learning. *Educational Researcher, 18*(1), 32-41.

Bruder, I. (1991). Multimedia: How it changes the way we teach and learn. *Electronic Learning, 11*(1), 22-26.

Calfee, R. & Nelson-Barber, S. (1991). Diversity and constancy in human thinking: Critical thinking as amplifier of intellect and experience. In: E. H. Hiebert (Ed.), *Literacy in a diverse society: Perspectives, practices, and policies* (pp. 44-57). New York: Teachers College Press.

Chandler, M. (1973). Egocentrism and antisocial behavior: The assessment and training of social perspective-taking skills. *Developmental Psychology, 9*, 326-332.

Clements, D. H. & Nastasi, B. K. (1988). Social and cognitive interactions in educational computer environments. *American Educational Research Journal, 25*(1), 87-106.

The Cognition and Technology Group at Vanderbilt (1990). Anchored instruction and its relationship to situated cognition. *Educational Researcher, 19*(6), 2-10.

Daiute, C. (1986). Do 1 and 1 make 2? Patterns of influence by collaborative partners. *Written Communication, 3*(3), 382-408.

Daiute, C. (1989). Play as thought: Thinking strategies of young writers. *Harvard Educational Review, 59*(1), 1-23.

Daiute, C. & Dalton, B. (1988). "Let's brighten it up a bit": Communication and cognition in writing. In: B. A. Rafoth & D. L. Rubin (Eds.), *The social construction of written language* (pp. 249-269). Norwood, NJ: Ablex.

Damon, W. (1984). Peer education: The untapped potential. *Journal of Applied Developmental Psychology, 5*, 331-343.

DeVillar, R. A. & Faltis, C. J. (1991). *Computers and cultural diversity: Restructuring for school success*. Albany: NY: State University of New York Press.

Dewey, J. (1933). *How we think* (rev. ed.). Boston: Heath.

Dickinson, D. K. (1986). Cooperation, collaboration, and a computer: Integrating a computer into a first-second grade writing program. *Research in the Teaching of English, 20*(4), 357-378.

DiPardo, A. & Freedman, S. W. (1988). Peer response groups in the writing classroom: Theoretical foundations and new directions. *Review of Educational Research, 58*(2), 119-149.

Duin, A. H., Jorn, L. A., & DeBower, M. S. (1991). Collaborative writing–Courseware and telecommunications. In: M. M. Lay & W. M. Karis (Eds.), *Collaborative writing in industry: Investigations in theory and practice* (pp. 146-169). New York: Baywood Publishing.

Dyasi H. (1991). Assessing "imperfect" conceptions. In: K. Jervis & C. Montag (Eds.), *Progressive education for the 1990s: Transforming practice* (pp. 101-110). New York: Teachers College Press.

Flavell, J. H. (1985). *Cognitive development* (2nd ed.). Englewood Cliffs, NJ: Prentice Hall.

Freedman, S. W. (1987). *Response to student writing*. Urbana, IL: National Council of Teachers of English.

Freeze, D. R. (1991). *An evaluation of the writing for meaning project*. (Unpublished manuscript). University of Manitoba, Winnipeg, MB.

Fullan, M. G. & Stiegelbauer, S. (1991). *The new meaning of educational change* (2nd ed). New York: Teachers College Press.

Gaffney, J. S. & Anderson, R. C. (1991). Two-tiered scaffolding: Congruent processes of teaching and learning. In: E. H. Hiebert (Ed.), *Literacy in a diverse society: Perspectives, practices, and policies* (pp. 184-198). New York: Teachers College Press.

Galegher, J. & Kraut, R. E. (1990). Technology for intellectual teamwork: Perspectives on research and design. In: J. Galegher, R. E. Kraut, & C. Egido (Eds.), *Intellectual teamwork: Social and technological foundations of cooperative work* (pp. 1-20). Hillsdale, NJ: Erlbaum.

Galegher, J., Kraut, R. E., & Egido C. (Eds.). (1990). *Intellectual teamwork: Social and technological foundations of cooperative work.* Hillsdale, NJ: Erlbaum.

Gebhardt, R. (1980). Teamwork and feedback: Broadening the base of collaborative writing. *College English, 42*(1), 69-74.

Glynn, S. M., Oaks, D. R., Mattocks, L. F., & Britton, B. K. (1989). Computer environments for managing writers' thinking processes. In: B. K. Britton & S. M. Glynn (Eds.), *Computer writing environments: Theory, research, and design* (pp. 1-16). Hillsdale, NJ: Erlbaum.

Greif, I. (Ed.). (1988). *Computer-supported cooperative work: A book of readings.* San Mateo, CA: Morgan Kaufmann.

Guthrie, J. T. & Dreher, M. J. (1990). Literacy as search: Explorations via computer. In: D. Nix & R. Spiro (Eds.), *Cognition, education, and multimedia: Exploring ideas in high technology* (pp. 65-113). Hillsdale, NJ: Erlbaum.

Harasim, L. M. (1989). Online education: An environment for collaboration and intellectual amplification. In: L. M. Harasim (Ed.), *Hypertextual perspectives on educational computer conferencing* (pp. 39-64). New York: Praeger Press.

Hartman, K., Neuwirth, C. H., Kiesler, S., Sproull, L., Cochran, C., Palmquist, M., & Zubrow, D. (1991). Patterns of social interaction and learning to write: Some effects of network technologies. *Written Communication, 8*(1), 79-113.

Hawkins, T. (1980). Intimacy and audience: The relationship between revision and the social dimension of peer tutoring. *College English, 42*(1), 64-68.

Hiebert, E. H. & Fisher, C. W. (1991). Task and talk structures that foster literacy. In: E. H. Hiebert (Ed.), *Literacy in a diverse society: Perspectives, practices, and policies* (pp. 141-156). New York: Teachers College Press.

Higgins, L., Flower, L., & Petraglia (1990). *Planning text together: The role of critical reflections in student collaboration.* Paper presented at the American Educational Research Association annual convention, Boston, MA.

Hoffman, D. (1991). Summer news update: Software seen and heard at NECC. *Technology & Learning, 12*(1), 67-69.

Houlette, F. (1991). Write Environment: A window on the writing process. *T.H.E. Journal,* pp. 9-11. Special Insert by Zenith Data Systems, Masters of Innovation II Competition, Liberal Arts and Sciences.

Inhelder, B. & Piaget, J. (1958). *The growth of logical thinking: From childhood to adolescence.* New York: Basic Books.

Jervis, K. & Montag, C. (1991). *Progressive education for the 1990s: Transforming practice.* New York: Teachers College Press.

Johnson, D. W. & Johnson, R. T. (1987). *Learning together and alone: Cooperative, competitive, and individualistic learning* (2nd ed.). Englewood Cliffs, NJ: Prentice-Hall.

Kozma, R. B. (1991). Learning with media. *Review of Educational Research, 61*(2), 179-211.

Krauss, R. M. & Fussell, S. R. (1990). Mutual knowledge and communicative effectiveness. In: J. Galegher, R. E. Kraut, & C. Egido (Eds.), *Intellectual teamwork: Social and technological foundations of cooperative work* (pp. 111-145). Hillsdale, NJ: Erlbaum.

Lakin, F. (1990). Visual languages for cooperation: A performing medium approach to systems for collaborative work. In: J. Galegher, R. E. Kraut, & C. Egido (Eds.), *Intellectual teamwork: Social and technological foundations of cooperative work* (pp. 453-488). Hillsdale, NJ: Erlbaum.

Landow, G. P. (1990). Hypertext and collaborative work: The example of hypermedia. In: J. Galegher, R. E. Kraut, & C. Egido (Eds.), *Intellectual teamwork: Social and technological foundations of cooperative work* (pp. 407-428). Hillsdale, NJ: Erlbaum.

Lay, M. M. & Karis, W. M. (Eds.). (1991). *Collaborative writing in industry: Investigations in theory and practice.* New York: Baywood Publishing.

Lehrer, R. (1993). Authors of knowledge: Patterns of hypermedia design. In: S. Lajoie & S. Derry (Eds.), *Computers as cognitive tools* (pp. 197-227). Hillsdale, NJ: Erlbaum.

Lehrer, R., Erickson, J., Love, M., & Connell, T. (1994). *Learning by designing hypermedia documents.* Computers in the schools, *10*(4).

Levine, J. M. & Moreland, R. L. (1991). Culture and socialization in work groups. In: R. B. Resnick, J. M. Levine, & S. D. Teasley (Eds.), *Perspectives on socially shared cognition* (pp. 257-279). Washington, DC: American Psychological Association.

MacArthur, C. A. (1988). The impact of computers on the writing process. *Exceptional Children, 54*(6), 536-542.

Mead, G. H. (1934). *Mind, self, and society.* Chicago: University of Chicago Press.

Montague, M. (1990). *Computers, cognition, and writing instruction.* Albany, NY: State University of New York Press.

Muuss, R. E. (1988). *Theories of adolescence* (5th ed.). New York: Random House.

Newman, D. (1990). Opportunities for research on the organizational impact of computers. *Educational Researcher, 19*(3), 8-13.

Palincsar, A. S. (1986). The role of dialogue in scaffolded instruction. *Educational Psychologist, 21*(1, 2), 73-98.

Pea, R. D. (1985). Beyond amplification: Using the computer to reorganize mental functioning. *Educational Psychologist, 21*(4), 167-182.

Peyton, J. K. & Bruce, B. C. (1993). Understanding the multiple threads of network-based classrooms. In: B. Bruce, J. K. Peyton, & T. Batson (Eds.), *Network-based classrooms: Promises and realities* (pp. 50-64). New York: Cambridge University Press.

Piaget, J. (1963). *Psychology of intelligence.* Paterson, NJ: Littlefield, Adams & Co.

Rafoth, B. A. (1988). Discourse community: Where writers, readers, and texts come together. In: B. A. Rafoth & D. L. Rubin (Eds.), *The social construction of written language* (pp. 131-146). Norwood, NJ: Ablex.

Riel, M. (1990). Cooperative learning across classrooms in electronic Learning Circles. *Instructional Science, 19,* 445-466.

Riel, M. (1991). Approaching the study of networks. *The Computing Teacher, 19*(4), 5-7, 52.

Rogoff, B. (1990). *Apprenticeship in thinking: Cognitive development in social context.* New York: Oxford University Press.

Rubin, D. L. (1988). Introduction: Four dimensions of social construction of written communication. In: B. A. Rafoth & D. L. Rubin (Eds.), *The social construction of written language* (pp. 1-33). Norwood, NJ: Ablex.

Salomon, G. (1988). AI in reverse: Computer tools that turn cognitive. *Journal of Educational Computing Research, 4*(2), 123-139.

Salomon, G. (1993). On the nature of pedagogic computer tools: The case of the *Writing Partner.* In: S. Lajoie & S. Derry (Eds.), *Computers as cognitive tools* (pp. 179-196). Hillsdale, NJ: Erlbaum.

Salomon, G., Globerson, T., & Guterman, E. (1989). The computer as a zone of proximal development: Internalizing reading-related metacognitions from a reading partner. *Journal of Educational Psychology, 81*(4), 620-627.

Salomon, G., Perkins, D. N., & Globerson, T. (1991). Partners in cognition: Extending human technologies with intelligent technologies. *Educational Researcher, 20*(3), 2-9.

Sarin, S. & Greif, I. (1988). Computer-based real-time conferencing systems. In: I. Greif (Ed.), *Computer-supported cooperative work: A book of readings.* San Mateo, CA: Morgan Kaufmann.

Saunders, W. M. (1989). Collaborative writing tasks and peer interaction. *International Journal of Educational Research, 13*(1), 101-112.

Scardamalia, M. & Bereiter, C. (1991). Higher levels of agency for children in knowledge building: A challenge for the design of new knowledge media. *Journal of the Learning Sciences, 1*(1), 37-68.

Scardamalia, M., Bereiter, C., McLean, R. S., Swallow, J., & Woodruff, E. (1989). Computer supported intentional learning environments. *Journal of Educational Computing Research, 5*(1), 51-68.

Schoenfeld, A. H. (1988). Mathematics, technology, and higher order thinking. In: R. S. Nickerson & P. P. Zodhiates (Eds.), *Technology in education: Looking toward 2020* (pp. 67-96). Hillsdale, NJ: Erlbaum.

Schrage, M. (1990). *Shared minds: The technologies of collaboration.* New York: Random House.

Schrum, L. M. (1991). *Telecommunications: Working to enhance global under-*

standing and world peace. Paper presented at the American Educational Research Association annual meeting, Chicago, IL.

Selman, R. (1971). The relation of role-taking to the development of moral judgment in children. *Child Development, 42*, 79-91.

Selman, R. L. (1980). *The growth of interpersonal understanding: Developmental and clinical analysis*. New York: Academic Press.

Slavin, R. E. (1987). Developmental and motivational perspectives on cooperative learning: A reconciliation. *Child Development, 58*(5), 1161-1167.

Soloway, E. (1988). It's 2020: Do you know what your children are learning in programming class? In: R. S. Nickerson & P. P. Zodhiates (Eds.), *Technology in education: Looking toward 2020* (pp. 121-138). Hillsdale, NJ: Erlbaum.

Soloway, E. (1991). *MediaText*. Paper presented at the American Educational Research Association annual meeting, Chicago, IL.

Stefik, M., Foster, G., Bobrow, D. G., Kahn, K., Lanning, S., & Suchman, L. (1988). Beyond the chalkboard: Computer support for collaboration and problem solving in meetings. In: I. Grief (Ed.), *Computer-supported cooperative work: A book of readings*. San Mateo, CA: Morgan Kaufmann.

Swallow, J., Scardamalia, M., & Olivier, W. P. (1988). *Facilitating thinking skills through peer interaction with software support*. Paper presented at the American Educational Research Association annual meeting, New Orleans, LA.

Tharp, R. G. & Gallimore, R. (1988). *Rousing minds to life: Teaching, learning, and schooling in social context*. New York: Cambridge University Press.

Tharp, R. G., Note, M., & O'Donnell (1991). *Intersubjectivity, shared planes of consciousness*. Paper presented at the American Educational Research Association annual meeting, Chicago, IL.

Thralls, C. (1992). Bakhtin, collaborative partners, and published discourse: A collaborative view of composing. In: J. Forman (Ed.), *New visions of collaborative writing* (pp. 63-81). Portsmouth, NH: Boynton/Cook Publishers.

Toews, O. B. (1989). Challenge to learn: Building knowledge and writing. *River East School Division Journal, 1*(1), 50-78.

Tripp, S. D. & Roby, W. (1990). Orientation and disorientation in a hypertext lexicon. *Journal of Computer-Based Instruction, 17*(4), 120-124.

Vygotsky, L. S. (1978). *Mind in society: The development of higher psychological processes*. In: M. Cole, V. John-Steiner, S. Scribner, & E. Souberman (Eds.). Cambridge, MA: Harvard University Press.

Vygotsky, L. (1986). *Thought and language* (rev. ed.). Cambridge, MA: The MIT Press.

Webb, N. M. (1982). Peer interaction and learning in cooperative small groups. *Journal of Educational Psychology, 74*(5), 642-655.

Webb, N. M. (1989). Peer interaction and learning in small groups. *International Journal of Educational Research, 13*(1), 21-37.

Wertsch, J. V. (1985a). Adult-child interaction as a source of self-regulation in children. In: S. R. Yussen (Ed.). *The growth of reflection in children*. (pp. 69-97). Orlando, Fl: Academic Press.

Wertsch, J. V. (1985b). *Vygotsky and the social formation of the mind.* Cambridge, MA: Harvard University Press.
Wilson, K. (1991). New tools for new learning opportunities. *Technology & Learning, 11*(7), 12-13.
Wolfe, R. (1989). Hypertextual linkages on educational computer conferencing. In: L. M. Harasim (Ed.), *Hypertextual perspectives on educational computer conferencing.* (pp. 215-228). New York: Praeger Press.
Zellermayer, M., Salomon, G., Globerson, T., & Givon, H. (1991). Enhancing writing-related metacognitions through a computerized writing partner. *American Educational Research Journal, 28*(2), 373-391.

APPENDIX A
IMPORTANT FEATURE CONSIDERATIONS OF COLLABORATIVE WRITING

(1) *Maximum Number of Terminals*

The number of terminals that can be connected together is a function of both the type of network and software package capabilities. In the case of *Aspects*, for instance, the maximum number of terminals (16) is set by the software.

(2) *Multiple Windows*

In an ideal situation, collaborative writing software would include windows or boxes for the following features: student compositions, text outlining, concept mapping, knowledge bases, private messaging, and teacher dialogue. Users should have access to window resizing and repositioning. In addition, linking of one's screen position with others would enable participants to more readily share information and conceptual understanding.

(3) *Teacher/Coach Options*

Collaborative writing packages offer several options for teacher management and monitoring during the collaborative writing process. Options include access control, teacher dialogue boxes for commenting and assistance during the group writing process, and concurrency control (that is, deciding who has writing privileges over situations that involve turn-taking).

(4) *Tracking Comments and Dialogue*

The ownership of group products is a sticky issue and the track record of e-mail indicates that communication tends to get chaotic and complex at times. Hence, the ideal software package would include some way of tracking who made what changes to the shared document, and when. Tracking features also enhance researcher understanding of social and cognitive writing acts. For instance, students could retrospectively recount their thinking processes from a transcript of their activities or an electronic replay of participant interchanges. Considering the opportunities and extensive decision making surrounding Level 5 tools (i.e., cooperative hypermedia), tracking may be the most underexplored feature of collaborative writing.

APPENDIX B
TOOLS AVAILABLE FOR ELECTRONIC WRITING (NAME AND PUBLISHER/DEVELOPER)

Note: The following listing is primarily from asynchronous to synchronous communication.

Level 1. Electronic Mail and Delayed Messaging Tools

cc:mail (cc:Mail, Inc.)
DaynaMail (Dayna Communications)
Inbox (Sun Microsystems)
Microsoft Mail (Microsoft; Note: also has Level 3 applications)
QuickMail (CE Software; Note: also has Level 3 applications)
SchoolMate Plus (Radio Shack Education Division)

Level 2. Remote Access/Delayed Collaborative Writing Tools

AppleShare File Server Software (Apple Computer, Inc.)
Bank Street Writer III (Scholastic Software, Inc.)*
Carbon Copy (Microcom, Inc.)
Collaborative Writer (Research Design Associates)
For Comment (Access Technologies)
Instant Update (On Technology)
Mac-to-Mac (Caravelle; also has Level 3 applications)
Mark-Up (Mainstay)
Podium (Ideal Learning, Inc.)
Prep Editor (College of Humanities and Social Sciences at Carnegie Mellon University)
Prose (McGraw-Hill Book Company)
SEEN (CONDUIT; provides remote commenting on ideas not completed text)

Screen Share (White Knight Technology)
Timbuktu (Farallon, Inc.)

Level 3. Real-Time Dialoguing and Idea Generation
Conference Writer (Research Design Associates)
DIScourse (Daedalus Group, Inc.)
Group Writer (Sunburst Communications)

Level 4. Real-Time Collaborative Writing (Text Only)
Live Writer I (Research Design Associates)
Realtime Writer (Realtime Learning Systems; used mainly for Level 3 purposes)

Level 5. Cooperative Hypermedia
Aspects (Group Logic; formerly, Group Technologies)
BBN Slate (BBN Software Products)
CSILE (Ontario Institute of Studies in Education)
HyperAuthor (Hypermedia and Cognition Group at Wisconsin)**
IRIS Intermedia (Brown University, Institute for Research in Information and Scholarship)
KnowledgeBuilder (Dr. Robert W. Cross)**
Language Writer (Research Design Associates)
MediaText: Grades 7 to Adult (Wings for Learning)**
My MediaText Workshop: Grades K-6 (Wings for Learning)**

*Offers some hypermedia linkage capabilities.

**Tool may not yet satisfy all Level 5 criteria. However, future releases of two of these tools, *HyperAuthor* and *KnowledgeBuilder*, will include additional cooperative hypermedia features. The other two tools, *MediaText* and *My MediaText Workshop*, are compatible with System 7 software for the Macintosh, thereby offering at least delayed collaboration options.

APPENDIX C
SAMPLE COLLABORATIVE WRITING TOOLS

Level 1: *Electronic Mail and Delayed Messaging Tools*–***QuickMail***

Like most e-mail systems and messaging tools, *Quickmail* allows users to send messages or files from one computer to the next. However, *QuickMail* provides a convenient interface for both Macintosh and IBM users. *QuickMail* uses the store-and-forward transfer strategy (explained in text), with a centralized server for routing messages. This package can sort incoming mail by either history, priority, subject, sender, or date sent. Messages can be forwarded "as is" or "with changes." Up to 16 files of any type can be attached to any message and passed between PCs or PCs and Macintoshes. *QuickMail* captures all messages in a Mail Log, even those never sent. A QuickConference feature (similar to Level 3 dialoguing and brainstorming) enables potential participants of a meeting to "quickly" discuss open issues and problems (e.g., checking their calendars and confirming schedule openings). In effect, communication with *QuickMail* can take place regardless of time.

Level 2: *Remote Access/Delayed Collaborative Writing Tools*–***Mac-to-Mac***

Mac-to-Mac is a remote access program that works on an AppleTalk network. Using this package, students can connect to each other's computer and exchange files and messages. Users set separate access privileges for individual folders and disks. Folder access options include password protection and read, write, and overwrite privileges. Disk access options include password protection and read/write privileges. A log file consisting of the guest user's name, the names of files transferred, and the connection date and time is created by default in this program. In addition to file sharing, *Mac-to-Mac* allows for real-time dialoguing between two people at a time (i.e., Level 3 capabilities). The dialogue appears in a conversation window and text can be pasted from other applications to this window. The contents of the conversation window can be saved to a file or clipboard. As indicated, *Mac-to-Mac* also allows for delayed dialoguing. Delayed dialoguing options are similar to those on regular answering machines. Users can leave an announcement message, change the default number of rings before the announcement appears, play messages, and have messages read through "MacinTalk." In a writing classroom, this package can be used for real-time brainstorming and file sharing between students or the teacher and students.

Level 3: *Real-Time Dialoguing and Idea Generation*–***Conference Writer***

Conference Writer is a Hypercard stack that was developed specifically for the purpose of collaborative writing in the classroom. It works on a basic AppleTalk network and therefore does not require additional file server hardware or software. The main screen in *Conference Writer* consists of three windows: a compose window, a transcript window, and a group window. In the compose window, students can create and edit text. The contents of this window can be pasted into a full-screen editor. The transcript window displays all messages received. The group window lists the names of all students in a particular group. Messages can be copied and pasted from the transcript and compose windows to the editor. After messages are typed into the compose window, they can be displayed in the transcript windows of other participants or group members by pressing a "Send" button. Students can save both transcript and compose windows. One advantage of *Conference Writer* is that it allows students to work in groups. Students can join different discussion groups and move back and forth between groups by simply pressing a few buttons. *Conference Writer* is ideal for brainstorming and idea generation, peer critiquing of papers, and producing group products.

Level 4: *Real-Time Collaborative Writing (Text Only)*–***Live Writer***

Live Writer, like *Conference Writer*, was designed explicitly for use in the writing classroom. It works on an inexpensive AppleTalk network. *Live Writer* software comes in two versions: an instructor version and a student version. The instructor software allows the teacher to work in one of two modes: the preview mode or the coach mode. In the preview mode, the teacher can view student documents but cannot make changes to them or send messages to the student. In the coach mode, the instructor can edit student documents while the student is watching and carry on real-time conversations with students by typing messages in the message box. Students have the option of signing-off and working independently at any time. Both teachers and students can save messages and papers. Peer critiquing is possible if a student takes on the role of the instructor. Using a projector and an LCD pad, the teacher can show interesting portions of students' papers to the entire class. Recent enhancements to *Live Writer* to incorporate sound as well as text transfer have resulted in *Language Writer*, a Level 5 collaborative writing program.

Level 5: *Cooperative Hypermedia*–***Aspects***

Although *Aspects* was first developed for use in workgroups, its user friendly interface and extensive features make it an ideal collaborative writing tool in the classroom. *Aspects* requires no special server hardware (i.e., just cabling) since it works off a basic AppleTalk network. With *Aspects*, up to 16 students can work simultaneously on the same document. Students can import and export text (ASCII) and *Word*, *MacWrite*, PICT and *MacPaint* files. *Aspects*' word processor, drawing and painting applications have features similar to those of other Macintosh word processors and drawing programs. Thus, *Aspects* currently has more multimedia than hypermedia capabilities. In terms of hypermedia, students can link and unlink screen views, use pointer to draw attention to special parts of a shared document, and work off-line and later rejoin the conference. Teachers can create multiple conferences on different topics (or the same topic), and students can move freely from one conference to the next. The teacher can choose from three different degrees of structure for collaboration. For example, (a) in a free-for-all mode, everyone can edit at the same time; (b) in a medium mediation mode, students can take turns editing; and (c) in a full mediation mode, the teacher decides who can edit at any point of time. A convenient chat box allows for real-time dialoguing between members of the group.

APPENDIX D
SOFTWARE DEVELOPERS OR PUBLISHERS REFERRED TO IN THIS ARTICLE

Access Technologies, Inc.
2 Natick Executive Park
Natick, MA 01760
(508) 655-9191
(***For Comment***–*DOS compatibles on Novell Network*)

Apple Computer, Inc.
Cupertino, CA
(800) 538-9696
(***Apple System*** *7–Macintosh*)

BBN Software Products
150 Cambridge Park Drive
Cambridge, MA 02140
(617) 873-5000
(***BBN/Slate***–*Sun Workstation*)

Caravelle
301 Moodie Drive
Suite 306 Nepean
Ontario, CN K2H 9C4
(613) 596-2802
(***Mac-to-Mac***–*Macintosh*)

Carnegie Mellon University
College of Humanities and Social Sciences
Pittsburgh, PA 15213-3890
Contact: Chris Neuwirth or Rob Chandhok
(412) 268-2468
(***Prep Editor***–*Macintosh*)

cc:Mail, Inc.
385 Sherman Ave.
Palo Alto, CA 94306
(800) 448-2500
(***cc:Mail***–*Macintosh, DOS compatibles, and OS/2*)

CE Software
1801 Industrial Circle
P.O. Box 65580
West Des Moines, IA 50265
(800) 523-7638; (515) 224-1995
(***QuickMail***–*Macintosh and DOS compatible*)

Dr. Robert W. Cross (developer/contact)
292 Strood Avenue
Winnipeg, Manitoba R2G 1A7
(204) 668-2401
(***Knowledge Builder***–*Macintosh*)

Daedalus Group, Inc.
300 E. Huntland Drive, Suite 222
Austin, TX 78752
(512) 459-0637
(***DIScourse***–*Macintosh*)

Dayna Communications
50 S. Main St., Suite 530
Salt Lake City, UT 84144
(801) 531-0600
(***DaynaMail***–*Macintosh and DOS compatible*)

Farallon, Inc.
2150 Kitteridge Street
Oakley, CA 94704
(415) 849-2331
(***Timbuktu***–*Macintosh*)

Group Logic (formerly, Group Technologies)
Contact: Dimitri Korahais
1408 North Fillmore Street, Suite 10
Arlington, VA 22201
(800) 476-8781; (703) 528-1555
(***Aspects***–*Macintosh*)

Ideal Learning, Inc.
8505 Freeport Parkway, Suite 360
Irving, TX 75063
(800) 999-3234
(***Podium***–*Macintosh and Apple II*)

Institute for Research in Information and Scholarship
Brown University
155 George Street, Box 1946
Providence, RI 02912
(800) 282-2732; (401) 863-2001
(***IRIS Intermedia***–*Macintosh*)

Interactive Communication Systems, Inc.
8050 North Port Washington Road
Milwaukee, WI 53217
(414) 352-4404
(***Discourse System***–*DOS compatible*)

Learning with Hypermedia Group
Contact: Richard Lehrer
University of Wisconsin-Madison
1025 West Johnson
Madison, WI 53706
(608) 262-0836
(***HyperAuthor***–*Macintosh*)

Mainstay
5311-B Derry Drive
Agoura Hills, CA 91301
(818) 991-6540
(***MarkUp***–*Macintosh*)

McGraw-Hill Publishing Company
Comp Processing and Control
P.O. Box 454
Highstown, NJ 08520
(212) 512-2000
(***Prose***–*Macintosh*)

MECC
3490 Lexington Avenue North
St. Paul, MN 55126
(612) 481-3500
(***Wagon Train 1848***–*Macintosh*)

Microcom, Inc.
55 Federal Road
Still River Corporate Center
Danbury, CT 06810
(203) 798-3800
(***Carbon Copy Plus*** *6.0–Macintosh*)
(617) 551-1000
(***Carbon Copy***–*IBM*)

NTERGAID
2490 Black Rock Turnpike
Suite 337 Fairfield, CT 06430
(***HyperWriter***–*DOS compatible*)

Ontario Institute of Studies in Education
Contact: Marlene Scardamalia
252 Bloor Street West
Toronto, Ontario M5S 1V6
(***Computer-Supported Intentional Learning Environments–CSILE***)

On Technology
155 Second Street
Cambridge, MA 02141
(617) 876-0900
(***Instant Update***–*Macintosh*)

Radio Shack
Education Division
1600 One Tandy Center
Fort Worth, TX 76102
(800) 321-0160; (817) 390-3832
(***SchoolMate Plus***–*DOS/SchoolMate*)

Realtime Learning Systems
2700 Connecticut Ave., N.W.
Washington, DC 20008-5330
(800) 832-2472; (202) 483-1510
(***Realtime Writer***–*DOS compatible*)

Research Design Associates, Inc.
10 Boulevard Avenue
Greenlawn, NY 11740
(800) 654-8715
(***Collaborative Writer, Conference Writer, LiveWriter***–*Macintosh*)

Scholastic Software
730 Broadway
New York, NY 10003
(800) 541-5513
(***Bank Street Writer III***–*Macintosh, DOS and Apple II*)

Sunburst Communications
39 Washington Avenue
Pleasantville, NY 10570
(800) 628-8897
(***GroupWriter***–*Macintosh and Apple*)

Sun Microsystems, TOPS Division
950 Marina Village Pkwy.
Alemeda, CA 94501
(800) 445-TOPS; (415) 769-9669
(***InBox***–*Macintosh and DOS compatible*)

The University of Iowa
CONDUIT
Oakdale Campus
Iowa City, IA 52242
(800) 365-9774
(***Writer's Helper***–*IBM, Macintosh, and Apple*
SEEN–*DOS compatible and Apple*)

White Knight Software
P.O. Box 564
810 West Broadway
Vancouver, BC
Canada V5Z 4C9
(604) 290-4855
(***ScreenShare***–*Macintosh*)

Wings for Learning
Customer Service Department
P.O. Box 660002
Scotts Valley, CA 95067
(800) 321-7511; (408) 438-5502
(***MediaText*** *[Grades 7-Adult]* & ***My MediaText Workshop*** *[Grades K-6]–Macintosh*)
(Note: MediaText software was designed by Constructive Instruments, Inc., Elliot Soloway, and University of Michigan)

Anette M. DeNardo
Anthony S. Pyzdrowski

A Study of the Effectiveness of Computer-Based Simulations in Teaching Computer Architecture

INTRODUCTION

A computer-based simulator is a program that models a realistic situation because it requires active participation by the user in initiating and performing inquiries, decisions, and actions. In addition to providing an opportunity to acquire skills, attain new concepts, and engage in problem solving, a simulation can provide a student with immediate feedback and rapid repeatability without concern for the time and expense involved in using real materials (Gorrell, Cuevas, & Downing, 1988; Lunetta & Hofstein, 1981; McGuire, 1976; Spain, 1984; Strickland & Poe, 1989). Most educational settings require simple forms of simulators. Details are changed or omitted to provide thought or engage the student in participation (Strickland & Poe).

Currently, the literature suggests that the use of simulators is advantageous for students; however, not all claims are accompanied by documented evidence (Gorrell et al., 1988). A variety of educational settings use

ANETTE M. DENARDO and ANTHONY S. PYZDROWSKI, Associate Professors, Department of Mathematics and Computer Science, California University of Pennsylvania, California, PA 15419.

[Haworth co-indexing entry note]: "A Study of the Effectiveness of Computer-Based Simulations in Teaching Computer Architecture." DeNardo, Anette M. and Anthony S. Pyzdrowski. Co-published simultaneously in *Computers in the Schools* (The Haworth Press, Inc.) Vol. 10, No. 1/2, 1994, pp. 125-140; and: *Multimedia and Megachange: New Roles for Educational Computing* (eds: W. Michael Reed, John K. Burton, and Min Liu) The Haworth Press, Inc., 1994, pp. 125-140. Multiple copies of this article/chapter may be purchased from The Haworth Document Delivery Center [1-800-3-HAWORTH; 9:00 a.m. - 5:00 p.m. (EST)].

computer-based simulations. The study of computer architecture is one such area. Because students cannot study the internal architecture of a computer system, computer programs to simulate the architecture are frequently used. Unfortunately, research on their effectiveness is almost nonexistent.

Three simulators were written for incorporation in a college-level course in computer architecture. This paper reports on a study of the simulators and their effect on student understanding of the architecture of computers.

REVIEW OF THE LITERATURE

The literature contains many discussions of computer-based simulations in relation to their instructional uses. Computer-based simulations are efficient, effective, highly motivational, serve the need for individualization, and enhance the transfer of learning by teaching complex tasks in a real world setting (Reigeluth & Schwartz, 1989) and should be used to augment classroom instruction (Bender, 1989; Spain, 1984; Strickland & Poe, 1989).

Although the use of computer-based simulations was well established by the mid-70s (Magin & Reizes, 1990), their use varies from one application to another. Some simulators establish a game-like environment (Taylor, 1987), while others are quite realistic (Lunetta & Hofstein, 1981). Simulators have been used in chemical (Smith, Jones, & Waugh, 1986) and biological experiments (Angier, 1983), in business (Remus, 1977), counseling (Halpain, Dixon, & Glover, 1987), computer programming (Hooper & Thomas, 1990), and environmental (Fortner, Schar, & Mayer, 1986) education.

Simulators provide the means to reproduce, or simulate, the essential parts of a real situation. While they should appear as lifelike as possible (Strickland & Poe, 1989), research has shown that high levels of physical and visual fidelity are not always required to obtain valid results (Alessi, 1987; Thompson, 1989).

There is some evidence that knowledge gained through the use of a simulation may generalize more freely to real-life situations (Alessi & Trollip, 1985). Students using computer simulations of chemistry (Cavin & Lagowski, 1978; Jackman, Moellenberg, & Brabson, 1990) and physics (Boblick, 1972) laboratory experiments performed as well as or better than students who did not use the simulations.

Other researchers have looked at the effects of computer-based simulations on student attitudes. Most students react favorably to computer-simulated situations (Gorrell et al., 1988; Louscher & Van Steenburg, 1977;

Taylor, 1987). Their use has promoted an increase in student interest (Taylor, 1987), increased student confidence (Gorrell et al., 1988), and caused students to attempt more problem solutions (Hooper & Thomas, 1990).

Computer simulations have helped students score significantly higher than their control group counterparts on knowledge tests (Fortner et al., 1986) and improve research design and applied skills (Collet & Shiffler, 1985). Structured simulation activities have proved to be as effective as conventional practices among nontraditional students (Rieber, Boyce, & Assad, 1990). And, in some cases, the students preferred the simulation format over the more traditional approach (Halpain et al., 1987).

In a review of recent research in the use of computers in instruction (Roblyer, Castine, & King, 1988), several important observations were made about simulations. They may assist in teaching problem-solving skills if used in ways that help students identify and use information to improve decision-making. Simulations used in science applications and at college and adult levels provide promising results. Yet, more research and field testing is needed to confirm or deny the variety of theories regarding their use (Reigeluth & Schwartz, 1989).

PURPOSE OF THE STUDY

This research was motivated by the need for supportive learning materials for students in a computer architecture course. With the support of interactive computer learning aids, the researchers expected to find that students had a better understanding of the course material. This research was conducted to study the effect of computer architecture simulations on student understanding of computer architecture.

RESEARCH QUESTIONS

Several research questions were addressed in this study:

1. To what extent does the use of computer-based simulators affect the students in low, medium, and high ability groups?
2. To what extent does the use of computer-based simulators affect student achievement in the computer architecture course?
3. How do students perceive the use of simulators in a computer architecture course?

DESIGN OF THE STUDY

Sample

Fourteen undergraduate students enrolled in a computer architecture course served as the subjects in this study. The students were computer science majors in a small state university in southwestern Pennsylvania.

Independent Variables

Blocking Variable. The students were separated into low, medium, and high ability-level groups based on their quality point average (QPA) for computer science courses. The average QPA score ($\bar{x} = 3.16$, $s = 0.71$) for all students in the study was calculated. Two students scored at least one standard deviation above the mean and were placed in the high-ability group ($QPA_H > 3.87$); four students scored at least one standard deviation below the mean and were placed in the low-ability group ($QPA_L < 2.45$); the remaining eight students were placed in the medium-ability group ($2.45 \leq QPA_M \leq 3.87$).

Treatment. Students from all ability groups began the semester with an introduction to the first simulator. It provided students with an introductory, self-paced tutorial of a hypothetical computer architecture, a content quiz, and an interactive machine-code program simulator that accepted student-written or "canned" programs. The first simulator contained three parts. The first part graphically presented basic information, introduced the architecture of the hypothetical machine, and presented the first 11 primary machine instructions.

A graphically animated quiz was used to evaluate the content learned in the first part of the first simulator. The quiz sequenced through three progressively difficult sections. An 80% competency rate was required for progress between sections; only then was the student exposed to an animated positive reinforcement.

In the third part of the first simulator, the operation of the hypothetical computer was demonstrated through a graphical presentation of its program execution and included the registers and memory (Figure 1). Several example programs were provided. As a program executed, the simulator changed the contents of the displayed components. An outline of the execution cycle, with the current step highlighted, appeared on the screen. By selecting a designated button, the student initiated the execution of an instruction. This provided a self-paced learning environment. Students could also enter their own programs in the simulator using binary or octal machine code.

FIGURE 1. Sample Screen from *Simulator One*

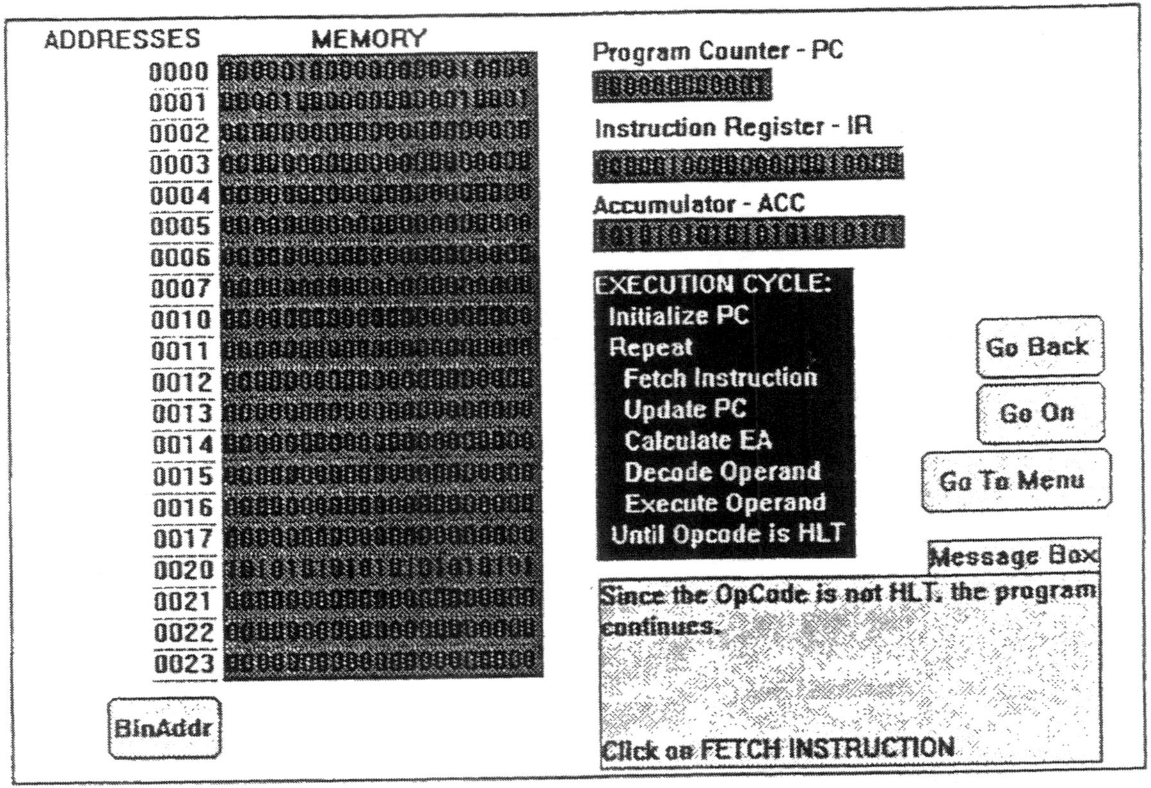

Near the midpoint of the course, students used a second simulator that demonstrated data flow at the machine level. The simulator supported class lectures on microsequences and contained a complete graphical rendering of the computer structure with buttons leading to further explanations of the components.

Following the graphical presentation of the computer, the simulator displayed a menu of 26 instructions. The student selected one instruction and a speed of presentation. The simulator displayed the microsequences for the selected instruction. The student selected one microsequence at a time and the simulator, using colors, traced the flow of data throughout the structure (Figure 2). These colored paths flowed throughout the structure at a rate proportional to the real operation time. The colored trace remained on the display for student scrutiny. The student could repeat this microsequence or select the next one. When all microsequences for the instruction were complete, the simulator returned to the menu.

The last simulator, written in C, was given to the students near the end of the semester. It accepted programs written by the students and demonstrated the execution sequence for the programs. Unlike the previous simulators, this package did not provide any educational instruction. The student entered a program from either the keyboard or a file. The output of the simulator could be sent to the display or another output file for a permanent record of the program execution. The output contained the contents of all registers for each instruction executed and the contents of memory upon program termination. There was no error detection or help within this simulator; its task was to test the effectiveness of the students' programming abilities with the new machine presented in the previous two learning simulators.

Dependent Measures

Pretest. At the beginning of the semester, the students were administered a pretest designed by the course instructor and validated by experts. It was used to evaluate student understanding of computer architecture at the beginning of the course.

Achievement Tests. The subjects were administered two instructor-prepared tests during the semester. A posttest was also used to measure student achievement.

Programming Assignments. The subjects wrote two programs using the third simulator. These programs were graded by the instructor of the class.

Surveys. The subjects completed a 13-item survey. It examined the time they spent on each of the three simulators, their perceptions of the effects the simulators had on their understanding of computer architecture con-

FIGURE 2. Sample Screen from *Simulator Two*

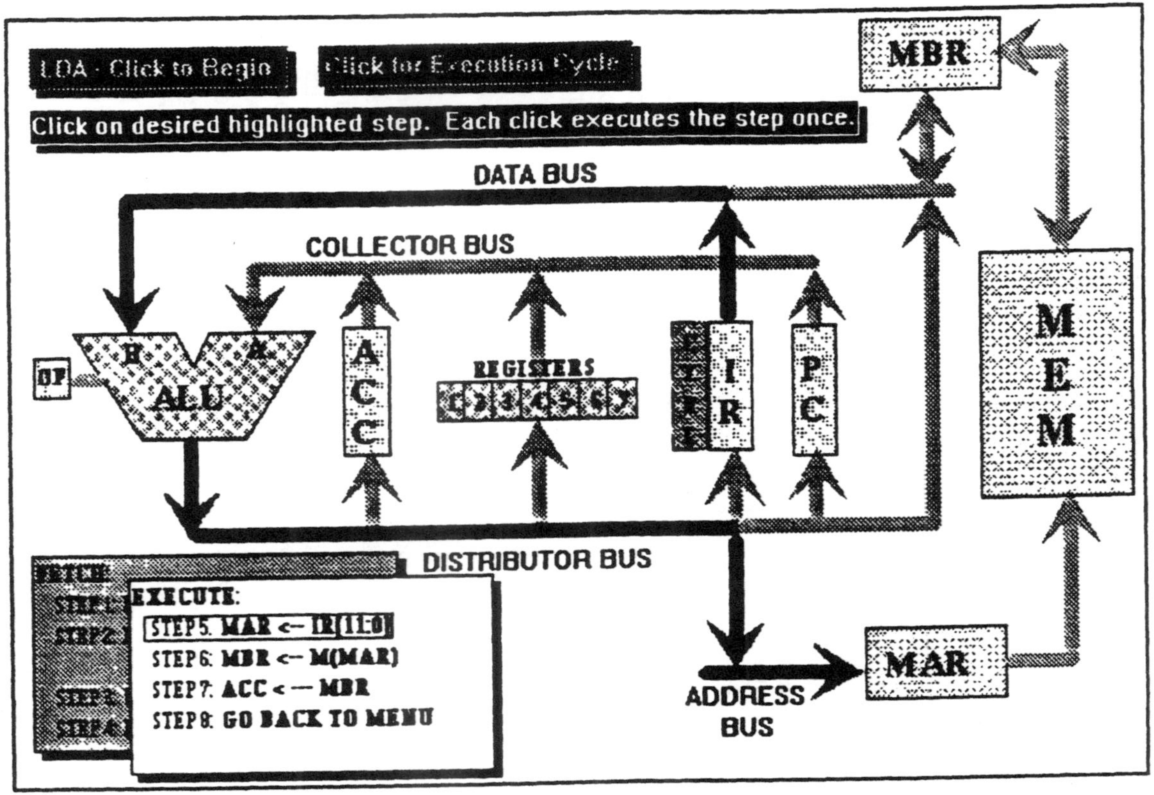

cepts and the instruction set of the computer, their perceptions of the effects of the simulators on their abilities to write programs and on the overall effectiveness of the simulators.

Procedures

The students were administered the pretest on the second class of the 30-class course. The first simulator was available for their use during the sixth class. Examination one was administered to the students during the 10th class. The second simulator was presented to the students during the 18th class. During the 24th class the final simulator was made available. The first two simulators were available on laboratory computers throughout the duration of the course. A copy of the final simulator was provided to the students for their individual use. No time restrictions were placed on usage, except that the students were expected to have used the simulators prior to the end of the course. Additionally, instructor assistance was available upon student request. Two programming exercises were assigned that made use of the third simulator. These assignments were made during the 25th and 27th classes. The second examination was administered during the 26th day of class. During the last day of class, the posttest was given.

Analysis of the Data

To what extent does the use of computer-based simulators affect the students in low, medium, and high ability groups? Five one-way ANOVAs were used to compare the mean scores on the two regular course examinations, the posttest, and the two programming assignments of the students in the three ability groups. In each ANOVA, ability grouping was the independent variable. If a statistically significant difference was detected, the Scheffé's test was used to determine the source of the difference.

To what extent does the use of computer-based simulators affect student achievement in the computer architecture course? T-tests were performed to determine whether or not significant gains were made between the pretest and first examination, the first and second examinations, the second examination and the posttest, and the pretest and posttest. These calculations were performed on all subjects and then on the subjects in each of the three ability groups.

How do students perceive the use of simulators in a computer architecture course? The results of a 13-item survey were examined. Trends in the subjects' responses were reported. The survey polled the subjects concerning the amount of time they spent on each of the three simulators, their understanding of computer architecture concepts and the instruction set of the hypothetical computer, their perceptions of the effects the simulators had on their ability to write programs, and the subjects' perceptions of the overall effectiveness of the simulators.

RESULTS

Achievement Measures

A one-way ANOVA was used to compare the means of the pretest, first examination, second examination, and posttest scores in the three ability groups (Table 1). There were nonsignificant differences for the pretest ($\bar{x}_L$ = 35.42; $\bar{x}_M$ = 28.02; $\bar{x}_H$ = 54.12). Significant differences were found for the

TABLE 1. Analysis of Variance of Pretest, Exam 1, Exam 2, and Posttest Scores for the Low, Medium, and High Ability Groups

SOURCE	df	SS	MS	F
Pretest:				
Between	2	1107.02	553.51	1.52
Within	11	4008.71	364.43	
Total	13	6222.75		
Exam 1:				
Between	2	1649.71	824.86	6.87*
Within	11	1320.66	120.06	
Total	13	2970.37		
Exam 2:				
Between	2	1037.49	518.75	4.95*
Within	11	1153.28	104.84	
Total	13	2190.77		
Posttest:				
Between	2	458.45	229.23	0.78
Within	11	3232.69	293.88	
Total	13	3691.14		

*$p < .05$

first regular course examination ($\bar{x}_L$ = 67.76; $\bar{x}_M$ = 89.48; $\bar{x}_H$ = 97.37). Using a Scheffé's test, significant differences were found between the low and medium group means and between the low and high group means. The low ability group performed significantly lower than the medium or high ability groups. Significant differences were found for the second regular course examination ($\bar{x}_L$ = 75.00; $\bar{x}_M$ = 91.05; $\bar{x}_H$ = 100.00). Using a Scheffé's test, significant differences were found between the low and high groups means, favoring the high ability group. There were nonsignificant differences found on the posttest ($\bar{x}_L$ = 76.67; $\bar{x}_M$ = 81.04; $\bar{x}_H$ = 95.00).

T-tests were performed to determine whether or not significant gains were made between the various examinations for all students and for students in each of the ability groups. Those results can be found in Table 2. Significant differences were found between the pretest and examination one, examination two and the posttest, and the pretest and posttest scores for all students. For the low ability group, there were significant gains pretest to examination one and pretest to posttest. For the medium ability group, there were significant gains pretest to examination one, examination two to posttest, and pretest to posttest. There were nonsignificant gains for the high ability group.

A one-way ANOVA was used to compare the means of the two programming assignments for the subjects in the three ability groups. There were nonsignificant differences on both programming assignments (F_{prog1} = 0.26; F_{prog2} = 1.22).

Percentage changes were calculated for the three ability groups from pretest to posttest. The medium ability group made the greatest gains of 289.22%, followed by the low ability group whose gains were 216.46%. The high ability group had the lowest gains of 175.37%.

Attitude Measures

Each of the 14 students in the study anonymously completed a survey. The survey asked for a self-reported indication of the time spent using the three simulators. The amount of time each student spent on the three simulators varied from less than one hour to more than three hours. One student used the first simulator for less than one hour; eleven students used it for one to three hours; two used it for more than three hours. All but one of the students used the second simulator for three or fewer hours. One student used the third simulator for less than one hour; seven students use it for one to three hours; six students use it for more than three hours. The third simulator was used for more hours than the first two simulators since the students were required to write two programs using that simulator.

The students who participated in the study indicated that the simulators

TABLE 2. Results of t-Tests on Various Examinations for All Subjects, Low Ability Group, Medium Ability Group, and High Ability Group

EXAMINATIONS	M_1	SD_1	M_2	SD_2	t
Pretest–Exam 1:					
All Subjects	33.87	19.84	84.40	15.12	8.25[1]
Low Ability	35.41	5.97	67.76	15.99	2.97[2]
Medium Ability	28.02	22.04	89.48	8.78	9.50[3]
High Ability	54.17	22.39	97.37	3.72	2.34
Exam 1–Exam 2:					
All Subjects	84.40	15.12	87.74	12.98	1.12
Low Ability	67.76	15.99	75.00	11.68	–0.95
Medium Ability	89.48	8.78	91.05	10.31	–0.41
High Ability	97.37	3.72	100.00	0.00	1.00
Exam 2–Posttest:					
All Subjects	87.74	12.98	81.79	16.85	–1.40[4]
Low Ability	75.00	11.68	76.67	19.00	–0.13
Medium Ability	91.05	10.31	81.04	17.43	2.36[5]
High Ability	100.00	0.00	95.00	4.71	1.50
Pretest–Posttest:					
All Subjects	33.87	19.84	81.79	16.85	8.28[1]
Low Ability	35.41	5.97	76.67	19.00	4.46
Medium Ability	28.02	22.04	81.04	17.43	6.07[3]
High Ability	54.17	22.39	95.00	4.71	3.27

$df_{ALL} = 13$ $df_L = 3$ $df_M = 7$ $df_H = 1$

[1] $t_{crit} = 2.65$, $p = .01$ [2] $t_{crit} = 2.35$, $p = .05$ [3] $t_{crit} = 5.41$, $p = .0005$
[4] $t_{crit} = 1.17$, $p = .05$ [5] $t_{crit} = 1.90$, $p = .05$

helped them to understand the concepts relating to the specific machine demonstrated in the simulators, helped them to understand the concepts relating to computer architecture, and made learning about computer architectures more concrete. Student responses were less strong when asked about using the simulators to write or understand programs written for the hypothetical machine. However, the majority of them agreed that the simulators had been helpful in these areas. They also agreed that the simulators helped them to understand the instruction set and microsequences of instructions for the hypothetical machine. The students agreed that the simulators helped them to better understand how other computer structures operate. And, although some students felt that they could have learned about the architecture of the hypothetical machine without the simulators, they recommend its use when the class is next taught.

DISCUSSION

Achievement Measures

The ANOVA performed on the pretest means for the three ability groups (F = 1.52) showed no significant differences between the means. This was expected since the content examined on the pretest consisted of information which the students should not have known. Therefore, the three groups were relatively equal in their knowledge of computer architecture concepts at the beginning of the semester-long study.

The significant differences between the pretest scores and the scores on the first examination were expected. Overall, there was a significant gain (t = 8.25) for all students in the study. Additionally, the increases for the low (t = 2.97) and medium (t = 9.50) groups were significant. These values were reflected in the percentage gains for these two groups (PG_L = 191.30%, PG_M = 319.34%). However, the gain for the high ability group was not significant (PG_H = 179.75%). A one-way ANOVA comparing the mean scores for the three ability groups on the first examination was significant (F = 6.87). The Scheffé test determined that the means for the high and medium ability groups were significantly higher than the mean of the low ability group.

It was expected that the high ability group would outscore the low and medium ability groups. What is important here is that the gains made by the low and medium groups were significant, while the gains made by the high ability group were not. Also, the percentage gain for the low ability group was greater than that for the high ability group. The reason the high ability group did not perform significantly better was that this group started out high; there was simply little room for improvement.

No significant differences were found in the score changes between the first and second examinations. However, the ANOVA performed on the means of the three ability groups on the second examination produced significant results (F = 4.95). The Scheffé test showed that the significant difference was between the low and high ability group means. On the first examination, both the medium and high ability groups significantly outscored the low ability group. On the second examination, only the high ability group significantly outscored the low ability group. If the percentage increases are examined (PG_L = 110.68%; PG_M = 101.75; PG_H = 102.70), it can be seen that each group increased their means; however, the greatest increase was within the low ability group. The reduced differences between the scores of the students in the different ability groups is attributed partially to the leveling off of the high ability group and improvement on the part of the medium and low ability groups.

A significant difference was found in the test scores between the second examination and the posttest. Overall, the scores dropped between the second examination and the posttest. When the ability groups were examined, the scores for the low ability group dropped while those for the medium and high ability groups rose. The gain for the medium ability group was statistically significant ($t = 2.36$). Perhaps the drop in overall scores can be explained by the nature of the examinations. The second examination tested the information covered after the first examination; the posttest was comprehensive.

A one-way ANOVA performed on the scores of the entire group on the posttest indicated no significant differences between the three group means ($F = 0.78$). This might show that the simulators had a leveling effect on the scores. However, the low and medium ability groups had significant gains in average scores ($t_L = 4.46$, $t_M = 6.07$) while the high ability group did not ($t_H = 3.27$). When these gains are expressed as percentage changes, the low and medium ability groups, as expected from the *t* scores, outperformed the high ability group (PG_L = 216.46%; PG_M = 9.22%; PG_H = 175.37%).

The same comprehensive examination was used as both the pretest and the posttest. The high ability group made nonsignificant gains in scores between all examinations. There was not much room for improvement in the scores of the subjects in the high ability group.

However, there were significant gains in examination scores for the low and medium ability groups. Subjects in the low ability group made significant gains pretest to examination one and pretest to posttest. Those in the medium ability group made significant gains pretest to examination one, examination two to posttest, and pretest to posttest. We hypothesize that these gains were due, at least in part, to the equalizing effect the simulators had on the subjects in the low and medium ability groups.

There were no significant differences between the set of scores of either programming assignment (program 1: $\bar{x}_L = 96.25$, $\bar{x}_M = 85.00$, $\bar{x}_H = 95.00$, $F = 0.26$; program 2: $\bar{x}_L = 83.75$, $\bar{x}_M = 61.25$, $\bar{x}_H = 95.00$, $F = 1.22$). These are not surprising results. The students were permitted to work on their programming assignments for a specified period of time; however, if the output was not correct, the students could alter the code. Perhaps use of the first two simulators influenced the subjects in the low and medium ability groups so that their resulting programs were not significantly different from those produced by the students in the high ability group.

Another reason for the lack of statistically significant differences in the group means on the pretest and posttest may be due to the small sample size ($n_L = 4$, $n_M = 8$, $n_H = 2$). With a larger sample size, the degrees of freedom would, of course, be greater and a smaller calculated F value would have been significant. If the means of the groups on the pretest ($\bar{x}_L = 35.42$; $\bar{x}_M = 28.02$; $\bar{x}_H = 54.12$) and posttest ($\bar{x}_L = 76.67$; $\bar{x}_M = 81.04$; $\bar{x}_H = 95.00$) are examined, it can be seen that they are different from each other; yet, the small sample size did not allow for significant differences.

Our results support the findings of other researchers who studied subjects in treatment and control groups. They often found that subjects who used simulations performed better than those who did not (Boblick, 1972; Cavin & Lagowski, 1978; Collet & Shiffler, 1985; Fortner et al., 1986; Jackman et al., 1990).

However, our findings contradict those of other researchers (Rieber et al., 1990; Schloss, Cartwright, Smith, & Polka, 1986-87). Schloss et al. (1986-87) studied low- and high-achieving college students who used simulation exercises; they found that the high-achievement group significantly outperformed the low-achievement group. Rieber et al. (1990) found that learning among non-traditional students was not influenced more by a simulation approach, although the structured simulation activity was as effective as the conventional method of presentation.

Attitude Measures

Based on the informal student surveys, the students favored the use of the simulators. These findings are in support of conclusions drawn by other researchers (Gorrell et al., 1988; Halpain et al., 1987; Hooper & Thomas, 1990; Taylor, 1987).

CONCLUSIONS

The use of the simulators benefitted the students, especially those in the low and medium ability groups, and may have equalized student achievement in the three ability groups. As reported in the surveys, the students have positive attitudes about the advantages of using the simulators.

Although these first findings are encouraging, more research needs to be done in this area. Larger sample groups should be studied. Student QPAs are based, in part, on the number of courses taken. Since this varies from student to student, the pretest should be used to separate the subjects into low, medium, and high ability groups. We feel this would be a better determiner of ability levels at the beginning of the course. Also, a more equal distribution of the subjects into the three groups is needed.

Individual interviews with the subjects should be conducted to gain the subjects' perspectives on the use of the simulators. An interview approach would permit researchers to gain a better perspective on student views of the architecture simulators. Additionally, other areas of the computer architecture, such as the ALU, can and should be simulated. This is an area of research that deserves further study.

REFERENCES

Alessi, S. (1987). *Fidelity in the design of instructional simulations.* Paper presented at the Annual Meeting of the American Educational Research Association, Washington, DC.

Alessi, S. M. & Trollip, S. R. (1985). *Computer-based instruction: Methods and development.* Englewood Cliffs, NJ: Prentice-Hall.

Angier, N. (1983). The electronic guinea pig. *Discover*, September. pp. 76-78,80.

Bender, D. A. (1989). Combining a computer simulation with a laboratory class–The best of both worlds? *Computers and Education, 13*, 235-243.

Boblick, J. M. (1972). Discovering the conservation of momentum through the use of a computer simulation of a one-dimensional elastic collision. *Science Education, 56*(3), 337-344.

Cavin, C. S. & Lagowski, J. J. (1978). Effects of computer simulated or laboratory experiments and student aptitude on achievement and time in college general chemistry laboratory course. *Journal of Research in Science Teaching 15*(6), 455-463.

Collet, L. S. & Shiffler, N. L. (1985). A computer simulation approach to teaching research and evaluation skills. *Journal of Educational Computing Research, 1*(3), 339-354.

Fortner, R. W., Schar, J. F., & Mayer, V. J. (1986). *Effect of microcomputer simulations on computer awareness and perception of environmental relationships among college students.* Columbus, OH: Ohio State University, Office of Learning Resources. (ERIC Document Reproduction Service No. Ed 270 311)

Gorrell, J., Cuevas, A., & Downing, H. (1988). Computer simulations of classroom behavior problems. *Computers and Education, 12*(2), 283-287.

Halpain, D. R., Dixon, D. N., & Glover, J. A. (1987). The great therapists program: Computerized learning of counseling theories. *Counselor Education and Supervision, 26*(4), 255-259.

Hooper, E. J. & Thomas, R. A. (1990). Investigating the effects of a manipulative model of computer memory operations on the learning of programming. *Journal of Research on Computing in Education, 22*, 442-456.

Jackman, L. E., Moellenberg, W. P., & Brabson, G. D. (1990). Effects of conceptual systems and instructional methods on general chemistry laboratory achievement. *Journal of Research in Science Teaching, 27*(7), 699-709.

Louscher, D. & Van Steenburg, R. (1977). Effectiveness of a short-term simulation as a teaching device in political science courses. *Simulation and Games, 8*(4), 439-460.

Lunetta, V. N. & Hofstein, A. (1981). Simulations in science education. *Science Education, 65*(3), 243-252.

Magin, D. J. & Reizes, J. A. (1990). Computer simulations of laboratory experiments: An unrealized potential. *Computers and Education, 14*, 263-270.

McGuire, C. (1976). Simulation technique in the teaching and testing of problem-solving skills. *Journal of Research in Science Teaching, 13*(2), 89-100.

Reigeluth, C. M. & Schwartz, E. (1989). An instructional theory for the design of computer-based simulations. *Journal of Computer-Based Instruction, 16*(1), 1-10.

Remus, W. (1977). Who likes business games? *Simulation and Games, 8*(4), 469-480.

Rieber, L. P., Boyce, M. J., & Assad, C. (1990). The effects of computer animation on adult learning and retrieval tasks. *Journal of Computer-Based Instruction, 17*(2), 46-52.

Roblyer, M. D., Castine, W. H., & King, F. J. (1988). *Assessing the impact of computer-based instruction*. New York: The Haworth Press, Inc.

Schloss, P. J., Cartwright, G. P., Smith, M. A., & Polka, B. A. (1986-87). Effectiveness of computer-assisted special education administration simulations. *The Journal of Special Education, 20*(4), 503-513.

Smith, S. G., Jones, L. L., & Waugh, M. L. (1986). Production and evaluation of interactive videodisc lessons in laboratory instruction. *Journal of Computer-Based Instruction, 13*(4), 117-121.

Spain, J. D. (1984). Computer center: It's time to take inventory. *The American Biology Teacher, 46*(6), 347-349.

Strickland, R. M., & Poe, S. E. (1989). Developing a CAI graphics simulation model: Guidelines. *Technological Horizons in Education Journal, 16*(7), 88-92.

Taylor, M. (1987). The implementation and evaluation of a computer simulation game in a university course. *The Journal of Experimental Education, 55*, 108-115.

Thompson, D. R. (1989). Transfer of training from simulators to operational equipment–Are simulators effective? *Journal of Educational Technology Systems, 17*(3), 213-218.

Mary J. Henry
Thomas W. Southerly

A Comparison of the Language Features of BASIC and *HyperCard*

The potential value of learning to program can have a dual nature. Besides learning to control the computer, the programmer is learning a form of problem-solving (Linn, 1985). The cognitive effects of programming instruction have been well documented (Dalbey & Linn, 1986; Linn, 1985; Mandinach & Linn, 1986). Generally speaking, programming has been described as having a series of stages, each requiring different cognitive activities. Specification, design, coding, and debugging are typical tasks involved in solving a programming problem (Dalbey & Linn, 1985).

Dalbey and Linn (1986) have provided a model of outcomes that could result from programming. Called a chain of cognitive outcomes, it indicates how various learning results are needed to produce technological expertise. Language features (instruction), design skills (access), and general problem solving skills (ability) are the three categories of potential learning outcomes included in the model. Instructional outcomes include knowledge of features and functions of the language being studied, that is, specific, detailed statements and outcomes of those statements. Access outcomes are considered to be template and procedural skills. Templates are patterns or recurrent elements in a solution to similar problems. Proce-

MARY J. HENRY is Assistant Professor of Instructional Technology, Indiana University-East, Richmond, IN.
THOMAS W. SOUTHERLY is a doctoral student, West Virginia University, Morgantown, WV 26506.

[Haworth co-indexing entry note]: "A Comparison of the Language Features of BASIC and *HyperCard*." Henry, Mary J. and Thomas W. Southerly. Co-published simultaneously in *Computers in the Schools* (The Haworth Press, Inc.) Vol. 10, No. 1/2, 1994, pp. 141-153; and: *Multimedia and Megachange: New Roles for Educational Computing* (eds: W. Michael Reed, John K. Burton, and Min Liu) The Haworth Press, Inc., 1994, pp. 141-153. Multiple copies of this article/chapter may be purchased from The Haworth Document Delivery Center [1-800-3-HAWORTH; 9:00 a.m. - 5:00 p.m. (EST)].

dural skills are used to combine templates and language features to invent and refine new programs. The chain of outcomes culminates in the acquisition of problem-solving skills that allow the programmer to learn new formal systems and transfer already learned skills to solving problems in other languages.

Obviously, the chain cannot be completed if the student does not have a good grasp of the features of the language. Putnam, Sleeman, Baxter, and Kispa (1986) have argued that a lack of knowledge of the basic features will prevent students from developing the higher-level cognitive skills. They continue by saying that learning enough about the specific constructs of a language is a major component of learning to program. Sophisticated programming activities that require expertise necessitate a good model of the structure of the language (Kurland, Pea, Clement, & Mawby, 1986). In a study of programming recall, Magliaro and Burton (1988) found that beginning programmers tended to group like commands together syntactically, while advanced programmers attempted to recall programs in a procedural order.

A question posed by Dalbey and Linn (1986) was whether or not learners can be moved along the chain of cognitive consequences more efficiently and effectively. They investigated interventions to improve instruction by using methods that would assist the move from specific knowledge to general skills. Their implementation of a special purpose programming language, Spider World, allowed students to plan and test programs without spending too much time learning language features. Results showed that students, after 12 weeks of use, benefitted in different ways from their respective instruction, but that, beyond limited gains in language features, none moved far along the chain of cognitive accomplishments.

In describing computer-assisted instruction, Cook (1989-90) has asserted that media in itself does not influence learning–he feels that content and method do, however. Content is usually an important component of any learning activity. The purpose of this paper is to examine the structure of the Applesoft BASIC programming language and the Macintosh authoring language, *HyperCard*. The language features of each will be presented and then the same program written in each language will be examined for comparison purposes. In effect, language structures will be scrutinized as the building blocks for moving along the chain of cognitive outcomes.

BASIC

BASIC was first developed at Dartmouth in the middle 1960s. Its widespread use in schools has been the reason researchers have often used it as the vehicle for their programming studies (Dalbey & Linn, 1986). Critics of BASIC have suggested that many of its features are not easily used in designing well-organized programs (Linn, 1985). However, efficient program design can be accomplished through a top-down instructional approach using modular program construction, according to research in this area (Kurland, Pea, Clement, & Mawby, 1986; Magliaro & Burton, 1988; Reed, Palumbo, & Stolar, 1988).

BASIC has two modes: (a) immediate–used for results that are desired as soon as the command is issued and (b) delayed–used for sequencing program lines and delaying action of the commands until the program is completed and then run. Programs can be constructed in text or graphic format. Two forms of graphics in BASIC are high-resolution and low-resolution. The distinction between the two is the number of pixels (dots) on the screen that are involved. Both can present animation with the use of appropriate command statements.

Data storage is accomplished with the use of numeric or alpha-numeric (string) variables and arrays. Assignment, INPUT, and READ/DATA statements are the language features that allow the data to be deposited in computer memory. Mathematical manipulation of data is done with the usual math functions of addition, subtraction, division, and multiplication, which can be used in a number of different ways to achieve desired results. The LEN command will help create a centering routine for text; the RND command will randomize numbers; and the INT command will round off decimal numbers.

Program control statements allow the programmer to govern the flow of action with the use of loops (FOR NEXT), conditionals (IF THEN and GOTO xx), subroutines (GOSUB) and the END statement. The logical operators AND and OR are used in conjunction with conditional statements for program flow. Internal documentation, which allows clarity upon later examination of the program, is performed by the use of REM statements.

DOS (disk operating system) commands such as RUN, LOAD, and SAVE are also important components in the acquisition of the language structure of BASIC. These commands allow the programmer to use the disk as a storage device from which files can be retrieved when desired. RUN will cause the designated program to be executed. LOAD is the command that will transfer a copy of a program from the disk to RAM. SAVE is the command that will transfer a copy of the program in the computer's memory to the disk for storage.

The majority of the BASIC commands are not DOS commands–essentially they do not access the disk drive. They include LIST, NEW, and

HOME. LIST gives a line-by-line display of the current program in RAM. NEW erases the program in RAM. And, HOME clears the screen.

BASIC has two modes of programming: graphics and text. The graphics command statements include GR for low resolution and HGR for high resolution graphics which allow entry to the graphic screen and mode. COLOR = XXX (low-resolution) and HCOLOR = XXX (high resolution) are the commands for changing background and drawing colors. In low resolution the programmer is given a choice of 16 colors; in high resolution graphics, the choice is limited to six (white and black are double listed). Graphics programs can be linked to text programs with the use of embedded DOS commands. One of the text mode command statements is PRINT, which is often accompanied by screen formatting commands of VTAB, HTAB, FLASH, INVERSE, SPEED = XXX, NORMAL. PRINT allows specified output to the screen; VTAB changes the vertical position on the screen, while HTAB changes the horizontal position; FLASH rapidly alternates background and foreground colors; TERSE changes the background; SPEED = XXX allows the programmer to control the speed with which text is presented on the screen (XXX being any number up to 255); NORMAL negates the INVERSE and FLASH commands.

In summarizing the language features of Applesoft BASIC, the concepts of mode, command statements, data storage, program control, math functions, and internal documentation have been addressed. Next a relatively new authoring language, *HyperCard*, will be summarized using the same concepts.

HYPERCARD

HyperCard is the most widely used Macintosh authoring language and can be described as a "hypertext generator based on the concepts of hypermedia functioning as an intuitive personalized database" (Cook, 1989-90, pp. 112-113). Basically, it is "a software product that serves as a platform for constructing computer applications that integrate text, numbers, sound, and graphics within an information storage and retrieval system" (Adams, 1990, p. 22). It has been called a "software erector set" by Harris and Cady (1988, p. 33), one that can emulate the way a person thinks. They feel that teachers who have no programming experience can customize their information to fit an individual lesson and that *HyperCard* is capable of incorporating content acquisition with active involvement of the student in the thinking process. La Passardiere (1989) describes it as a developmental tool and a database connected to an object-oriented language.

Harris and Cady (1988) state that the set of pre-programmed linking tools present in *HyperCard* accounts for its ease of authoring. New materials can be added to the source material (content) in a *HyperCard* database and new links and paths can be added so that the user can browse through it in any direction desired. Thus, one can rapidly pursue a wide variety of topics and subtopics (Crane & Mylonis, 1988).

The Macintosh environment allows *HyperCard* certain functions such as mouse-driven commands, icons, and pull-down menus. The objects in *HyperCard* that act as building blocks for structuring programs are *cards*–individual screens holding textual or graphical information or data (comparable to a record); *stacks*–cards of related information (comparable to a file); *background*–domain of all cards that defines its format and appearance; *fields*–containing text of either alphabetic or numeric data; *buttons*–which link cards and stacks, and are located at an area of the screen that is sensitive to a pointing device (mouse) and transfers control to another card. Stacks can be linked and control passed between them with the use of the Home Card, which serves as an index and visually represents all stacks that can be accessed within the *HyperCard* system (Figure 1).

The programming language of *HyperCard* is *HyperTalk*. Scripts are used to control stack processing and allow the user to control the actions of *HyperCard* objects. Links are established by keywords embedded within displayed text and then by linking these words with screens containing further information on the topic. Whenever an object is activated, the script for that object is executed, causing the desired action to take place. Both text and graphics modes can be accommodated on the same card in a stack. Graphics can be imported from another application, another file, or drawn by the programmer using the Tool menu. Animation can be accomplished by three methods: (a) showing all cards, (b) a repeating loop, or (c) selecting an object and scripting it to be "dragged" from one set of coordinates to another.

A number of command statements control various actions in a *HyperCard* stack. Commands that allow the user to navigate through the stack include Go, Find, Push, and Pop. The Go command can be used to script a button to take the user to any card in the stack; the Find command will retrieve a text string or a variable; Push and Pop commands can be used within scripts to control the sequencing of card viewing and create modularity for the program. On, Set, Show, and Hide are object manipulation commands through which the programmer can control the visual display on the screen. On receives and takes action on messages while Set can be used with many different commands–for example, to change user levels. User levels include browsing, typing, painting, authoring, and scripting, each allowing a different level of programming control. The Hide com-

FIGURE 1. *HyperCard* Home Card

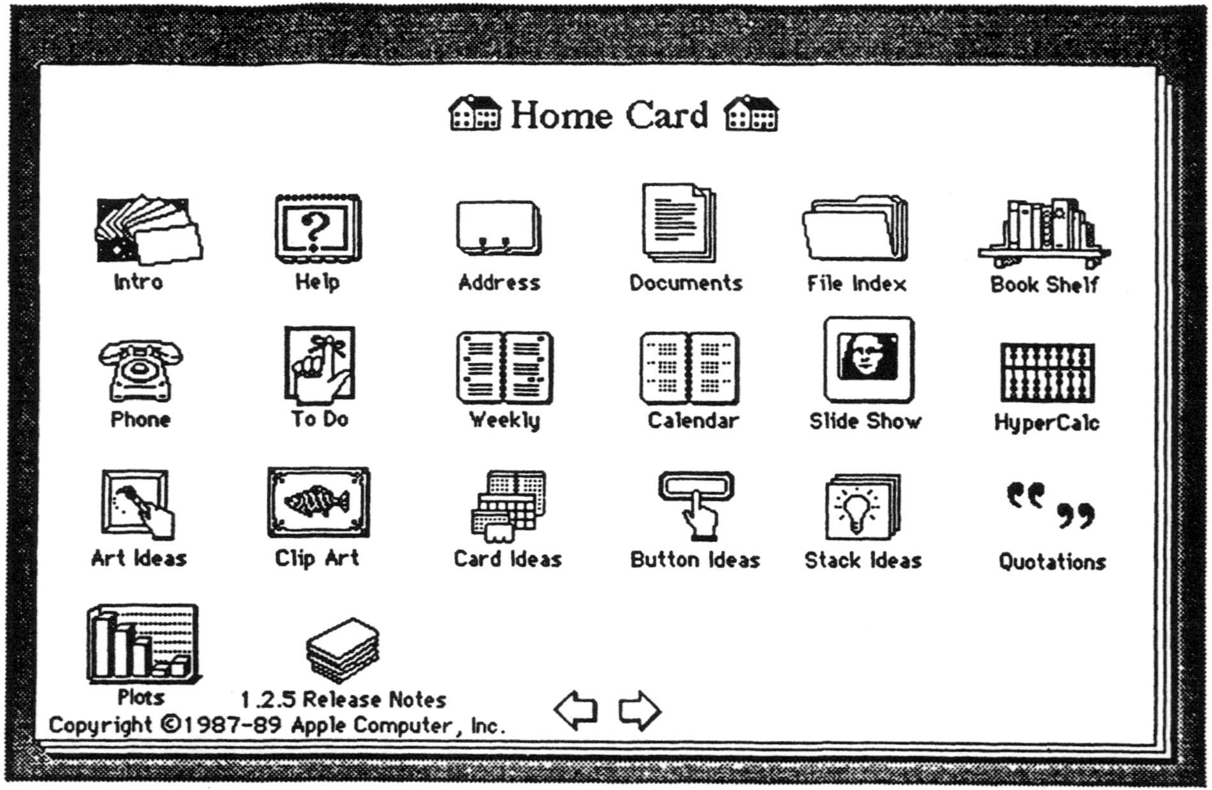

mand allows any object to be hidden from view on the screen; its opposite command, Show, makes visible an object that has been hidden.

Screen manipulation commands include Visual, Ask, and Answer. Visual allows varied optical effects in transition from one card to the next. The Ask and Answer commands are methods of soliciting information from the user. Dialog boxes appear containing a prompt asking for specified information with the Ask command; the Answer command can supply up to three responses to a prompt.

Action commands include Wait, Put, Drag, Sort, DoMenu, and Choose. Wait causes any action to be delayed for a specified time; Put is one way to assign values to variables and fields; Drag is an animation command to move from one spot to another; Sort arranges cards; DoMenu permits you to write scripts containing any of the menu commands; and Choose allows the choice of various tools from the tool menu.

Local and global variables are used for data storage; the PUT command is the accompanying statement that assigns the value to the variable. Arithmetic operators include addition, subtraction, multiplication, division with the usual remainder, division producing a whole number, mod division ignoring the whole number and producing the remainder, exponential operator, and parentheses used to group expression to control order of evaluation. Logical operators include Is, Contains, Is in, True, False, and Empty, each of which returns certain values to be used by the program. Combining logical operators with the operators And, Or, and Not, along with parentheses, allows the programmer to construct complex expressions.

Program control loops include Repeat, Repeat . . . Until, Repeat . . . While, and Repeat . . . With. Conditional statements that contribute to program control are If . . . Then, and If . . . Then . . . Else. Internal documentation is indicated by the inclusion of two hyphens (–) in front of any statement. Table 1 presents the language features of BASIC and *HyperCard.*

To illustrate how both languages address a similar problem, a simple animation program in low-resolution graphics BASIC would involve the use of the FOR . . . NEXT loop and a variable. The same program in *HyperCard* could be scripted in a button and include the Drag command. The BASIC program lines to accomplish the action of moving a box on the screen from left to right include:

```
10 GR (Sets graphics mode]
20 FOR BOX = 0 to 35 [Box is drawn at 36 different points across the
        screen]
30 COLOR = 2 [Sets color for box]
```

```
40 GOSUB 1000 [Sends control of program to Subroutine 1000 to
      draw box]
50 COLOR = 0 [Sets color to default background color]
60 GOSUB 1000 [The box is now being drawn in the background
      color, as if being "erased," thus seeming to move]
70 NEXT BOX [Sends control back to line 20 until 36 iterations are
      completed]
999 END
1000 REM ****************BOX*********************
1010 HLIN BOX,BOX+4 AT 7 [Use of variable BOX to represent
      points from 0 to 35 in loop; changes the x value]
1020 HLIN BOX,BOX+4 AT 8
1030 HLIN BOX,BOX+4 AT 9
1040 RETURN
```

Programming in *HyperCard* involves drawing the box first, then dragging it to the desired location by scripting a button. The steps include:

1. Choose rectangle tool from Tools Menu. Draw box in desired area of screen.
2. Choose button tool from Objects Menu. Create button and script the following:

```
on mouseup
   Choose select tool
   Drag from 10,80 to 100,200 [selects area on screen to be moved;
      explains the x,y values]
   Set dragspeed to 200 [sets speed for animation]
   Drag from 10,200 to 400,200 [x,y values for old and new posi-
      tion]
   Choose browse tool [returns control to browsing mode]
end mouseup
```

SIMILARITIES AND DIFFERENCES

HyperCard is mouse-driven in the Macintosh environment, while on the Apple the BASIC commands must be typed into the computer's memory. Both *HyperCard* and BASIC have text and graphics modes, and both can accommodate animation in graphics. The speed of animation is controlled by a STEP command in BASIC, while in *HyperCard* the command Set Dragspeed is used. The Home Card in *HyperCard* is comparable to the CATALOG listing in BASIC, and it serves to link programs (stacks) as does the embedded DOS command in BASIC. Data are stored in arrays in BASIC, while in *HyperCard* data are stored in fields or variables. Program modularity for top-down programming is accomplished in BASIC through the use of subroutines and the GOSUB statement. *HyperCard* is modular in nature, as its five objects are independent of each other. The change in the script of one object does not affect the script of the other objects. A program in *HyperCard* can consist of several stacks (modules) which can be linked together by buttons.

TABLE 1. Comparison of Language Features

LANGUAGE FEATURES		
	BASIC	*HyperCard*
Mode	Text Graphics: Low, High Res Animation	Text Graphics: Imported, Drawn Animation
Command Statements	PRINT VTAB HTAB FLASH SPEED = XXX NORMAL END	Go Find Hide Show Set Visual Ask Answer Wait Put Drag Sort DoMenu Choose
Data Storage	Variable: Numeric, String Arrays: One, Two Dimensional	Variable: Numeric, String Local, Global
Program Control	Conditionals: IF...THEN GO TO GO SUB Loops: FOR...NEXT Modularity: GOSUB	Conditionals: If...Then If...Then...Else On Loops: Repeat Repeat...Until Repeat...While Repeat...With Modularity: Push Pop
Math Functions	+ − * / ** ( ) LEN RND INT	+ − * / ^ ( ) Div Mod
Documentation	REM	--

High school honors students from a mid-Atlantic state received *HyperCard* training at a summer Honors Academy and were asked to enumerate any similarities and/or differences between *HyperCard* and BASIC (Reed & Rosenbluth, 1991). Their responses regarding ease of use contained expressions such as "similar in linking processes, but *HyperCard* is much easier to work with"; "creation of programs is much easier in *HyperCard*"; "*HyperCard* is much simpler and faster to use and learn"; and "application is user friendly."

In relation to actual programming, comments from transcriptions of assignments were found such as: "*HyperCard* doesn't appear to require as much technological knowledge about programming. It doesn't rely on symbols as much"; "mouse allows you to do with a button click what BASIC would require lines of code for"; "icons make tasks easier than typing in commands"; "the ability to move through the program while it is being designed makes the programming process less complicated"; "placing and moving text, graphics, or whole cards is simpler than trying to pick out individual parts of the BASIC program"; "*HyperCard* can use pictures not drawn in the programming" and "*HyperCard* is able to create pictures and backgrounds with its own programming before the program is run."

CASE STUDY

An instructional program written in *HyperCard* was duplicated as closely as possible in BASIC to use as a case study in order to examine the similarities and differences between the two languages. The program was originally designed in *HyperCard* to illustrate to the user how the computer may be useful in the process of conducting a social research telephone survey. Content of the program consists of a telephone questionnaire from an applied social research study, and includes providing step-by-step instructions to the interviewer (the program user) as an interview is conducted, asking the respondent on the phone, requesting permission to participate in the study, asking six survey questions, displaying ways to document answers, and providing the interview's closing comments.

In many cases, *HyperCard* entails orchestrating pre-existing programming to suit individual purposes, while the BASIC language requires the programmer to create and direct simultaneously. For example, in *HyperCard* the introductory text in the case study was typed with the aid of preprogrammed tools. Menus and options such as centering text, different text styles and size, and cut, copy, and paste text were selected by a simple click of the mouse. BASIC required that all features needed for text entry and manipulation be written in lines of command codes. Although *HyperCard* allows the user to combine language features to form a program that performs some activity or solves a problem, many of *HyperCard*'s functions are built in. BASIC allows many similar activities or problem-solving strategies, but the programmer must write code for all of the required functions.

In general, both languages allowed for user-friendly programs. In both, it is possible to allow the user to move around within the programs with the use of conditionals and optional directions. For example, it was possible to allow the user to move from the menu to various parts of the survey and back in both programs. But, overall, *HyperCard* was easier to program than BASIC. The use of fields in *HyperCard* was convenient and easy to program for features such as changing the respondent's name and number for multiple interviewing. Field use in *HyperCard* was also a great facilitator in allowing the user to input answers from the multiple choice responses.

One of the major differences between the programs was found in the telephone process of the survey. In *HyperCard*, there is a special phone feature which allows for automatic dialing. A graphic representation of a telephone was sensitized through the use of fields to list the name, identification number, and telephone number of the person called. A click on the telephone visual allowed the user to call automatically through the computer; in BASIC. the automatic telephone feature was not possible. Instead, the computer screen was utilized to list the respondent's name and number, and to direct the interviewer to manually dial the telephone.

Another major difference found between *HyperCard* and BASIC is in the use of graphics. In the *HyperCard* program, it was possible to copy a well-drawn picture from the Art Ideas stack. In the BASIC program, the picture was omitted. It would have been possible to utilize a picture by drawing one with the BASIC graphic features, but the programmer would need good drawing skills in order to obtain a quality picture. A similar difference was also found in the use of Button icons as graphic descriptors in *HyperCard*; these were not available in BASIC.

CONCLUSION

In order to acquire design skills and problem-solving skills, one must first be fluent in the language itself. Without basic knowledge of the command statements, program control, and modularity, the programmer will probably have a difficult time advancing along the cognitive course of outcomes described earlier.

The language features of BASIC and *HyperCard* have been presented and then contrasted for similarities and differences. Whether one is preferable to the other probably depends upon the purpose of learning the language. One must ask what the objective is for the study of programming in either language. A study conducted by Reed and Liu (this volume) concluded that *HyperCard* simplifies programming so much that certain thinking processes necessary for problem-solving skills may not develop. Their study showed that *HyperCard* students performed better on the probing exercises than did the BASIC students; however, the problem-solving skills of the BASIC group improved pre-treatment to post-treatment, while the *HyperCard* group did not. If software development is the outcome desired, then perhaps *HyperCard* is the preferable language; if problem-solving is desired, then the BASIC language has proven superior in that area.

REFERENCES

Adams, D. R. (1990). HyperCard and Macintosh: A primer. New York: McGraw-Hill.

Cook, E. K. (1989-90). The use of Macintosh authoring languages in effective computer-assisted instruction. *Journal of Educational Technology Systems, 18*(2), 109-122.

Crane, G. & Mylonas, E. (1988). The Perseus project: An interactive curriculum on Classical Greek civilization. *Educational Technology, 28*(1), 25-32.

Dalbey, J. & Linn, M. C. (1985). The demands and requirements of computer programming: A literature review. *Journal of Educational Computing Research, 1*(3), 253-274.

Dalbey, J. & Linn, M. C. (1986). Cognitive consequences of programming: Augmentations to BASIC instruction. *Journal of Educational Computing Research, 2*(1), 75-93.

Harris, M. & Cady, M. (1988). The dynamic process of creating hypertext literature. *Educational Technology, 28*(1), 33-40.

Kurland, D. M., Pea, R. D., Clement, C., & Mawby, R. (1986). A study of the development of programming ability and thinking skills in high school students. *Journal of Educational Computing Research, 2*(4), 429-458.

La Passardiere, B. (1989). *Lecture notes on computer science: Computer assisted learning*. Springler Verlag: Gt. Goos & J. Hartmanis.

Linn, M. C. (1985). The cognitive consequences of programming instruction in classrooms. *Educational Researcher, 14*(5), 14-25-29.

Magliaro, S. B. & Burton, J. K. (1988). Adolescents' chunking of computer programs. *Computers in the Schools, 4*(3/4), 129-138.

Mandinach, E. B. & Linn, M. C. (1986). The cognitive effects of computer learning environments. *Journal of Educational Computing Research, 2*(4), 411-427.

Putnam, R. T., Sleeman, D., Baxter, J. A., & Kuspa, L. H. (1986). A summary of misconceptions of high school BASIC programmers. *Journal of Educational Computing Research, 2*(4), 459-471.
Reed, W. M. & Liu, Min. (1994). The Effect of BASIC programming versus HyperCard programming on problem-solving and computer anxiety.
Reed, W. M. & Rosenbluth, G. S. (1991, June-July). *Governor's Honors Academy*. Morgantown: West Virginia University.
Reed, W. M., Palumbo, D. B., & Stolar, A. A. (1988). The comparative effects of BASIC and Logo instruction on problem-solving skills. *Computers in the Schools, 4*(3/4), 105-118.

Stephen W. Harmon
Sharon H. Dinsmore

Novice Linking in Hypermedia-Based Instructional Systems

INTRODUCTION

By now almost everyone involved in education acknowledges that we are in the midst of an information explosion. We are no longer all that surprised by proclamations such as the one made by futurist Marvin Cetron (1988) that by the year 2000, high school seniors will come into contact with as much information in the course of a year as their grandparents did in the course of a lifetime. Indeed, we sometimes fail to be astonished when we hear people like Ivan Trujillo (1989) tell us that the body of scientific information is doubling every 18 months. We are becoming accustomed to the information explosion just as our forebears became accustomed to air travel, color television, and sliced bread. But one aspect of the information explosion appears to be sneaking up on us.

Technological innovation has necessarily kept pace with the expansion of readily accessible information. To be sure, the information explosion is directly attributable in large part to technological innovation. New technologies allow us to deal with more massive and disparate sources of information than ever before, and to do so more easily than we were able to

STEPHEN W. HARMON is Assistant Professor of Instructional Technology, University of Houston-Clear Lake, Houston, TX 77058-1098.
SHARON H. DINSMORE is a graduate student in Instructional Technology, University of Houston-Clear Lake, Houston, TX 77058-1098.

[Haworth co-indexing entry note]: "Novice Linking in Hypermedia-Based Instructional Systems." Harmon, Stephen W. and Sharon H. Dinsmore. Co-published simultaneously in *Computers in the Schools* (The Haworth Press, Inc.) Vol. 10, No. 1/2, 1994, pp. 155-170; and: *Multimedia and Megachange: New Roles for Educational Computing* (eds: W. Michael Reed, John K. Burton, and Min Liu) The Haworth Press, Inc., 1994, pp. 155-170. Multiple copies of this article/chapter may be purchased from The Haworth Document Delivery Center [1-800-3-HAWORTH; 9:00 a.m. - 5:00 p.m. (EST)].

deal with much smaller, more localized information just a few years ago. When microcomputers first became popular, almost everyone who owned one was a computer programmer; users almost had to be programmers in those days. But as time went on and computers became easier to use, they became more complicated to program. The number of amateur computer programmers dropped correspondingly. This decrease continued until the advent of object-oriented, natural language authoring systems in the late 1980s. Almost overnight, virtually anyone who had access to a microcomputer and wanted to create computer programs could–and many of them did. However, it is this very ease of programming that may be leading educators into trouble.

The number of new computer programs available, particularly educational programs, has increased dramatically over the last five years. Since most software authors want their programs to be in the vanguard of educational theory, and since one of the first widely distributed authoring systems dealt with an exciting new concept in cognitive theory, most of these new authors began making what they said were cutting-edge programs. If you have followed computer-based education over the last few years, you must be aware by now that it is hypermedia of which we speak. The promise of these hypermedia authoring systems was that "any expert on any subject should be able to produce . . . attractive, accessible, and powerful instructional applications with a moderate investment of time and energy" (Morariu, 1988, p. 17). With the advent of HyperCard in 1987 and Apple Computer, Inc.'s decision to bundle it free with every new Macintosh computer they sold, the hypermedia bandwagon was off and rolling. What few people realized was that it was rolling down a pretty steep hill. Today it is in some danger of rolling out of control.

Hypermedia is a combination of text, sound, still pictures, graphics, and motion video arranged nonlinearly in linked nodes so that a user can go directly from one node to any other. It should not be confused with multimedia, which combines text, sound, still pictures, graphics, and motion video but is unconcerned with the way nodes are linked together (Halasz & Conklin, 1989; Reeves & Harmon, 1991). What makes the concept of hypermedia exciting for educators is that it closely models semantic network theory (Jonassen, 1989). Semantic network theory holds that people store information in linked weblike node structures (Anderson & Bower, 1973). People create networks by relating different nodes of information to one another in what becomes a meaningful way for them. For one person a node for the color green might be linked to nodes for grass, money, elves, and men from Mars. For another person green might be linked to eggs and ham, cheese, and a golf tournament. Cognitive psychologists and educational researchers believe that the best way to help learners acquire new knowledge is to present the knowledge in structures that the learner can easily relate to existing networks within his or her own memory (Jonassen, 1989). As Dede and Palumbo (1991, p. 16) put it, "our adeptness in quickly storing and retrieving large amounts of information seems to stem from this property of associativity."

So it is no wonder that developers of computer programs systems have embraced hypermedia wholeheartedly. In fact, development of hypermedia systems has far outstripped research on them (Heller, 1990; Jonassen & Grabinger, 1990; Tsai, 1988). Most developers assume that, because hypermedia *ought* to be good for instruction, it *is* good for instruction. Those of us who have been involved in educational research for any length of time recognize this as a potentially dangerous assumption. As Heller (1990, p. 436) so ably points out, "The problem areas within hypermedia and HAI [hypermedia-assisted instruction] are well documented but there needs to be more research done on how one comes to understand the extent and interconnections of the material represented in a hypermedia system." One method of arriving at some understanding of the innate instructional ability of hypermedia systems is to examine the ways in which learners actually use them. This study looks at how learners used a hypermedia system to form semantic associations among nodes of information that were not formally linked by the system designers in advance. Hypermedia proponents assume that learners will form semantic networks similar to those formed by experts, and many of today's educational hypermedia systems are based on this assumption (Fischer & Mandl, 1990). This study begins to examine the validity of that assumption.

METHODOLOGY

The goal of this study was to evaluate how subjects, who were novices at learning with hypermedia systems, would carry out a task of linking nodes of information in a hypermedia system that presented a relatively unfamiliar topic. We constructed a very simple-to-use hypermedia system that provided subjects the opportunity to read about and watch video clips of topics related to the conflicts between the Israelis and Palestinians over the land now called Israel. The hypermedia system was designed to present the topics as separate entities with no pre-imposed structure so that it would not suggest any relationships between topics.

The subjects were asked to spend one hour browsing the system and constructing links between the topics in any way that made sense to them.

In addition to having the subjects browse the hypermedia system and construct links, we asked questions occasionally about the reasoning behind a linkage. These data were collected to help determine the types of links they were constructing. In addition, subjects completed a pre-treatment survey, a post-treatment questionnaire, and a post-treatment individual differences measurement test.

Subjects

Students in two graduate level "Introduction to Educational Computing" courses were chosen as subjects for several reasons. First, these students already had a general knowledge of computers and a specific knowledge of how to use the treatment system, the Apple Macintosh. Second, as newcomers to educational computing they were likely to be inexperienced in learning or teaching with hypermedia systems. Third, we felt that a few students at most might already have a more than general knowledge of the chosen topic–the conflict over the Holy Lands in the Middle East. Fourth, as graduate students in the College of Education, these students have a similar education level.

Subjects were recruited by asking students in the two classes to volunteer to participate in a study of "Hypermedia and Learning." Initially, everyone in the two classes signed up, but due to scheduling conflicts, only 24 actually completed the study.

Instrumentation

The hypermedia system was created using the Apple Macintosh, *HyperCard 2.0*, a laser videodisc player, and the ABC News Interactive Videodisc entitled *In the Holy Land*. So the subjects could complete the task in one hour, *HyperCard* was used to construct a system which provided access to a limited set of the topics (or nodes) in the videodisc and allowed the subject to browse the nodes and link them easily.

The main screen (card) of the hypermedia system displayed the 25 available nodes as icons. The icons were purposefully presented as separate entities scattered on the screen in no predefined order. To view a node, a subject simply clicked on the appropriate icon. Each node presented one card of information with options for viewing related video-clips or occasionally for getting more detailed information. Each node card also included a button for returning to the main system screen.

The hypermedia system also included a very simple to use mechanism for setting up links between related nodes. Buttons for setting up the link appeared on the bottom of the main screen. The subject simply pressed the "link to" button followed by the icon for the first node to be linked. Next, he or she pressed the icon for the second topic to be linked and pressed a second button to confirm the link. As each link was constructed, a line showing the link between the two node icons appeared on the main screen. The system was constructed in this manner, so that subjects could quickly alternate between browsing and linking and also keep track of the links they had established.

The hypermedia system was designed to record all the links that each subject made to ensure that complete, accurate data were available for analysis.

Pre-Treatment Survey

A computer-based pre-treatment survey was constructed to gather general background data from each subject. In addition to demographic questions, the survey included questions regarding hobbies, special interests, teaching specialities, knowledge of and experience with hypermedia systems, and familiarity with the conflicts over the Holy Lands. The purpose of these additional questions was to determine whether any subjects had more than general knowledge of either hypermedia learning or the Holy Lands conflicts and issues. Students completed this survey in class prior to using the hypermedia system.

Post-Treatment Interview

After using the hypermedia system, subjects were interviewed to provide insight into their experience in using the system and what they "learned" from using it. A structured interview process (Bogden & Biklen, 1982) was employed as well as a constant-comparative data analysis/gathering strategy (Glaser & Strauss, 1967). Structured questions included:

1. What was your strategy for going through the system?
2. Who is right?
3. How do you feel about using this sort of hypermedia system to learn something?
4. How would you describe your reading habits?
5. What did you know about the topic (Holy Lands conflict) prior to using this system?
6. What other comments do you wish to share regarding this system or hypermedia?

Interaction Procedure

Prior to participating in the study, all subjects took the pre-treatment questionnaire during their regularly scheduled class time. The "interaction" with the hypermedia system was conducted on an individual basis due to the nature of a videodisc-based hypermedia system and the need for the researchers to observe each subject during the treatment. Upon arrival for the treatment, subjects were given brief instructions on how to use the customized hypermedia system and asked to express how much they felt they knew, as well as to report what they actually knew about the content area. Next, they were asked to spend the next hour browsing the nodes and setting up links between any nodes they felt were related. Subjects were ask to verbally report (Ericsson & Simon, 1984) on the types of links they were making. They were also advised that one of the researchers would be available to assist them, would be observing them, and would occasionally ask for a more detailed explanation of why a particular link was constructed.

When an hour had passed, the subject was told that time was up and was interviewed. The researcher recorded the subject's oral answers to the post-treatment questions, thanked him/her for participating, and finally gave a brief synopsis of the purpose of the study. After the subject left, the researcher chose an option from the system to save a list of links that the subject had created.

RESULTS

Twenty-four subjects completed the study. Complete data sets were retained for all subjects. Subjects generally had little trouble becoming familiar with the interface. They typically were immediately able to browse from one node to the next and were able to confidently make links on their second attempt. Only two of the subjects reported any extensive prior knowledge of the content area beyond having heard of the some of the names and events included in the study. Interestingly, each of these subjects either was currently or had at one time been a career military officer. One had read several books on the content area. Some descriptive statistics were compiled in order to give an overview of the data sets. Three hundred different links were mathematically possible in the system, though not all nodes bore any semantic relationship to each other. The mean number of links made by subjects in the study was 20.71, with a standard deviation of 11.82. The range of links was from 8 to 69.

Statistics were also compiled for links by node. For the 25 different nodes combined, a mean number of 39.8 total links were created by participants, with a standard deviation of 13.99. Each node had a mean of 13.44 different links established, with a standard deviation of 3.94. Each node had a mean number of 3.8 instances in which it was not linked at all, with a standard deviation of 2.93. Table 1 presents the means and standard deviations obtained in the study.

As might be expected, a fairly strong significant correlation ($p = .0001$) was observed for total links by topic and number of different links ($r = 0.673$), indicating that, where more links were made, more different topics were linked together. Somewhat surprisingly, there was also a fairly strong positive correlation ($p = .0001$, $r = 0.672$) between total number of links per card and instances of cards receiving no links. This correlation indicates that subjects linked some topics either quite a lot or not at all. One reason for this might be that some nodes were difficult to understand and subjects either failed to see that they related to anything or else failed to see how they didn't relate to everything. Table 2 shows all of the nodes with the total number of links, number of different links, and instances of no links for each node.

Types of Links

More interesting themes emerged from the qualitative analysis of the interview and verbal report data. Eight different types of links were identified by the subjects. This sort of emic (subject-generated) categorization is of particular interest since, as Boas remarks, "If it is our serious purpose to understand the thoughts of a people the whole analysis of experience must be based on their concepts, not ours" (1943, p. 314). In each case the term

TABLE 1. Means and Standard Deviations of Links by Subjects and Nodes

Category	Mean	Std. Dev.
Total links per subject	20.71	11.82
Total links for all nodes	39.8	13.99
Total links per individual node	13.44	3.94
Instances where nodes were left unlinked per node	3.8	2.93

TABLE 2. Links by Individual Node

Node	Total # links	Links to different nodes	Instances of no links to any node
Balfour Declaration	36	11	2
United Nations	44	13	2
Terrorism	65	19	0
Security for Israel	54	22	2
PLO Violence	52	16	4
War and Refugees	42	17	3
Deir Yasin Massacre	22	11	8
Sanctuary	43	14	3
The Intifadah	18	9	9
Yom Kippur War	30	14	6
Palestinian Homeland	59	20	2
Fedayeen Attacks	20	9	7
UN Resolution 242	31	7	6
War of Independence	30	9	5
Children of Palestine	39	14	0
Camp David	28	11	6
Sabra and Shatilla	18	9	9
British Mandate	34	9	4
The Holocaust	54	16	0
State of Israel Proclaimed	61	16	0
Children of Israel	45	15	0
Arafat and the UN	41	11	4
Six day War	61	17	2
Munich Olympics	33	11	3
The Three Religions	35	16	8

used here to describe the type of link was used by at least one subject. In many of the instances, subjects used different but equivalent expressions to identify a particular type of link. We have chosen the words we feel best describe the types of links subjects made and have occasionally changed the case of the words used as link types in order to maintain consistency. To increase inter-rater reliability, each investigator coded links separately, before combining to discuss and resolve discrepant cases. In the few instances where we disagreed, the disagreement was caused by different, but synonymous, terms used to describe a particular link. Note that no attempt was made to determine the frequency of occurrence of any particular link type; we were interested primarily in identifying the different types.

Comparative. The first two of these eight link types are similar and opposite links. Subjects would identify a similar link when one node shared characteristics with another node. For example, several subjects linked a node about "Children of Israel" with a node about "Children of Palestine" because they were both about children. Subjects would identify an opposite type link when they felt nodes were opposites of each other. For example, many subjects linked "Terrorism" to "Sanctuary" because they felt they were diametrically opposed to each other. (Interestingly, some subjects linked the same two nodes because they felt terrorism caused the need for sanctuary.) Since these two categories appear to us to be different sides of the same coin, we treat them together and suggest that they be simplified into one category called comparative links. Nineteen of the 24 subjects made at least one link of this type.

Causal. The third type of link identified by subjects is causal. Subjects would call a link causal when they felt that one node was the result of another node. For instance, one common causal link subjects made was between the node for "State of Israel Proclaimed" and the "War of Independence." They felt that the War of Independence was a direct result of the proclamation of the state. Another was linking "PLO Violence" to "Security for Israel" because the violence created (or caused) the need for security. However, as with comparative linking of "Terrorism" to "Sanctuary," several subjects linked these two nodes together for a different reason. All of the subjects made at least one link of this type.

Sequential. The fourth type of link is sequential. Subjects identified a link as sequential when they felt that one node occurred chronologically soon before or soon after another, or even when they felt that two nodes occurred at the same time. For example, some subjects linked the "Six Day War" and "U.N. Resolution 242" because resolution 242 was passed immediately after the Six Day War. Again though, different subjects would make the same links for different reasons. At least as many subjects identified the link between "State of Israel Proclaimed" and the "War of Independence" as sequential as did causal. These two link types do seem logically related. Eight of the 24 subjects made at least one sequential link. Interestingly, the two subjects who had more extensive prior knowledge than the rest of the sample made no sequential links.

Associative. The fifth type of link identified by subjects is associative. Subjects used this word to describe links they made where one node explicitly mentioned another, or when they felt that one node was vaguely related to another and were unable to express a more concrete relationship. Subjects often identified "The Children of Israel" and "The Holocaust" as an associative link because the text for "The Children of Israel" node mentions that the children of Israel "are well schooled in the horrors of the Holocaust." They would identify "Arafat and the UN" and "PLO Violence" as being associated, but were not clear how. Twenty-two of the 24 subjects made at least one associative link.

Exemplary. The sixth type of link is exemplary. Subjects called links between nodes that illustrated each other exemplary. For instance, some subjects identified the link between "The Munich Olympics" and "Terrorism" as exemplary because the events which occurred at the Munich Olympics were an example of terrorism. Similarly, they identified the link between "PLO Violence" and "Terrorism," as exemplary, saying terrorism was an example of PLO violence. Likewise they identified the link between "PLO Violence" and "The Munich Olympics" as exemplary, saying the acts at the Munich Olympics were an example of PLO violence. Subjects rarely had trouble expressing this type of link. Eighteen of the 24 subjects made at least one exemplary link.

Componential. The seventh link type is componential. A link between two nodes was said to be componential when one node was a component of another one. For example, some subjects called the link between "UN Resolution 242" and the "Security for Israel" componential because one part of resolution 242 guarantees Israel's security. Similarly they called the link between "PLO Violence" and "Terrorism" componential because terrorism was one part of the grand scheme of PLO violence. Five subjects made at least one componential link. Both subjects who had greater prior content knowledge made links of this type.

Accidental. The eighth type of link identified by subjects is accidental. Subjects occasionally slipped when they were clicking the mouse or else misread a title when linking two nodes. They invariably noticed when this had occurred and were quick to call it to the researcher's attention. Accidental links were the least common type of link observed in this study. This link type is interesting because of its potential to lead to serendipitous learning. Although no direct evidence for it was obtained in this study, it is possible that subjects could come to a new understanding of a relationship initially made accidentally.

Although subjects weren't always able to classify every link that they made, of the 497 total links made by subjects, all were either immediately placed into one of the seven categories (combining similar and opposite into comparative) by the subjects themselves or in retrospect by the researchers. It is important to remember that these seven link types may not represent every possible link type. They only represent every link type made in this study with this particular set of nodes. Further research with different subjects and subject matter is needed to find the limits of the utility of this categorization.

Higher and Lower Order Links. Apart from the seven link types, two other major themes emerged from the study. The first deals with levels of links and the second with video and node size. In looking at link types on another level, two other classes of links emerged from this study, direct and indirect, or higher and lower order links. Direct or lower order links follow the pattern of: A is related to B. Indirect or higher order link types follow the pattern of: if A is related to B and B is related to C then A is related to C. Lower order links were the most common type observed in this study. All of the links mentioned above can be classified as lower order links. All of the subjects made lower-order links, while only three made higher-order links. Higher order links occurred only among those subjects who indicated having a greater conceptual knowledge of the topic area prior to beginning the study. The one subject who made higher-order links who did not indicate having a broad prior knowledge of the content area did indicate having a good knowledge of, and a strong interest in, history in general.

One example of a higher order link was made by a subject when he, in rapid succession, linked "Arafat and the UN" to "PLO Violence," "PLO Violence" to "Terrorism," then "Arafat and the UN" to "Terrorism." In another example, that same subject likened "Sanctuary" to "PLO Violence" because in his words "countries around the world give sanctuary to the PLO." He then linked "Sanctuary" to "Terrorism" because since PLO violence is most often expressed as terrorism, "those same countries are supporting terrorism when they give sanctuary." Interestingly, this subject had read several books about the content area. This subject made 69 links overall, 4 standard deviations above the mean. Higher-order linking appears to indicate a greater degree of assimilation of information than direct linking, hence the higher and lower order distinction.

Video Nodes. One final interesting theme to emerge from the study is that the video segments appeared to be detrimental to purposeful linking. Subjects were frequently observed watching a video segment, then appearing to have forgotten what they were doing before they watched the video. In fact, subjects almost invariably had a hard time making any links at all for a few minutes after watching a video segment. This phenomenon is also reflected in the fact that the students who made the most links watched the least video and vice-versa. One possible explanation for this observance is that the video segments were too long in length. They typically lasted between forty-five seconds and two minutes. The video segments may have actually represented several nodes worth of information. After watching a video segment, subjects appeared to be unclear as to which node they were on, perhaps because they had just encountered several nodes disguised as one. Three subjects actually expressed being confused by the video. One subject remarked, "I'm not watching any video because there's too much to do. I can't make connections and watch video at the same time, that's too much stimulation." Twenty-three of the 24 subjects looked at video at least once; 17 looked at video only once.

GENERAL CONCLUSIONS

The results of our research indicate that subjects gave seven types of reasons for creating their links. We consider this to be a positive finding. The variety of link types that subjects created without prompting from us is a positive indication of the diverse goals which similar hypermedia systems can be designed to address. In addition, because comparative, associative and causal linkages were among the types of links subjects created, hypermedia systems organized in similar ways may be useful for developing critical thinking skills. One of the goals mentioned by many educators and education reform advocates is that to survive and prosper in the 1990s and beyond, American students need to develop critical thinking skills. Hypermedia enthusiasts have been claiming that hypermedia has the potential to help students develop those skills. While we cannot claim to have proven this for all hypermedia systems, we believe that our subjects did demonstrate the use of critical thinking skills in establishing those links. In Bloom's taxonomy of learning (1956), comparison, association, and causation are analytical skills. Since the subjects in this study generated links which they subsequently classified as being of one or the other of these types, it would seem that they used these analytical thinking skills to arrive at the linkages. Because subjects were able to relate previously unrelated pieces of information in a nonrandom fashion, they must have to some extent analyzed that information in the process, when these analyses led them to create. However, we feel that our findings were definitely influenced by the fact that we forced active linking of information. We also believe that the subject and nodes of information chosen for our system could have influenced the type of links subjects chose to create.

Dansereau (1978; Dansereau, Collins, MacDonald, Holley, Garland, Diekhoff, & Evans, 1979) advocates a general schema training approach called "networking." In networking he suggests that learners be trained to recognize six types of links between nodes of information. These are Part links, Type links, Leads-to links, Analogy links, Characteristic links, and Evidence links. Learners read a passage of text, then create a "node-link map" on paper. They can then relate or link information nodes on the map by classifying them as one of these link types. Links represent the way the ideas represented by the nodes are interrelated. Clearly this strategy relates closely to the link types identified in this study. It may be that experts in a content domain or in working in hypermedia environments would exhibit link types more closely related to those suggested by Dansereau. Although McKeachie (1984) suggests that this networking strategy is difficult and time-consuming to learn and employ, it would be well worthwhile to examine how well it works in hypermedia environments. This study suggests that training in networking is highly applicable to work in hypermedia environments and should be researched. Subjects in this study had no training in networking. Whereas Dansereau's link types are etic, the types identified in this study are emic, coming from the subjects, not the researchers. At the time that analysis of the data for this study was conducted, neither researcher was familiar with Dansereau's work.

However, we feel that the results of our study also suggest that caution should be used before choosing hypermedia to address some educational goals. Based on our observations of the subjects, their answers to our questions and the linkages they established, it is clear to us that there is no way to guarantee that specific learning objectives will be met with a completely nonlinear, unstructured system such as that used in this study. Based on post-treatment interviews, we felt that some subjects left the study with an incomplete and/or inaccurate understanding of some of the facts presented in the system. (One subject left the study thinking Camp David was a concentration camp in World War II.) Because of this finding, we believe that we can only say that these systems allow learners to construct their own world views and that there is no evidence that these newly constructed views will be consistent with the norm. More research must be performed before it is clear what features hypermedia systems must incorporate in order to allow learners to achieve more specific learning objectives.

This study gave us the opportunity to observe subjects actually using a hypermedia system and to gain some new insights into potential advantages and disadvantages of non-linear, learner-controlled instructional systems. One aspect of that observation was eye-opening for us, and we believe it should be considered carefully in the development and implementation of hypermedia instructional systems (HIS). To be precise, subjects occasionally mentioned during their interaction that they were avoiding particular topics (like violence and terrorism) because, although they knew things like that happened, they didn't like to hear or see the details. This suggests that allowing students to choose the topics they review in a hypermedia system could actually allow them to bias their learning because they are unwilling to explore certain topics. Much emphasis has been placed on giving students access to raw information so that their learning is not biased by the opinions held by their teacher; however, we have not seen anyone mention this equally unsettling prospect of students censoring their own learning due to personal preferences. While most hypermedia proponents extol the virtues of students being able to come to their own conclusions based on raw, uncensored data, we wonder if they have considered how valid those conclusions might be if the learner refuses to expose himself/herself to certain facts or theories.

Further, the size of a hypermedia system may turn out to be a critical factor in its success. Although much emphasis has been placed on how we can develop hypermedia systems which encompass great volumes of information, we believe that too large a system might actually hamper the hypermedia learning process. Our system used only 25 nodes of information taken from a larger system of over 400 nodes. The subjects had a difficult time reviewing that much information in the one hour allotted and some of them said they had difficulty maneuvering among that many options.

Limitations Evident Within the Study

Due to the nature of the topic chosen for this hypermedia system, certain types of links might not have been possible or likely. Therefore, we do not believe that our seven link types are necessarily the full extent of link types possible or that they are completely representative of link types likely to be found in all hypermedia knowledge construction systems.

Due to the limited time available for the study, the subjects were artificially limited to one hour to explore the topics. This limitation possibly precluded the viewing of many videodisc clips and/or the careful reviewing of data nodes. This time limitation, therefore, could have impacted our findings.

Subjects often found it difficult to verbalize link types. This difficulty may have had two impacts on the study: (a) in identifying all of the different link types subjects made and (b) in interfering with the subjects' progress through the system. Being forced to stop and verbalize reasons for links may have caused the subjects to progress through the system in a manner different from what they might have done otherwise. The verbalization may have also affected the number of links subjects made.

The video-clips available were often too big to be single nodes, often containing information about more than the topic they represented. This was distracting to subjects in some cases and possibly caused confusion in what nodes were appropriate to link. The structure of the system utilized video-clips as part of the nodes (or topics) rather than as separate entities.

One other major consideration is that subjects had no extrinsic motivation for learning about this particular topic area. They were rewarded for participating in the study by being given extra credit in their courses, but they had no reason to want to learn about the Israeli/Palestinian conflict. Findings may have been different given a sample already studying this content area.

Suggestions for Further Research

Some of the conclusions already mentioned suggest the need for further research. For instance, investigation will be necessary to understand the optimal size of hypermedia instructional systems. Also, as mentioned earlier, research must continue into how hypermedia can be designed to ensure that specific educational objectives are met by learners. There are two additional research directions that we would like to introduce here.

First, extensive research into the active versus passive hypermedia instructional systems is needed. Many proponents of hypermedia in education are emphasizing the virtues of hypermedia as a teacher presentation tool. While it may be more than multimedia due to its non-linear capabilities, it still amounts to relatively passive learning for students. In other cases, hypermedia systems are designed for use by individual students but still do not promote active learning by students. We feel that hypermedia systems that promote active learning by forcing learners to construct their own links between nodes of information will prove to be the most beneficial. However, we feel that more research is needed into how active versus passive hypermedia instructional systems will impact learning.

Second, our research results indicate that subjects with a richer prior knowledge of the subject created more links between nodes. We expect that there will be a difference between the way domain experts and novices create links between nodes. We feel that there is a need for further research to examine the way learners at different levels construct links in hypermedia systems compared to the way experts in the field construct them. If a goal of instruction is for learners to become experts in whatever area they are studying, every stop on the path to expertise should be mapped out and road signs put up for the travelers.

Hypermedia-based instructional systems have the potential to become the vehicle that carries education into the 21st century. They also have the potential to become the out-of-control bandwagon that plummets off a cliff.

REFERENCES

Anderson, J. R. & Bower, G. H. (1973). *Human associative memory.* Washington, DC: Winston & Sons.

Bloom, B. S. (1956). *Taxonomy of educational objectives: The classification of educational goals. Handbook I: Cognitive domain.* New York: Longman.

Boas, F. (1943). Recent anthropology. *Science, 98,* 311-314, 334-337.

Bogden, R. C. & Biklen, S. K. (1982). *Qualitative research for education: An introduction to theory and methods.* Boston: Allyn and Bacon.

Cetron, M. J. (1988). Class of 2000: The good news and the bad news. *The Futurist, 23*(6), 915.

Dansereau, D. F. (1978). The development of a learning strategy curriculum. In: H. F. O'Neill, Jr. (Ed.), *Learning strategies* (pp. 1-29). New York: Academic Press.

Dansereau, D. F., Collins, K. W., McDonald, B. A., Holley, C. D., Garland, J. C., Diekhoff, G. M., & Evans, S. H. (1979). Development and evaluation of an effective learning strategy program. *Journal of Educational Psychology, 79,* 64-73.

Dede, C. J. & Palumbo, D. B. (1991). Implications of hypermedia for cognition and communication. *Impact Assessment Bulletin, 9*(1-2), 15-27.

Ericsson, K. A. & Simon, H. A. (1984). *Protocol analysis: Verbal reports as data.*

Fischer, P. M. & Mandl, H. (1990). Toward a psychophysics of hypermedia. In: D. H. Jonassen & Mandl, H. (Eds.), *Designing hypermedia for learning* (pp. XIX-XXV). Berlin: Springer-Verlag.

Glaser, B. G. & Strauss, A. L. (1967). *The discovery of grounded theory: Strategies for qualitative research.* New York: Aldine.

Halasz, F. & Conklin, J. (1989). Issues in the design and application of hypermedia systems. In *CHI '89,* Tutorial #26 . Austin: Texas.

Heller, R. S. (1990, Summer). The role of hypermedia in education: A look at the research issues. *Journal of Research on Computing in Education,* pp. 431-441.

Jonassen, D. H. (1989). *Hypertext/hypermedia.* Englewood Cliffs, NJ: Educational Technology Publications.

Jonassen, D. H. & Grabinger, S. R. (1990). Problems and issues in designing hypertext/hypermedia for learning. In: D. H. Jonassen & H. Mandl (Eds.), *Designing hypermedia for learning* (pp. 3-26). Berlin: Springer-Verlag.

McKeachie, W. J. (1984). Spatial strategies: Critique and educational implications. In: C. D. Holley & D. F. Dansereau (Eds.), *Spatial learning strategies: Techniques, applications, and related issues* (pp. 301-312). Orlando, FL: Academic Press.

Morariu, J. (1988). Hypermedia in instruction and training: The power and the promise. *Educational Technology, 28*(11), 17-20.

Reeves, T. C. & Harmon, S. W. (1991). What's in a name: Hypermedia vs. multimedia. *Interact, 3*(1), 28-30.

Trujillo, I. (1989). Academic Computing: The los andes project.

Tsai, C. J. (1988). Hypertext: Technology, applications, and research issues. *Journal of Educational Technology Systems, 17*(1), 3-14.

David B. Palumbo
Andrea B. Bermúdez

Using Hypermedia to Assist Language Minority Learners in Achieving Academic Success

Much of the discussion about the potential impact of hypermedia has centered on ways that such systems may become infused into our society. Current applications tend to focus on the presentation of information; a few wrestle with the challenges of representing information in an advanced storage and retrieval system. Some developers are proposing a next generation of hypermedia that will target the construction of knowledge.

The power of hypermedia applications can be seen in three characteristics that relate directly to their uses as presentation tools, representation tools, and construction tools (Collier, 1987):

1. Printed knowledge is inherently linear and often has arbitrary ordering forced on it by the print medium. Hypermedia systems eliminate such constraints in the presentation of information, allowing users to browse more freely through a data structure.
2. Links enable semantically and logically related information to be tied together in conceptual webs. Using this representational archi-

DAVID B. PALUMBO is Director, The Advanced Knowledge Transfer Lab and Associate Professor of Instructional Technology, University of Houston-Clear Lake, Houston, TX 77058.
ANDREA B. BERMÚDEZ is Professor of Bilingual and Multicultural Education, School of Education, University of Houston-Clear Lake, Houston, TX 77058.

[Haworth co-indexing entry note]: "Using Hypermedia to Assist Language Minority Learners in Achieving Academic Success." Palumbo, David B. and Andrea B. Bermúdez. Co-published simultaneously in *Computers in the Schools* (The Haworth Press, Inc.) Vol. 10, No. 1/2, 1994, pp. 171-188; and: *Multimedia and Megachange: New Roles for Educational Computing* (eds: W. Michael Reed, John K. Burton, and Min Liu) The Haworth Press, Inc., 1994, pp. 171-188. Multiple copies of this article/chapter may be purchased from The Haworth Document Delivery Center [1-800-3-HAWORTH; 9:00 a.m. - 5:00 p.m. (EST)].

tecture allows hypermedia systems to mirror some of the associational power of human memory.

3. Linear information systems support only part of the potential web of interconnections. Authors choose which interconnections to present based on a hypothetical "typical" user. Since the prior knowledge, experiences, and learning style of all potential readers cannot be accommodated, many users may be unable to adequately transfer desired information into their cognitive structures; the appropriate semantic relationships may be missing. Hypermedia, on the other hand, holds the potential for users to access tools by which they can construct personalized transitions between the information to be accessed and their cognitive structure. This would truly individualize the information environment.

HYPERMEDIA AS A PRESENTATION SYSTEM

As a presentation system, the ability of hypermedia applications to exhibit information in a multimedia framework is emphasized. In fact, much of the excitement of lower end hypermedia systems, such as *HyperCard*™ and *SuperCard,*™ tends to focus on their multimedia aspects rather than on the nonlinear attributes critical to any hypermedia application.

This emphasis on hypermedia as a presentation system is exemplified in Oren's (1987) discussion positing that the designers of hypermedia applications should focus on constructing the most useful pathway for users to proceed through the information in a particular data structure. His position is that hypermedia design should anticipate the needs of the learner and present information accordingly.

However, hypermedia applications optimized as vehicles for capturing, structuring, and presenting information will not necessarily be used to their fullest potential as knowledge representation systems. For this to occur, the representational process within hypermedia will need to become more formal.

To facilitate the movement of hypermedia systems from presentation systems toward representation systems, more attention should be placed on the underlying processes required for human knowledge representation. It is not sufficient to present information on a computer screen and assume that this will be accurately, adequately, and completely transferred to the knowledge base of the learner. Even multiple modes of presentation (a current theme of hypermedia proponents) do not assure such transfer. As hypermedia systems move from knowledge presentation to knowledge representation, the issue of knowledge transfer will be key.

HYPERMEDIA AS KNOWLEDGE REPRESENTATION

As a representational architecture, much is made of the similarity of hypermedia to current models of long-term memory. In fact, the definition of *representation* as the capacity to picture in the mind a mental image or idea leads one to such parallels. A common terminology also promotes such a relationship; nodes and links are the metaphor for both cognitive models of memory and semantic webs in hypermedia.

Nodes and links are also a common ground between artificial intelligence and linguistics researchers, but practitioners in these disciplines have been hesitant to claim that they are referring to the same entities. In fact, the field of cognitive science has evolved to reconcile the psychological, linguistic, and computer science conceptions of knowledge representation and to promote a more multidisciplinary approach to study in this important area.

While one of the often touted aspects of hypermedia is its ability to support the emergent properties of the representation process, researchers are beginning to realize that current hypermedia systems have failed to fully develop this capability. Specific inquiry into the fundamental aspects of nodes and links are needed if hypermedia is to become a sophisticated knowledge representation system.

For example, current systems differ in the way information is captured by the nodes in a hypermedia web. One difference is that, in systems such as *Intermedia,*™ the information is stored as nodes; other systems, such as *Thoth-II*, separate the nodes and the information they contain. The benefit of this second type of system is that more complex connections between units of information are empowered, allowing an explicit conception of the knowledge representation to be conveyed from the designer to the user (Collier, 1987).

Hypermedia applications also differ in the amount of information that may be placed in the nodes of this second type of system. One type, exemplified by *Textnet*, allows only one unit of information to be placed in a particular node. The principle behind the *Thoth-II* system, on the other hand, is to allow for multiple units of knowledge to be placed in any node.

An extension of such a system would promote levels of structure within a hypermedia environment. Information at one level of complexity could be combined and collapsed into a larger composite node. For example, the HAKCS hypermedia system for physics instruction (Lidwell, Hobbins, Troutman, & Palumbo, 1991) breaks the physical domain into certain expertly defined concepts, which are then further broken into specific units of information. As users demonstrate mastery of prespecified sub-domains, HAKCS collapses the micronetwork presenting that sub-domain into a composite node. For example, if the primary domain is wave dynamics, one sub-domain would be the Doppler effect. Once the user has demonstrated mastery of the micronetworks comprising the concept of Doppler effect (by constructing appropriate associations between nodes), then those micronetworks would be collapsed into a composite node representing Doppler effect. That node, then, may be associatively linked with other composite nodes, and so on, until the entire network has been constructed and then may be collapsed into the primary domain node.

As hypermedia systems move from mere presenters of information to more sophisticated knowledge representational vehicles, the use of linkages is also a critical issue. "In many representations, a key decision centers around the distribution of meaning–should links or cards carry the semantic burden?" (Marshall 1987, p.265). Ideally, the semantic weight of a hypermedia system needs to be equably distributed between its nodes and links, as neither entity is capable of conveying the full associational meaning in isolation.

While much of the semantic weight was placed on the nodes in early hypermedia networks, current implementations are moving more of this burden to links. The possibility of making "value" a link property would be beneficial in developing more complete knowledge representation systems in hypermedia.

Such systems would more readily parallel its human counterpart. It is clear to see that simply stating that a node "apple" *is associated with* a node "fruit" does not convey as much information as stating the "apple" *is an example* of "fruit." However, if link types are used for too many semantically orthogonal purposes, performing a representational task or interpreting the results of an analysis may become confusing.

One future direction of hypermedia is to develop systems that are capable of capturing knowledge representations via some type of concrete structure that could then be reapplied to other knowledge bases. Such systems would parallel human metacognition, in that they could begin to address generalizable association that could then be applied to novel information. With the incorporation of artificial intelligence components, such systems could self-generate meaningful associational links between nodes, as well as assign them appropriate "values."

HYPERMEDIA AS KNOWLEDGE CONSTRUCTION

A key claim of hypermedia proponents is that these systems will be effective as a teaching medium: Users can access a large knowledge base and seek out information that meets their particular needs, in terms of both their prior knowledge and their preferred learning style. The development of systems to achieve these ends seems possible. However, simply providing an advanced presentation system, or even a more elaborate information storage and retrieval system that parallels the way the human brain represents knowledge, does not guarantee that more effective or efficient learning will occur (Locatis, Letourneau, & Banvard, 1989).

A more constructivist environment–where the user not only browses the information base but also has the ability to build additional nodes and links–holds more promise to promote learning.

One key to such environments is the level of interactivity promoted by the system. While a system that provides the user with a choice of direction in terms of information presentation does promote some level of user control, and therefore interactivity, such interaction is focused at a very basic level. On the other hand, a system that also challenges the user to actively connect information to other nodes, to add additional information, and even to question and/or extend the relationships defined by the hypermedia designer, provides a much higher level of interactivity. Many hypermedia systems support such an environment, yet little has been done to promote this obvious advantage.

Raskin (1987) laments that hypermedia has been heralded with mostly uncritical attention. While he does state that current implementations of hypermedia are worth pursuing, he strongly cautions that they may fail to realize the expectations currently promised. His criticisms focus mainly on technological and user-interface design limitations that seem addressable in the near term. However, this line of argument also leads to more daunting concerns in that current directions in hypermedia development may focus too heavily on the presentational features and storage/retrieval capabilities necessary for sophisticated representational systems. Instead, to achieve the full potential of hypermedia systems, developers should target empowering users to actively construct information via typed linkages. Developmental research in creating such constructive systems would be more strongly grounded in the psychological literature on learning and transfer than in the human factors and technological design community.

Such research needs to focus on critical issues of knowledge construction and knowledge transfer. The optimal degree of user-centered control also needs to be addressed, as purely discovery environments do not tend to produce effective or efficient knowledge construction or transfer to other domains. Construction of hypermedia systems that support the construction of metacognitive and problem-solving environments also merit considerable attention.

A key issue in the emergence of hypermedia is the ability of these systems to promote learning in an effective and efficient manner. The term HAI (hypermedia-assisted instruction) has been proposed to describe the use of such systems (Heller, 1990). To extend hypermedia beyond the traditional uses of computers in instructional settings (drill and practice, tutorials, simulations), Heller believes that current hypermedia systems must be augmented. However, the issues that she addresses focus on presentation and interface concerns rather than on allowing the user to construct knowledge from within the hypermedia environment. To build effective hypermedia learning environments, the focus of such systems needs to include essential characteristic of effective learning environments as well as successful implementations of computer technologies.

CREATING HYPERMEDIA-BASED INDIVIDUALIZED LEARNING ENVIRONMENTS

The ability to individualize information access to accommodate the diversity of possible users has traditionally been a strength of instructional technology. As our society continues to evolve toward a diverse world-wide village, developing single-mode instruction designed for the needs of a "typical" learner is increasingly ineffective; no ethnic or cultural majority dominates the user population. Technologies that can individualize to the multiple, wide-ranging differences inherent in the global marketplace are needed.

Traditional computer-assisted instruction (CAI) is limited in that it can realistically only accommodate differences in the rate at which users progress through the information base. Approaches more sophisticated than CAI to individualizing educational tools are necessary; proponents of hypermedia believe that their systems, if used for knowledge construction, could fill the need to tailor learning environments for the evolving demands of a global information society.

Hypermedia and Learning Styles

Research supports the claim that cultural influences have an effect on the cognitive learning styles exhibited by individuals (Ramirez & Price-Williams, 1974; Witkin, 1967). Learners' cultural background may effect differences in both their cognitive skills and intellectual performance. Children of different cultural and linguistic groups exhibit significant variations in both cognitive and sensory perceptions.

Cohen (1969) has identified two basic learning styles: analytic and relational. Those who learn in an analytic style view information as bounded, objective, and isolated (rather than intrinsic to some context). Those who exhibit a relational learning style instead see information as embedded in a larger environment and as inherently unbounded and subjective. Kirby (1979) indicates that, to address the cognitive learning styles of all students, information environments should be structured bicognitively. Otherwise, the many pupils who do not function effectively in the analytically structured environment typical of current educational practice will be poor achievers.

A crucial, and yet often neglected, aspect of effective information transfer is ascertaining and accommodating users' learning styles (Ausubel, 1968). Research suggests that learners who were taught by their preferred method achieved better, were more interested in the subject matter, liked the way the subject was taught, and wanted other instructional situations to be taught in a similar manner (Smith & Rezulli, 1984). Matching the presentation style of the information with the desired learning style of the pupil enhances cognitive outcomes and encourages students to become more involved in the learning process.

Hypermedia as a Flexible Instructional Environment

Hypermedia-based systems allow the user to redefine both the structure and content of the material to be learned. When compared to traditional forms of information presentation, this capability alters the constraints and opportunities for conveying information. The power of such a tool can be seen as both subtle and incremental; yet we need to harness this power to effectively and efficiently develop training programs that meet the requirements of the information age (Conklin, 1987).

In traditional forms of instruction, learners most often are presented with information in a sequentially formatted environment. Hypermedia, on the other hand, allows the learner to determine the order of access for any information in the knowledge base (Jonassen, 1988). Learners need not be constrained by the initial structure imposed by either the database designer or the instructor. Since learners each have unique knowledge structures based on their experiences and abilities, the ways that they choose to access, interact, and interrelate information in the knowledge base will also vary. Hypermedia-based learning environments allow the knowledge base to accommodate the learner rather than the learner accommodating the knowledge base.

A major characteristic of hypermedia environments is that they enable users to link information together in multiple ways and to make these relationships explicit. Instructors and learners may create different pathways through the hypermedia knowledge base. Users can also annotate the knowledge base by creating notes, explanations, and analogies.

To realize maximum effectiveness from this type of environment, learners should be encouraged to explore information, to make associational links and relationships, and even to alter the knowledge base as a means of achieving greater understanding, given their previous experiences and learning style. Hypermedia offers the potential to construct an environment that allows for these beneficial activities (Jonassen, 1986).

A major goal of hypermedia is to provide a learning environment that facilitates exploration. This type of learning environment provides immediate access to large collections of information. The most distinct aspect of hypermedia learning environments is their ability, in a node-link framework based upon semantic structures, to portray an accurate structural description of the knowledge base they are representing. Hypermedia offers advances from previously available technologies since it is strongly connected with a cognitive conceptual framework; yet this framework does not limit or constrain its possible application.

Cognitive Load

A second potential benefit of hypermedia-based individualized learning environments is the possibility of decreasing the cognitive load associated with accessing information from within such an environment. Any information presentation/retrieval system has some load associated with its operation: Users must wrestle with issues of learnability, efficiency, ease of remembering, and error frequency. The amount of time a user must devote to such operational issues directly increases the amount of time and cognitive energy required to effectively interact with the information system. In turn, the efficiency of usage is adversely affected; systems that decrease cognitive load enable more effective utilization.

Nielsen (1990) addresses five usability parameters that are directly related to cognitive load. These include the ease with which the operation of the hypermedia system is learned, how efficiently the system can be used once the user has learned its effective operational structure, how easily the operation of the system is remembered from one interaction to the next, the number and cost of errors associated with system operation, and how pleasant the system is to use.

If hypermedia systems can optimize the usability parameters addressed above through knowledge construction features, this would decrease the cognitive load they require. However, compared with other methods of information access, cognitive load may still remain as one of the largest drawbacks of hypermedia environments.

The question of how much and at what level information should be presented to the user is often at the heart of such concerns. Issues of how many simultaneously displayed nodes should be allowed on any given screen and of how many links any one node of information should support are questions that need further investigation. To see how strongly these issues are tied to the theme of cognitive load, one of the prevailing sentiments in this area is that the number of nodes displayed and the number of links allowed per node should be limited to seven: a direct connection to Miller's (1956) assessment of the limits of human working memory.

Novice/Expert Users of Hypermedia

Another key issue in the use of hypermedia as an individualized learning environment is the prior expertise and knowledge requirements of the intended user. While knowledge presentation systems may be very useful to those considered expert in the content area of a particular hypermedia, such presentation systems do not hold the key learning tools required by novices beginning to use a particular knowledge base.

Learning theorists are beginning to view learning as the construction of mental models. Norman (1983) notes that such mental models are characteristically unique, incomplete, and lack essential information. Current implementations of hypermedia as individualized learning environments presume the existence of specific prerequisite knowledge and the ability of the learner to draw successfully from that knowledge. However, since these required mental models are inherently incomplete for the novice learner, information presentation systems will not successfully accommodate their construction of correct and complete mental models in the desired domain.

While there is a continuum between novices and experts in a particular knowledge area, a bi-polar distinction between experts and non-experts is appropriate in interpreting the potential of hypermedia as a learning tool. Problems with cognitive overload, user disorientation, superficial browsing and disinterest often reported by users of hypermedia may well center on the issue of the level of experience of the user. Thus, while current hypermedia systems may well decrease the cognitive load of those users closer to the expert end of the continuum, they may well increase the load on users less familiar with the content of the knowledge base or the navigation of nonlinear structures. Even more devastating would be if such systems would promote the development of incorrect mental models for novice learners, which would then prove difficult to correct or modify (Fisher & Lipson, 1985).

Thus, while hypermedia does provide a potential environment for the construction of individualized learning environments, hypermedia does not stand alone as such an environment. Several critical issues, including the construction of appropriate mental models, transfer of knowledge, cognitive learning style, and cognitive load need to be more fully investigated if hypermedia systems are to provide the type of individual learning environment needed to meet the needs of our society as we move into the 21st century.

HYPERMEDIA'S POTENTIAL FOR LANGUAGE MINORITY LEARNERS

These issues are exacerbated by the fact that the new literacy created by these emerging technologies and the inherent need to constantly update information has widened the gap between the mainstream and the various minority groups, particularly language minorities. Ethnic minorities and women, for instance, have been historically underrepresented in science, mathematics, and technology careers. In 1986, women accounted for 15% of the employed scientists; African-Americans, 2%; and Hispanics, 2% (National Science Foundation, 1988). In addition, access to technology has been substantially unequal for these groups (Tichenor, Donohue, & Olien, 1970; Paisley, 1985).

Concurrently, labor market projections indicate a strong demand for literacy, science, mathematics, and technology to satisfy the needs of the information-intensive society of the 90s. Because fewer students are pursuing careers in mathematics, science, and technology, a labor supply/demand crisis is projected. This scenario is particularly critical for minority students and women who by third grade are already exiting the scientific pipeline to nonacademic curricular tracks that keep them unexposed to the skills needed to succeed in the labor market (Oakes, 1990).

These facts, coupled with the rapidly changing demographics and the uneven distribution of educational resources, call for fundamental changes in the infrastructure of the schools. The 1990 U.S. Census reported a dramatic increase in minority populations during the last decade. Hispanics, for example, increased by 53%; Asians by 108%; and African-Americans by 13.2%; while the Anglo population increased moderately (4.4%). By the year 2000, it is predicted that the Hispanic school population will increase to 35% (Oxford-Carpenter et al., 1984). Demographic trends indicate that the white youth population will be declining after the year 2000, while its nonwhite counterpart will increase 8% from 1990 to 2010 (Hodgkinson, 1991). It has been reported that in the nation's largest 15 school districts minority enrollment already comprises 70 to 96% of the total school population (Hodgkinson, 1986).

In examining the escalating dropout rates of minority populations, it becomes evident that schools have failed in meeting the educational needs of these students (e.g., U.S. General Accounting Office Report, 1987). Approximately 682,000 American teenagers dropped out of school during the 1985-1986 academic year, producing an average of 3,789 dropouts a day over 180 school days (OERI, 1987). Thus, students who drop out of school will have limited occupational and economic opportunities.

Failure to achieve academically is correlated to the student's ability to understand the language of the classroom (Valverde, 1984). Additionally, having parents with low level education and limited English proficiency is a critical factor in placing students at-risk of dropping out of school (Hodgkinson, 1991). These issues force educational reforms to take into consideration the population that is to benefit. The issue of linguistic and cultural differences, therefore, cannot be overlooked in planning strategies to deal with the school dropout population (Bermúdez & Rakow, in press). According to the 1980 U.S. Census, approximately sixteen million homes communicate in a non-English language. In addition, from 3.5 to 5.5 million limited English proficient (LEP) students are currently enrolled in our public schools (Waggoner, 1986).

Schools lack training in how to deal with these increasing populations of students. Knowledge about language and cultural acquisition remains elusive for the largely monolingual/monocultural school personnel making instructional and, therefore, life-decisions for LEP students. Three critical instructional areas need to be examined in order to adequately address the educational needs of language minority students: (a) role of the student, (b) negotiation of meaning, and (c) the impact of social interaction and cognitive interaction on second language development.

Hypermedia and the LEP Student

Role of the Student

Hypermedia enables intuitive, "how-to" learning opportunities for students in contrast to the more traditional approach which underscores teacher-generated and controlled instruction. Since hypermedia is self-paced and student-centered, it offers students unique opportunities to tap into their prior knowledge and experiences by allowing them to create their own paths through the information web presented. Levels of fluency, knowledge, motivation, and interest are addressed individually; hence, inclusion of culturally and linguistically-diverse populations is ensured in the learning process.

The need for students to develop an internal locus of control in learning is critical in language and cultural development as students must become their own monitors of comprehension, language production, and behavior. Using a student-controlled medium for learning activates the strategies necessary for self-evaluation and cognitive augmentation.

Social and Cognitive Interaction

Second language classroom research suggests that teacher tendency to dominate the classroom speech jeopardizes student opportunities to interact and develop conceptually and linguistically (Legarretta, 1977; Ramírez et al., 1986). Newman (1985) stresses the importance of student participation in classroom exchanges if language is to develop naturally as happens when young children develop it at home.

Because hypermedia is interactive, it helps to enhance the inherent social nature of language. Meaning is negotiated as students construct and manipulate information, interact with peers, teachers, and other significant individuals. Concepts and language become associated and relationships between and among concepts strengthened. Students discover novel relationships and learn to relate them to already established knowledge. Hypermedia focuses attention on relationships rather than isolated facts, thus facilitating important language development processes, including concept formation, comprehension, remembering, retention, and retrieval.

This conceptual flow and interconnection of ideas is facilitated in hypermedia by the fact that the presentation of information is not constrained to a physical space (i.e., one page, one chapter, one book, etc.). In addition, hypermedia provides ample opportunity for concept exploration (prior and new knowledge). This exploration must be purposeful to avoid losing the student in "hyperspace." Since schemas are idiosyncratic because of their dependence upon student prior experiences, links can become a personal journey. This fact poses a great challenge to teachers who are trained in a linear, outcome-based pedagogy. Furthermore, the non-linear presentation of materials emulates knowledge acquisition by facilitating associations (*links*) between and among concepts (*nodes*) (e.g., Horn, 1989).

Focus on Context

Particularly important to second language learners is a clear context that facilitates comprehension and retention of concepts. Graphics, sound, animation, and other forms of information transfer that simulate real-life situations, are possible with hypermedia. Activities that are authentic, interactive, context-embedded, and purposeful contribute to the attainment of meaning and thus promote second language acquisition (Enright & McCloskey, 1985).

Hypermedia and Language Development

Researchers and linguists have identified the following necessary, but not sufficient, conditions for second language development: (a) language is acquired more naturally as learners share a concrete task that removes the anxiety associated with the "learning" of a second language (Chamot & O'Malley, 1987; Bermúdez & Rakow, in press); (b) language acquisition/learning is an involved cognitive, affective, and psychomotor process; therefore, instructional tasks must emphasize problem solving, critical thinking, and social interaction (Padrón & Bermúdez, 1988; Bermúdez & Prater, 1990); (c) a meaningful context must be provided for vocabulary and concept development with opportunities for students to relate concepts in unique ways; (d) listening, speaking, reading, and writing practice must be provided concurrently to ensure access to the learner's strongest learning modality; and (e) attention to various learning modalities must be provided as different activities or media are brought into the learning situation.

Concrete Tasks: A Key to Negotiation of Meaning. Hypermedia provides an opportunity to enhance the visual presentation with other modalities such as sound and animation. As a result, the real world can be integrated into the classroom experience. As the learning environment becomes less abstract, associations between concepts and words are strengthened without the usual anxiety created by traditional language classrooms. Sharing these experiences with other learners enhances the process of negotiating meaning.

Language Acquisition: A Complex Process. Because language development involves several domains, the cognitive, affective, and psychomotor aspects of learning have to be considered in order to provide a comprehensive language medium. Working in a multimedia environment allows for opportunities to think, feel, create, dialog, and physically act and control learning. Student empowerment is evidenced through the multiple decisions that he/she must make for learning to take place.

The Need for a Meaningful Context to Enhance Associations. Because of the similarity between hypermedia and current models of long-term memory and semantic webs, a potential for language and concept development for LEP learners is apparent. Meaning is enhanced as the context becomes tangible and tailored to the individual's prior knowledge and ability to construct further associations. Pace and the amount of learning in conjunction with the sequence of information are key issues in providing meaning for individual learners. Traditional methodologies tend to standardize these issues based on the false assumption that all learners are a homogeneous target who apply the same strategies to the learning task, share a similar learning focus, and define the roles of learner/teacher in the same fashion. It is evident that hypermedia–with its potential to offer students opportunities to learn at a different pace, to choose how much learning can take place, and to be in control of this decision-making process–can be more effective in providing access to learning for culturally and linguistically diverse populations.

Whole Language Environment. Whole language activities are those that support students in the development and use of meaningful language (Newman, 1985). Students learn about reading and writing while listening; they learn about writing from reading and gain insights into reading from writing. They can best learn to read and write in much the same way they learned to speak (Hollingsworth & Reutzel, 1988). This approach to learning is particularly successful with LEP learners (Goodman, Goodman, & Hood, 1988). Many students, especially linguistically different students, have few opportunities to read or write prose during the school day (Goodlad, 1984) because their instruction usually focuses on remedial rather than developmental activities. In addition, most language instruction is extensively part to whole (Freeman, 1987). Any strategy or approach based on dissecting language into mutually exclusive components jeopardizes second language acquisition by not drawing on the prior knowledge and strengths of the learner and by not providing information in an integrated fashion (Bermudez & Prater, 1990; Freeman, 1988).

Teachers can support the language learning capabilities of students through a variety of hypermedia activities that promote the transference of skills across languages (i.e., the ability to shift information back and forth from listening, speaking, reading, and writing to produce language). An appropriate level of instruction slightly above students' output level can be used to encourage language development (Bereiter & Scardamalia, 1982).

Providing for Individual Differences in Learning. Three learning modalities have been identified in literature as the most common methods of acquiring information: visual, auditory, and tactile-kinesthetic. Although most people learn through a combination of all three modalities, each person has a preferred style of learning. Visual learners use their eyes as a primary medium for gathering information. Text, graphics, and illustrations, for example, reinforce this approach to learning. Auditory learners, on the other hand, require sound as the main access to retain information, while the tactile-kinesthetic learner needs to become physically involved through touch and motion to be successful in learning. In order to provide for a variety of teaching/learning experiences, exposure to all modalities is critical. It is evident that a hypermedia environment has the potential for integrating all three modalities thus facilitating the matching between learning and instruction.

SUMMARY AND CONCLUSIONS

Hypermedia environments are not inherently instructional (Nelson & Palumbo, 1991); however, they do hold the promise of providing an environment for the development of instruction. A central feature of these environments will be active student involvement. Students need to become active builders of knowledge, inherently challenged to create new insights from the information provided. An old adage states that "knowledge is power." As we move into the information age, some have proposed a change to "access to knowledge is power." This does not seem to hold true, however. With rapidly accessible information dissemination and retrieval tools, almost everyone will have access to unlimited stores of information. A key component of our educational system, therefore, will require a shift from presenting information to successfully interacting with available information to solve the variety of problems that will be present as our society continues to evolve.

Concurrently, we are faced with an ever-changing student population base, one in which there is the need to accommodate various cognitive and cultural differences. It is no longer wise to assume that everyone will obtain academic success in the same fashion. Nor is it feasible to continue to design educational environments that attempt to teach everyone the same material. If our society is to continue to advance, we will need to harness the intellectual and creative potential that our diversity brings.

Hypermedia environments seem to allow for the development of the type of educational environments that are required as we move into the next century. However, potential does not always lead to successful implementation. The costs of developing such environments will be significant. We must also begin to incorporate new insights from the field of cognitive science into our educational system. As we continue to gain broader understanding of the learning process, this needs to be successfully integrated into our instructional systems. Hypermedia holds the potential of providing tools for such an enterprise.

REFERENCES

Ausubel, D. (1968). Educational psychology: *A cognitive view*. New York: Holt, Rinehart and Winston.

Bereiter C. & Scardamalia, M. (1982). From conversation to composition: The role of instruction in a developmental process. In: R. Glaser (Ed.), *Advances in instructional psychology*, Hillsdale, New York: Lawrence Erlbaum.

Bermúdez, A. B. & Rakow, S. J. (in press). Enhancing science achievement and attitudes in LEP students. *The Journal of Educational Issues of Language Minority Students, 11*.

Bermúdez, A. B. & Prater, D. L. (1990). Using brainstorming and clustering with LEP writers to develop elaborative skills. *TESOL Quarterly, 24*, 523-527.

Chamot, A. U. & O'Malley, I. M. (1987). The cognitive academic language learning approach: A bridge to the mainstream. *TESOL Quarterly, 21*(2), 227-249.

Cohen, R. (1969). Conceptual styles, culture conflict, and nonverbal tests of intelligence. *American Anthropologist, 71*, 828-856.

Collier, G. H. (1987). Thoth-II: Hypertext with explicit semantics. *Hypertext '87 Proceedings* (pp. 269-290). New York: Association for Computing Machinery Press.

Conklin, J. (1987). Hypertext: A survey and introduction. *IEEE Computer, 20*(9), 17-40.

Enright, D. S. & McCloskey (1985). Yes, Talking! Organizing the classroom to promote second language acquisition. *TESOL Quarterly, 19*(3), 431-453.

Fisher, K. M. & Lipson, J. I. (1985). Information processing interpretation of errors in college science learning. *Instructional Science, 14*, 49-79.

Freeman, Y. S. (1988). Do Spanish methods and materials reflect current understanding of the reading process? *Reading Teacher, 7*, 654-662.

Freeman, Y. S. (1987). *The Contemporary Spanish Basal in the United States*. Unpublished doctoral dissertation, University of Arizona, Tucson, AZ.

Goodlad, J. I. (1984). *A place called school: Prospects for the future*, New York: McGraw Hill.

Goodman, K. S., Goodman, Y. M., & Hood, W. J. (1988). *The whole language evaluation book*. Portsmouth, NH: Heineman.

Heller, R. S. (1990) The role of hypermedia in education: A look at the research issues. *Journal of Research on Computing in Education, 22*, 431-441.

Hodgkinson, H. (1991). Reform versus reality. *Kappan, 73* (1), 9-16.

Hodgkinson, H. L. (1986). Texas: The state and its educational system. Washington, DC: The Institute for Educational Leadership.

Hollingsworth, P. M. & Reutzel, D. R. (1988). Whole language with LD children. *Academic Therapy. 23* (5), 477-487.

Horn, R. E. (1989). *Mapping hypertext: The analysis, organization, and display of knowledge for the next generation of on-line text and graphics*. Lexington, MA: The Lexington Institute.

Jonassen, D. H. (1986). Hypertext principles for text and courseware design. *Educational Psychologist, 21*(4), 269-292.

Jonassen, D. H. (1988). Designing structured hypertext and structuring access to hypertext. *Educational Technology*, pp. 13-16.

Kirby, P. (1979). Cognitive style, learning style, and transfer skill acquisition. Information Series Number 195. Columbus: Ohio State University, National Center for Research in Vocational Education.

Legaretta, D. (1977). Language choice in bilingual classrooms. *TESOL Quarterly, 11*, 9-16.

Lidwell, W., Hobbins, W., Troutman, T., & Palumbo, D. (1991). *HAKCS: A Hypermedia-assisted knowledge construction system.* Paper presented at the annual conference of the Southwest Educational Research Association, San Antonio, TX.

Locatis, C., Letourneau, G., & Banvard, R. (1989.) Hypermedia and instruction. *Educational Technology Research and Development, 37* (4), 65-77.

Marshall, C. C. (1987). Exploring representation problems using hypertext. *Hypertext '87 Proceedings* (pp. 253-268). New York: Association for Computing Machinery Press.

Miller, G. A. (1956). The magical number seven, plus or minus two: Some limits on our capacity for processing information. *Psychology Review, 63*, 81-97.

National Science Foundation (1988). *Women and minorities in science and engineering*. Washington, DC: National Science Foundation.

Nelson, W. A. & Palumbo, D. B. (1992). Learning, instruction, and hypermedia. *Journal of Educational Multimedia and Hypermedia, 1*, 287-299.

Newman, J. M. (1985). *Whole language in context.* Boston: Heinie & Heinie.

Nielsen, J. (1990). *Hypertext and hypermedia.* Boston: Academic Press.

Norman, D. A. (1983). Some observations on mental models. In: D. Gentner & A. Stevens (Eds.), *Mental models.* Hillsdale, NJ: Lawrence Erlbaum Associates.

Oakes, J. (1990). *Lost talent: The underparticipation of women, minorities, and disabled persons in science.* (RAND/R-3774-NSF/RC). Washington, DC: National Science Foundation.

Office of Educational Research and Improvement (1987). *Dealing with dropouts: The urban superintendents' call to action.* Washington, DC: Office of Educational Research and Improvement.

Oren, T. (1987). The architecture of static hypertext. Hypertext '87 Proceedings (pp. 291-306). New York: Association for Computing Machinery Press.

Oxford-Carpenter, R., Pol, L., López, D., Stupp, P., Gendell, M., & Peng, S. (1984). *Demographic projections of non-English-language-background and limited-English-proficient persons in the United States in the Year 2000 by state, age, and language group.* Rosslyn, VA: Interamerica Research Associates, National Clearinghouse for Bilingual Education.

Padrón, Y. N. & Bermúdez, A. B. (1988, Spring). Promoting effective writing strategies for ESL students. *Southwest Journal of Research Into Practice, 2*, 19-27.

Paisley, W. (1985). Children, new media, and microcomputers. In: M. Chen, & W. Paisley (Eds.), *Children and microcomputers* (pp. 19-35). Beverly Hills: Sage Publications.

Ramirez, M. & Price-Williams, D. (1974). Cognitive styles in children: Two Mexican communities. *Interamerican Journal of Psychology, 8*, 93-101.

Raskin, J. (1987). The hype in hypertext: A critique. Hypertext '87 Proceedings (pp. 325-330). New York: Association for Computing Machinery Press.

Smith, L. H. & Renzulli, J. S. (1984). Learning style preferences: A practical approach for teachers. *Theory into Practice, 23*(1), 44-50.

Tichenor, P. J., Donohue, G. A., & Olien, C. N. (1970). Mass media flow and differential growth in knowledge. *Public Opinion Quarterly, 34*, 158-170.

U. S. General Accounting Office (1987). *School dropouts: Survey of local programs*. Washington, DC: U. S. General Accounting Office.

Valverde, L. (1984). Underachievement and underrepresentation of Hispanics in mathematics and mathematics-related careers. *Journal for Research in Mathematics Education, 15* (2), 123-133.

Waggoner, D. (1986). Estimates of the need for bilingual education and the prospects of children being served. *IDRA Newsletter*, pp. 2-6.

Witkin, H. A. (1967). A cognitive style approach to cross-cultural research. *International Journal of Psychology*, 2, 223-250.

William M. Lidwell
David B. Palumbo
Thomas Troutman

Promoting Learning Through Hypermedia: Local versus Global Interfaces

INTRODUCTION

Hypermedia systems (nonlinear, associative multimedia) have received considerable attention as next-generation learning and communication environments. Exponents have referred to such systems as the first "knowledge medium" (Stefik, 1986), "peripheral brains" (Carlson, 1990), a "psychological landscape" (Shirk, 1991), and "the next step in civilization" (Nelson, 1989). The comments do not, of course, refer to existing hypermedia systems, but rather to the more elaborate (and literally safe) integrated systems of the future. This is as it should be, for there is current-

WILLIAM M. LIDWELL and THOMAS TROUTMAN, Senior Research Associates, The Advanced Knowledge Transfer Lab, University of Houston-Clear Lake, Houston, TX 77508.
DAVID B. PALUMBO is Director, The Advanced Knowledge Transfer Lab and Associate Professor of Instructional Technology, University of Houston-Clear Lake, Houston, TX 77058.
This research was supported through funding from the Texas Center for Educational Technology (TCET).

[Haworth co-indexing entry note]: "Promoting Learning Through Hypermedia: Local versus Global Interfaces." Lidwell, William M., David B. Palumbo, and Thomas Troutman. Co-published simultaneously in *Computers in the Schools* (The Haworth Press, Inc.) Vol. 10, No. 1/2, 1994, pp. 189-197; and: *Multimedia and Megachange: New Roles for Educational Computing* (eds: W. Michael Reed, John K. Burton, and Min Liu) The Haworth Press, Inc., 1994, pp. 189-197. Multiple copies of this article/chapter may be purchased from The Haworth Document Delivery Center [1-800-3-HAWORTH; 9:00 a.m. - 5:00 p.m. (EST)].

ly little, if any, empirical support favoring hypermedia-based instructional or communication systems over traditional, linear systems or approaches (Jonassen, 1991; Locatis, Letourneau, & Banvard, 1989). Much of the excitement surrounding hypermedia arises amidst talk of a new medium of communication. Hypermedia is often represented as the latest in an evolutionary progression of communication media whose phylogeny includes artifacts such as the spoken word, written word, still images, and full-motion images (Dede & Palumbo, 1991). With regard to education, however, we must be careful to evaluate hypermedia as a medium of education rather than a medium of communication. Communication is, after all, a necessary, but insufficient condition for learning (Gilbert, 1982).

Determining the respective quality of a genre of learning systems requires some standardized, baseline interpretation of that genre. No such baseline currently exists for hypermedia (Gygi, 1990). Interpretations range from Dede's (1990) general "associative, non-linear interconnection of multimedia materials" to Gaines and Vickers' (1988) more specific "knowledge support systems that integrate existing human knowledge transfer processes with information technology, instrumentation, and control technology, and the full range of media" (p. 1). And, although any serious, empirical attempt at evaluating hypermedia versus alternative environments is weakened by an absence of consensus of what hypermedia is, a foundation of empirical and theoretical support is absolutely necessary if hypermedia is to be taken seriously as complement to either communication or learning. Issues abound: how do (should) humans interface with hypermedia, what are the learning effects (if any), what constitutes a "sufficient" treatment in hypermedia research, to what extent does hypermedia reflect the architecture of knowledge in long-term memory, what pedagogy is appropriate for hypermedia, etc.? Dealing with these issues will require not only better research regarding the implementation of hypermedia systems, but also research regarding pedagogical and learning processes.

The present study investigated the differences between two interfaces of a single hypernetwork using brief treatment interventions (5-15 minutes). Semantic network theories (e.g., Collins & Quillian, 1972) suggest that the storage architecture of long-term memory is functionally equivalent to networks comprised of nodes (concepts) and pathways or links (directional, semantic associations between nodes). Hypermedia, based on a comparable node-link architecture, appears, at least superficially, to be an ideal medium for representing semantic networks both functionally and visually. It will be difficult to test the analogical validity of this observation, however, as long as interface issues cloud the testability of hypermedia as a medium.

The global and local interfaces used in this study represent two possible "windows" of interactions with hypermedia. Existing systems have used a wide variety of interfaces–ranging from traditional browsers to three-dimensional hyperwebs. These interfaces generally share many common themes–for example, most support some form of navigational browser. They also tend to employ system-specific approaches to revealing and concealing complexity, directing user-interaction (locus of control), customizing the hypernetwork, and browsing.

It can be said whimsically that the many faces of hypermedia have just as many interfaces, but the heterogeneity of these systems confounds general, empirical research of the basic premises of proponents: i.e., advantage of nonlinearity, associativity, multimedia, and similarity with human long-term memory. Until some consensus is achieved regarding acceptable definitions and interfaces for hypermedia, the principal claims of hypermedia will remain untestable.

METHOD

Sample

Thirty-six students enrolled in introductory instructional technology courses at a southern, land-grant university participated in this study.

Dependent Measure

A multiple choice measure requiring recall, transfer, and deductions of treatment information on Doppler Effect served as the dependent measure.

Independent Variable

Treatment. Subjects were randomly assigned to one of two treatment groups. The underlying hypernetwork in both treatments was identical as each dealt with the content domain of Doppler Effect. Subjects interacted with one of two possible interfaces in this study: (a) a global interface, or (b) a local interface. The global interface represented the whole of the hypernetwork of Doppler Effect as a two-dimensional map with "typed" links displaying their respective semantic relationships. Subjects were free to click on nodes that provided further information in the form of multimedia sequences about that node.

The local interface represented only two nodes from the network at a time, separated by a menu of possible semantic relationships. As with the global interface, subjects were free to click on the nodes to view corresponding multimedia sequences. In the local interface, subjects were asked to select the semantic relationship they thought was appropriate for describing the relationship between two nodes in the hypernetwork. Selections were deemed correct or incorrect based on their correspondence with the expert-created hypernetwork.

The main difference between these environments was that the global interface allowed the user to see (and thus browse) all the nodes and their corresponding expertly defined semantic relationships in the hypernetwork. The local interface required subjects to select the correct semantic relationship between two computer-selected nodes in the hypernetwork.

Procedures

Subjects were pre-tested on knowledge of Doppler Effect and related concepts. Subjects were then randomly placed in one of two treatment conditions and given written instructions on how to interact with the system. Both treatments were subject-centered and self-paced. Subjects were told that they could discontinue the task at any time. Upon completion of the task, subjects were given a post-test.

Analysis

To determine changes in participants' understanding of the Doppler Effect, a two-factor analysis of variance (ANOVA) with repeated measures was conducted, comparing instrument scores taken at the pre-test and post-test points. *Duncan's Multiple Range post hoc* tests were conducted to determine the actual sources of the effect.

RESULTS

A two-factor analysis of variance (ANOVA) with repeated measures yielded no significant treatment effect measures between the global interface group and the local interface group. There was no significance for the repeated measures main effect. There was, however, a significant AXB interaction: $F(1,34) = 9.706$, $p = .0037$. *Duncan's Multiple Range post hoc* analysis revealed that there was a significant performance decrease from pre-test to post-test for the global interface group (-7.556); the local interface group showed a significant increase in their performance

(11.000). (See Table 1 for the ANOVA summary information; see Figure 1 for a graph of the mean scores for each group.)

DISCUSSION

The results of this study suggest that local interfaces, which emphasize specific inter-node relationships, might foster more effective instructional interactions with hypernetworks than global interfaces, which emphasize holistic architectures. The treatment group that interacted with the local interface demonstrated significant, positive pre-test/post-test differences. The treatment group which interacted with the global interface demonstrated significant, negative pre-test/post-test differences.

It is interesting that the global interface negatively affected user knowledge of Doppler Effect. After examining pre- and post-test measures, it appeared that the subjects who interacted with the global interface retained strong visual-spatial impressions of the map, but failed to recall and/or sufficiently process the specific ways in which the various nodes within the map were related. Obviously, for post-test scores to decrease, many of the items on the pre-test that were answered correctly were later answered incorrectly on the post-test. Invariably, the items in which this occurred involved allusions to terms or experiences found in the hypernetwork not relevant to the item at hand. Hence, it seemed that knowledge that the nodes were associated in a general sense, without knowledge of the specific way in which they were associated, often led to incorrect categorizations and inferences about Doppler Effect.

TABLE 1. ANOVA Summary Information

Source	*df*	Sum of Squares	Mean Square	*F*-test	*P* value
Treatment (A)	1	.5	.5	.002	.966
subjects within groups	34	9222.111	271.239		
Repeated Measure (B)	1	53.389	53.389	.334	.5669
AB Interaction	1	1549.389	1549.389	9.706	.0037
B × subjects within groups	34	5427.222	159.624		

FIGURE 1. Mean Scores for Local and Global Interface Groups

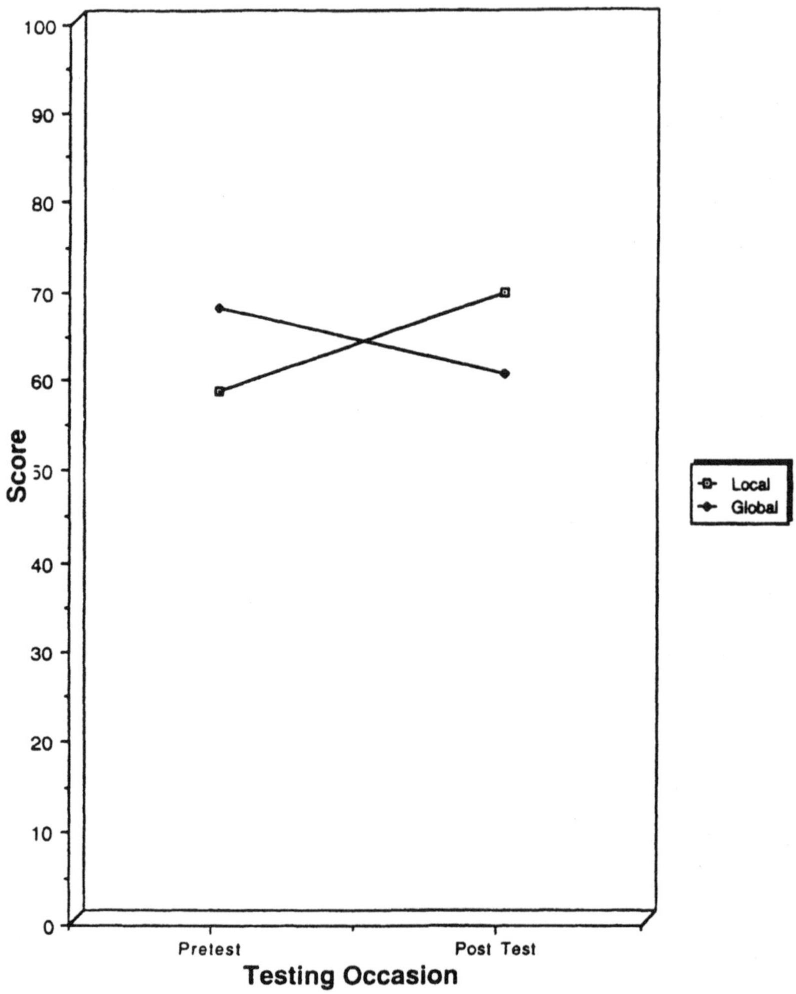

The improved performance of the local interface group is no doubt attributable to a number of possibilities. Four possible advantages seem particularly salient: (a) reduced cognitive load, (b) absence of navigational load, (c) directed interaction, (d) deeper processing of information.

The local interface reduced cognitive overhead by localizing visual representation to two nodes (versus 18 nodes on the global interface). The local interface made no provision for user browsing or navigation, requiring only that the user select the correct semantic relationship. Since further interaction with the local interface was contingent upon the selection of a semantic relationship, the local interface, in effect, directed user interaction throughout the intervention. The local interface, as stated, required users to identify specific semantic relationships between nodes. Having to consciously process the way in which two nodes were semantically related to continue the interaction might have enhanced the integration of that information into user knowledge bases. Bobrow and Bower (1969) found that the depth at which information is meaningfully processed is positively related to recall performance. This would adequately explain both the improved performance of the local interface group and the diminished performance of the global interface group.

Conklin (1987) suggested that the unique representational and navigational difficulties associated with hypermedia predisposes hypermedia systems to problems of user disorientation and cognitive overhead. A number of hypermedia-based system designs have since emerged in an attempt to address these problems (Lidwell, Palumbo, & Troutman, 1991; Dede, 1991; Fairchild & Wexelblat, 1989), but little empirical support has been provided to corroborate the instructional validity of the various designs.

The results of this study are consistent with Conklin's claim that issues of disorientation and cognitive overhead are problematic. They point to other issues of navigational load, directed interaction, and intensity of treatment. The results also suggest possible advantages for interfaces which foster "deep" processing of information, rather than traditional navigational browsers or paging models. These issues, collectively, represent necessary directions of future research if hypermedia is ever to become more than the "programmed instruction" of yesteryear.

CONCLUSION

Philosopher Arthur Schopenhauer advocated what he called the "natural method" of education. To Schopenhauer, depth of knowledge required depth of experience. The whole of the experience, its essence, is only attainable through natural experiences (first-hand exposure). Natural education, then, was defined as an education comprised entirely of natural experiences. The trend in education, even in Schopenhauer's time, was toward "artificial" experiences (second-hand experiences; e.g., reading, listening about, etc.).

The idea of a wholly natural education is obviously impractical–or is it? Providing students with hands-on experience is the current fad in education. Children are conducting actual scientific investigations, creating computer programs in a variety of programming languages, and building robots using construction kits like Lego/Logo. These activities are genuine, fulfilling experiences that get at the heart of Schopenhauer's philosophy.

But what of those experiences that do not involve the physical construction or manipulation of something? What of experiences like seeing the Grand Canyon, hearing the fugues of Bach, or exploring the moons of Jupiter? How can such experiences be presented in an economically feasible and "natural" fashion? The answer might be hypermedia. Certainly, Schopenhauer had no conception of the types of technologies that are or soon will be. Presently, most experiences can be presented in near complete form through hypermedia technology. In the future, virtual realities will provide even more complete, and perhaps perfectly authentic experiences to the user.

Hypermedia potentially circumvents the impracticalities of Schopenhauer's natural method by bringing the experiences to the user. Experiences can be presented free from the chaos and distractions of truly natural experiences and permit system developers to emphasize the relevant elements. In this sense, technology has done nature one better. Presentations can be augmented through the use of process highlighters, voice guidance, and computer-enhanced video to concentrate user attention on those elements relevant to the linking task. It is important, however, not to confuse the potential of hypermedia with the actuality. It may be that hypermedia holds tremendous promise as a powerful, new medium of communication and learning, but the jury is still out.

REFERENCES

Bobrow, S.A. & Bower, G.H. (1969). Comprehension and recall of sentences. *Journal of Experimental Psychology, 80*, 455-461.

Carlson, P. (1990). Hypertext, typographic man, and the notion of literacy. Proceedings of *Hypermedia & Information Reconstruction Conference* (pp. 3-15). Houston, TX: University of Houston-Clear Lake.

Collins, A.M. & Quillian, M.R. (1972). How to make a language user. In: E. Tulving and W. Donaldson (Eds.), *Organization of memory* (pp. 309-351). New York: Academic Press.

Conklin, J. (1987). Hypertext: An introduction and survey. *IEEE Computer, 20*(9), 17-41.

Dede, C.J. (1990). Hypermedia as medium. Proceedings of the *Hypermedia & Information Reconstruction Conference* (pp. 181-192). Houston, TX: University of Houston-Clear Lake.

Dede, C.J. (1991). Designing a tool for imaging mental models. *Proceedings of the International Conference on the Learning Sciences* (pp. 125-135). Evanston, IL: Erlbaum.

Dede, C.J. & Palumbo, D.B. (1991). Implications of hypermedia for cognition and communication. *Impact Assessment Bulletin, 9*, 15-27.

Fairchild, K.F. & Wexelblat, A. (1989). *Navigation through cyberspace* (MCC Technical Report Number STP-161-89). Austin, TX: Microelectronics and Computer Technology Corporation.

Gaines, B.R. & Vickers, J.N. (1988). Design considerations for hypermedia considerations. *Microcomputers for Information Management, 5*(1), 1-27.

Gilbert, T.F. (1982). Human incompetence: The autobiography of an educational revolutionist. *Journal of Organizational Behavior Management, 3*, 55-67.

Gygi, K. (1990). Recognizing the symptoms of hypertext . . . and what to do about it. In: B. Laurel (Ed.), *Human-computer interface design* (pp. 273-298). Reading, MA: Addison-Wesley.

Jonassen, D.H. (1991). Representing the expert's knowledge in hypertext. *Impact Assessment Bulletin, 9*, 93-105.

Locatis, C., Letourneau, G., & Banvard, R. (1989). Hypermedia and instruction. *Educational Technology Research and Development, 37*, 65-77.

Nelson, T.H. (1989, September 15). Titanic Change. *Statement to the Senate Commerce Committee.*

Schopenhauer, A. (1892). *Essays of Arthur Schopenhauer.* New York: A.L. Burt.

Shirk, H.N. (1991). Communicating in the global village: Hypermedia & McLuhanism. *Impact Assessment Bulletin, 9*, 159-170.

Stefik, M. (1986). The next knowledge medium. *The AI Magazine, 7*, 34-46.

Alex Romiszowski
Andrew Abrahamson

The Structural Communication Methodology as a Means of Teaching George Orwell's *Animal Farm*: Paper and Computer-Based Instruction

When it is done well, instruction allows the student to actively participate in the learning process. Teachers of children talk about collaborative learning, where students work together to come to a full understanding of the subject. Schön (1983) suggests that people *reflect-in-action* and *know-in-action* throughout the learning process. Craik and Lockhart (1972) suggest that active participation allows the learner to integrate new material into existing knowledge, resulting in deeper processing of understanding.

Structural Communication is one attempt to achieve this deeper processing. The technique, first developed in the 1960s in England, engages the learner in a challenging, game-like problem-solving exercise. As a response to programmed instruction, Structural Communication (SC) "was developed largely in reaction to those linear and branching programs on which many people pinned such extravagant hopes not so long ago" (Egan, 1976, p. 6). Originally intended for interactive, computer-based

ALEX ROMISZOWSKI is Professor, Department of Instructional Design, Development and Evaluation, Syracuse University, Syracuse, NY 13244.
ANDREW ABRAHAMSON is a doctoral candidate, Syracuse University, Syracuse, NY 13244.

[Haworth co-indexing entry note]: "The Structural Communication Methodology as a Means of Teaching George Orwell's *Animal Farm*: Paper and Computer-Based Instruction." Romiszowski, Alex and Andrew Abrahamson. Co-published simultaneously in *Computers in the Schools* (The Haworth Press, Inc.) Vol. 10, No. 1/2, 1994, pp. 199-226; and: *Multimedia and Megachange: New Roles for Educational Computing* (eds: W. Michael Reed, John K. Burton, and Min Liu) The Haworth Press, Inc., 1994, pp. 199-226. Multiple copies of this article/chapter may be purchased from The Haworth Document Delivery Center [1-800-3-HAWORTH; 9:00 a.m. - 5:00 p.m. (EST)].

"conversational" tutorials, SC attempts to individualize instruction for each learner, affording a pace suitable for all students. Similar to programmed instruction, it provides the instructor with control over the medium and content. It differs, however, by allowing the learner to control the process and outcomes of the exploration of the content.

COMPONENTS OF STRUCTURAL COMMUNICATION

The simplest and most common form of Structural Communication (SC) study unit is a booklet of between 10 and 15 pages, suitable for approximately one hour of individual study. It usually contains six portions: the Intention, the Presentation, the Investigation, the Response Matrix, the Discussion, and Viewpoints. Figure 1 shows the relationship among these six portions.

Intention	The intention is the opening portion of the lesson. It provides the author's purpose and goals. It may include objectives. It may also include an "advanced organizer" or rationale.
Presentation	In this section, the material to be studied or read is presented. It provides the learner with the first contact with the content. The presentation often includes a written text. However, it may be a video, case study, simulation or real life experience. It can accommodate nearly any content area.
Investigation	The investigation is a set of approximately four questions or problems based on the presentation. These questions, or "challenges" (Egan, 1976), are designed to investigate a different aspect of the study unit theme.
Response Matrix	The response matrix is an array of between 10 and 30 items that restate the key themes, concepts and principles described in the presentation. The student composes a response for each question by selecting any number of items from the response matrix.
Discussion	The discussion contains two parts: a discussion guide and a set of discussion comments. Based on the response items selected by the learner, the discussion guide directs the learner to a specific discussion comment or set of discussion comments which describe in depth the rationale for including or excluding certain items from the response matrix.

Viewpoints

The viewpoints section may be viewed as a conclusion to the lesson. It describes what the authors have attempted to achieve in the lesson, and those biases or emphases they may have imposed on the material. Ideally, the viewpoints section plays a final, interactive role between author and learner.

RESEARCH ON STRUCTURAL COMMUNICATION

In 1946, J. G. Bennett founded a private research organization called the Institute for the Comparative Study of History, Philosophy, and the Sciences. The Institute, located in Great Britain, conducted research into the methods of analyzing, interpreting, and organizing knowledge, with the aim of creating practical instructional techniques which lead to more insightful understanding. During the mid 1960s the Hirst Research Laboratories of the General Electric Company funded Bennett's research on teaching machines using the newly developed Structural Communication methodology. Success with teaching machines in business settings suggested that the technique was ready to be used in schools. In 1968 the Centre for Structural Communication was founded in London, Great Britain, under the directorship of Tony Hodgson. This organization, now defunct, was responsible for both research on and development of Structural Communication lessons.

One of the best features of Structural Communication is that it provides a practical application of cognitive psychology principles. Over the past two decades, there has been a shift in emphasis from behavioral explanations of learning to cognitive approaches to understanding learning. Most research on cognitive processes has resulted in a descriptive understanding of learning rather than prescriptive methods of developing and implementing instructional materials. Structural Communication stands as one of the few attempts to implement an instructional practice based on cognitive

FIGURE 1

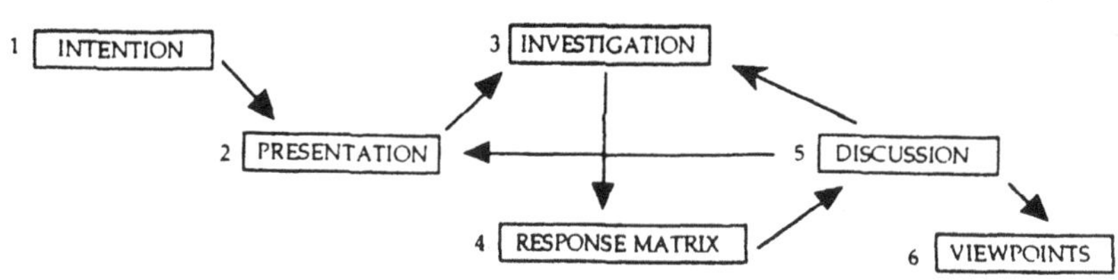

theory. Unfortunately, since the early 1970s and the closure of the Centre for Structural Communication, little research or development has been conducted concerning Structural Communication.

In a series of articles in the *Harvard Business Review,* Hodgson and Dill (1971, 1970a, 1970b) discuss the benefits of an SC approach to the teaching of management issues. Readers were invited to mail in their responses to a Harvard Business Case, presented by the means of the Structural Communication methodology. One interesting result was that the reader response was higher for these articles than any other case studies presented in the *Harvard Business Review.*

Romiszowski (1976) performed a feasibility study that compared existing instructional materials and a Structural Communication unit for teaching set theory. The Structural Communication unit was found to be successful in teaching concepts and principles of set theory at a greater depth of understanding. However, the Structural Communication unit was found to have limitations based on the reading level of the learners. This is not a limitation of Structural Communication, but of the specific materials used.

Mitchell and Meilleur-Baccanale (1982) compared a Structural Communication systems analysis unit to traditional text presentations. The study, which focused on both immediate recall and delayed understanding, found that students in the experimental group outscored the traditional group by 58% on the test of immediate recall and by 51% on the delayed post-test.

Romiszowski, Grabowski, and Damadaran (1988) discuss the use of a Structural Communication (SC) lesson as part of an interactive video (IV) unit. The authors discovered that during successive uses of an IV case study aimed at teaching management skills, students did not improve their scores with successive attempts. The authors designed a Structural Communication (SC) unit as a supplement to the IV case study. The authors found that those students who participated in the Structural Communication (SC) "debriefing" lesson improved their scores as they worked through the IV simulation.

STRUCTURAL COMMUNICATION AND *ANIMAL FARM*

The remainder of this article will discuss the development and initial use of a Structural Communication unit developed for helping eighth grade students gain a better understanding of George Orwell's novel *Animal Farm.* The format of this article will highlight the basic elements of a Structural Communication lesson.

Intention

Orwell's *Animal Farm* can be a difficult novel for eighth grade students (age 13-14) to understand. Allegory, metaphor, and symbolism play a major, if not most important, role in the book. English teachers have suggested that students read for "facts," memorizing plot events and character names, rather than reading for understanding of the author's intention and meaning. A Structural Communication lesson was developed for *Animal Farm* with the hope that it would provide the following benefits:

1. Challenging, game-like study unit
2. Higher-level processing/thinking
3. Creative means of generating new insights
4. Discovery of key relationships and structures
5. A "socratic" dialogue between student and teacher

Whereas a traditional SC unit allows the teacher/developer to explain why he/she chose specific responses to questions (the discussion section), the unit developed for *Animal Farm* allowed the students, after reading the teacher-generated discussion comments, to generate discussion comments of their own.

Presentation

A paper-based SC unit of eight pages was developed for *Animal Farm*. An English teacher in a private school in the northeast United States used the unit for those students in her eighth grade English class who chose to read the novel. Thirteen students read the novel and completed the SC lesson. Students were provided one class period of 40 minutes to complete the unit. They were allowed to work independently or in groups.

The *Animal Farm* unit differs from the traditional SC unit in two important ways. First, as mentioned previously, a traditional SC unit does not allow the student to respond to the teacher/developer after reading the discussion section. The unit developed for *Animal Farm* encourages students to respond to the teacher-generated discussion comments. After each discussion comment, space is provided for the students to respond to the teacher-generated comments. In the pilot test of this unit, some, though not all, students chose to respond to the teacher discussion comments.

A second variation from standard SC presentation format was the lack of traditional intention and presentation sections. The intention consisted of the classroom teacher telling the students that they could participate in the SC unit for extra credit. The students were told that this unit would help them understand the novel better. The teacher informed the students that since the exercise was not a test, the students were allowed to work either in groups or individually, as they preferred. Only one group of three students opted to work together. The "presentation section" was the actual reading of the novel, which the students completed prior to receiving the SC unit.

Investigation

Students were asked to respond to four questions concerning the novel. Figure 2 presents one of those four questions.

One goal of this type of question is to help students understand that, in this case, corruption is not necessarily caused by a single event, but by an amalgam of events which, over time, result in change. Whereas students traditionally would look for one answer to a particular question (traditional matching technique), this question, as with the other three questions, forced students to view human nature as a much larger condition than can be answered by one response.

A second goal of this question was to shift the attention of the students from plot and characterization (both common emphases in eighth grade English instruction) to a more global concern with meaning and metaphor. The question suggests a relationship among plot, characterization, and *interpretation* of events of the novel. The question requires students to defend a position based on their interpretation and understanding of the events provided in the response matrix.

FIGURE 2

QUESTION 2

It has been said that "Power corrupts, and absolute power corrupts absolutely," meaning that those who have total power over other persons usually use that power for evil. In *Animal Farm*, the pigs gain absolute power. From the response matrix, construct an argument which supports the notion that absolute power corrupts those who hold it.

Write the letters of your selected items here: ____________________

Response Matrix

The response matrix consists of 20 "facts" or events concerning the novel. Figure 3 presents the response matrix that the students received.

The response matrix in Figure 3 presents those facts and events that the

FIGURE 3

RESPONSE MATRIX

After the rebellion, Molly still wants to wear ribbons and eat sugar. 1	The pigs control all information. 2	Squealer often revises the commandments. 3	Benjamin says "Life will go on as it had always gone on...that is badly." 4
Leadership is described as a sacrifice that few would be willing to make. 5	It is believed that only the pigs need to be educated, as they are the thinkers of the farm. 6	The pigs say they need the milk; therefore the milk is mixed with the pigs' food. 7	Animals call each other comrade. 8
Boxer neglects his health in order to build the windmill. 9	Napoleon confers honors and titles on himself. 10	The pigs break many of the original commandments. 11	Boxer often says "Napoleon is always right." 12
The pigs learn to walk on two legs. 13	The pigs train the sheep to bleat "four legs good, two legs bad." 14	Moses the raven is criticized for believing in Sugarcandy Mountain. 15	The animals did not have to work extra hours. But if they did not, their food rations were cut in half. 16
Snowball is accused of destroying the windmill. 17	The animals create the seven commandments. 18	The retirement pasture is planted with barley for the pigs' beer. 19	Some say that Animal Farm is more productive at the end of the novel than it was at the beginning. 20

developers deemed important in the novel. In many ways, the response matrix serves as a concept map or concept organizer for the student, allowing the student to see what the teacher has learned from the instruction and how the teacher processes that information. The response matrix and discussion sections provide a means of structuring communication between teacher and learner (hence the name Structural Communication).

It is possible for students to create millions of possible answers from the matrix provided in Figure 3. Even if the students were told to select only five answers from the matrix, a total of 1.5 million separate answers is possible. The large number of potential answers creates a dilemma for the teacher/developer: it would be nice to have a discussion comment for each possible response; however, it is nearly impossible (time and space being two factors which come quickly to mind) to create as many discussion comments as there are possible student responses. For the purposes of this SC unit, four discussion comments per investigation question were provided for the student.

Discussion

One of the advantages of Structural Communication is that the methodology allows the developer to anticipate a variety of student responses. In fact, a quick glance at the response matrix suggests that millions of answers are possible. If the student was limited to selecting at most five responses for each question, over one million responses could be created. A successful SC discussion section will anticipate the variety of student responses and provide feedback for each combination of answers. This is not to suggest that millions of discussion comments are necessary. Often, responses link with other responses, creating patterns easily identified within the Discussion Section. Figure 4 displays the four responses that were created for each question.

The Discussion Guide used in this unit could be intimidating to many adults, never mind a 13-year-old, as the paper-based presentation form requires great precision. The unit developers and classroom teacher anticipated that students might have difficulty routing themselves to the appropriate response. It was hoped that students would work collaboratively and therefore have a better chance of turning to the appropriate discussion comment.

Figure 5 presents *Discussion Comment E,* the comment provided to students who created the same response as the unit developers. The developers attempted to create a conversational comment that would elicit a response from students. Rather than say something like, "This is the correct answer," the discussion comment attempts to *build* a series of responses that answer the question.

FIGURE 4

QUESTION 2

- If you omitted three or more of items 2, 3, 6, 7, 10, 11, and 13, read Comment E.
- If you included three or more of items 1, 4, 9, 14, 15, 17, 18 and 20, read Comment F.
- If you included any of items 5, 8, 12, 16, and 19, read Comment G.
- If you included five or more of items 2, 3, 6, 7, 10, 11, and 13, read Comment H.

FIGURE 5

E. We think that responses 2, 3, 6, 7, 10, 11, and 13 all support the notion that absolute power corrupts those who hold it. By controlling all information (response 2) and refusing to let other animals become educated (response 6), the pigs retain power for themselves. Revising and breaking the commandments (responses 3 and 11), keeping the milk for themselves (response 7), and conferring honors and titles on themselves (response 10) further demonstrate the pigs' misuse of power. The pigs abuse their privilege by learning to walk on two legs (response 13), thus becoming more like the corrupt humans who precede them.

Do you have any other ideas on this?

The items included in *Discussion Comment E* are those the developers deemed essential to answer the question. Other items in the response matrix could be included in an appropriate answer to the question, though those items may not be essential to answer the question. Figure 6 presents *Discussion Comment G*, which draws items from the response matrix that could be included in an answer but are not essential elements of an answer. This type of response communicates to students the relationship between essential and supporting evidence.

Viewpoints

Unfortunately, students did not respond favorably to the SC unit. The following list describes some of the students' complaints:

1. It was difficult for students to route themselves to the appropriate discussion comment.
2. Students did not like having to read eight pages in one class period.
3. Students did not like the idea that one question can have more than one answer.
4. Students were not convinced that the unit was not a test.
5. Students did not want to respond to the teacher-generated discussion comments.

Some of these complaints suggest limitations to either the SC methodology or our educational system. Students who do not like the idea of a question having more than one correct answer may be uncomfortable because they have never been asked to think that way before. This may reflect more on our educational system than it does on the SC unit itself, and may suggest that by eighth grade, students already have a pretty good idea how to answer a question. The complaint that students were not convinced that the unit was not some form of test reflects not only on our educational system, but on the relationship between student and teacher. These may or may not be issues which the SC methodology can influence.

Other student issues, however, can be addressed by considering alternative presentation forms for the SC unit. Those students who complained about the difficulty of routing themselves to the appropriate discussion comment could be aided by a computer that does the work for them. Students who complained about having to read eight pages during a class period might be happy to find that the lesson can be viewed on a few screens in a computerized lesson. Students who did not want to respond in traditional writing form to the teacher-generated discussion comments

FIGURE 6

G. We think that responses 5, 8, 12, 16, and 19, though not essential, help to support the notion that absolute power corrupts absolutely. Response 5 suggests an attempt on the part of the pigs to make the other animals believe that leadership is a sacrifice (do you believe their argument?). The term comrade (response 8) has been used in other totalitarian societies where absolute power has also corrupted those who hold it. Boxer's belief that Napoleon is always right gives Napoleon the power to abuse other animals. Responses 16 and 19 demonstrate the pigs' control over farm resources and over the actions of the other animals.

Tell us what you think. Do you agree that these items are essential to answering the question? Do they help support the notion that power corrupts?

might be interested in responding if they knew that they would have a computer-generated dialogue with the teacher and/or other students.

COMPUTER BASED IMPLEMENTATION OF STRUCTURAL COMMUNICATION UNITS

Even in the late 1960s, when the Structural Communication methodology was still under development, its inventors were planning to deliver their study units by means of computer (Bennett & Hodgson, 1967). An early version was running in 1968, in a typical mainframe environment of that period. Students would study the intention and presentation sections off-line, from a book or from other appropriate media. They would then be given a two-page exercise. The first page would present a set of challenging questions on the material studied, and the second page was in the form of a response matrix, similar to the one shown in Figure 3. All the questions could be responded to by selecting different combinations of items from the matrix. The page with the response matrix would be placed on a special touch-sensitive response tablet. By pressing a number of the cells on the page, students would input the pattern of their response to the computer. The computer, in turn, would apply a response-analysis algorithm developed by the author of the exercise (similar to Figure 4), select the appropriate discussion comments (e.g., Figures 5 and 6), and present them to the student, one after another, on the screen or teletype terminal. Many of the early units developed for management training were thus presented (Wilson 1970).

The Harvard Business Review experiment, mentioned earlier, applied an adaptation of this method in a distance education environment. Readers received the intention, presentation, problems and response matrix as an article in the *Review*, together with a preprinted response postcard on which they recorded their choices. These postcards (over 2,000 were received) were processed by data input clerks, and the computer printed a personalized feedback letter to each responding reader, including the particular selection of discussion comments that matched the pattern of the reader's responses to the problems posed in the case material (Hodgson & Dill, 1971, 1970a, 1970b).

Little further work has been done on the computer-based presentation of Structural Communication units. It is notable that none of the widely available courseware authoring systems has a built-in capability for generating feedback on the basis of a combination of responses. Some authoring languages may be used to create such exercises, but few published CAI units have attempted to utilize such strategies. The programming issues involved are not complex. The typical response-analysis algorithm for a given question may be composed of four to eight rules (if-and/or-then logic statements) that relate a particular set of inclusions and/or omissions from the response matrix to a specific discussion comment generated by the author. The early experiments described herein implemented their response-analysis algorithms in Fortran. No sophisticated artificial intelligence languages are required, and yet a surprisingly intelligent-seeming dialogue may be initiated between student and software.

In an attempt to develop a personal computer-based shell for the authoring of S.C. units, Romiszowski, Grabowski, and Pusch (1988) utilized a similar approach. The Fortran routines were so developed as to give authors a menu-driven front-end into which they could plug the logic statements that represented their rationale for presenting a particular discussion comment. The discussion comments would then appear as a scrolling text file, devoid of the finer points of screen design. It was obviously necessary to link this "logic engine" to a set of routines for the generation and presentation of courseware, such as is commonly included in commercially available courseware. This was not immediately done, as the attractiveness of Hypercard as a courseware development tool captured our attention.

Our initial attempts to implement Structural Communication study units in a Hypercard environment utilized some already existing exercises developed by one of the present authors to teach some of the critical thinking skills utilized by instructional designers. One such skill (the analysis of performance deficiencies and their causes, or "front-end" analysis) involves the application of a complex schema of interrelated concepts and principles to the analysis of a particular case of human performance deficiency problems (Romiszowski, 1981). The teaching of this skill can be achieved effectively by means of the case study method. The case-related information may be presented as a role-play or simulation, as a real-life analysis task, or by printed text. The case discussion (the most important element for achieving the in-depth processing required to master the skill) would typically be a teacher-led group discussion. If a computer-based version of such exercises were to be developed, it would seem to be an appropriate application for the Structural Communication methodology.

A computer-based version of one case study was developed in Hypercard. The case-related information was presented as a loosely structured hypertext, which contained both relevant and irrelevant information, requiring an effective search strategy on the part of the student in order to efficiently discover the most pertinent facts of the case.

The specific front-end analysis model that students are expected to use in this particular set of exercises contains a list of 20 different types of solutions or solution elements that can be used in combination in order to develop a total multi-faceted solution to a complex multi-faceted human performance problem. In Figure 7, these 20 items are incorporated as the elements of the response matrix. The student, having studied the case material, now makes a proposal on how to solve the problem by selecting any combination of these 20 types of solutions.

Naturally, the student has also studied the model and, therefore, the short two-word phrases are fully meaningful as each of them represents a section of a chapter and previously presented examples. There should be no doubt in the student's mind of the differences between, for example, job enlargement and job enrichment, nor, for example, of the meaning that should be ascribed to the term *punishment*. If such previous study had not been performed, the short, cryptic terms presented here would not, by themselves, be meaningful. They would have to be elaborated in more detail, and then the limited size of the Macintosh screen would make it very difficult to include all 20 items of the response matrix in one presentation.

As the student selects a combination of items from this response matrix by clicking in the boxes provided, the response appears in the bottom window, presenting the cumulative outline of the proposal being formulated as a solution to the case problem. On completing and editing this selection, the student clicks on the right-hand button, which then presents the discussion guide that is illustrated here in Figure 8.

The discussion guide to this particular case problem reveals that there are as many as 13 different discussion comments that are linked to particular patterns of inclusion or omission of elements from the response matrix. Typically, a student may receive a prescription to read a lesser or greater selection of these items, depending on the amount of convergence or divergence between the student's approach to solving the problem presented and that which would be adopted by the expert author of the exercise. There is no implied criterion of how many items indicate good or inferior performance on the part of the student at this point, as learning is deemed to occur principally through the reading of the discussion comments which follow.

As the student clicks on a particular comment button, this comment will appear and the student will be able to read it and then return to the discussion guide in order to make further selections. Although a limited number of the discussion comments have been flagged as particularly relevant to the student's initial response pattern (those which are marked in Figure 8 by the word "click"), the network of comments is in fact an open

FIGURE 7

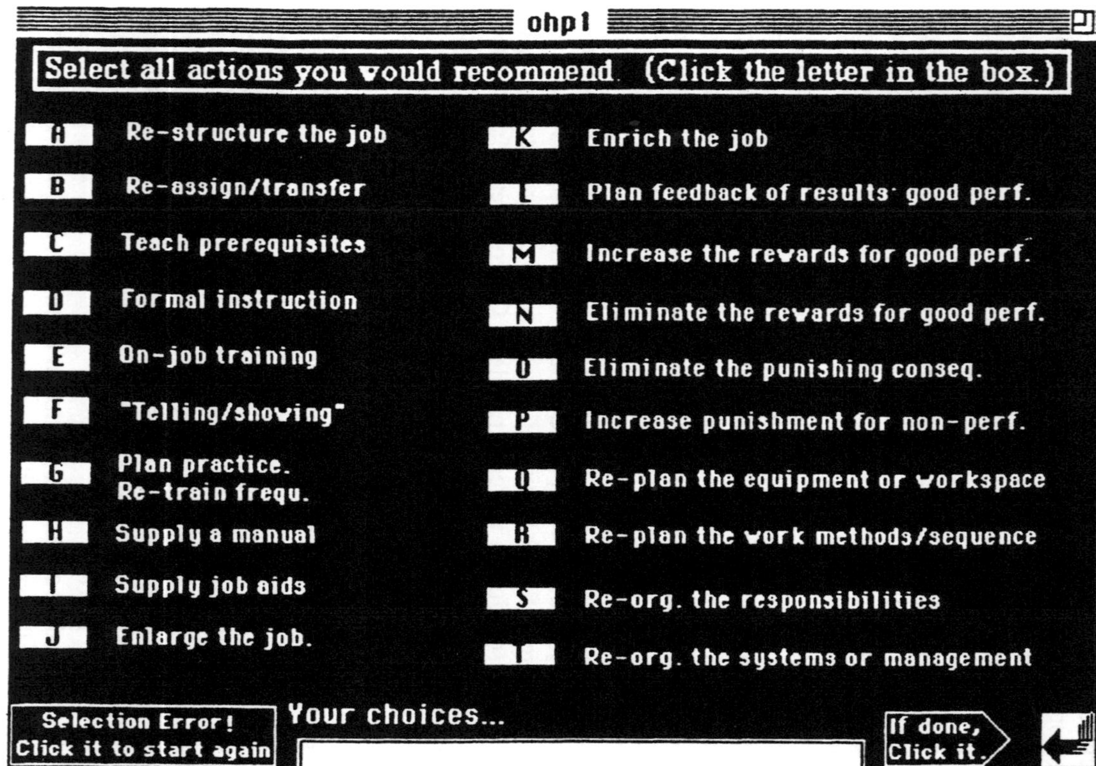
ohp1
Select all actions you would recommend. (Click the letter in the box.)
A Re-structure the job
B Re-assign/transfer
C Teach prerequisites
D Formal instruction
E On-job training
F "Telling/showing"
G Plan practice. Re-train frequ.
H Supply a manual
I Supply job aids
J Enlarge the job.
K Enrich the job
L Plan feedback of results· good perf.
M Increase the rewards for good perf.
N Eliminate the rewards for good perf.
O Eliminate the punishing conseq.
P Increase punishment for non-perf.
Q Re-plan the equipment or workspace
R Re-plan the work methods/sequence
S Re-org. the responsibilities
T Re-org. the systems or management
Selection Error! Click it to start again
Your choices...
If done, Click it.

FIGURE 8

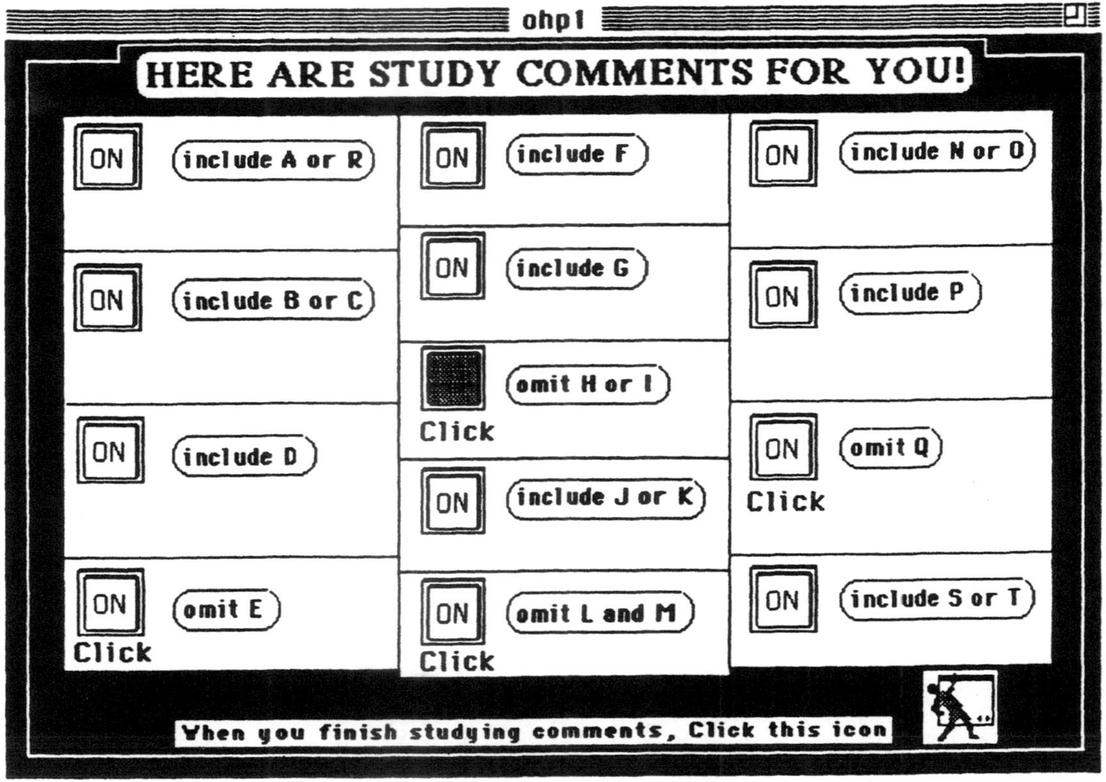

ohp1
HERE ARE STUDY COMMENTS FOR YOU!
ON
include A or R
ON
include B or C
ON
include D
ON
omit E
Click
ON
include F
ON
include G
omit H or I
Click
ON
include J or K
ON
omit L and M
Click
ON
include N or O
ON
include P
ON
omit Q
Click
ON
include S or T
When you finish studying comments, Click this icon

hypertext, capable of being browsed at will by the student. As different choices are made, the buttons change to indicate to the student what comments have already been read and which ones remain to be read if so desired. Also, these 13 buttons indicate the reasons for which a particular comment has been written and is being recommended for reading, by specifying the pattern of inclusions or omissions of response items that is associated with each of the feedback comments.

A typical comment presented in this particular exercise is shown in Figure 9. The student reads the quite extensive constructive feedback, which analyzes reasons why the particular element chosen could be considered valuable or not so valuable from a number of points of view. Often, the student is asked to think again or to consider whether the previous opinion or viewpoint still stands. In the classical structural communication exercise, this is where the dialogue would cease. In our implementation, however, we have incorporated a student opinion window at the bottom of each discussion comment card. Here the student may type in at will any comment on the material as presented, asking for more help, for further explanation, or taking issue with a comment, disagreeing, or having some other bright idea that is worthy of sharing with others.

The simplest implementation of this system requires the tutor to check through the student's work and then respond personally to any comments that have been made. The tutor is helped in this because all student responses are tracked and a student register card is prepared at the end of the exercise that shows not only what the student has selected from the response matrix but also what the student read and in what specific cards the student made any original comments. In a more sophisticated application, which we are now setting up, the student comments made within the hypercard environment are automatically captured by a program running in the background and are stored as flagged messages within a file that later is capable of being uploaded to a network.

The adult training environment in which we are working with this implementation utilizes an existing mainframe supported network that links universities worldwide (Bitnet). This enables instructional design students in many different universities and even on different continents to interact on an exercise of this nature as a "virtual group." To do so, they use their own copy of the courseware in their own Macintosh and then, on finishing, upload the file of secondary comments they have created to a listserver, using the file manipulation and electronic mail capabilities that are available on the university mainframe to which their Macintosh is connected as a terminal. Any other student at any other location who is participating in the same exercise would have his or her own copy of the

FIGURE 9

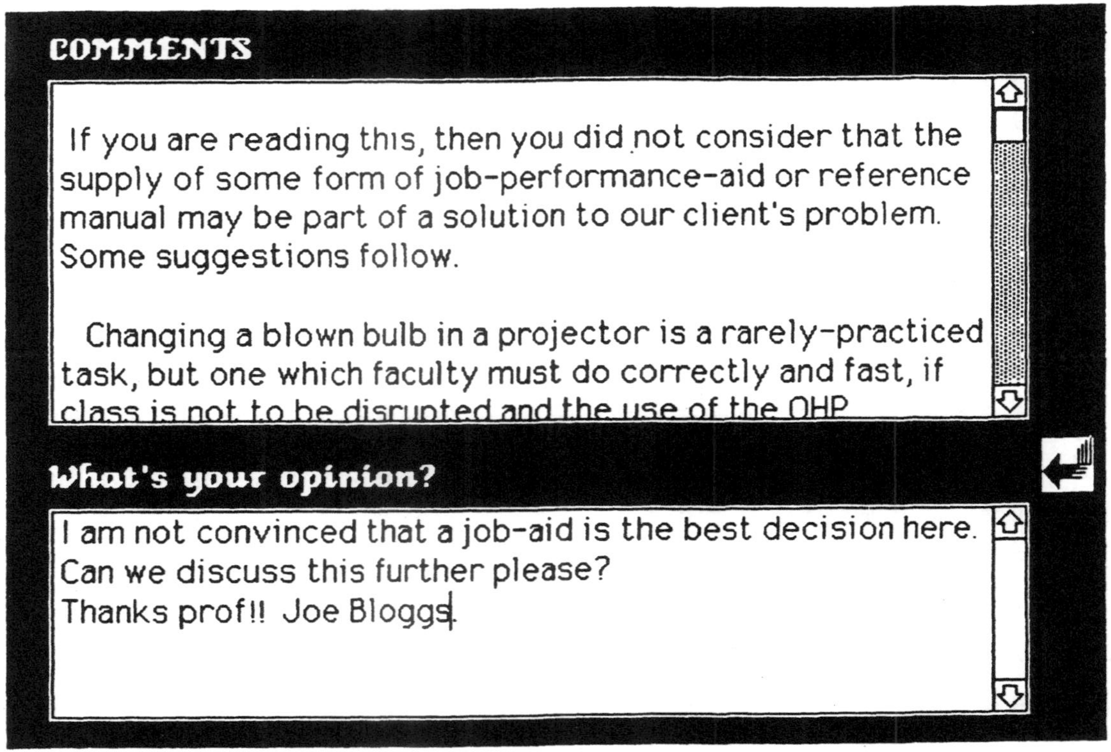
COMMENTS
If you are reading this, then you did not consider that the supply of some form of job-performance-aid or reference manual may be part of a solution to our client's problem. Some suggestions follow.
Changing a blown bulb in a projector is a rarely-practiced task, but one which faculty must do correctly and fast, if class is not to be disrupted and the use of the OHP
What's your opinion?
I am not convinced that a job-aid is the best decision here.
Can we discuss this further please?
Thanks prof!! Joe Bloggs

courseware in the hard disk of the local Macintosh and would update this by logging onto E-mail and receiving from the listserver at Syracuse University the files that have been created by all other students who have worked on the exercise since the last time that this student accessed it.

On receiving these files into the Macintosh's hard disk, the software automatically "unpicks" them into the separate messages, and each of these messages is placed in the comment space on the particular card in which it was generated on some other student's copy. In this way, a cumulative collection of these messages is created as a group of students interacts in a conversational discussion on the finer points of the case study being used. While this system is somewhat cumbersome and requires a fair amount of familiarization with both PC and mainframe environments, it is simple to implement as it requires no networks or hardware systems that are not already available on the various computers present in the environment in which we work.

In a school environment, where often there is no access to a mainframe, some of the aspects of this implementation may be not feasible. In our current work related to the *Animal Farm* exercise, we have been trying to replicate the environment described above in its essential aspects and adapt it to the context of a typical school computing environment and to the characteristics of the content.

ANIMAL FARM IN HYPERCARD: SOME PROBLEMS

In continuing the experiments described earlier, using *Animal Farm* as a paper exercise, we are currently developing a computer-based version. In doing this, we have met with some problems that to some extent render it necessary to re-think how to implement an exercise of this nature within a Hypercard environment.

The first problem is concerned with the nature of the response matrix that was developed for use with the paper exercise (Figure 3). Each of the response elements within this matrix is a sentence, and it would be unreasonable to expect students who have read *Animal Farm* only once to make sense of anything much shorter than these elements. It could even be argued that a longer paragraph of text may sometimes be required to recall a particular event that is being used as a building block in the construction of a complex response to a complex question.

The problem mentioned earlier of the size of a Hypercard presentation now becomes a major issue. To divide a card screen into 20 or more buttons and within each button put the element descriptor with the detail that is required for an exercise like *Animal Farm* would necessitate the use of print size so small as to be totally impractical and not at all user friendly. The solution we have adopted is shown in Figure 10. Here we have used the capability of creating scrolling windows to transform the response matrix of 20 items into a scrolling list. We have also included the relevant question in the scrolling window at the top so that the student on this one card has both question and response elements. Finally, at the bottom of the card is a pad of buttons on which the selections from the response elements can be recorded.

This would seem to be a very neat solution since it doesn't look as complicated as the multi-page paper exercise that seemed to frighten some of the participants in the study reported earlier. The matrix no longer appears as a complicated chart. The four questions are spread out on separate cards, and only one at a time is visible to the student. Finally, the number of comments and the size of the discussion comments are hidden from the student until they are accessed by making a particular selection. It is probable that this form of presentation of the exercise may appear much less threatening to a high school or middle school student who is not very familiar with self-study from complex learning materials.

On the other hand, the presentation of the exercise in this form has thrown away some of the visual aspects of representing structure that are present in the paper version. The presentation of all four questions on one page, alongside one another, does have, in theory, the advantage of illustrating not only the questions individually but also how they hang together. The reading of the four questions together before attempting any of them could be recommended as an exercise that would act as some form of advance organizer of what is coming, and indeed may help some students to better organize their thoughts about the questions individually.

Similarly, the presentation of the response elements as a "matrix," or more accurately, as a structured array that attempts to be nonlinear in its format, was developed by the inventors of Structural Communication as a means of presenting the elements in such a way that it would encourage students to see relationships and patterns by visually scanning the total domain of key points rather than by considering them separately. In scrolling the list shown in Figure 10, only two or sometimes three response items can be seen at any one time, and the relationships and mutual exclusions and redundancies must be held in the mind of the learner while looking at later items. It is probable that some structural learning difficulties may arise from having transformed the nonlinear visual "matrix" into a linear list.

Both of these possible deficiencies in this new approach to implementing the exercise are yet to be subjected to experimental testing. It may be

FIGURE 10

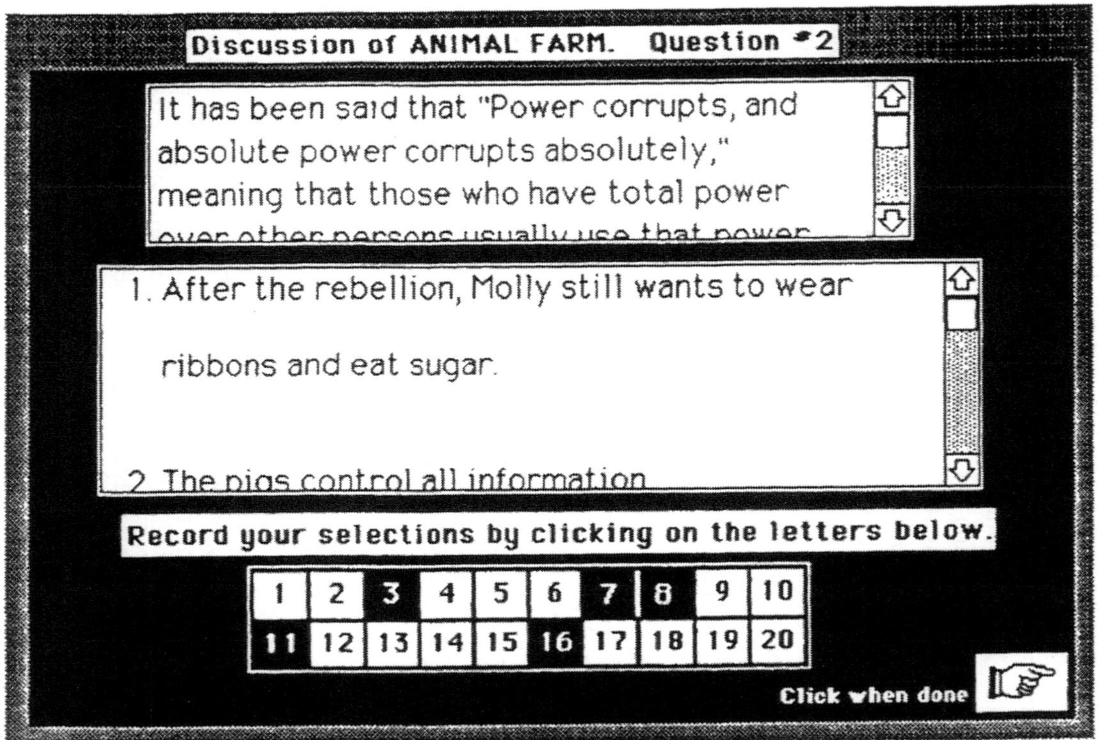
Discussion of ANIMAL FARM. Question #2
It has been said that "Power corrupts, and absolute power corrupts absolutely," meaning that those who have total power
1. After the rebellion, Molly still wants to wear
ribbons and eat sugar.
Record your selections by clicking on the letters below.
1 2 3 4 5 6 7 8 9 10
11 12 13 14 15 16 17 18 19 20
Click when done

that we are not, in fact, losing any learning effectiveness by transforming the exercise into the format shown here. It may even be that forcing the student to keep more of the structure in mind, as the separate elements are browsed, may even enhance learning for some participants. These questions are part of our ongoing research agenda which we will implement in our next stages of work with the *Animal Farm* exercise.

A second problem encountered in creating this exercise is illustrated in Figure 11. This figure is essentially equivalent to Figure 4 presented earlier. In the paper version, the student had to do the process of comparing the elements selected with the particular prescription and identifying whether the requisite number of items in the category had been included or omitted. It is now the computer that is to carry out this task for the student. Here we hit an interesting problem, however, since we have been unable to find a way of implementing the particular algorithm as represented by this figure in Hypertalk. While Hypertalk is a very powerful language for controlling visual presentations, it is not sufficiently powerful as a general purpose computer program to handle complex looping and recursion. It would seem that in order to create this sort of exercise with an easy-to-program shell, we would be required to build a subroutine to implement an algorithm, utilizing a programming language such as Pascal. The previous experience in developing such a shell in Fortran should stand us in good stead for creating a Pascal version compatible with Hypertalk, thus extending its power in this particular respect.

Another interesting research question appears at this stage. In delegating to the computer the analysis of the student response, we are taking away one step of the learning process from the student. Early research on Structural Communication has failed to categorically demonstrate whether delegating to the computer the analysis is detrimental to the actual learning that takes place. It may be that the process of analyzing one's own choices and comparing them with a printed version of the algorithm may, in fact, enhance learning. This may not appear very likely with the *Animal Farm* exercise, as it was found in practice with the paper exercise that, due to the rather complex nature of the analysis involved, students took some considerable time on this stage and also often made errors, directing themselves to feedback comments that maybe they need not have read. As there is no definitive research on this issue, another aspect of our current research agenda is to investigate this question with different age groups of students, different types of content, and different levels of complexity of the response analysis that is demanded in order to select appropriate discussion comments.

The discussion comments themselves are presented in much the same

FIGURE 11

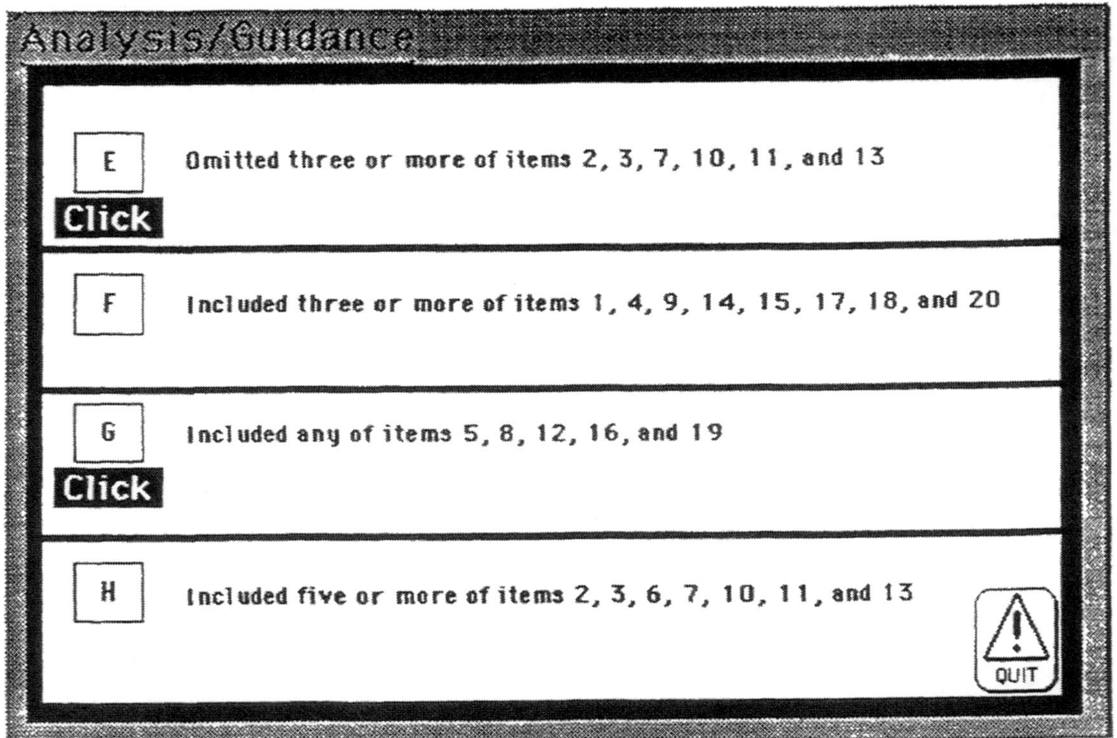
Analysis/Guidance
E
Click
Omitted three or more of items 2, 3, 7, 10, 11, and 13
F
Included three or more of items 1, 4, 9, 14, 15, 17, 18, and 20
G
Click
Included any of items 5, 8, 12, 16, and 19
H
Included five or more of items 2, 3, 6, 7, 10, 11, and 13
QUIT

way as they were in the front-end analysis case study that we have used with adult learners, as illustrated in Figures 12 and 13. The same format of a scrolling window for the quite extensive teacher or author comment is followed by a scrolling window in which the student can write a response that is absolutely open-ended. In the paper-delivered version, the students were encouraged to write their comments on the papers and hand them in to the teacher, but in fact very few wrote comments that were related to the content of the exercise as opposed to their attitude toward it.

It is expected that the computer-based presentation may encourage students to make comments, particularly if the system is set up so that each student's comments are circulated to all. Teachers often notice that a small proportion of students raise their hands to respond during class discussions; however, teachers would like to receive the responses of all students. Those students who require more time to think through questions and responses than a typical classroom discussion allows may benefit from the networking advantages of a computerized SC unit. Those students who are shy to offer answers in a personal, in-class setting may feel more comfortable responding via a less-personal computer network. The resulting open discussion is not just between a student and the teacher but between all members of the group, as students would be encouraged to read each others' responses.

In order to do this and avoid a lot of searching of each copy of the software, the computers would, of course, have to be networked. Many schools now have local area networks and utilize file servers to distribute software to the various computers in the clusters. This sort of environment could be utilized in a manner that is much more automated than the part PC-based/part E-mail-based system that we are using with our students at Syracuse University. It could be set up to be completely automatic so that students do not have to carry out any uploading or downloading of files between computers. One way that we have attempted to do this is to set up just one copy of the courseware on a file server and download this to each computer as a student uses it. In the typical computer network, this has the disadvantage of allowing only one student at a time to work on the software without the danger of some students overriding some of the input made by other students. There are methods to overcome this by setting up the network in appropriate ways, but in fact most networks available to schools are not thus organized, and consequently this would be a significant problem.

Another problem we encountered in trying to use such exercises on our own local area networks at Syracuse University is administrative in nature. The dozen or more computer clusters spread around the campus are all

FIGURE 12

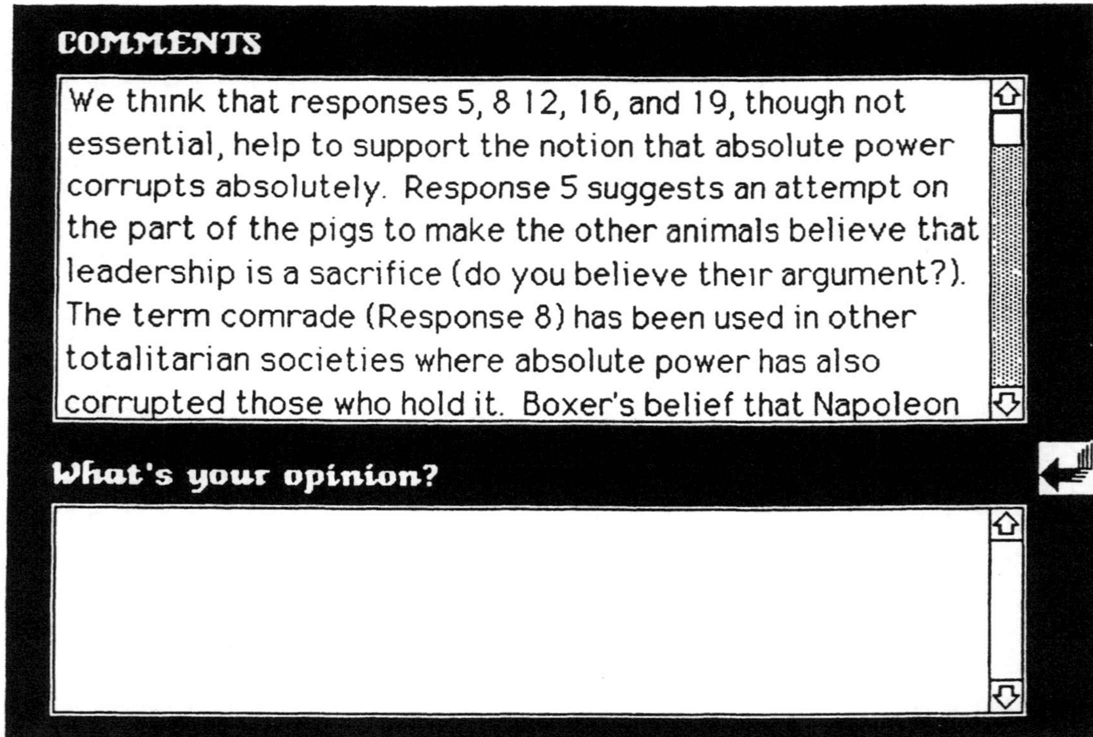
COMMENTS
We think that responses 5, 8 12, 16, and 19, though not essential, help to support the notion that absolute power corrupts absolutely. Response 5 suggests an attempt on the part of the pigs to make the other animals believe that leadership is a sacrifice (do you believe their argument?). The term comrade (Response 8) has been used in other totalitarian societies where absolute power has also corrupted those who hold it. Boxer's belief that Napoleon
What's your opinion?

FIGURE 13

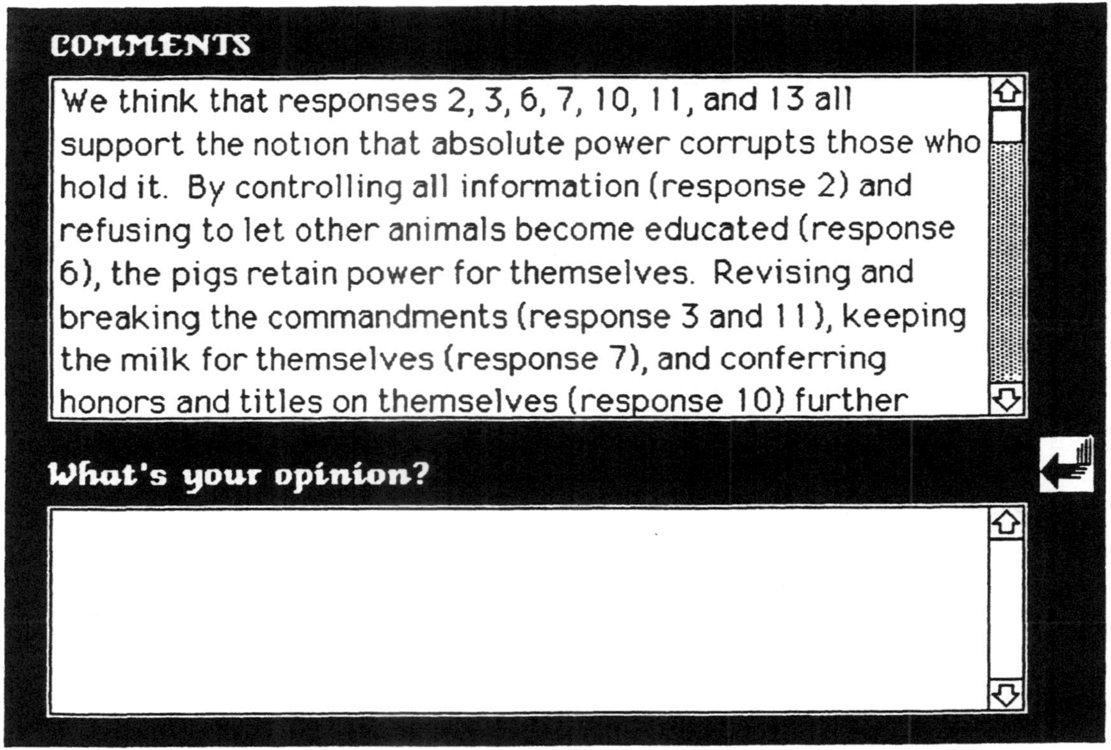
COMMENTS
We think that responses 2, 3, 6, 7, 10, 11, and 13 all support the notion that absolute power corrupts those who hold it. By controlling all information (response 2) and refusing to let other animals become educated (response 6), the pigs retain power for themselves. Revising and breaking the commandments (response 3 and 11), keeping the milk for themselves (response 7), and conferring honors and titles on themselves (response 10) further
What's your opinion?

linked to one file server that can distribute the exercises we described herein to any one of the computers and allow students to work at their own pace without having their own copy on a diskette. However, due to fears of contamination of the system by virus or by vandals, the network is so set up that no student input is accepted from the networked computers to the file server. It is therefore impossible on a system like this to build a cumulative file of student-generated comments as we do with the exercises we have designed.

This, of course, is mainly an administrative problem; however, it is not easy to overcome. Suffice it to say that on our campus we have in excess of one hundred CAI packages on file servers. These are used by thousands of students a year; however, only those run on the mainframe environment collect any data on what students did, how far they got, what they got wrong, etc. This would seem a particularly strange situation since the aspect of computer-based instruction for which the computer is uniquely suited is the number crunching involved in tracking student progress and consequently allowing authors and teachers to make more intelligent decisions about future work or about revising existing materials. All data generated in our networks are thrown away because of the fear of viral infections. It is worth remembering that some of the problems of implementing CAI effectively are not so much technological but bureaucratic or social.

CONCLUSION

We are currently developing a computer-based version of the *Animal Farm* unit discussed in this paper. In many ways, this article mirrors the dialogue the authors are having concerning the best medium and presentation form for this SC unit. We would like to combine the interactive, number-crunching benefits of a computerized SC lesson with the spatial, gamelike, structured benefits of the paper version.

At present it is unclear whether or not a Hypercard, computer-based presentation form of the *Animal Farm* SC study unit will be an improvement over the original paper-based prototype. The potential limitations of a Hypercard version may suggest that a computer-based page-turner format will not achieve the advantages of the spatial simulation properties of a traditional paper-based SC lesson. If Hypercard is considered one aspect of a more complete hypermedia presentation form including sound, video, still graphics, and computer images, it may be possible to enhance the spatial, simulation, and game-like qualities of Structural Communication.

A further avenue of study would be a determination of the value of the

SC methodology as an assessment tool for the teacher. The SC unit, comprised of an investigation, matrix, and responses, validated by a team of "experts" on *Animal Farm*, could be part of an experiment to measure the value of SC as an assessment measure of comprehension and understanding. Previous research on SC has suggested that the methodology is a powerful means of assessing student comprehension. If validated, this unit would provide the classroom teacher with the ability to assess student comprehension of the more salient portions of the novel. Similarly, a paper-based version could be compared with a computer/hypermedia version of the same lesson, aiding researchers in determining the advantages of various media.

Along with our emphasis on producing an SC unit employing the best aspects of the computer and paper versions of an SC unit, and the potential use of other hypermedia advantages, we are also sensitive to the needs of the classroom teacher who may or may not have computers (or the skill to use them) on which to run the lesson. Though many schools have computer facilities, not all teachers are prepared to use the technology. It is possible that the best of all products developed may not be used by the classroom teacher for whom the SC methodology may be a powerful tool. It will be important to provide the teacher with the support necessary to implement any computerized version developed.

The discussion of paper versus computer media is not a new issue. The computer revolution predicted in the sixties and seventies has not impacted education for children in the ways that many persons anticipated during those early years of the computer. Structural Communication has not impacted education as many of its initial proponents may have anticipated. But the link of Structural Communication methodology and the computer (via hypermedia) may now be a ripe field for research and application. Current and future research may indicate an effective means of linking the best of powerful media with an interactive problem-solving instructional methodology.

REFERENCES

Bennett, J. G. & Hodgson, A. M. (1967, December). Structural communication. *Systematics*, (Special issue devoted entirely to Structural Communication).

Craik, F. I. M. & Lockhart, R. S. (1972) Levels of processing: A framework for memory research. *Journal of Verbal Learning and Verbal Behavior, 11*, 671-684.

Egan, K. (1976) *Structural Communication*. Fearon Publishers Inc.

Hodgson, A. M. & Dill, W. R. (1971, January/February). Programmed case: Reprise of the misfired missive. *Harvard Business Review*, pp.140-45.

Hodgson, A. M. & Dill, W. R. (1970 a, November/December). Programmed case: Sequel to the misfired missive. *Harvard Business Review*, pp.105-110.

Hodgson, A. M. & Dill, W. R. (1970b, September/October). Programmed case: The misfired missive. *Harvard Business Review*, pp.140-46.

Mitchell, P. D. & Meilleur-Baccanale, D. (1982). Differential effects of holist and serialist learning style on learning with Structural Communication. *Cybernetics and systems research.* New York: John Wiley and Sons; Washington Hemisphere Publishing Corp.

Romiszowski, A. J. (1981). *Designing instructional systems*. London, UK: Kogan Page.

Romiszowski, A. J. (1976). A study of individualized systems for mathematics instruction at the secondary levels. Unpublished doctoral dissertation, The University of Technology, Loughborough, United Kingdom.

Romiszowski, A. J., Grabowski, B. L., & Damadaran, B. (1988). Structural Communications, expert systems, and interactive video: A powerful combination for a non-traditional CAI approach. *Proceedings of Association for Educational Communications and Technology.*

Romiszowski, A. J., Grabowski, B. L., & Pusch, W. (1988). Structural Communication: A neglected CAI methodology and its potential for interactive video simulations. *Proceedings of the 1988 International ADCIS Conference.* Association for the Development of Computer-based Instructional Systems.

Schön, Donald A. (1983). *The reflective practitioner: How professionals think in action.* New York: Basic Books.

Wilson, J. C. (1970). *Structural Communication in management.* London, UK: Structural Communication Systems Ltd.

Richard Lehrer
Julie Erickson
Tim Connell

Learning by Designing Hypermedia Documents

At the turn of the century, Dewey (1910) advocated progressive education–education designed to link purpose and structure. To this end, he advocated such projects as designing a clubhouse, as well as other activities that placed students in the role of developing rather than receiving knowledge. Unfortunately, schools rarely have adopted this philosophy, in part because the metaphor of learning in schools is often one of knowledge transmission rather than of knowledge construction (Perkins, 1986), and in part because the construction of physical artifacts is limited both materially and intellectually. Having built one clubhouse, how easy is it to revise, elaborate, or extend it to other constructions? Instead of designing clubhouses and other physical artifacts, Perkins suggests that teachers and learners design knowledge. The design approach is best understood by example: instead of telling students about a topic like "animals of the prairie,"

RICHARD LEHRER is Professor of Educational Psychology, University of Wisconsin-Madison, Madison, WI 53706.
JULIE ERICKSON and TIM CONNELL are doctoral candidates, Department of Educational Psychology, University of Wisconsin-Madison, Madison, WI 53706.
Parts of this research were funded by the University of Wisconsin-Madison Outreach Initiative and by the Robert M LaFollette Institute of Public Affairs, and may not reflect the views of either organization. Copies of the HyperAuthor software may be obtained by corresponding with the first author.

[Haworth co-indexing entry note]: "Learning by Designing Hypermedia Documents." Lehrer, Richard, Julie Erickson, and Tim Connell. Co-published simultaneously in *Computers in the Schools* (The Haworth Press, Inc.) Vol. 10, No. 1/2, 1994, pp. 227-254; and: *Multimedia and Megachange: New Roles for Educational Computing* (eds: W. Michael Reed, John K. Burton, and Min Liu) The Haworth Press, Inc., 1994, pp. 227-254. Multiple copies of this article/chapter may be purchased from The Haworth Document Delivery Center [1-800-3-HAWORTH; 9:00 a.m. - 5:00 p.m (EST)].

students design an animal that could live on the prairie, justify their design, and critically compare their designs to those of nature.

Perkins' knowledge-design approach has close links to traditional project-based learning (Katz & Chard, 1989), but the design approach is more concerned with the authenticity and extensibility of the knowledge artifacts that students develop. Thus, while traditional projects are often displayed to wider audiences, they are rarely, if ever, used. It is even more unlikely that students in one year will build upon their project or someone else's project of the previous year. Yet, most communities of practice develop in this incremental manner. Hence, project work in the schools, and other similarly constructivist approaches, often wither on the vine despite the strong push of progressive education.

Although Perkins intends that the metaphor of design be construed quite broadly to embrace most of thinking, we use the idea in a more limited way to refer to the mental processes and activities involved in the development of technologically-based knowledge artifacts (Harel & Papert, 1990). In our classrooms, students and teachers collaborate to design artifacts that structure information, such as Logo tutorial programs or hypermedia documents (Lehrer, 1991, 1993; Lehrer, Lee, & Jeong, 1991; Lehrer, Littlefield, & Wottreng, 1991). Here we report our observations of a classroom where ninth-grade American history students worked in teams to design and develop hypermedia documents about different epochs in American history. Their purpose was to develop documents that their classmates could use as learning aids, and that could be placed in the school's media center for the benefit of the entire school.

We begin by describing the instructional model that guided our introduction of hypermedia authoring tools. We then describe the implementation of the instructional model in the classroom, followed by our observations of student learning. We conclude with a discussion of the implications of our research for school restructuring and reform.

THE INSTRUCTIONAL MODEL

Images for instruction such as knowledge-as-design typically underspecify practice even as they orient the direction of that practice. In this instance, the task is to specify the nature of hypermedia-based design in more detail so that principles of practice can be deduced more confidently. Lehrer (1991,1993) distinguished among four primary types of cognitive processes when students compose with hypermedia: planning, transforming, evaluating, and revising, all of which are similar to those involved in written composition (Hayes & Flower, 1980). However, there are important differences as well.

Planning. Planning the design of a hypermedia document involves deciding upon the nature of the problem, developing ideas about the overall structure of the document, and deciding upon the respective roles and responsibilities of the design team. Thus, the goal of "design a hypermedia presentation about immigration" leaves much to the imagination of the designer. Essentially, designers must decide which questions they would like to answer, and how to constrain their search among the space of all possible partitionings of the subject-matter. The first three cognitive skills listed in Table 1 are most applicable to this phase of the design process. Unlike the individually-centered authorship of conventional text, we assume collaborative authorship in the hypermedia design approach. This assumption follows from the vision of hypermedia as a diffuse, multiple-voiced document (Barrett, 1989; Nelson, 1987; Nielson, 1990). The educational virtue is that collaborative authorship provides students with opportunities to view knowledge as distributed, to see one another as resources and sources of knowledge, to develop critical skills in arguing for one's own viewpoint, and to collectively develop ideas that might be out of the reach of individuals (Rogoff, 1990; Vygotsky, 1978).

Transforming. The next phase of the design process involves transforming information into knowledge. Knowledge is distinguished from information by its systematicity–a network of relationships that sustain one or more themes. The transformation phase of hypermedia design entails many of the cognitive skills depicted in Table 1, ranging from finding information to developing representations of that information, to relating one representation to another. The design process then lends coherency to the development of a wide range of skills.

Although many forms of media, including conventional text, could encompass many of these skills, hypermedia has an important educational advantage–it can be used to encourage students to think about how to represent an idea, to think about how to link different representations of an idea, and to think about relationships among ideas (Lehrer, 1991, 1993). We assume that a focus on external representations or systems of notation leads to a mapping of the key attributes of these notations onto a mental or internal form of representation (or some hybrid form where the external notation supports internal activity). Multiple and linked mental representations are the cornerstone of understanding (Janvier, 1987). Students who develop multiple representations of concepts can apply these representations flexibly to resolve impasses. For example, given a physics problem involving falling bodies, graphical representations allow one to check on

TABLE 1. Cognitive Components of Hypermedia-Based Design

Design Component	Primary Skills Involved
Defining the Nature of the Problem	Question posing
Problem Decomposition	Team collaboration
Project Management	Task & Role Assignments, Developing timelines
Finding Information	Document search techniques Using keywords in electronic search
Developing New Information	Interviewing, Developing questionnaires, etc.
Selecting Information	Note taking, Summarization, Data analysis
Organizing Information	Use of database tools, Semantic mapping
Representing Information	Segmenting video & sound Interleaving media, Graphics & video production
Evaluating the Design	Articulating intentions Public speaking Use of display tools
Revising the Design	Taking design as an object for thought Soliciting peer feedback

the sensibility of conclusions drawn from the application of equations or other algorithmic forms of representation. More generally, multiple representations sustain the rich web of ideas that support substantive interpretations of events.

Representing an idea also implies that one has segmented or categorized it in some way. With hypermedia, this segmentation extends from the mental plane into multiple forms of media–text, video clips, sound clips, animation clips, illustrations, and so on (Lehrer, 1991, 1993). Hence, there is an increased functional role for different systems of notation in the organization of one's thought and in the communication of knowledge. For example, eighth grade students who designed a hypermedia document about the Civil War used a sound clip from one of Martin Luther King's speeches to complement text that addressed how the Civil War continues in some ways today (Lehrer, 1991). Interestingly, students in another design team used the same clip to illustrate a very different point about the Emancipation Proclamation. Hence, students had the opportunity to see how the same piece of information could be transformed in multiple ways through its participation in different systems of knowledge.

Evaluation. Authoring is not sufficient. The designers of hypermedia documents must attend to what Bolter (1990) refers to as the "restlessness" of hypermedia; readers of hypermedia are not limited to any particular path through the document, so it is impossible to fully anticipate their reactions to any document. Hence, perhaps even more than is the case for text, which at least has a body of conventions to sustain a writer's efforts to anticipate the actions of the reader, the reactions of readers to hypermedia designs must be sampled empirically. This phase relies upon designers' abilities to solicit feedback which in turn relies upon their skills in articulating their goals and intentions to others. As noted in Table 1, this phase also includes multiple skills ranging from public speaking to the use of display tools. It also requires students to think carefully about who should provide feedback, at what point in the design cycle, with what frequency, and so on.

Revision. As with writing conventional text, once is not enough. Successful design, like successful composition, requires multiple cycles of drafting and revision. Although most of the skills displayed in Table 1 are implicated in this process, the most important skill is the ability to take the hypermedia document as an object of thought. This may entail skills such as listing and describing the problems that readers report, generation of hypotheses about their causes, and generation of potential repairs.

Theoretical Issues in Classroom Implementation. Specification of the design process provides a framework for its implementation in the classroom. However, the method and organization of instruction are not carried by the specification of the design process, although the thinking skills that we intend students to develop serve as instructional goals. Hence, we need to turn elsewhere for the organization of instruction.

Action and Meaning. Vygotsky (1978, p. 100) noted that during the course of early development "a child is able to do more than he can understand" and that action is dominant over meaning. Meaning here refers to an intersubjectively available typification or interpretation of events. Similarly, in classrooms, activity can supersede meaning. For example, a commonplace observation in mathematics education is that conceptual understanding, or grasp of the larger interpretative framework intended by teachers, often lags behind procedural understanding (Hiebert, 1986).

Vygotsky (1978) went on to assert that meaning arose through interactions with others in a "zone of proximal development." Meaning is created in such a zone through a variety of processes ranging from simple signifying (one part of an activity is crucial for understanding–for example, of all the possible motions of a saw, this one is most effective for cutting; of all the possible novels that you could read, these provide the best doorways to understanding the genre) to the more complex scaffolding of activity characteristic of coaching. This sociocultural perspective then emphasizes both "tacit structuring of communication" (Rogoff, 1990) and outright teaching in the creation of meaning. The outcome of this process is a gradual growth in the autonomy of sense-making as a person transforms the knowledge acquired in the social plane into an individual system of meaning, although the meaning is still reliant on some form of participation in the community in which it evolved.

Cognitive Apprenticeship. To translate sociocultural principles into instructional practice, Collins, Brown, and Newman (1989) suggest a "cognitive apprenticeship model" of instruction. This model provides guidelines for sequencing instruction so that students become autonomous learners, and for engineering educational setting so that the communities of practice required from the sociocultural perspective are created. The cognitive apprenticeship model differs from traditional models of apprenticeship in its emphasis on mental skills.

We focused on two themes of the cognitive apprenticeship model as we developed a learning environment to support student design. First, thinking must be made visible so that teachers and students can participate jointly in the development of knowledge. For example, one might decide that posing questions or organizing information are worthy of learning, but teaching these skills involves the additional step of making thought indexical, meaning that thought is referred to by acts that everyone can see. To illustrate, Palinscar and Brown (1984) make the tacit reading skill of prediction indexical by having students and teachers state their predictions verbally. This makes a formerly invisible mental process visible to all. With respect to the skills displayed in Table 1, we attempted to find ways of making the thought processes involved in each more visible so that they could be treated as objects for classroom conversation.

The cognitive apprenticeship model also provides guidelines about methods of instruction and the sequencing of instruction. For example, Collins et al. suggest that one begin by modeling a skill (direct instruction), proceed incrementally to provide less and less support for the student's learning of that skill, and then attempt to motivate students to explore a domain autonomously. With respect to skills, the cognitive apprenticeship model suggests learning global skills before specific ones. For example, Carver (1991, personal communication) had students investigate a small design problem (using *HyperCard* as a design tool) that required the integration of several skills before they developed any one skill in depth.

In summary, our approach to developing a classroom context to support student design with hypermedia tools was informed by an image of teaching as assisted performance (Tharp & Gallimore, 1988) and the practical problem of specifying and making visible the design skills we believed important to support students' efforts to design. Several critical components of the classroom context were left unspecified by our prior knowledge, including how to create a classroom community that would make student design subject to evolution, how to assess student learning in a way that could be used to inform practice, and how to understand the match between the role of student designer and the larger institution of the school.

METHOD

Participants

Twenty ninth-grade students in one American history class participated. The school was a suburban school in the MidWest region of the country. Although the school is located in a suburb, many of its students lived in rural settings. Occupations of parents included farming, light industry, and the professions.

Instructional Methods

Goals. Students were asked to develop a hypermedia presentation about a topic in American history for use as an educational tool for their peers. A list of potential topics was generated by the classroom teacher, and the top four interests of students were retained as the topics for the presentations: (a) World War I, (b) lifestyles between 1870-1920, (c) immigration, and (d) imperialism.

Setting. Students met in design teams of five students each in a portion of the school's library media center. The design teams were determined by common interests. Students met daily for 50 minutes for approximately 10 weeks. Most students also worked occasionally during study halls, after-school, or on weekends. The instructors consisted of various combinations of the authors and the classroom teacher.

Tools. Each design team had one MacIntosh II (cx or si) computer configured with 4MB RAM, an 80MB hard disk, and a 13 inch color monitor. In addition, one optical scanner was provided for the class, driven by a Mac SE 30. On each computer, we provided *HyperAuthor*, a software system to facilitate the design and development of hypermedia (Lehrer, 1991, 1993). *HyperAuthor* provided students with tools for word processing and for creating notecards, graphics, charts, animation clips, video clips, and sound clips. *HyperAuthor* also provided a linking menu so that any notecard could be linked to any other notecard and to any video, sound, or animation clip. For example, Figure 1 displays a note-card from the presentation developed by the World War I design team. The movie projector icon denotes a link to a video clip about trench warfare.

We also provided other software to help students develop knowledge. One such tool was a simple database manager linked to the authoring tools provided by *HyperAuthor*. Other software included tools for scanning graphics (Hewlett-Packard's *DeskScan* and *DeskPaint*), recognizing characters optically (*OmniPage*), and developing more complex graphs (*Cricket Graph*).

Assisting Student Performance

We scaffolded student design in several ways, including (a) modeling cognitive skills and providing systems of notation to support skill development, (b) providing computer tools, (c) asking leading questions, and (d) creating alternative forms of assessment. We discuss each in turn.

Scaffolding by Modeling. Scaffolding of student activities took many forms. One was direct instruction and modeling of many of the design skills presented in Table 1. For example, to teach students how to summarize text, we provided instruction that decomposed the skill into several distinct steps or metarules (Brown & Day, 1983), and we also provided examples of good and poor summaries. The declarative portion of the instruction was as follows:

"Summaries are good ways to help you figure out what you have read or seen really means. Summaries should only contain the main ideas.

FIGURE 1. A student notecard with a link to video

Summaries state the important information in the text in briefer form. The major steps in writing a summary are:

1. *Read* the passage once quickly and write a list of the major ideas.
2. Then go back and try to *find the supporting ideas for the major ideas*. Arrange each major idea and its supporting ideas in the form of a wheel with the major idea in the hub and the supporting ideas at the rim. Other ways to do this include forming a concept web or developing an outline. Do whatever works best for you!
3. *Write a first draft* of the summary (you might want to put it into *HyperDatabase)*. Be sure that you include the main ideas and some supporting statements.
4. *Look for too much detail* and eliminate it, unless it's some detail that you are sure that you want to include in your presentation.
5. *Interpret what you read.* After you summarize a topic, you may wish to make a note about your own views about what the author has said. Do you agree with the author? Does the author make a good argument? Does the author back up his or her claims? What does it all mean to *you?*

In addition to modeling cognitive acts like summarization, we provided systems of notation. For example, we developed aids to *student planning* in the form of worksheets where students drew a likeness of each notecard as well as a description of the associated text, its themes, and its links to other topics or representations, like sound, video, and animation. Similarly, when teaching students about principles of linking nodes, we modeled first deciding on the nature of the relationship, then selecting an *icon* representative of this relationship, and lastly using the *HyperAuthor* software to create the link. We then coached students in the use of this skill with their own stacks and finally let them explore and develop relationships autonomously. These direct forms of instruction about design skills were recorded in a "student design guide" that was distributed to each student as a reference.

Scaffolding with Computer Tools. A second, less direct form of scaffolding was embedded in the design of the tools for hypermedia composition. In this regard, *HyperAuthor* allowed students to segment and store different types of media so that they could develop multiple representations of concepts. This was implemented by *HyperAuthor*'s sound, video, and animation facilities, all of which stored "clips" in a library. A more conceptually compelling form of scaffolding was provided by *HyperAuthor*'s Linking facility. This facility required students to decide about and iconically label the semantic relationship between two nodes before they could link them electronically. This both highlighted the importance of semantic relatedness, a key component of the indexicality of hypermedia, and nudged students toward more reflective consideration of the nature of the relationship.

We also used some of the organizational features of *HyperAuthor* to stimulate students' own conceptual organization. Every time a student created a notecard, an icon of that card and its title was placed on a separate notecard called the "user's guide." This guide was intended to serve as a potential navigational structure for readers in that each icon was linked to its notecard. Hence, when readers clicked with the mouse on the icon, they would be transported to that card. However, to realize this potential, students had to develop a structure for these icons. To this end, *HyperAuthor* provides students with tools to move the icons around, and to draw graphics indicating connections and categories among these icons. Hence, by its choice of what it made easy (creation of media) and more difficult (linking media), the *HyperAuthor* software itself constituted a weak form of scaffolding (Lehrer, 1993).

Scaffolding Through Inquiry. The third form of scaffolding provided to students was the daily emphasis on inquiry by all of us. That is, we asked students leading questions and often asked them to justify their choices of representations, links, media, and the like. We also attempted to provide more direct forms of instruction only after it was clear that students had reached impasses with their own approaches. This instructional approach follows from previous research where inquiry-based instruction has proven a necessary adjunct to computer-mediated learning (Lehrer, Guckenberg, & Lee, 1988a; Lehrer, Guckenberg, & Sancilio, 1988b).

Scaffolding Through Alternative Assessment. A final form of scaffolding was the introduction of alternative forms of assessment practices to replace multiple-choice achievement tests. Although this took many forms, one of the most significant from the student's point of view was the practice by the teacher of grading student work along the following dimensions: (a) group cooperation (cooperative feedback to peers, cohesiveness of group, incorporation of feedback from peers/instructors), (b) design product and content (research notes for at least six sources, depth of individual focus, inter-connectedness of the individual part of a project to the group presentation, integration of topics in the presentation, evidence of proofreading of text, and the presence of a well-developed user's guide), and (c) competence in using computer tools.

Evaluation of Learning

Learning by design involves many component skills and processes. Our assessment focused on only a few of these: student discourse, student perceptions of design, self-report of mental activities relevant to design, student competence with *HyperAuthor*, and the structure of the organization imposed by students on the subject, both internally (mental cognitive structure) and externally (the organization of their hypermedia presentation). Other aspects of our assessment practices are provided in Carver, Lehrer, Connell, and Erickson (1992).

Student Discourse. We videotaped students working together during the course of the design and development of their hyperdocuments. We analyzed student discourse using a modification of a design discourse analysis scale presented in Lehrer (1993). Although this scale assesses many components of the design process, here we report only the percentage of time students engaged in off-task behaviors shortly after they began working on their projects and shortly before they finished them. Off task behaviors are those that bear no obvious relationship to the conduct of inquiry (e.g., talking about an NFL game). We randomly sampled six two-minute segments at each time period (early, late), and cataloged the number of off-task behaviors in each 30-second interval.

Student Perceptions of Design. One form of assessment measured students' perceptions of the design process. As noted by Shavelson (1972), teachers may intend a particular model of instruction, but students may perceive one that is very different. Accordingly, we developed three measures of student perceptions: (a) a design interview (Lehrer, 1991, 1993), (b) elicitation of the tasks that students thought they needed to accomplish in order to create a hypermedia document and of the strategies they used that either helped them or hindered them in accomplishing these tasks, and (c) a ranking of the importance of a standard set of 21 tasks that had been elicited from students in (b).

The design interview questions reflected the four processes of the instructional model of hypermedia design and the taxonomy of skills presented in Table 1. For example, we asked about the purpose of the presentation, its structure, students' rationale for various representations (e.g., sound, illustrations), their rationale for a particular form of organization and the alternatives that they considered, the nature of the collaboration with other members of the team, and their general likes and dislikes.

The task elicitation procedure followed from Cantor and Kihlstrom's (1987) work on life tasks and strategies. Here students listed all of the tasks or "things you had to do" to develop their presentations. After writing their list of tasks, students wrote the label for each task on a separate page and then listed strategies that helped them achieve this goal and strategies that hindered them. For example, for "I found information," one student listed electronic search with keywords and using the card catalog as helpful strategies, and another, "getting impatient," as a strategy that hindered the attainment of this goal.

A related assessment, the task rankings measure, consisted of student rankings of a standard list of 21 tasks such as search for information with the card catalog, interview someone, decide on how two cards are related, develop a plan of who will do what, and so on. The result was a list of 21 tasks for each student with his/her judgment of its relative importance expressed as a rank.

Self-Report of Mental Activities. Students responded to 66 statements about the design process, like "I think a lot about how ideas are connected in my presentation," by indicating their degree of agreement with each statement. The statements reflected seven categories of design: planning, searching for information, representing information, deciding on the nature of relationships between pieces of information, audience, collaboration, mental effort and involvement.

Competence with HyperAuthor. We developed a dynamic form of assessment for measuring student's competence with *HyperAuthor*. The assessment involved the creation of a "mini-presentation" with performance measures of each student's ability to use the authoring and organizational tools provided by *HyperAuthor*. The dynamic form of the assessment involved a series of hints, beginning with global hints (e.g., select the graphic) and culminating in specific hints (e.g., press the delete key).

Evaluating Mental Organization. We used students' questions about a topic as a guide for selecting 16 key concepts. The concepts were printed on a page, each labeled with a letter, and students were asked to order them so that concepts that "belonged together" would be placed adjacently (Naveh-Benjamin, McKeachie, Lin, & Tucker, 1986). We then repeated this procedure three more times, except that each of the succeeding trials was cued by a concept we selected. For example, given a set of 16 concepts about World War I, we asked students to start their ordering with the concept of attrition. We then applied a clustering technique that represents each student's ordering as an "ordered tree"–a directed graph (Reitman & Reuter, 1980).

Evaluating the Organization of the Presentation. We examined each design team's hyperdocument by classifying the nature of the links between cards and by developing a graphical representation of the structure. We classified links according to their semantic roles: structural (e.g., continuation of an idea, part-whole relationship, characteristic-of), explanatory (e.g., causes, leads-to), or elaborative (e.g., example-of, alternative-representation-of, personal comment).

Procedure

Students worked in design teams as noted above for 10 weeks. We interviewed them about their perceptions of design approximately every other week. After eight weeks, we assessed their competence with the *HyperAuthor* software. The project questionnaire was administered before and after the completion of their hyperdocuments. During the first eight weeks, students designed and developed their hyperdocuments. At this time, they completed the cognitive structure, task elicitation, and task ranking assessments. After eight weeks, students attempted to use the hyperdocuments to learn about the topics that their peers had explored. We asked students to think aloud as they used the document so that its authors could "hear" the effects of their organization on potential readers. We then interviewed them once again about their perceptions of the design approach toward learning and about their perceptions of hypermedia composition.

RESULTS

Student Discourse

Analysis of the percentage of time students engaged in off-task behaviors revealed a dramatic decline from nearly 30% during the early phase of design process to less than 3% during the late phase of the design process. This result is similar to one obtained previously (Lehrer, 1993).

Student Perceptions of the Design Process

Student perceptions of the design process were measured in a variety of ways: interviews, questionnaires, and the task elicitation and rankings measures. Together, these methods allowed us to triangulate students' perceptions.

Student Perceptions of Design Tasks. Students' responses to the task elicitation measure (students wrote down the tasks they had to complete and things that helped or hindered their accomplishment of these tasks) indicated that their perceptions of the design process corresponded well with the instructional model: More than half the students made explicit mention of the skills involved in the planning and transforming phases of the instructional model. For example, all students mentioned the task of searching for information, and the majority mentioned the tasks of note-taking ("write rough notes from the source material," "took notes"), interpreting information (e.g., "separate the meat from the source," "decided on what info to use"), organizing information ("organize the notes, combining them together in subtitles," "used the data-base manager to organize," "talked with group about how to link"), and representing information ("experimenting with graphics," "deciding on pictures to go with the presentation"). All students mentioned learning to use the various components of *HyperAuthor* as a means to achieve these ends. However, it was comparatively rare for students (15%) to mention considerations of audience ("imagine it wasn't your project, how would you react to it then") or explicit ways of soliciting feedback from others.

Student Rankings of Design Tasks. The task rankings assessment complemented the elicitation of tasks in that it required students to make judgments about the relative importance of the tasks for achieving the goal of developing a hyperdocument. It also relieved students of the burden of explicitly recalling all the potentially relevant tasks. The five most salient tasks, according to their median rank, were: (a) taking notes, (b) discussions and coordination with other members of the team, (c) finding information, (d) writing interpretations, and (e) thinking about the best way to present an idea to someone. The five least salient tasks (arranged from least to most salient) were: (a) getting someone to try out the presentation, (b) making animation clips, (c) making video clips, (d) making graphs, and (e) making colorful graphics.

Generally, student choices reflected an emphasis on higher level skills with less emphasis on those tasks used in service of these higher level skills. For example, making video or animation clips serves the goal of thinking about the best way to present an idea. Moreover, with *HyperAuthor*, these lower level tasks were relatively easy to perform, so they did not receive much attention for their own sake. An interesting and important contradiction to this trend is the stark contrast in the rankings between thinking about the best way to present an idea to someone and actually getting someone to try out the presentation. It seems that the component of the instructional model dealing with multiple representations for ideas was communicated, but the importance of building self-evaluation into the process was not. Students apparently thought that their inner audience and reactions from other members of their team made the test afforded by a real audience less important and perhaps trivial. We shall present the consequences of this belief shortly.

Questionnaires. To examine which design processes were most salient to students, we calculated the median response to each item, with a possible range of 1 (does not describe me at all) to 7 (describes me very well). We then selected those items that were responded to either very positively (median score of 6 or more) or very negatively (median score of 2 or less).

This resulted in the selection of 14 positively rated and 2 negatively rated items. Taken collectively, the responses indicated high levels of student report of (a) mental effort and involvement (e.g., "I think a lot about ideas when I do a project," "I often lose track of time when I'm working on a project"), (b) interest (e.g., "I like to work on projects" and a low rating for "I think projects are boring."), (c) planning (e.g., a low rating for "I find that winging it is the best way to get through a project"), (d) collaboration (e.g., "Overall, we accomplish more as a team than I could working alone"), and (e) individualization (e.g., "Doing projects gives me a chance to develop my own point of view"). In addition, students believed that projects increased the likelihood that they would later recall something about the topic. With the exception of the last belief, all of these beliefs about projects were not evident in students' responses to the project questionnaire before their experiences with the hypermedia design project.

Interviews. Interviews with students largely corroborated the portrait of their perceptions developed by the analysis of the project tasks and questionnaire measures. However, the interviews did reveal the development of a constellation of students beliefs about *critical standards* for hypermedia compositions. Students in each group articulated criticisms about both their own work and that of their peers. Generally, most students criticized the documents on the basis of the use of multiple representations (e.g., "they should have used animation to make their hints come across," "too much text"), the nature of the navigational structure (e.g., "We think branches are easier to follow than a maze of links"), the attention to the interests of the audience (e.g., "That one had way too much information, presented in a boring way), and the quality of group processes such as planning (e.g., "I'm not happy with ours . . . We were too deadline driven . . . not enough blueprinting") and collaborating (e.g., "Some people stay isolated. They want lectures so they can just sit there and do nothing. But we won't let that happen.").

Another set of themes that emerged in these interviews was student dissatisfaction with both assessment practices and the organization of student time during the school day. With respect to the former, they stated often that their classroom teacher seemed to respect her point of view and interpretation of events more than theirs. They argued for a more individual-change view of assessment. One student stated: "So how about an advisor for each group rather than a grader? So then how students do with respect to this advice would be the basis for the evaluation." With respect to the organization of the school day, all students indicated that 50-minute periods were not sufficient to get any "real thinking" done. They also wanted more computers so that there would be fewer constraints on this resource.

Competence with *HyperAuthor*

Students' competence with the *HyperAuthor* tools was generally quite high; all students could use the tools to create cards, graphics, text, sound clips, and links. Some students experienced difficulty with the software associated with the scanner, and some had difficulty using the graphing tools. However, taken as a whole, all students mastered the software.

Organization of the HyperDocuments

The Effects of Literal Audience. Table 2 displays the characteristics of the hyperdocuments developed by each of the four design teams before and after the completion of the revision phase. Note the substantial effects of a literal audience on the number of links among the nodes on the hypermedia document; the number of each link type (structural, elaborative, explanatory) increases substantially after revision.

For the most part, these changes in quantity reflected the distribution of link types before revision, although, for the immigration design team, this isn't true: they developed a substantially greater number of explanatory links. Figure 2 displays the organization of the World War I hyperdocument before revision and Figure 3 displays this document after revision.

TABLE 2. Organization of HyperDocuments by Design Team

Design Team	Number of Cards	Structural Links	Elaborative Links	Explanatory Links	Total Links
WWI					
Pre-Revision	42	17	14	3	34
Post-Revision	43	48	26	10	84
Lifestyles					
Pre-Revision	32	9	6	3	18
Post-Revision	33	26	7	4	37
Immigration					
Pre-Revision	31	12	4	1	17
Post-Revision	31	13	8	15	36
Imperialism					
Pre-Revision	51	21	16	15	52
Post-Revision	64	29	19	19	67

FIGURE 2. Organization of a presentation about World War I before revision

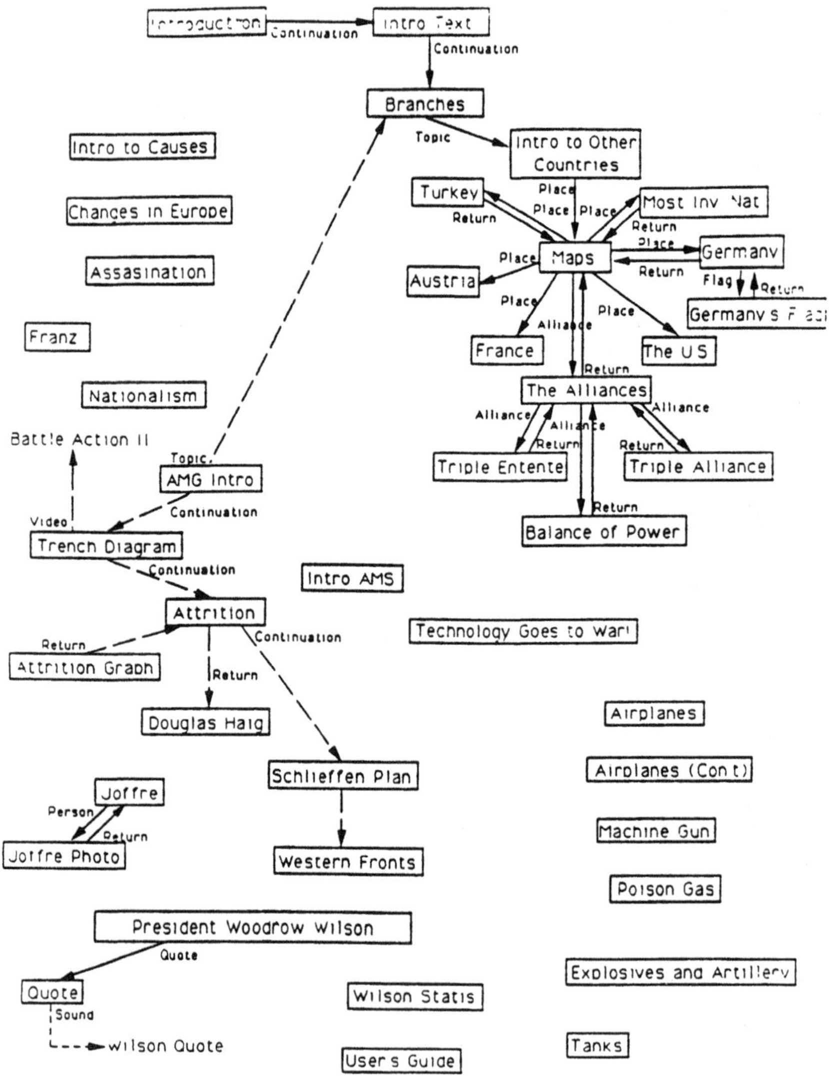

FIGURE 3. Organization of a presentation about World War I after revision

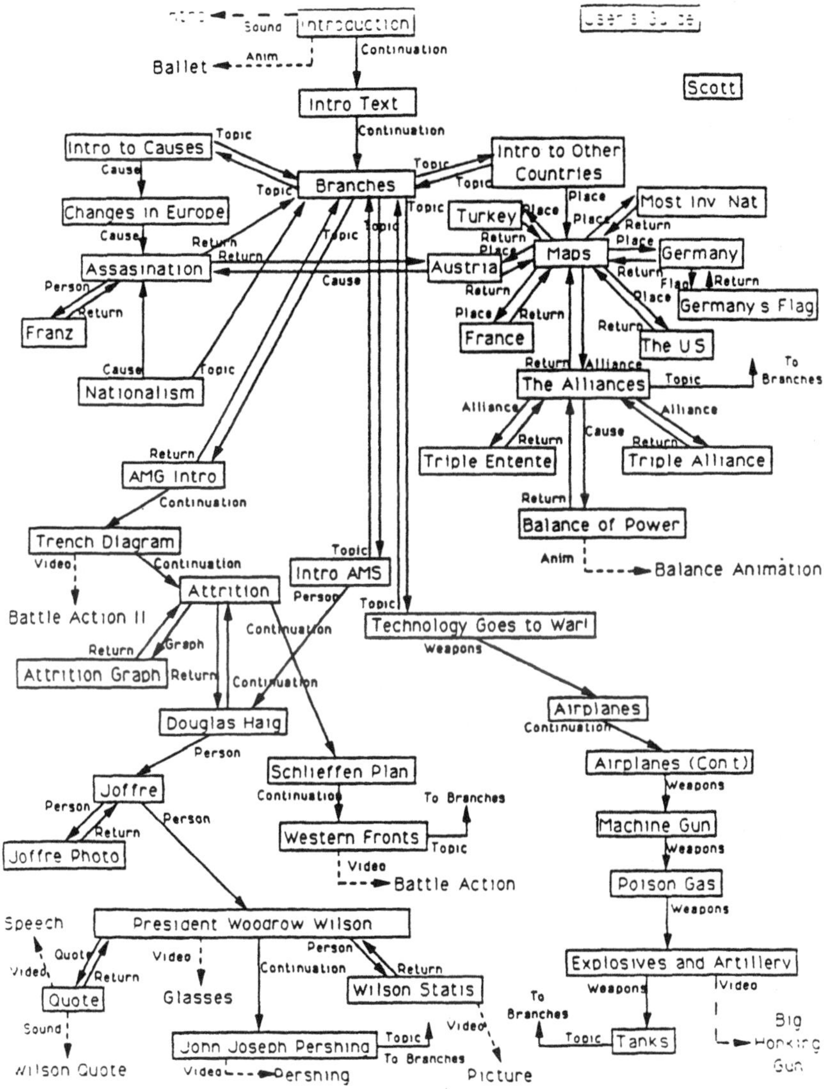

Inspection of these figures indicates the degree of configural change induced by the addition of additional links.

Our observations of the feedback provided to students by their peers generally suggested that designers were quite surprised about how opaque their documents were to potential readers. For example, the imperialism group presented a lot of information about a topic on each card, making reading and abstracting the main idea difficult. When another student complained about how hard the cards were to read, one of the students in the imperialism design team said: "But you can't have too much information!" At this point, a debate ensued between the student trying to read the card and its authors. The results of this argument did not lead the authors to a complete renunciation of their beliefs, but it did seem to at least plant a seed of doubt. Unfortunately, the classroom teacher had the same belief as the authors of the hyperdocument on imperialism. This may have contributed to their reluctance to discount the evidence at hand. Nevertheless, the literal audience generally induced students to reorganize and revise their documents.

Multiple Representations and Iconicity. Students frequently resorted to the use of multiple representations and iconicity to illustrate ideas. Figure 4 displays some examples. The pie charts displayed in the upper portion of Figure 4 were made to illustrate the chances of returning home unscathed if one was a soldier on either side in World War I. The text corresponding to these charts framed the problem in terms of what would happen to a group of 200 people. The illustration of the pan balance was intended to convey the idea of the balance of power among competing states, one of the causes of this conflict. This balance was also animated to convey some of the dynamics of shifting alliances. The picture of the corset was taken from a Sears catalog by a member of the lifestyles team to dramatize differences between contemporary and past lifestyles for women. Finally, the helmet icon was drawn by a member of this team to symbolize the fight for women's rights (black and white cannot do justice to its colorful balance).

Other instances of the powerful use of multiple representations were very evident in the other projects as well. For example, one member of the design team studying immigration noted that the founder of the Coca-Cola Corporation, Asa G. Candler, was a fan of child labor, so he placed the following quote on a card with the now familiar Coke logo: "The most beautiful sight we see is the child at labor."

Cognitive Structure

The creation of a hyperdocument was the result of a collaborative design process. Nevertheless, fitting the ordered tree model to individual patterns

FIGURE 4. Examples of iconicity in design

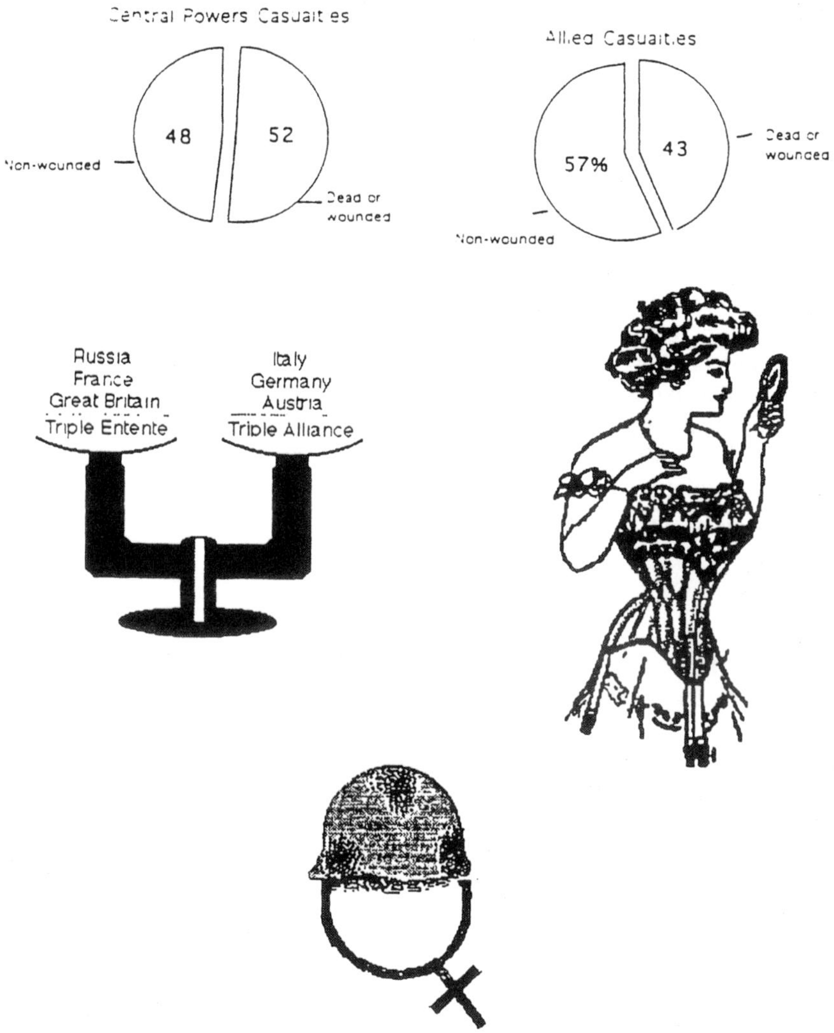

of recall of the concepts revealed substantial individual differences within each group. For example, taking the World War I team again as a representative sample, Figure 5 displays the cognitive structures of three members of the team. Note that the first student's structure (6a) is hierarchically arranged with a modal depth of 2 nodes between the root and the terminal nodes (e.g., concepts like Triple Entente). In contrast, the cognitive structure for the second student (6b) was fairly less well-organized, with less chunking of concepts and less overall depth to the structure of knowledge. The third student's (6c) organization is like the first student's in that it is hierarchically organized with a modal depth of 2 nodes, but it is significantly different with respect to how the concepts are clustered.

Generally, we observed that students with less well organized knowledge about the subject-matter tended also to focus on the surface features of the design process. Stated another way, they tended to identify the actions and tasks at a more concrete level, such as scanning, creating cards, and the like, without connecting these to higher level actions, such as developing alternate representations of an idea, and so on. However, we would have to follow up on this observation before drawing any conclusions about relationships between knowledge organization and how one thinks about the design process.

DISCUSSION

The results obtained from this descriptive study of students in one American history class suggests that design can serve as the fulcrum of the classroom. In this study, high levels of student effort and involvement were apparent, and students used the hypermedia authoring environment to create fairly complex documents about American history. Along the way, they developed a number of skills valuable in many areas, such as finding and interpreting information, articulating and communicating knowledge, and using computers as cognitive tools. They also had the opportunity to see knowledge in a fundamentally new way, as a result of their constructive efforts rather than as a set of givens from their teacher and text.

To date, our efforts to develop and implement a model of student designers is in its embryonic form. Nevertheless, the research results are encouraging: In a variety of contexts, students participating in design activities seem to explore topics more deeply, converse substantively about the topics, develop personal interests and involvement, and begin to develop critical standards for knowledge (Allen, 1992; Carver, 1991; Lehrer, 1993; Pea, 1991; Scardamalia & Bereiter, 1991). Taken as a whole, these studies

FIGURE 5. Examples of ordered tree representations of cognitive structure

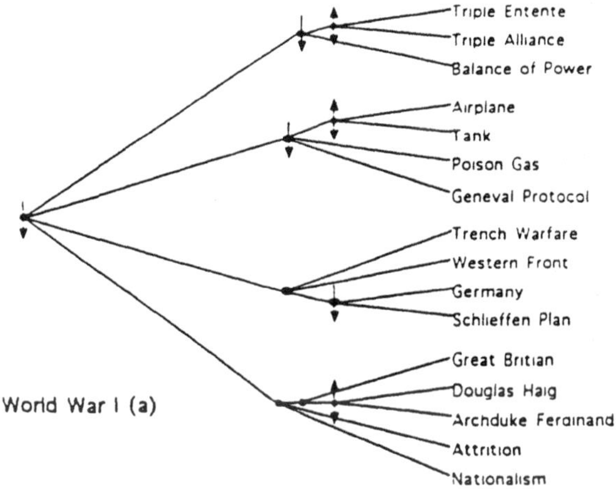

World War I (a)

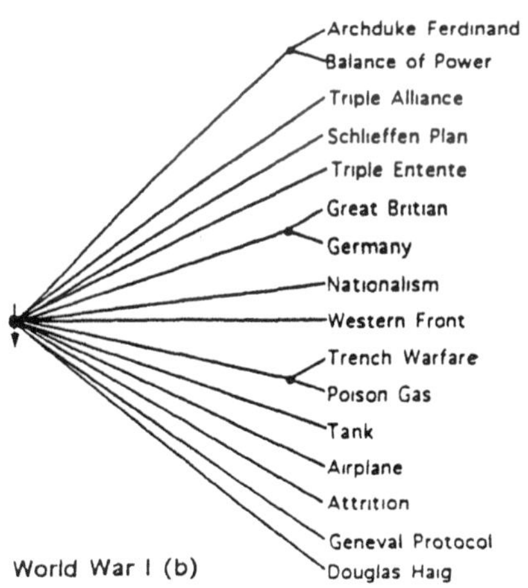

World War I (b)

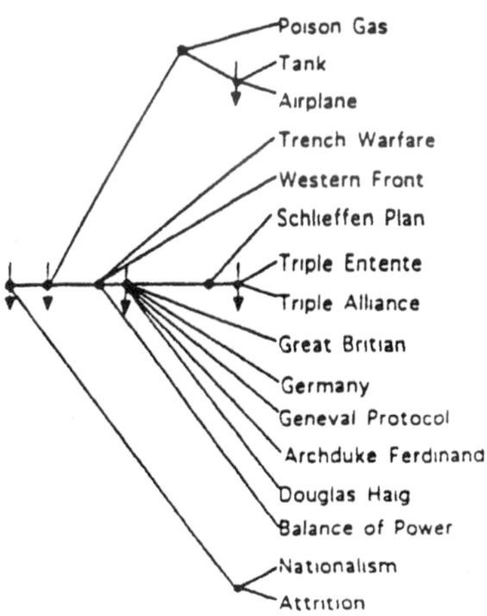

World War I (c)

suggest that the metaphor of design can help students develop conceptions of themselves as authors of knowledge. Nevertheless, the metaphor of knowledge design and its implementation with hypermedia composition tools still faces formidable challenges; their joint application implies the need to restructure schools.

Restructuring School

Ideally, implementing the design metaphor of instruction restructures schooling at several "levels" and along several "dimensions." Our use of levels refers to the organization of activity within the school. This ranges from the everyday activities of teachers and students, including their conceptions of their purposes, intentions, and respective roles in these activities, to more macroscopic activity structures such as the structure of the school day, and the broader role of the school in the community and in the society. In contrast, our use of dimensions refers to the components of learning that we believe important to the attainment of understanding about a topic. If one is placed in the role of a designer, such dimensions as defining the nature of a problem, finding and developing new information, and developing tools for use by others promote the evolution of a wide range of skills that are valued both in the classroom and beyond.

Nearly a decade ago, Goodlad (1984) observed: "If a predominance of rote learning, memorization, and paper-and-pencil activity is what people have in mind in getting the schools back to basics, they probably should rest assured that this is where most classrooms are and always have been" (p. 358). Unfortunately, Goodlad's description is apt today as well. In the current call for restructuring schools, Newmann (1990, 1991) observes that such restructuring, if it is to succeed, must go far beyond organizational change. Newmann calls instead for a close connection between restructuring and the development of classroom thoughtfulness. The latter refers to opportunities for "disciplined inquiry," inquiry that develops understanding, not rote recall, and where student achievement has "aesthetic, utilitarian, or personal value" (Newmann, 1991, p. 460).

The consequences of this type of restructuring include "a need to plan backwards" (Newmann, 1991, p. 461) starting with a conception of student thoughtfulness and then developing instruction accordingly. We suggest that the metaphor of students as designers is a fruitful place to begin such backward planning. As we noted earlier, adoption of this approach has lead to a specification of the kinds of mental skills that we would like to see students develop, a rethinking of the nature of assessment, the redesign of the classroom to place collaboration and criticism at its core, and careful consideration of how computer technologies can be used as design tools rather than as drill tools.

With regard to assessment, we must develop assessments that both guide practice, by serving as benchmarks of student performance, and that do not violate the students' conceptions of themselves as authors. The latter means that evaluation has to permit students to track their own progress as well as their relation to the critical standards of the group. In a follow-up study with some of the same students (but with different topics), we attempted to begin to change assessment practices to meet these criteria. To this end, we developed a narrative form of evaluation for each student. The narrative informed students about our judgments of their progress in each of ten skill areas: planning, question posing, data gathering, data interpretation, representations, computer skills, presentation, evaluation (soliciting feedback from others), research logs (we asked students to keep daily research diaries), and collaboration. For each of these skill areas, we developed a set of benchmark performances and informed students of these benchmarks both verbally and in writing. Thus, for planning, we established the following benchmarks: developing a timeline, specifying research topics, and their expected dates of completion, and assigning specific tasks to individuals in the design team. Similarly, for presentations, benchmarks included justification for the design of the user's guide from the viewpoint of a potential browser, development of a blueprint for the presentation with specific roles for each member of the team, summarizations of topics rather than literal reading of cards, appropriate eye contact with the audience, and clear evidence of connections among subtopics in the presentation.

Student report cards for history were then replaced with our narratives assessing competence with respect to performance benchmarks. For example, a portion of one student's narrative about her presentation skills was: "Your group's presentation was well organized, each member articulated an important topic, and the topics were nicely connected. Each member summarized his or her sub-topics well. However, Rebecca, you tended to talk to the computer instead of your audience. Try to think about this the next time you give a presentation–eye-contact is important."

The design approach has also lead us to more mundane considerations for school restructuring, such as the need for blocks of time for serious student engagement, and the need for greater amounts of space so that students can work collaboratively with technological tools that are commonplace in every other information environment (e.g., any professional office). The design approach also prompts some other long-overdue and decidedly intricate considerations: the development of organizational structures so that teachers can truly collaborate in instruction and develop a common vision of student thoughtfulness. It is this common vision that will be the glue of successful reform (Ladwig, 1991).

REFERENCES

Allen, C. L. (1992). Multimedia learning environments designed with organizing principles from non-school settings. In: E. de Corte, M. Linn, H. Mandl, & L. Verschaffle (Eds.), *Computer-based learning environments and problem-solving*. (pp. 463-484). New York: Springer-Verlag.

Barrett, E. (1989). *The society of text*. Cambridge, MA: MIT Press.

Bolter, J. D. (1990). *Writing space. The computer, hypertext, and the history of writing*. Hillsdale, NJ: Lawrence Erlbaum Associates.

Brown, A. L. & Day, J. D. (1983). Macrorules for summarizing texts: The development of expertise. *Journal of Verbal Behavior, 22*, 1-14.

Cantor, N. & Kihlstrom, J. (1987). *Personality and social intelligence*. Englewood Cliffs, Prentice-Hall.

Carver, S. (1991, April). *Interdisciplinary problem solving*. Paper presented at the annual meeting of the American Educational Research Association, Chicago, IL.

Carver, S. M., Lehrer, R., Connell, T., & Erickson, J. (1992). Learning by hypermedia design: Issues of assessment and implementation. *Educational Psychologist, 27*, 385-404.

Collins, A., Brown, J. S., & Newman, S. E. (1989). Cognitive apprenticeship: Teaching the crafts of reading, writing, and mathematics. In: L. B. Resnick (Ed.), *Knowing, learning, and instruction. Essays in honor of Robert Glaser*. (pp. 453-494). Hillsdale, NJ: Lawrence Erlbaum Associates.

Dewey, J. (1910). *How we think*. Boston: Heath.

Frederiksen, J. R. & Collins, A. (1989). A systems approach to educational testing. *Educational Researcher, 18* 27-32.

Goodlad, J. I. (1984). *A place called school: prospects for the future*. New York: McGraw-Hill.

Harel, I. & Papert, S. (1990). Software design as a learning environment. *Interactive Learning Environments, 1*, 1-32.

Hayes, J. R. & Flower, L. S. (1980). Writing as problem solving. *Visible Language, 14*, 388-399.

Hiebert, J. (Ed.) (1986). *Conceptual and procedural knowledge: The case of mathematics*. Hillsdale, NJ: Lawrence Erlbaum Associates.

Janvier, C. (1987). Representation and understanding: The notion of function as an example. In: C. Janvier (Ed.), *Problems of representation in the teaching and learning of mathematics*. (pp. 67-81). Hillsdale, NJ: Erlbaum.

Karmiloff-Smith, A. (1990). Constraints on representational change: Evidence from children's drawing. *Cognition, 34*, 57-83.

Karmiloff-Smith, A. (in press). *Beyond modularity: A developmental perspective on cognitive science*. Cambridge, MA: MIT Press/Bradford Books.

Katz, L. G. & Chard, S. C. (1989). *Engaging children's minds: The project approach.* Norwood, NJ: Ablex.
Ladwig, J. G. (1991). Organizational features and classroom thoughtfulness in secondary school social studies departments. *Theory and research in social education, 19,* 390-408.
Lehrer, R. (1993). Authors of knowledge: Patterns of hypermedia design. In: S. Lajoie & S. Derry (Eds.), *Computers as cognitive tools.* (pp. 197-227). Hillsdale, NJ: Lawrence Erlbaum Associates.
Lehrer, A. (1991, April). *Knowledge design in history.* Paper presented at the annual meeting of the American Educational Research Association, Chicago, IL.
Lehrer, A., Guckenberg, T., & Lee, O. (1988a). A comparative study of cognitive consequences of inquiry-based Logo instruction. *Journal of Educational Psychology, 80,* 543-553.
Lehrer, R., Guckenberg, T., & Sancilio, L. (1988b). Influences of Logo on children's intellectual development. In: R. E. Mayer (Ed.), *Teaching and learning computer programming: Multiple research perspectives.* (pp. 75-110). Hillsdale, NJ: Lawrence Erlbaum Associates.
Lehrer, R., Lee, O., & Jeong, A. (1991, April). *Reflective teaching of Logo.* Paper presented at the annual meeting of the American Educational Research Association, Chicago, IL.
Lehrer, R., Littlefield, J., & Wottreng, B. (1991). *Seeding mindstorms: Using Logo in the elementary classroom.* Fontana, WI: B&B Publishing.
Naveh-Benjamin, M., McKeachie, W. J., Lin, Y-G., & Tucker, D. G. (1986). Inferring students' cognitive structures and their development using the "ordered tree technique." *Journal of Educational Psychology, 78,* 130-140.
Nelson, T. (1987). *Literacy machines.* San Antonio, TX: Project Xanadu.
Newmann, F. W. (1991). Linking restructuring to authentic student achievement. *Phi Delta Kappan, 72,* 458-463.
Newmann, F. W. (1990). Higher order thinking in teaching social studies: a rationale for the assessment of classroom thoughtfulness. *Journal of Curriculum Studies, 22,* 41-56.
Nielson, J. (1990). *Hypertext and hypermedia.* New York: Academic Press.
Palinscar, A. S. & Brown, A. L. (1984). Reciprocal teaching of comprehension-fostering and monitoring activities. *Cognition and Instruction, 1,* 117-175.
Pea, R. D. (1991, July). Learning through multimedia, *IEEE Computer Graphics & Applications,* 58-66.
Perkins, D. N. (1986). *Knowledge as design.* Hillsdale, NJ: Lawrence Erlbaum Associates.
Reitman, J. S. & Rueter, H. H. (1980). Organization revealed by recall orders and confirmed by pauses. *Cognitive Psychology, 12,* 554-581.
Rogoff, B. (1990). *Apprenticeship in thinking.* New York: Oxford University Press.
Scardamalia, M. & Bereiter, C. (1991). Higher levels of agency for children in knowledge building: A challenge for the design of new knowledge media. *Journal of the Learning Sciences, 1,* 37-68.

Shavelson, R. J. (1972). Some aspects of the correspondence between content structure and cognitive structure in physics instruction. *Journal of Educational Psychology*, *63*, 225-234.

Tharp, R. G. & Gallimore, R. (1988). *Rousing minds to life*. New York: Cambridge University Press.

Vygotsky, L. S. (1978). *Mind in society. The development of higher psychological processes*. Cambridge, MA: Harvard University Press.

APPLIED

Martha Irwin
Margaret A. Moore
Judy Stevenson

Enhancing a Multicultural Program Through HyperText Links

The demographics of the elementary classroom are dramatically shifting in many schools throughout the nation, heightening the expectations of our educational systems to address the needs of students from diverse cultural backgrounds. The perplexing dilemma of the economically poor and the minority populations, whose numbers continue to mount, challenges the schools. In schools where demographic changes remain minimal, there is an increased awareness of the many cultures within our nation and the world. This heightened awareness is emerging as school personnel realize that

MARTHA IRWIN is Professor Emeritus; MARGARET A. MOORE is Associate Professor, Department of Teacher Education; JUDY STEVENSON is Educational Consultant; Eastern Michigan University, Ypsilanti, MI 48197.
Address correspondence to Margaret A. Moore, Department of Teacher Education, 714 N Pray Harrold, Eastern Michigan University, Ypsilanti, MI 48197.

[Haworth co-indexing entry note]: "Enhancing a Multicultural Program Through HyperText Links." Irwin, Martha, Margaret A. Moore, and Judy Stevenson. Co-published simultaneously in *Computers in the Schools* (The Haworth Press, Inc.) Vol. 10, No. 3/4, 1994, pp. 255-280; and: *Multimedia and Megachange: New Roles for Educational Computing* (eds: W. Michael Reed, John K. Burton, and Min Liu) The Haworth Press, Inc., 1994, pp. 255-280. Multiple copies of this article/chapter may be purchased from The Haworth Document Delivery Center [1-800-3-HAWORTH; 9:00 a.m. - 5:00 p.m. (EST)].

contacts with other countries are continuously expanding–the numbers of immigrants and people traveling or working in other parts of the world are escalating. Technological developments, furthermore, make it possible for people throughout the world to remain in close touch with one another via television, radio, and telecommunications.

Educators are realizing the need to help tomorrow's citizens acquire the knowledge, skills, and attitudes critical to functioning and interacting with people from varied cultures and backgrounds throughout the world. Yet, when we consider our current curricula, we find that the materials that relate to the diverse cultural backgrounds of our learners are very limited. Is this a hidden message that we do not value the history, traditions, and heritage of varied cultures? Can we expect learners to relate to materials that are incompatible with their prior experiences and background knowledge?

In order that the curricula might reflect and validate diverse cultures, information to enhance our appreciations and understandings of other people needs to be available. Multicultural literature and technology are two important sources for this information. By providing students access to a multicultural curriculum centered on reading and writing and enhanced with technology, we enable them to acquire multicultural understandings and perspectives and to become familiar with the tools of the information age.

To introduce a multicultural component to the curricula, a multicultural literacy project (MLP) has been successfully implemented in three school districts in southeastern Michigan. A hypertext program is being developed to support and enhance that project. In this article we will describe the use of hypertext materials to enhance the MLP.

Consistent with hypertext formats, the article will be organized so that you can determine the sections you wish to explore and the order in which you wish to pursue them. If you are a conventional, linear reader, you can simply read the article from beginning to end. However, if you are an interactive reader, you have your own ideas about what you would like to find about the MLP and its accompanying computer materials. Therefore, the article is organized in a hypertext fashion so that you can determine the sections you wish to explore and the order in which you wish to pursue them. You can seek information about a particular question by moving to the letter (A, B, C, D, E) denoting its section:

A. What is the overall content of *Multicultural Links*, the hypertext program?
B. What is the multicultural literacy project?
C. Why are hypertext materials needed to enhance the multicultural literacy project?

D. What are some of the specific features of the *Multicultural Links* program?
E. What are the implications of using hypertext materials to support curricula?

A. OVERVIEW OF *MULTICULTURAL LINKS*

In an attempt to meet the needs of the varied populations in our schools and to introduce students to the many cultures in the world, we are assembling a hypertext program called *Multicultural Links. Multicultural Links*, which will enhance the multicultural literacy project, is a resource bank of materials, including textual information about people and their cultures throughout the world, maps, pictures, music, and familiar phrases in different languages. With *Multicultural Links*, teachers and students can access quickly and easily various types of information, as diagrammed in Figure 1. For brief descriptions and illustrations of the components of the hypertext program, you can jump now–in hypertext fashion–to the related sections of this article listed below:

D.1. Maps of the world and of individual countries
D.2. Information about people and their cultures in countries throughout the world
D.3. Annotations of multicultural books and their relationship to specific cultures
D.4. Mini-biographies about prominent people from the various cultures and well-known authors of multicultural books
D.5. A multicultural calendar of historical events, holidays, and other information of interest

B. DESCRIPTION OF THE MULTICULTURAL LITERACY PROJECT

The Multicultural Literacy Project (MLP), a three-year program funded by the Fund for the Improvement and Reform of Schools and Teachers (FIRST), United States Department of Education, is designed to address the needs of the changing populations of the once monocultural school districts. Following the whole language approach to reading/writing instruction, we are integrating multicultural literature with the current reading program. We define "multicultural literature" as that literature

FIGURE 1. The components of *Multicultural Links* are inter-linked

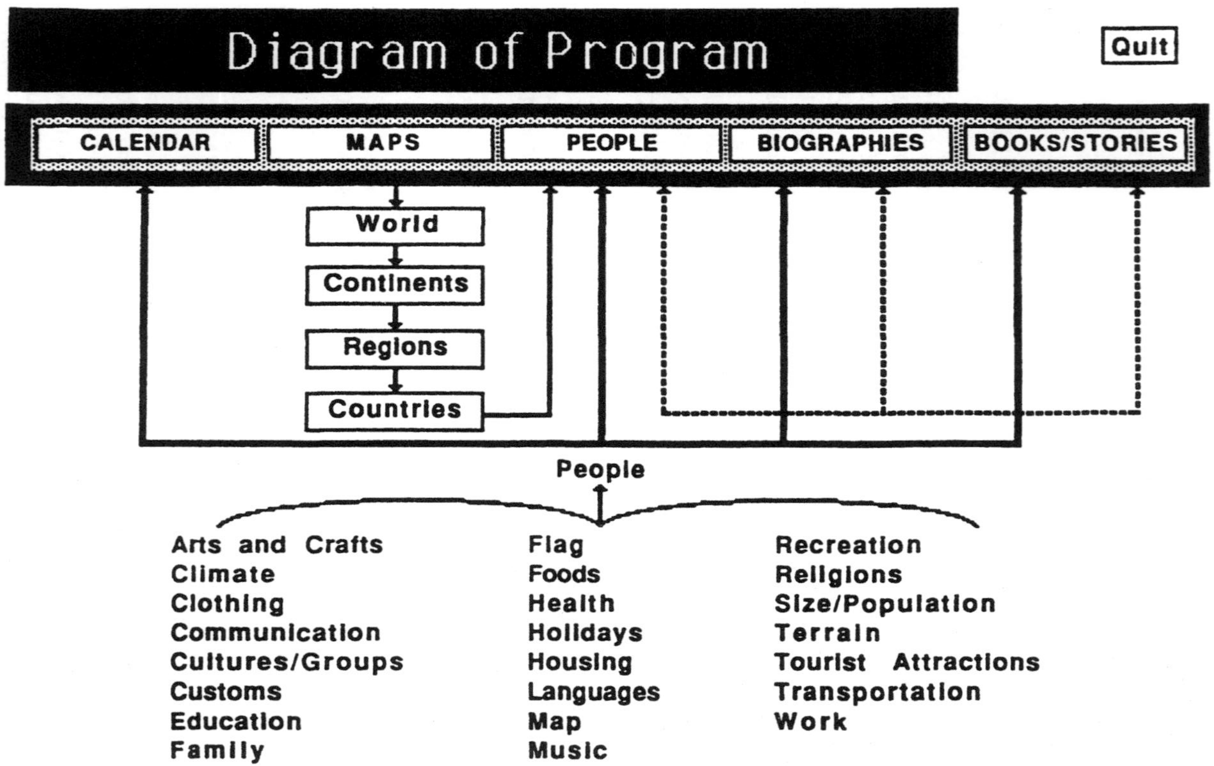

which focuses on specific cultures by highlighting and celebrating their cultural and historical perspectives, traditions and heritage, language and dialects, and experiences and life styles (Nauman, 1987). Examples of books that are used include: *Patchwork Quilt*, which highlights the life experiences and life styles of an African American family; *Knots on a Counting Rope*, which captures the traditions and heritage of Native Americans; and *Chasing the Moon to China*, which highlights cultural and historical perspectives of the Chinese. In this way, multicultural literature serves: (a) as a mirror which reflects and validates familiar cultures and experiences of our students, and (b) as a window which reveals similarities and differences between one's own culture and the culture of others. Through the use of literature, moreover, students are guided in reading and writing activities, creative responses to books, thematic learning experiences in the content areas, and cooperative learning groups.

In response to the needs of the changing populations of the classrooms and the widespread patterns of educational failure of at-risk students, we designed the program to be consistent with recent research studies that report educational gains in the performance of minority and economically deprived students. Following the suggestions of these studies, we incorporate: (a) minority students' language and culture with the reading/writing curriculum (Campos & Keatinge, 1984; Cummins, 1983, 1986); (b) the active use of language in order to generate and construct one's own knowledge (Au & Jordan, 1981, 1990; Cummins, 1986; Wong-Fillmore, 1983); (c) one's life experiences and background knowledge as a foundation for learning (Mason & Au, 1990; Martinez, Cheyney, McBroom, Hemmeter, & Teale, 1989; Vacca, Vacca, & Gove, 1991); and (d) cooperative small-group learning environments that include a mixture of ability levels (Cohen, 1987; Goodlad & Oakes, 1988; Slavin, 1983; Stevens et al., 1987).

Consistent with these studies, we provide a variety of literacy experiences for our students that emerge from their language and cultural background. Through the use of multicultural books, we lay the foundation for literacy learning so that students might enjoy literature and learn to appreciate their own culture and the culture of others. To support literacy learning, we also build on our students' life experiences and background knowledge in the context of an emotionally supportive environment–an environment that is risk-free, that encourages students to explore and experiment with language. We believe that *all* of our students can develop communicative competence, and we set high expectations for *all* students. Thus, the major goals of the multicultural project are to: (a) use the cultural backgrounds, language, and experiences of diverse population groups as foundations for reading and writing; (b) improve reading, writing, and vocabulary performance; (c) develop positive attitudes toward reading and writing; and (d) promote understanding and appreciation of one's own culture and the cultures of others.

In order to accomplish these goals, teachers attend five inservices, spaced throughout the year, to acquire methods and techniques of integrating multicultural literature-based activities with their reading program. After the first two inservices, teachers begin implementing the program within their classrooms, guiding their students through literature-based activities and cooperative learning experiences two days per week or one-half hour per day. Examples of multicultural literature-based activities include interactive reading and writing activities; choral reading; readers' theater; mapping and knowledge-generating activities; writing responses to literature; interactive discussion; and creative responses to literature through drama, art, music, and folk dancing. To further support and assist teachers in the implementation of the MLP, university personnel visit classrooms bi-monthly, providing assistance, guidance, and constructive feedback to the teachers as they integrate these activities with their current reading/writing curriculum.

To determine the impact of the project on varying populations, the MLP is currently being implemented and evaluated in three school districts in southeast Michigan. School District A is a predominantly black, economically deprived population, whose performance is ranked in the bottom 10% of the state; School District B is a racially balanced, economically varied population whose academic performance is diversified, including a large number of below-average students; and School District C is a predominantly white, economically sufficient population whose academic performance is ranked as educationally advantaged, with a large number of above-average students.

Evaluation of program implementation and its effects on educational performance is ongoing throughout the three-year study. Preliminary results of program evaluation indicate that all students, including minority and underachieving students, significantly improved their reading comprehension, vocabulary development, and writing skills (Moore & Diamond, 1991). Results further suggest that students significantly improved their attitudes toward writing and other cultures. The results of the observations, student interviews, and questionnaires indicate that all teachers are implementing the program as designed. Moreover, the outside consultant reported, "In fifteen years I have been interviewing over two hundred teachers across the country who have implemented over a dozen different innovations. I have never encountered the level of enthusiasm, understanding and commitment to a project as I have with Drs. Diamond and Moore's project."

C. NEED FOR HYPERTEXT MATERIALS TO ENHANCE THE READING AND WRITING PROGRAM

The emergence of significant and meaningful change in the behaviors and attitudes of students and teachers might be attributed to the staff development model that promotes the acquisition of new skills within the context of the specific school and community, the specific classroom, and the specific concerns of the teachers. While the evaluations of the MLP demonstrate that it has been successful in achieving its goals, much of the success of the project depends on relating the multicultural literature to the many and varied cultures in our country and the world.

The teachers in the project, while knowledgeable about some cultures, lack a deeper understanding of many cultures and lack information about other cultures. In today's technological society, one can no longer keep up with the rapid pace of knowledge expansion and its impact on cultures in our country and the world. Books, materials, and resources about other cultures remain limited; the few sources that are available are often no longer current. Teachers, moreover, do not have the time and resources available to readily access the available information.

Educators and students need to have information readily available for classroom use, and they must know how to access this information. They, therefore, must assume new roles in the learning process. They need to become competent users of knowledge who access, retrieve, organize, analyze, synthesize, and evaluate information. If we are to achieve our goals to foster an understanding and appreciation of cultures, we need to facilitate opportunities for teachers and students to readily access multicultural resources in all core subject areas.

Using *Multicultural Links* will enhance the current MLP. Teachers and students will be able to access more quickly and easily a larger array of multicultural materials. As teachers and students become competent users of information and technology, culture might become a funnel for understanding content information for all students, especially underachievers and students of diverse cultural backgrounds. While relating their personal experiences and cultural background with new information gained from the hypertext materials, students will be able to construct their own knowledge and develop cognitive maps of interconnections among the concepts and facts.

Different from many other educational software programs, *Multicultur-*

al Links is being designed to match the curriculum and the needs and interests of students and teachers. The software will both correlate with goals and objectives of the MLP and enhance learning for teachers and students by making information readily available and accessible. Since the hypertext materials are organized to support a thematic approach to learning, students will be able to connect more easily their own experiences with the information they are studying.

Just as this article has been designed to be read in the order that is most meaningful to you as a reader, students and teachers are able to access information in ways that are purposeful and meaningful, according to their immediate requirements and choices. Experimentation and exploration, fundamental to the construction of knowledge, become a natural way of interacting with information. Throughout the development of the software, moreover, we have enlisted suggestions and feedback from both teachers and students. In this way, we hope the software will be compatible with their learning styles, cultural backgrounds, interests, and needs.

D. DESCRIPTION OF THE COMPONENTS OF *MULTICULTURAL LINKS*

The hypertext program, *Multicultural Links*, has five major sections as shown on the main menu (Figure 2). Students can enter the program by clicking on any item on the main menu. When they are within any section, such as maps, they can link to other parts of the program, such as information about the language or housing of the people in a selected country. Selected screens within each of the five sections of the main menu–maps, people, books and stories, mini-biographies, and calendar–are described and illustrated below. Some of the linkages among different parts of the program are indicated.

D.1. Maps

In this section, students can see a map of any country in the world. The countries are grouped by continents so that students will learn locations of countries in relation to continents. Students can access a map of a country in two ways: (a) they can simply type in the name of the country of their choice, or (b) they can choose a continent from the world map (Figure 3) and then choose from a list of countries in that continent (Figure 4).

When they reach the selected country, the map will appear on the left side of the screen, and its location in the continent will be shown on the right (Figure 5). The names of cities, mountains, and rivers are not shown

FIGURE 2. The main menu of *Multicultural Links* has five sections

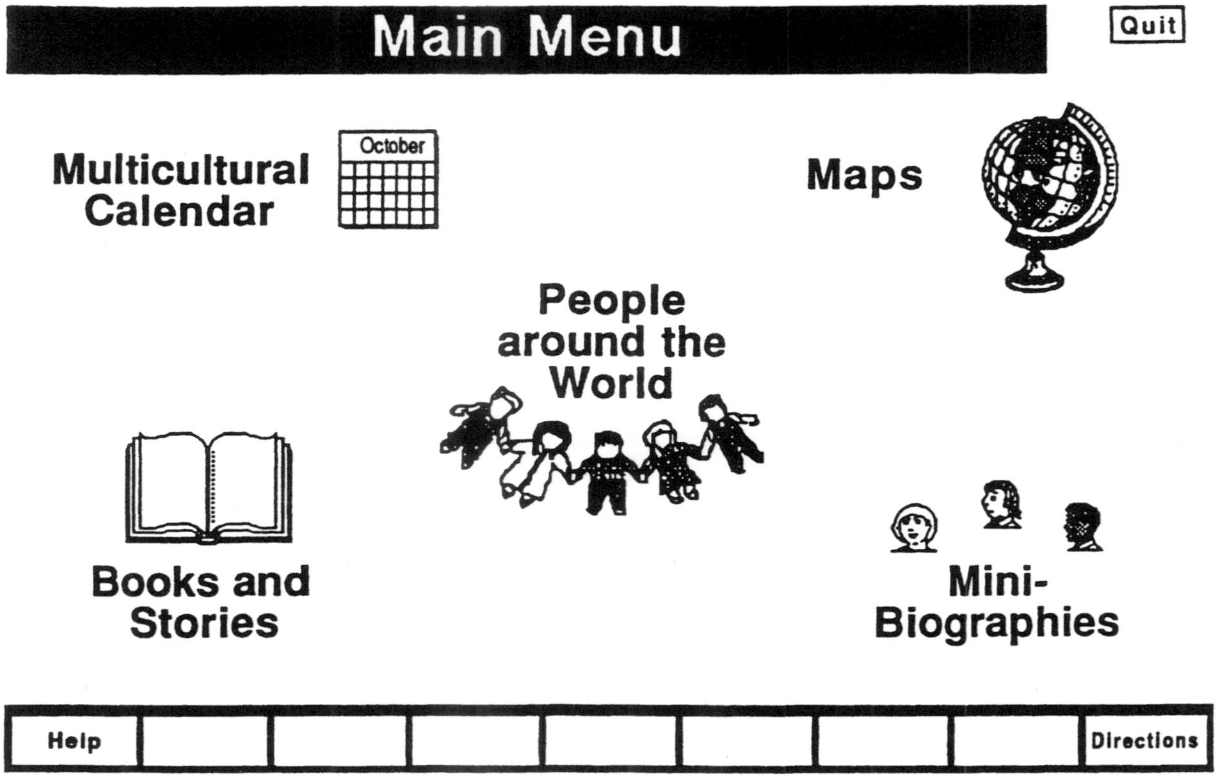

FIGURE 3. Students can select a continent from the world map

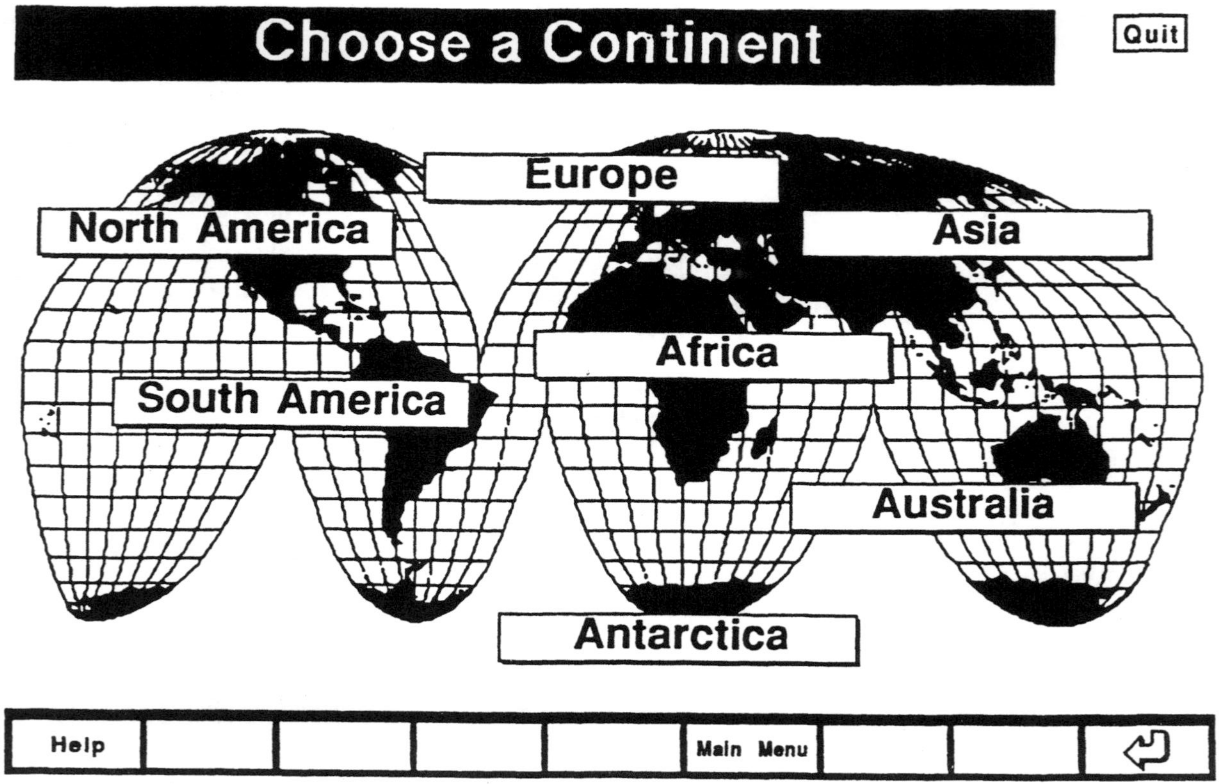

FIGURE 4. Students can select a country from a list for a particular continent

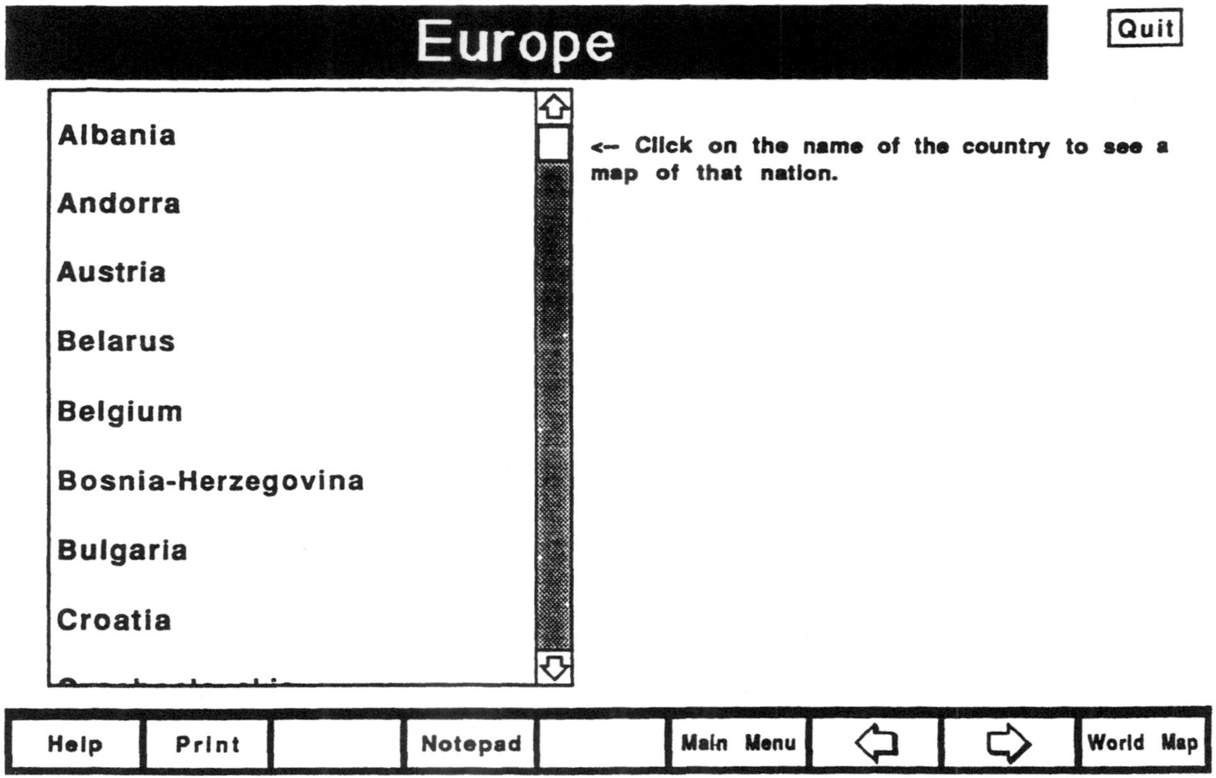

until the student clicks on the symbol or the word. For example, in Figure 5, the student has clicked on the star symbol to show the name of the capital city and on the word "river" to show its name, but has not yet clicked on other symbols.

Linkages to other parts of the program are consistently placed at the bottom of the screen. Note that on the map in Figure 5, the student could choose to get more information about that country or could return to the world map to find a map of another country.

D.2. People

The central part of *Multicultural Links* is the information about people in many of the countries of the world. When a country has been selected, an index of topics appears (Figure 6). By clicking on any of the topics on the index, the student will get information, pictures, or music related to that topic. Choosing housing, for example, will bring up text and perhaps a related picture on the same screen (Figure 7).

Boldfaced words in the text are indications that more information is available. Clicking on these words will bring up a picture, such as the Ninja village that was drawn by a Japanese elementary school student (Figure 8).

Music and languages have been included in *Multicultural Links*. The national anthem for many of the countries can be heard by clicking on the "Play National Anthem" button on the "music" card (Figure 9). If students click on the boldfaced words "traditional songs," they will hear some folksongs of Israel. For some countries, familiar words and phrases have been recorded by people from those cultures. By clicking on appropriate buttons, students are able to hear and see these words and phrases (Figure 10).

D.3. Books and Stories

The books and stories being used in the Multicultural Literacy Project are annotated in this section of the program (Figure 11). Students can locate books by authors or by titles, and they can search for books about particular countries they are studying. As the Multicultural Literacy Project continues, students will be encouraged to contribute their own writings or art work that have been done in relation to a book they are reading. When they click on the "More" button for that book, they will be able to see their contributions as well as those from other learners.

FIGURE 5. The map of a country shows its location on the continent and allows students to click to see names of cities, rivers, and other features

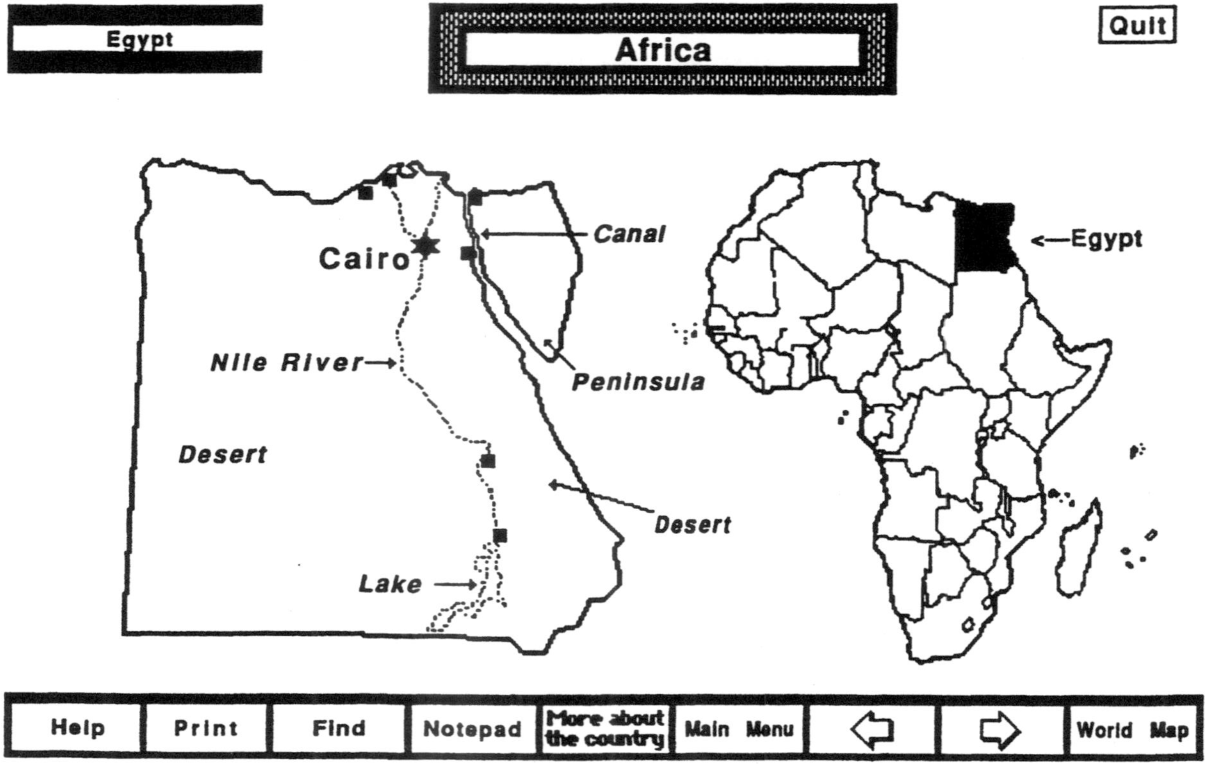

FIGURE 6. Several categories of information are available for the people in a selected country

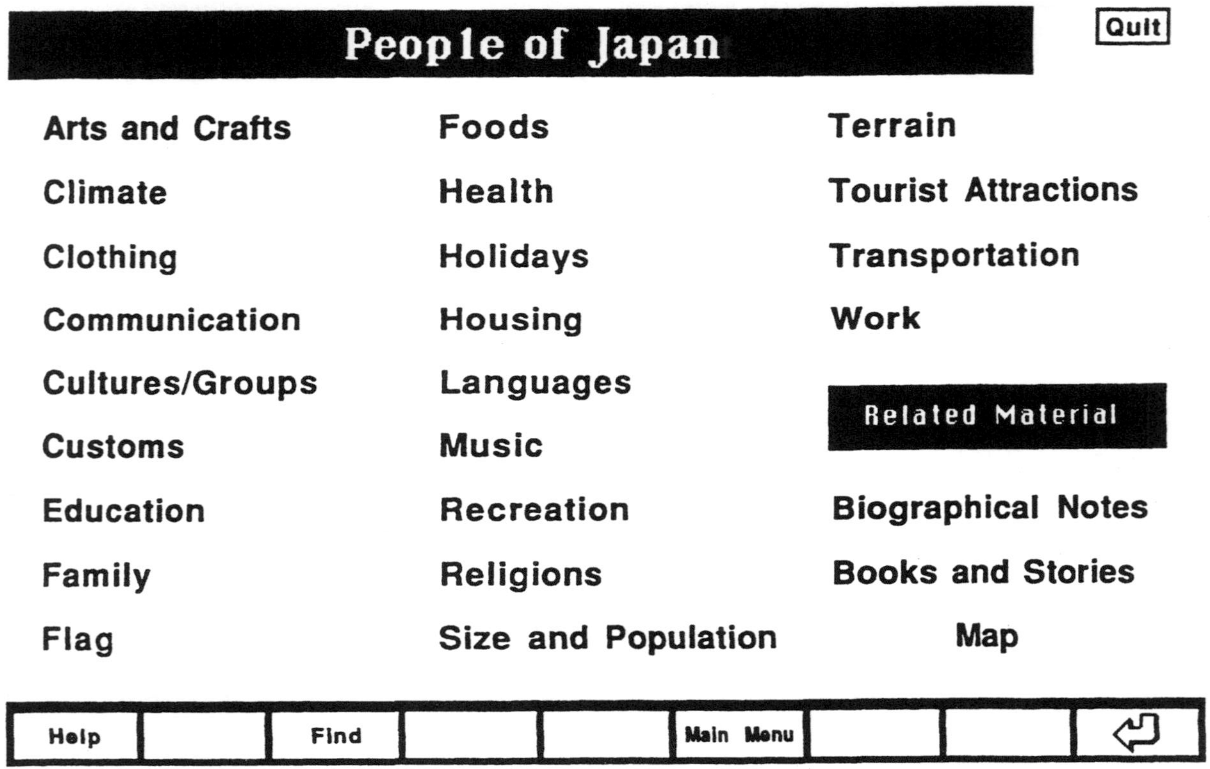

FIGURE 7. Information about a topic might be illustrated with a picture on the screen

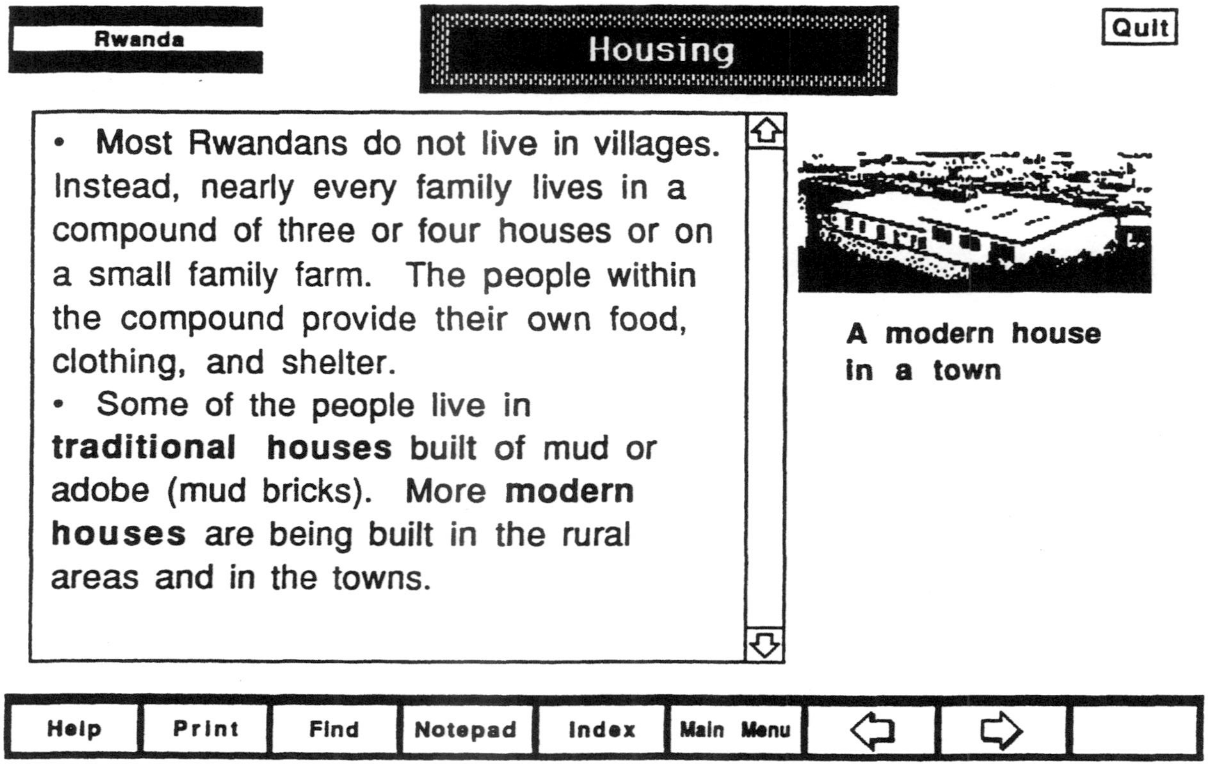

FIGURE 8. A full-screen picture can be seen by clicking on bold-faced words within the text

FIGURE 9. Students can choose to hear national anthems and traditional songs

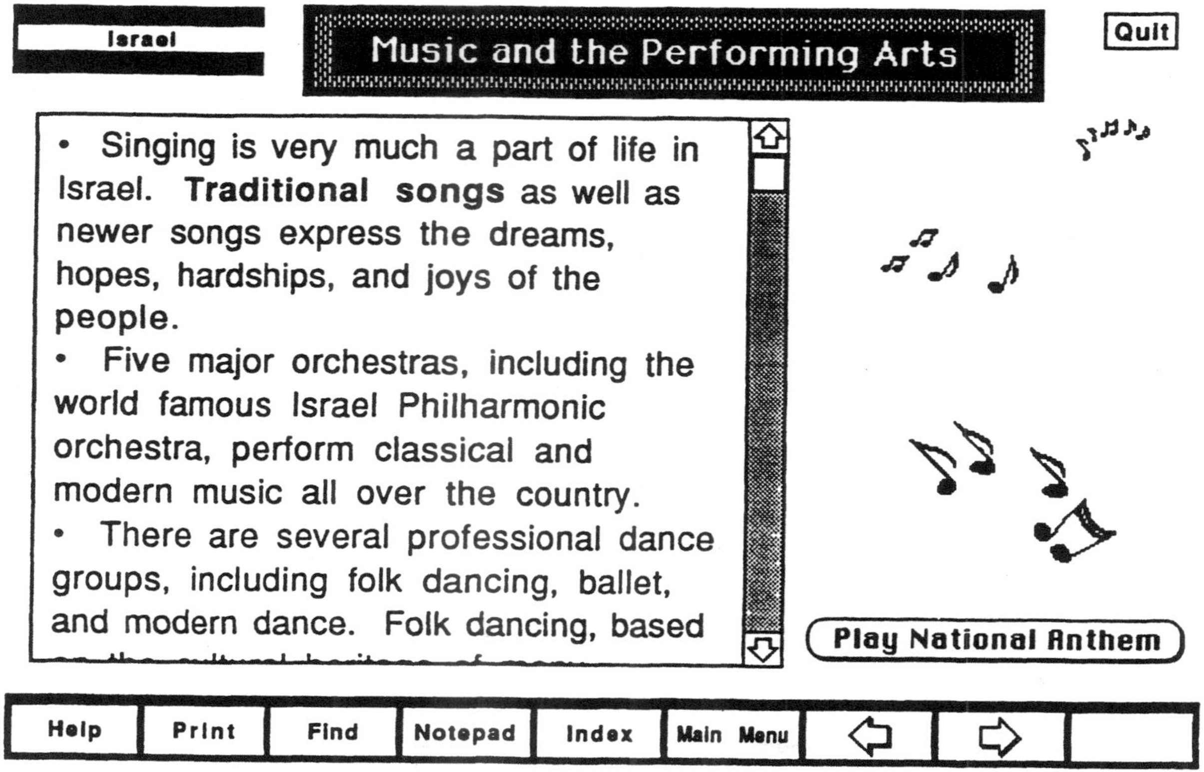

FIGURE 10. Words and phrases can be seen and heard in other languages

FIGURE 11. Information about multicultural books is provided

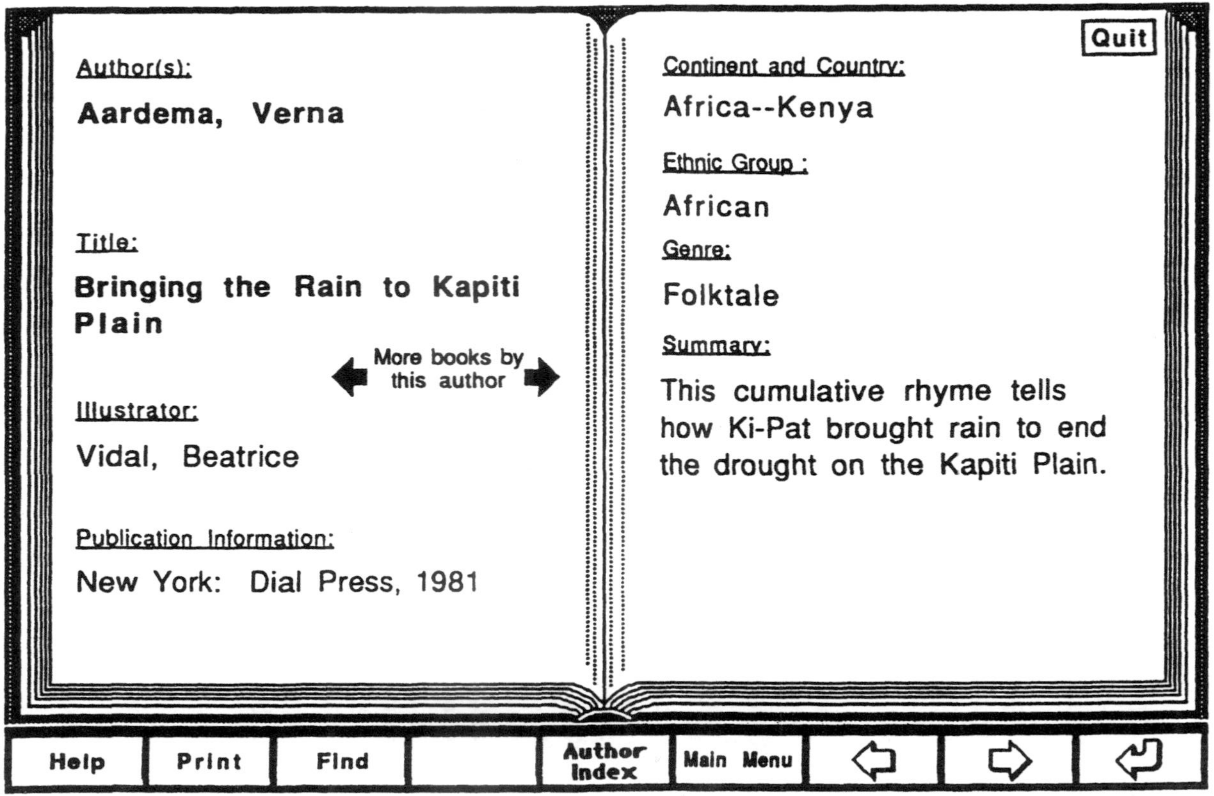

D.4. Mini-Biographies

In *Multicultural Links*, students will be able to read mini-biographies of people–historical figures, inventors, artists, musicians, athletes, authors, politicians–from various cultures (Figures 12 and 13). Students need role models and opportunities to read about people from their own cultures. They need to be aware of people who have made contributions to world society, but perhaps have not been recognized in typical school textbooks and curricula. By including these biographical sketches, we hope learners will be inspired and will develop a greater appreciation for the contributions by these people to a global society.

D.5. Calendar

Almost every day of the year, somewhere in the world, a country is celebrating a holiday, an author was born, an invention was recorded, or a special event happened. In the multicultural calendar, the students can find out which events are connected to a particular day (Figure 14). This might motivate them to link to a mini-biography of a person, a description of an author's books, a map of a country, or information about how the people celebrate a holiday or event. A challenge for each day of the year will further lure students to explore one of the day's events by going other places within *Multicultural Links*, by seeking information from other sources, and by relating the day's events to their own lives. For example, in the challenge activity for John Steptoe (Figure 15), the students can access more information about Steptoe in the Mini-biographies section and more information about his books from the Books and Stories section of the program.

E. IMPLICATIONS OF USING HYPERTEXT MATERIALS TO SUPPORT CURRICULA

Hypertext materials offer many new opportunities for adding breadth, depth, meaning, and interest to the learning environment. These values will be realized when the materials are developed specifically to correlate with the curriculum and contribute to the stated goals and objectives of the curriculum. Fortunately, the ease of programming hypertext materials now makes it possible for more educators to create materials rather than rely solely on commercially developed software.

Consistent with learning styles, students can explore hypertext materi-

FIGURE 12. The first screen of a mini-biography gives factual data

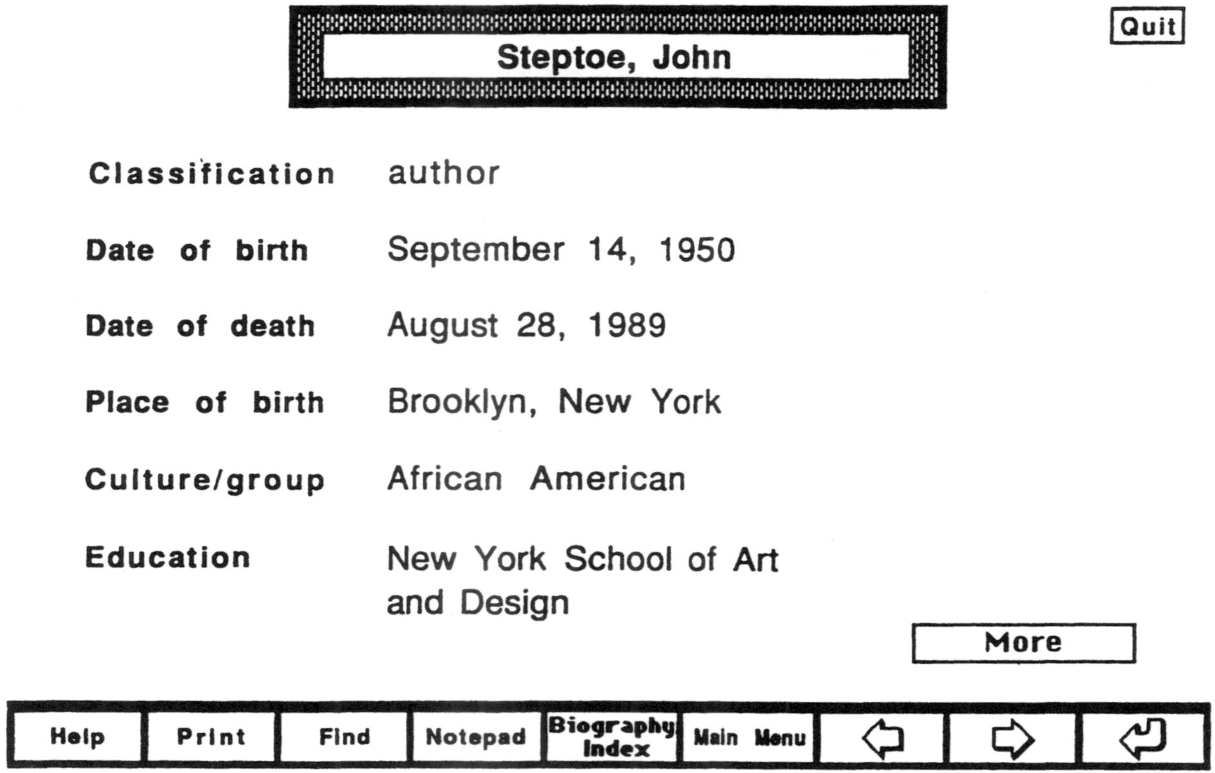

FIGURE 13. The second screen of a mini-biography gives a brief insight into the person's life and contributions

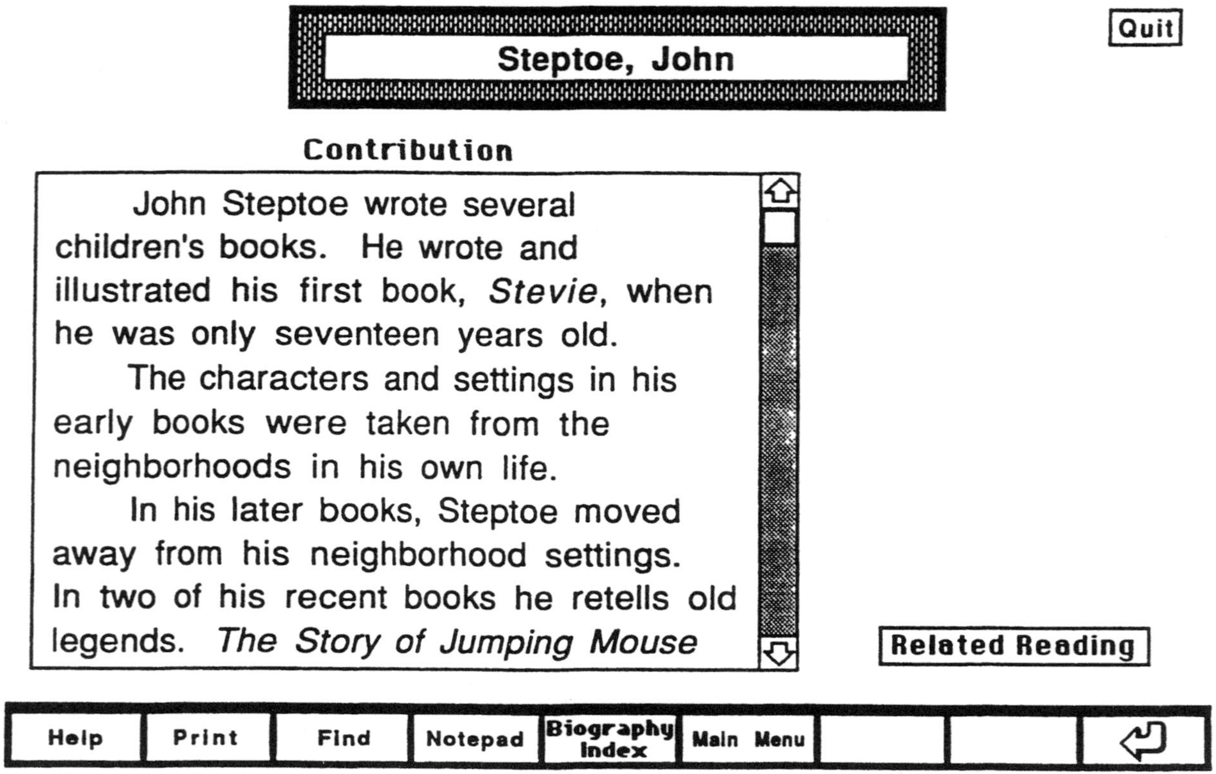

FIGURE 14. The calendar shows events for each day of the year

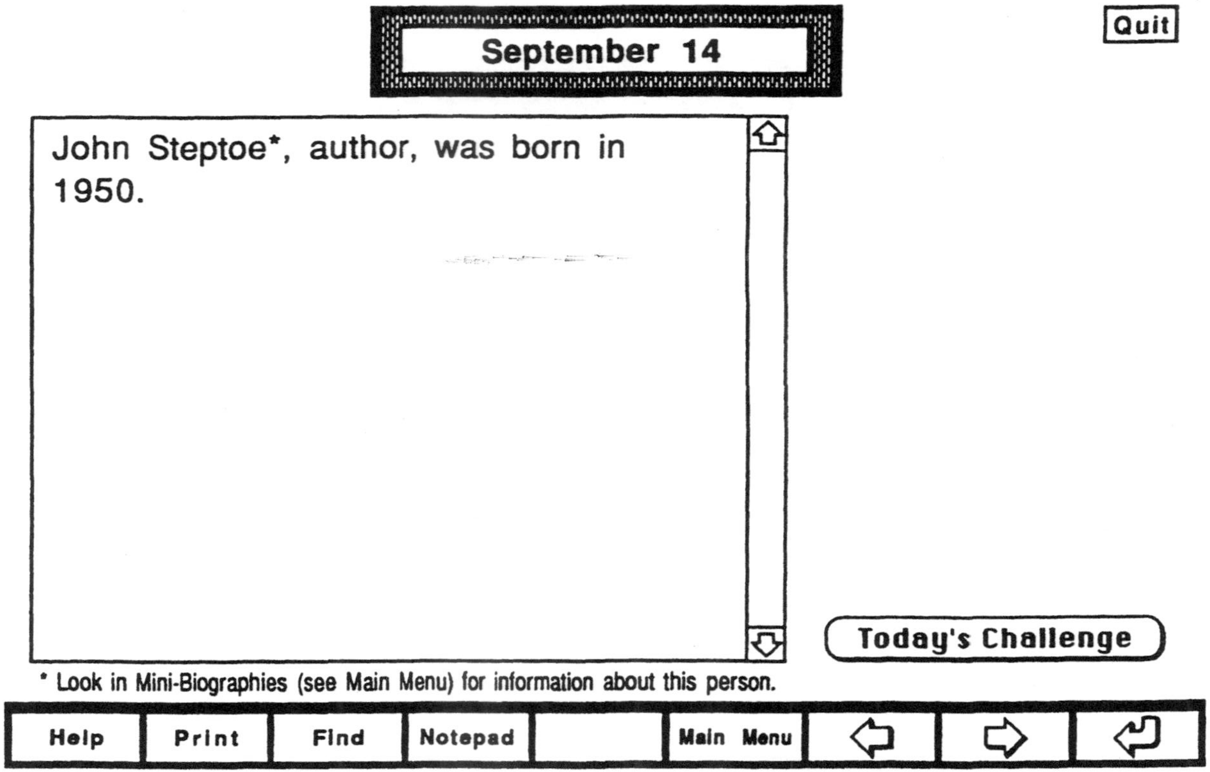

FIGURE 15. Challenge questions for the calendar encourage students to explore further or apply the information

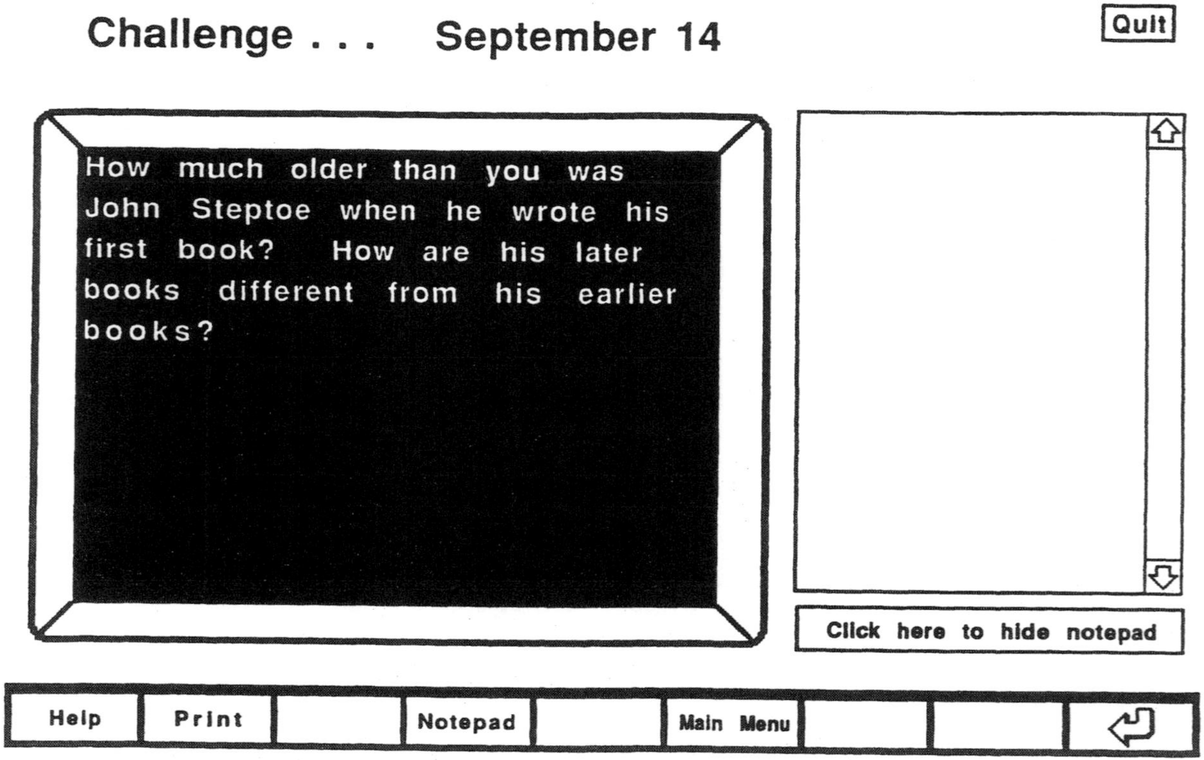

als according to their interests and needs. When hypertext materials are organized thematically, students can make connections between their prior experiences and background knowledge. Concurrently, they extend and deepen their understanding and appreciation of new information.

When hypertext materials are designed to be used interactively, they provide opportunities for optimizing learning. Organizing materials so that students might add information and drawings, moreover, enables students to construct their own knowledge. Due to the ease with which hypertext materials can be programmed, students will quickly learn to create their own reports with hypertext formats.

Multicultural Links is only the first step in our attempt to provide materials to support and enhance the Multicultural Literacy Project. Interactive videos are exciting new directions to pursue. Audiotapes and videotapes can be made of resource people from various cultures who tell folktales and legends, describe multicultural activities, and share artifacts. Tapes can be made of students singing traditional songs, playing games, and doing folk dances from other cultures. Students can exchange stories, poems, and drawings with students around the world, and their materials can be added to the hypertext program. With the use of interactive videos, learners can view movies based on multicultural literature and then compare and contrast movies and books. They can access video clips on cultural, geographic, and scientific features of people and countries they are studying. Not only will these features add new dimensions to the program, but students will be directly involved in accessing and retrieving information in ways that are consistent with a technological society.

REFERENCES

Au, K. & Jordan, C. (1981). Teaching reading to Hawaiian children. Finding a culturally appropriate solution. In: H. Trueba, G. P. Guthrie & K. H. Au (Eds.), *Culture and the bilingual classroom: Studies in classroom ethnography* (pp. 139-152). Rowley, MA: Newbury House.

Campos, J. & Keatinge, B. (1984). *The Carpinteria preschool program. Title VII second year evaluation report.* Washington DC: Department of Education.

Cohen, E. (1987). *Designing group work: Strategies for the heterogeneous classroom.* New York: Teachers College Press.

Cummins, J. (1983). *Heritage language education: A literature review.* Toronto: Ministry of Education.

Cummins, J. (1986). Empowering minority students: A framework for intervention. *Harvard Educational Review, 56*, 28-46.

Goodlad, J. & Oakes, J. (1988). We must offer equal access to knowledge. *Educational Leadership, 45*, 16-22.

Martinez, M., Cheyney, M., McBroom, C. Hemmeter, A., & Teale, W. (1991). No-risk kindergarten literacy environments for at-risk children. In: J. Allen & J. Mason (Eds.), *Risk makers, risk takers, risk breakers: Reducing the risks for young literacy learners* (pp. 93-124). Portsmouth, NH: Heinemann Educational Books.

Mason, J. & Au, K. (1990). *Reading instruction for today.* New York: Harper Collins Publishers.

Moore, M. & Diamond, B. (1991). *A staff developmental model for promoting literacy and cultural awareness: A multicultural literature-based approach.* Paper presented at the Annual meeting of the American Educational Research Association, Miami Beach, FL.

Nauman, K. (1987). School librarians and cultural pluralism. *The Reading Teacher, 41*, 201-5.

Slavin, R. (1983). *Cooperative learning.* New York: Longman.

Stevens, R., Madden, N., Slavin, R., & Farnish, A. (1987). Cooperative integrated reading and composition: Two field experiments. *Reading Research Quarterly, 28*, 433-454.

Vacca, J., Vacca, R., & Gove, M. (1991). *Reading and learning to read.* New York: Harper Collins Publishers.

Wong-Fillmore, L. (1983). The language learner as an individual: Implications of research on individual differences for the ESL teacher. In: M. A. Clarke & J. Handscombe (Eds.), *On TESOL '82: Pacific perspectives on language learning and teaching.* Washington DC: Teachers of English to Speakers of Other Languages.

Ray Braswell

The Top Five Reasons Not to Use Multimedia

Too often, we as university personnel, forget the implications of our work and research for those working in a public school setting. This article will address some of the factors that we, as educators, need to keep in mind when espousing the use of multimedia in education. The benefits for the use of multimedia in educational settings have been well documented. These benefits, however, do not come without costs, both in terms of time and money and raise realistic issues with which we must deal. Several of these issues are:

1. THE DOLLAR FACTOR

Walk into almost any university setting and ask to see a computer lab. Many times we will see large labs of equipment, usually containing the latest in technology. You can usually find interactive videodisc equipment, laser printers, CD-ROM drives, large monitors, and other video equipment. Contrast this with many public school settings in which the school may have a computer lab with 15 Apple computers, two printers, and no other additional equipment. Should we expect this school system to spend thousands of dollars to purchase multimedia equipment? Far too often we

RAY BRASWELL is Associate Professor, Auburn University at Montgomery, Montgomery, AL 36117.

[Haworth co-indexing entry note]: "The Top Five Reasons Not to Use Multimedia." Braswell, Ray. Co-published simultaneously in *Computers in the Schools* (The Haworth Press, Inc.) Vol. 10, No. 3/4, 1994, pp. 281-284; and: *Multimedia and Megachange: New Roles for Educational Computing* (eds: W. Michael Reed, John K. Burton, and Min Liu) The Haworth Press, Inc., 1994, pp. 281-284. Multiple copies of this article/chapter may be purchased from The Haworth Document Delivery Center [1-800-3-HAWORTH; 9:00 a.m. - 5:00 p.m. (EST)].

tend to forget the initial costs of utilizing multimedia in a school setting. Purchase of videodisc players, CD-ROM drives, video equipment, video boards, plus videodiscs and compact discs needed to utilize multimedia can comprise an enormous outlay of funds. We need to be aware of this problem when we present workshops and in-service for our public school colleagues. One possible solution is to recommend that the school start with equipment that can be shared throughout the school. A videodisc player can cost less than a good quality VCR. Most schools already have at least one large monitor for use with these VCRs. Recommend that these monitors be used with the videodisc players. Emphasize the fact that the videodisc player need not be connected to a computer, at least until the school can afford this equipment.

Recommend that videodiscs and other multimedia materials be purchased and maintained at a central location, such as the central office for the school district. One school purchasing a $1,000 videodisc set for one teacher who has 100 students is making an outlay of $10 per student. One district purchasing a $1,000 videodisc for 10 teachers who each reach 100 students is only making a $1 outlay per student. This concept of making materials available through a central location is used for most other media and should also be utilized for those multimedia materials that can be used for instruction.

2. JUST ENOUGH TO BE DANGEROUS SYNDROME

Click here and this happens. Touch there and that happens. Click and touch, drag and choose, punch in a number and watch what happens. Workshops and in-service can provide valuable information and important introductions to the use of multimedia in the classroom. Too often, however, the attendee is provided with just enough information to go back to the classroom and be overwhelmed when trying to replicate what was demonstrated only a short time before. There is nothing wrong with the "WOW" experience. We must remember that what we may feel very comfortable with has taken time and effort to master. Provide information that can be utilized but provide follow-up. Offer handouts that cover step-by-step setup, instructions, and potential trouble-shooting pointers. At your workshops, leave plenty of time for questions and, if possible, hands-on work with the equipment. Don't allow your expertise to become a handicap. Programs such as *HyperCard* can be simple to use but can be frustrating to a programmer who can make the computer do anything in BASIC. We must remember that we are often dealing with someone who is excited about the information you have provided. The more useful information and structure you can provide, the more it will be appreciated.

3. THE HOLY GRAIL SYNDROME

Not since the advocacy of television's use in the classroom has one instructional strategy been so promoted. Multimedia will end all instructional problems from teaching Johnny to read and add to eliminating truancy and drop-outs. Sally won't need to dissect her frog–just multimedia-ize it. Too often, at conferences, presenters will offer multimedia as a panacea for too many educational problems. There are many instructional issues multimedia can address. There are many valid places and times where the use of multimedia is not only an appropriate instructional choice but is the best instructional choice. Those who advocate the use of multimedia must also provide guidance for those times when it would not be appropriate. Hannafin & Peck (1988) suggest that you ask yourself several questions (dealing with the need for motion, costs, availability of equipment, and motivation) before deciding to use multimedia. Provide realistic, real-life examples of when and how to best utilize multimedia. Offer suggestions for incorporating multimedia into the regular classroom lesson. Don't be afraid to dazzle but do remember to teach.

4. YOU DON'T NEED MUCH TIME

Simply and *just*: two words which should be removed from every educator's vocabulary. It's easy. Just type this. It's not hard. Just do that. To play this video segment, just type in these numbers. Little is said about the myriad of tasks needed before you can just type in the numbers. These include installing the videodisc driver, creating the prerequisite card or page, finding the frame numbers, and cataloging an hour of videodisc frames. Fortunately, many educators who utilize multimedia are aware of the amount of time needed to properly prepare lessons that involve the technology. These educators should insist on proper implementation of multimedia technology. Nothing can kill the benefits of this technology faster than its misuse or poor use in the classroom. Think of all the computer labs sitting empty in our schools. We should not allow multimedia to become another tool that is tried, found to be more work than initially thought, and then discarded.

5. THE PURPOSE BEHIND REPURPOSING

Not every videodisc is appropriate for every subject. Much has been made about the availability of inexpensive videodiscs that can be "adapted" for use in the classroom. These videodiscs, although more available and less expensive, often do not contain enough instructional material or material that can be repurposed to warrant purchasing. We must encourage companies (such as Apple) to continue to produce materials similar to *The Visual Almanac* that contain an abundance of video images, sound, instructional activities, and information. These videodiscs provide the tools needed for true repurposing: information that can be adapted by the instructor to meet a variety of needs and levels. We, as multimedia-using educators, must emphasize the power of repurposing videodiscs, yet along with that power comes the responsibility of quality assurance. This responsibility does not, however, preclude imaginative thinking. *All Dogs Go To Heaven* (an animated movie about the friendship between two stray dogs and a little girl) may not be the first videodisc thought of when selecting materials for use in a high school physics class, but imagine the fun and learning the students will experience when applying physics concepts to a rat race.

Multimedia can be a powerful instructional tool when utilized properly. It is our job to see that it is. We must be aware of these five issues when promoting the use of multimedia in the classroom. We must also be prepared to offer solutions to these and other problems as they arise.

REFERENCE

Hannafin, M. J. & Peck, K. L. (1988). *The design, development, and evaluation of instructional software*. New York: MacMillan.

Peter E. Smith

Enhancing Hypermedia Through the Use of Templates

Hypermedia has received much attention from educators. In this article the term *hypermedia* refers to programs such as *HyperCard* and others (e.g., *HyperStudio* for the Apple II) that are used to control interactive multimedia applications and are also used by themselves to create effective computer learning materials called stacks. For more information on definitions of hypermedia and interactive multimedia, the reader is referred to Schroeder (1992) and to Reeves and Harmon (1991). Numerous conference presentations and journal articles have praised hypermedia's effectiveness in helping teachers create and use computer-based learning materials. Some educational technology journals have devoted entire issues and supplements to this topic because of "the explosion of information" about it (Brady, 1989). In a review of hypermedia literature, Ambrose (1991) indicated that "hypermedia products are becoming important components in educational and training programs" (p. 51).

Why has hypermedia received so much attention? According to Lehrer (1989) "it's because the hypertools make it relatively simple for beginners to achieve dramatic results" (p. S-5). In addition, hypermedia's popularity probably stems from the widespread availability of the *HyperCard* program, bundled with all new Macintosh computers. Whatever the case, it is clear that many educators see hypermedia authoring programs as a possible answer to the long-awaited dream of having available easy-to-produce yet powerful computer-based learning materials.

PETER E. SMITH is Professor, School of Education, Seattle Pacific University, Seattle, WA 98119.

[Haworth co-indexing entry note]: "Enhancing Hypermedia Through the Use of Templates." Smith, Peter E. Co-published simultaneously in *Computers in the Schools* (The Haworth Press, Inc.) Vol. 10, No. 3/4, 1994, pp. 285-291; and: *Multimedia and Megachange: New Roles for Educational Computing* (eds: W. Michael Reed, John K. Burton, and Min Liu) The Haworth Press, Inc., 1994, pp. 285-291. Multiple copies of this article/chapter may be purchased from The Haworth Document Delivery Center [1-800-3-HAWORTH; 9:00 a.m. - 5:00 p.m. (EST)].

In contrast to the enthusiasm noted above, others have raised concerns over the possibility of teachers and students authoring hypermedia stacks (Marchionini, 1988; Johassen, 1988; Reeves, 1992). Do prospective teacher-authors have necessary prerequisite (a) competencies in instructional design and (b) knowledge of hypermedia authoring programs to be successful in developing stacks? Looking first at instructional design, stack developers might encounter problems such as writing suitable objectives, guiding learning through appropriate user interfaces, and presenting information in stacks with sufficient organization to avoid "intellectual indigestion" arising from information overload.

As if instructional design concerns are not enough to discourage prospective authors, additional obstacles may be encountered when authoring hypermedia stacks. Are *HyperCard* and similar authoring programs as easily learned as proponents would have us believe? In a query to a "Question Clinic" for teachers in a popular education journal, a reader asks: "I've been told that HyperCard is a simple-to-use authoring tool for education, but frankly, I don't find it that easy. Do you have any suggestions?" (Mageau, 1990, p. 80). Perhaps this call for help reflects widespread difficulties among teachers in the use of hypermedia authoring programs.

Is it really possible for teachers (and their students) to readily overcome instructional design and programming challenges or is it "unreasonable to expect them to have the time or skills to author their own hyperdocuments" as Marchionini (1988, p. 11) suggests. The answer probably lies somewhere in the middle. Undoubtedly, hypermedia authoring programs present powerful environments for creating computer-based learning materials. It is also likely that novices will experience difficulties in using these authoring tools for the reasons outlined above.

TEMPLATES

This article is intended as an introduction to the possibilities of using templates in connection with hypermedia authoring. Suggestions are given on how templates could address some of the problems encountered by novices when authoring hypermedia stacks. It presents a narrative description of how hypermedia templates were successfully employed in one elementary school. Potential advantages and disadvantages of templates are identified. Finally, directions for further research and development are advised.

Let us begin with a definition of *templates*. The writer offers the following definition as a starting point: A template is a customized mold, guide, or pattern designed to overlay a given format and structure on a particular software program. Templates for computer software are available in many forms and subjects. While a complete accounting of templates is beyond the scope or intent of this article, an example of their use in educational contexts is appropriate. A good illustration may be seen in the wealth of templates that have been developed and marketed for the popular *AppleWorks* program. Templates for gradesheets, lesson plans, school-year calendars, spreadsheets, and quiz-making databases are but a few of the many educationally oriented offerings available. In addition are numerous templates for out-of-school *AppleWorks* applications in areas ranging from recipes to personal finance and taxes. Noting the wide variety of templates available, one might observe that a vigorous and healthy "cottage industry" has grown around this popular product. A growing variety of templates is likewise available for other popular word processors, databases, and spreadsheets.

ADVANTAGES OF TEMPLATES

For those who would like to have powerful computer applications up and running with minimal time and effort in development, templates offer advantages. Perhaps the greatest of these is that only a very small subset of any program's commands must be learned to successfully employ templates. A deep and sophisticated knowledge of the host program's operational commands is not necessary for most template applications. As an example, prospective users of an *AppleWorks* spreadsheet template will require only a copy of *AppleWorks*, the most fundamental understanding of its operation, the template, and original data to "fill in the blanks."

USING TEMPLATES IN A SCHOOL

Recently this writer worked with several teachers at a local elementary school in a cooperative effort to explore the potential uses of hypermedia templates. We were not engaged in a formal research project; rather, the objective was simply to informally check the feasibility of using hypermedia templates in an elementary school and to explore directions for further study. For this project, we used Apple IIgs computers and *HyperStudio*, a hypermedia authoring program from Roger Wagner Software (Wagner, 1991).

With the overwhelming popularity of the Macintosh and *HyperCard*, the reader might wonder why the Apple IIgs and *HyperStudio* were selected. The reasons included:

1. The Apple IIgs remains popular in local area elementary schools. There is a large installed base of these computers in the school where the templates were developed. Both teachers and students were already familiar with the operation of the Apple IIgs and required no additional training .
2. Hypermedia is at its best when a variety of graphics can be made available for the creation of cards. *HyperStudio* includes a good collection of clip art as well as an adequate number of tools for creating original graphics. In addition, the participating teachers and the writer possessed additional Apple II clip-art. We were also familiar with Apple II graphics creation, digitizing, file transfers, etc.
3. The Apple IIgs provides a fine platform for the development of hypermedia stacks. Its color and sound capabilities are easily accessed through *HyperStudio*. Completed stacks can be run on individual computers or shown on large-screen television monitors because of the Apple IIgs composite video output. It is even possible to record the "playback" of a stack for later review using a standard videocassette recorder (Wagner, 1991).
4. At the time, *HyperStudio* was the only IIgs specific hypermedia program available. The writer was impressed by reports of its power. (A new and more powerful version 3.1 of *HyperStudio* is now available.)

In developing the templates, *HyperStudio* was first demonstrated for the faculty so that they could understand potential benefits of the program. Advantages and disadvantages of hypermedia in the teaching/learning process were discussed. Also explored were various ways hypermedia might be used by students. Finally, possible template ideas were generated in a brainstorming session. Among the ideas suggested by the group were:

1. *Timeline template*: Various timelines developed with students putting in appropriate material for given dates.
2. *Class newspaper template*: A newspaper with feature stories; editorials; sports; movie, television, and book reviews, etc.
3. *Open house template*: A report featuring activities and programs in the school to be set up and run during an open house for parents.
4. *School report template*: An aid for students preparing reports on various topics. This template also could provide structure for class presentations.

5. *Teacher report to parents template*: Similar in nature to the open house template, except this would feature particular students and would be sent to parents. If parents did not have a computer to run the stack, it could be recorded on a videocassette recorder and sent home for later viewing on a videocassette player.
6. *Action-adventure template*: A structural framework with organizational prompts for action-adventure stories.
7. *Family tree template*: A family history stack. Students would provide information on relatives that would be incorporated into the stack.
8. *School or room resource template*: A way for students to locate and find out more about available resources in a school or classroom.
9. *General purpose branching template*: A kind of catch-all miscellaneous template that could be adapted to many uses.
10. *Health room template*: A variant on the school/room template described above focusing on a health room.

After exploring the relative benefits of each of the possibilities above, the following templates were developed by the writer in consultation with the teachers:

1. *A Kiosk template*: Designed to announce school events and activities, showcase student work. Installed and run at the school library.
2. *An Animal report template*: To guide the development and preparation of reports on animals.
3. *A Story template*: To guide in the development and writing of stories.

The templates were complete in that they contained all of the final cards (although blank) and branching capabilities. What was missing was the particular information required for each card to complete the final stack. The cards provided an organizational structure for content that was later supplied by students. The students completed the stacks by filling in blank cards with original graphics and writings.

In keeping with the preliminary, exploratory nature of the project, no formal experimental procedures were followed in assessing the template effectiveness. Rather, narrative reports were gathered from the teachers who used the templates. Their reports indicated satisfaction in use of the templates. Students could quickly and easily create colorful, attractive, and informative stacks. One unanticipated benefit was that the templates appeared to whet their appetites to go on and develop their own original stacks.

ADDITIONAL TRAINING BENEFITS OF TEMPLATES

As the template development team continued to think about using templates with hypermedia, additional potential benefits soon became apparent. Perhaps templates could be helpful in the teaching of hypermedia authoring. When one has had no previous experience with computer program authoring, the creation of an original hypermedia stack from scratch could be viewed as a formidable task. If, however, prospective authors could work within a previously developed stack template in which cards, backgrounds, and some buttons had been already placed, stacks could be completed quickly, thereby keeping motivational levels high.

For training purposes, one might envision a series of templates, each teaching various sub-skills necessary for authoring, such as creating and placing buttons, creating backgrounds, graphics, text, branching strategies, etc. Rather than being faced with the daunting task of learning a number of sub-skills simultaneously, prospective authors could build competencies in sub-skills one at a time, while constructing useful stacks. Templates could thus serve a useful training function in providing students with guided practice as they develop various authoring skills. Various combinations of simultaneous versus successive learning of component authoring skills could be systematically explored.

DISADVANTAGES OF TEMPLATES

Templates are not without disadvantages. These include the possibility that they might not fit the needs of the application for which they are used and, from the training perspective, the possibility that the built-in structures inherent in templates could discourage the development of creative new forms of hypermedia. That is, it is possible that working within the built-in constraints of the template, prospective authors might tend to prepare conventional rather than creative stacks.

CONCLUSIONS

This exploratory and informal project was undertaken to determine the feasibility of using templates in connection with hypermedia stacks in an elementary school. While no formal study was attempted, the preliminary and informal findings would suggest that the use of templates has potential benefit for helping "non-authors" produce useful hypermedia stacks quickly and easily. It is also possible, as noted earlier, that templates might be employed for teaching authoring skills. In any case, it is this writer's firm belief that the use and development of templates for hypermedia have untapped potential and deserve to be systematically explored.

REFERENCES

Ambrose, D. (1991). The effects of hypermedia on learning: A literature review. *Educational Technology, 31*(12), 51-54.

Brady, H. (1989). HyperCard K-12. *Classroom Computer Learning (HyperCard supplement), 9*(7), S2.

Jonassen, D. (1988). Designing structured hypertext and structuring access to hypertext. *Educational Technology, 28*(11), 13-16.

Lehrer, A. (1989). HyperCard K-12: What's all the commotion? *Classroom Computer Learning (HyperCard supplement), 9*(7), S4-S7.

Mageau, T. (1990). Question clinic. *Instructor, C*(4), 80.

Marchionini, G. (1988). Hypermedia and learning: Freedom and chaos. *Educational Technology, 28*(11), 8-12.

Reeves, T. & Harmon, S. (1991). What's in a name-hypermedia versus multimedia. *Interact, 3*(1), 28-30.

Reeves, T. (1992). Evaluating interactive multimedia. *Educational Technology, 32*(5), 47-52.

Schroeder, E. (1992). Interactive multimedia computer systems. *Educational Technology, 32*(2), 59-60.

Wagner, R. (1991). *The VCR Printer.* El Cajon CA: Roger Wagner Publishing.

Min Liu

Hypermedia Assisted Instruction and Second Language Learning: A Semantic-Network-Based Approach

INTRODUCTION

Let us consider a scene (as adapted) Duchastel (1990) described in his article "Discussion: Formal and Informal Learning with Hypermedia": You are viewing the evening news on television about Chinese imperial dynasties. A news item about a recent archaeological finding in Kiangsu province has aroused your curiosity. You interrupt the newscast momentarily to get further information. By touching the words "Chinese" and "dynasties" on the TV screen, you are led to an overview given in the form of a graphical representation of the hypermedia information bank. You begin to explore information related to this news item. Since the information items in this hypermedia bank are related to each other, a touch on the screen will branch you to various topics in which you are interested. Some information presented is textual, some graphical, some video, and other in map forms. Your exploration continues until your curiosity is satisfied. Then you resume watching the evening news at the point where you left off, which is now a video-recording.

What is described here is an example of hypermedia. Compared with print materials that we are so accustomed to, accessing information in this

MIN LIU is Assistant Professor, Department of Curriculum and Instruction, University of Texas at Austin, Austin, TX 78712.

[Haworth co-indexing entry note]: "Hypermedia Assisted Instruction and Second Language Learning: A Semantic-Network-Based Approach." Liu, Min. Co-published simultaneously in *Computers in the Schools* (The Haworth Press, Inc.) Vol. 10, No. 3/4, 1994, pp. 293-312; and: *Multimedia and Megachange: New Roles for Educational Computing* (eds: W. Michael Reed, John K. Burton, and Min Liu) The Haworth Press, Inc., 1994, pp. 293-312. Multiple copies of this article/chapter may be purchased from The Haworth Document Delivery Center [1-800-3-HAWORTH; 9:00 a.m. - 5:00 p.m. (EST)].

situation is different in a number of ways. It not only involves the textual information but also information in the form of graphics, sound, and video. These multimedia information elements are interconnected and are presented in such a way that a touch on the screen will bring the relevant materials to a user. There is no particular linear sequence of accessing the information imposed upon a user. The process of exploring is interactive, nonlinear, user-controlled, and often determined by a user's interest and curiosity. These characteristics of hypermedia technology have provided a new way to present and organize information.

Hypermedia, first conceived by Vannevar Bush in 1945, is a new form of computer technology being popularized and technologically made possible during the recent few years. It refers to an associative, nonlinear information presentation and representation system built around a network of multimedia materials such as text, graphics, sound, and motion (Conklin, 1987; Hammond, 1989; Heller, 1990; Jonassen, 1989). Applying hypermedia techniques to teaching and educational software development is sometimes called hypermedia-assisted-instruction (HAI) (Heller). In the past two or three years, we have seen a growing interest in hypermedia technology. There is a growing body of literature on hypermedia's educational relevance because the technology of hypermedia has provided breakthroughs to the traditional methods of learning and teaching. Attempts have been made to integrate this technology in different disciplines. Research examining the impact of hypermedia technology upon learning and teaching is beginning to emerge. This paper examines a hypermedia learning environment from a semantic network basis and the application of such an environment to second language learning (learning a language by non-native speakers for the purpose of communication).

ADVANTAGES AND LIMITATIONS OF HYPERMEDIA

As a tool for learning and teaching, hypermedia has both advantages and limitations. Consideration of these attributes is a necessary background to discussion of a semantic-network-based hypermedia learning environment. The following is an overview of some of the well-documented advantages and limitations of hypermedia technology.

Advantages of Hypermedia

Nonlinearness. Unlike printed materials, there is no specific sequence of proceeding from one point to another in a hypermedia environment. There are no obvious beginning or ending points. Learners can choose different ways to pursue the subject matter based upon their own interests and objectives. This nonlinear environment can better accommodate individuals' different needs and different learning styles and is more suitable for discovery learning. As Mayes, Kibby, and Anderson (1990) pointed out, "By requiring learners to move towards nonlinear thinking, they may also stimulate processes of integration and contextualization in a way not achievable by linear presentation techniques" (p. 229).

Associativity. Hypermedia mirrors some of the functions of human memory in that logically and semantically related information can be linked together to form a network. It is not only a tool suitable and capable of representing the knowledge base of an expert on a subject but also a tool that can enable learners to construct their own knowledge bases by making meaningful connections among the ideas as they perceive (Conklin, 1987; Dede & Palumbo, 1991; Hammond, 1989; Heller, 1990; Jonassen, 1989; Marchionini, 1988).

Flexibility. The flexibility of hypermedia is multi-fold. From the learner's point of view, he or she can follow the subject matter semantically but not necessarily physically from one page to the next. There is no arbitrary order imposed upon a learner as to how to proceed. The learner can jump freely from one idea to another without worrying if it is the right sequence or what sequence to follow. Learners can simply let their interests guide them. From a systems point of view, hypermedia is capable of revealing and concealing the complexity of a subject matter more easily than the linear method. The content of a subject matter can be presented with different levels of complexity. At each level, the system can let the learner be aware of the next level of content, but the learner does not need to activate it, if not interested. Therefore, the complexity of a subject can be concealed until the user asks for it. This can not only lessen the cognitive load on a learner, to some extent, but can also help the learner assimilate and accommodate ideas. Finally, from the designer's point of view, the designer can easily modify the information in specific nodes without affecting the entire system, since the information in a hypermedia system is modular in nature (Conklin, 1987; Dede & Palumbo, 1991; Hammond, 1989; Heller, 1990; Jonassen, 1989; Marchionini, 1988).

Efficiency. In a hypermedia environment, different forms of information such as text, graphics, animation, and sound can all be brought to the screen simultaneously. By a simple touch on the screen, a keypress, or a mouseclick, the user can activate a link from a node of text to a node of graphics or a combination. This is much easier and faster than juggling encyclopedias, a videoplayer, a cassette player, and an atlas at the same time (Conklin, 1987; Dede & Palumbo, 1991; Hammond, 1989; Heller, 1990; Jonassen, 1989).

Limitations of Hypermedia

Disorientation. One of the most obvious disadvantages of hypermedia is that users can easily become disoriented (lost) in the hyperspace. Unlike reading a book in which one usually knows exactly how many pages have been read and how many more are expected, one can easily lose sense of location in a nonlinear environment. There are no obvious beginning and ending points, especially when navigating through a large hypermedia system containing hundreds or thousands of nodes and links (Conklin, 1987; Dede & Palumbo, 1991; Hammond, 1989; Heller, 1990; Jonassen, 1989; Marchionini, 1988).

Cognitive Overhead. As a new way of learning, hypermedia imposes additional cognitive overhead upon a user as he or she tries to keep track of links, makes decision about how to proceed, and possibly creates new nodes herself. "The richness of a nonlinear representation carries a risk of potential intellectual indigestion, loss of goal directedness, and cognitive entropy" (Dede & Palumbo, 1991, p. 8). Using a hypermedia system requires a new type of literacy (i.e., hypermedia literacy) to handle such an environment effectively. Novice users often feel uncomfortable with such systems; and, as a result, the environment is less beneficial. Therefore, creating hypermedia systems involves a very large front-end investment of time and expertise (Jonassen, 1989).

Learner Control. As an instructional strategy, learner control suggests that instruction will be more motivating and meaningful if the learner is given control of instructional decisions. Because of its highly interactive nature, a hypermedia environment places a large amount of responsibility upon the learner. However, research shows that not all learners can benefit from this less structured learning environment. Some actually produce less satisfactory results (Jonassen, 1989). As such, the characteristics of learner control in hypermedia seem both a blessing and a curse.

THEORETICAL ASSUMPTIONS OF A SEMANTIC-NETWORK-BASED HYPERMEDIA LEARNING ENVIRONMENT

Rationale

From John Dewey's Educational Philosophy. One of the key points of John Dewey's philosophy for curriculum development is that one learns through experiences and meaningful interaction with the environment and other people (Dewey, 1966). Therefore, in order for learning to occur, schools and society must provide these meaningful experiences for learners. Learning takes place when one organizes and reorganizes, constructs and reconstructs one's experiences. The role of schools is to provide a proper environment where learners have the opportunities to fully realize their potentials. The role of a teacher is to provide proper guidance and direction for learners to exercise their judgments and decisions and to reach their goals. Dewey said that "the educational process is one of continual reorganizing, reconstructing, transforming" (p. 50). A semantic-network-based hypermedia learning environment where related ideas are linked to form a network of information is capable of providing meaningful experiences to a learner. Each information element in this network contributes in its own way to a better understanding of the subject. With the interrelatedness among ideas in such a network, learners are given an opportunity to view a subject from different perspectives in a multi-dimensional way.

From Norman's Mental Model Theory. While interacting with the environment and with others, people often form internal mental models of themselves and of the things with which they are interacting (Norman, 1983). The purpose of these mental models is to enable human beings to understand the subject matter or the object of their interaction; that is, to understand what they are learning. According to Norman, human beings' mental models are usually deficient because they are incomplete, unstable, unscientific, and parsimonious. They are unstable in that people often forget things, especially details. They are unscientific because people often have their own ways to proceed with an action. Especially after having encountered some difficulties and experienced the outcomes, they have formed certain beliefs as to how a particular sequence of actions will reduce or eliminate the difficulty. For example, some people, in working with computers, always go back to the main menu before proceeding to the next option, even though they can go directly from one option to another. The mental models can also be parsimonious as people are often reluctant to make mental efforts that would allow them to avoid performing extra physical operations.

The study of human mental models has the following implications in terms of learning new knowledge. First, because people's mental models are often incomplete, we must provide knowledge to learners in order to help them develop more coherent and usable mental models. Second, we cannot expect learners to remember everything they have learned. Learners need some kind of tools that can provide the overall structure of a new subject as well as its elaborative details. Third, it is the duty of educators to help learners develop more adequate, appropriate, and complete mental models through tools that can enable learners to see the interrelationships between the topics and subtopics. Fourth, because learners' mental models are often "unscientific," it is necessary to present, to a learner, more scientific mental models, rules, and techniques that have already been proven in order for them to learn more efficiently.

A semantic-network-based hypermedia learning environment, with its emphasis on the interrelationship among ideas, takes full advantage of the nonlinearity, associativity, flexibility, and efficiency characteristics of hypermedia technology and appears to be capable of providing a more coherent and complete mental model.

From Craik and Lockhart's Levels of Processing Theory. Many psychologists classify memory into three levels of storage; sensory store, short-term memory, and long-term memory (Craik & Lockhart, 1972). All information we receive through vision, hearing, or other senses goes directly to sensory store. Information only stays there in the form that it is received for a second or two, and then it is lost. The short-term memory, also called working memory by some, holds information considerably longer and not necessarily in its original form. However, information in the short-term memory is not remembered in any permanent sense, with only a limited number of items being kept at any one time. The amount of information that the short-term memory can hold at one time is about seven chunks or items (Miller, 1956). Long-term memory is the highest level of memory storage. Its capacity is unlimited, and, theoretically, nothing stored there will be lost.

Craik and Lockhart's theory of levels of processing has much to do with the differences between short-term and long-term memory. According to this theory, information received is processed at different levels (Craik & Lockhart, 1972). Information such as brightness, pitch, and loudness is processed at the preliminary stage of sensory analysis, whereas other information is processed through a deeper process such as pattern recognition, stimulus elaboration, and meaning extraction. Information in short-term memory is usually phonemic and visual in format; information in the long-term memory, which needs to be processed at a deeper level in order to be retained, is largely semantic. The more familiar and meaningful the stimuli, the deeper the level of processing, and the better and longer the information will be retained. Craik and Lockhart said that retention is a function of depth, not speed. In fact, it usually takes more time in order for information to be processed at a deeper level.

According to Craik and Lockhart (1972), in order to have longer retention, information not only needs to be repeated, but, more importantly, needs to be organized in a meaningful way (i.e., processed at a deeper level). If a word is presented only with its phonemic features, it probably will mean nothing to a learner and will quickly be forgotten. However, if this word triggers some associations from a learner with past experience, the word is more likely to be remembered. In teaching the word "apple" to a child, for example, instead of just showing her the word and reading the word aloud to her, the word "apple" can be shown along with the features of a real apple, its shape, its color, and its taste. The child is more likely to remember the word this way because this multidimensional approach can build meaningful associations in memory. The look, the feel, and the taste of an apple help a child remember and understand the concept of an apple. This is known as the "depth of processing." The deeper the level at which the information is processed, the greater the degree of semantic or cognitive analysis, and the longer one retains that information.

From Rumelhart and Norman's Modes of Learning Theory. The second theory supporting the semantic-network-based hypermedia learning environment is Rumelhart and Norman's modes of learning theory (Norman, 1978; Rumelhart & Norman, 1978). According to this theory, there are three basic modes of learning: accretion, restructuring, and tuning. Accretion is a straightforward addition of knowledge to the existing knowledge modules (KMs–Norman's term for memory structure). At the stage of accretion, one is simply adding new information to the existing knowledge without modifying the existing knowledge structure (i.e., accumulating knowledge). Accretion occurs through appropriate exposure to the concepts and facts to be learned. Accretion is important and necessary in order to establish a database upon which appropriate knowledge structures can be formed through restructuring. Accretion learning requires study and possibly deep levels of processing. When newly acquired information does not fit the current available memory structure, the existing knowledge structure is reorganized, and, in some cases, a new knowledge structure is created for interpreting new information. This is the stage of restructuring. At this stage, learners are expected to say "oh" and "aha" and have some jumps in understanding. Norman (1978) said that "if accretion is knowledge acquisition, restructuring is knowledge understanding" (p. 41). Because restructuring involves possible change of the existing knowledge, it takes place only after considerable time and effort. Tuning involves continuing modification of the existing knowledge so as to improve the accuracy, generalizability, and specificity of the existing knowledge (Rumelhart & Norman, 1978). Though making improvements, tuning does not change the existing knowledge structure. At the stage of tuning, the performance of a task becomes smoother, more efficient, less hesitant, automatic. In order to reach the stage of tuning, one needs to practice and do problem solving; that is, to use the knowledge repeatedly. Therefore, tuning can be a lifetime task.

According to this theory, these three modes of learning do not necessarily occur in sequence. They can sometimes happen simultaneously. For example, in the process of learning, one first acquires knowledge (facts and concepts). During the process of knowledge accumulation (accretion), restructuring can occur along with accretion, for learners often organize and reorganize their knowledge structures and create new structures. Tuning could also accompany accretion and restructuring. However, over the entire course of learning a subject, there will be stages when one mode of learning is dominant.

Both theories, the theory of levels of processing and the theory of modes of learning, center on the point that learning goes through different stages. In order to learn more effectively, new information must be integrated into the existing knowledge structure, and old information should be reorganized to accommodate new information. Learning is connecting, and humans are good learners because they can make many connections. But what can be used to help make meaningful connections between what is intended and what is actually learned? How can we represent closely what is in our mind? Craik and Lockhart (1972) stated that the information in long-term memory was largely semantic. In order to retain information in a more permanent sense, one must study the underlying structure of the information–the semantic information. Semantic networking is one tool that allows us to do that.

HYPERMEDIA AND SEMANTIC NETWORKS

Because of its capability of representing the mental process within human memory, a semantic network is one of the most popular formats used to represent the information in human minds. A semantic network is a conceptual representation of knowledge in human memory (Jonassen, 1990; Norman, 1976a; Norman, Gentner, & Stevens, 1976). It is characterized by a network structure of nodes and links and is often displayed by a directed graph in which concepts are represented as nodes and relationships between concepts are represented as links (Conklin, 1987). The theory of semantic networks states that (a) human memory is associative in nature, and ideas and information in memory are interrelated with one another; (b) this interrelatedness among ideas can be depicted by nodes and labelled links that connect nodes and can be represented by some precise and formal structures (Anderson & Bower,

1973; Lindsay & Norman, 1972; Norman, Rumelhart, & LNR Research Group, 1975). Because of its networking nature, a semantic network is capable of depicting and representing the "mess" of association in human memory. Hypermedia, using the same terminology of nodes and links, is a computerized way of representing the semantic network in human memory. Like human memory, concepts and ideas in hypermedia do not exist in isolation, but rather in association with other concepts and ideas. They are often packaged into nodes, whether they are cards, windows, or files; these nodes are, in turn, connected with and among each other through links, which can be referential, organizational, or keyword links (Conklin, 1987). This computerized information network structure is a better means of representing the complexity of the human mind. Through a hypermedia system, this complexity can be revealed or concealed since there can be many layers of information interwoven with one another, and yet only the most basic concepts of a subject are displayed at first. Upon a user's request, the elaboration on the subject can be provided. A user has the choice not to see certain detailed information if he or she does not want to, while still being aware of its existence. Thus, a more complete and adequate human mental model can be represented efficiently. Just as it is stored in human memory, information in a hypermedia system is nonlinear in nature. Because of the closeness between hypermedia and human memory, the analogy between them is direct. Nodes in a hypermedia system are like concepts (or schemata) in a semantic network of human memory; links are like the semantic interdependence among these concepts. The process of building a hypermedia network is a kind of knowledge engineering (Conklin, 1987; Jonassen, 1989). Hypermedia technology has provided a tool to help depict and display what occurs in human memory.

Grounded in the theory of semantic networks, a semantic-network-based hypermedia learning environment can not only display the interrelatedness of concepts through making full use of links, explicit or implicit, but will also emphasize the semantic relationships among the concepts. That is, in a semantic-network-based hypermedia, concepts are related through their semantic content rather than some arbitrary order, such as alphabetizing. Therefore, it is natural to use hypermedia to represent the semantic network of human memory. The technology of hypermedia makes the input of information more natural and direct, the display of information more active and realistic, the representation of information richer and more detailed, and the construction of information more flexible and efficient.

SEMANTIC-NETWORK-BASED HYPERMEDIA LEARNING ENVIRONMENT AND SECOND LANGUAGE LEARNING

The linking and networking among multimedia materials has given hypermedia the power to provide an alternative to the traditional and print-based learning and teaching. Currently, the power of hypermedia has been tested in many different subject areas. One of the areas that hypermedia can find a ready place is second language learning. In the following, the technology of hypermedia and second language learning has been examined from two perspectives: (a) a linguistic background for hypermedia-assisted-instruction and (b) a semantic-network-based hypermedia learning environment for second language learning.

Linguistic Background for Hypermedia-Assisted-Instruction

Communicative CALL. Computer-Assisted Language Learning, often termed CALL, has proven effective in second language learning and teaching (Chapelle & Jamieson, 1986; Hope, 1982; Jones, 1986; Morgan, 1986; Taylor, 1979). The use of CALL has been experiencing changes from focusing on drill and practice and tutorial to the possibility of using computers to teach communicative skills (Schaeffer, 1981). One of the purposes of promoting communicative CALL is to incorporate grammatical and lexical items into the context with which a learner is to interact during the process of learning. The linguistic background for communicative CALL is the teaching strategy of the communicative approach.

The basis of such an approach to language learning and teaching is the theory of communicative competence which states that a speaker's knowledge of language includes four aspects with regard to a linguistic utterance: (a) whether the utterance is formally possible; (b) whether it is feasible by virtue of the means of implementation available; (c) whether it is appropriate in the context; and (d) whether and how it is actually performed (Hymes, 1971). To apply this theory to language teaching, Widdowson (1979) suggested that what should be taught in the classroom is the use of a language; that is, how a learner can communicate properly in different situations. A proficient language user should be one who not only has the adequate knowledge of all aspects of the language but also is able to use the language *appropriately* and *correctly* in different situations.

Communicative CALL is also based upon the assumption of second language acquisition theory (L2 acquisition). Krashen (1982) discussed five factors in second language learning/acquisition, of which input and affective filter factors relate directly to the present discussion. The basic important principle based upon these factors states that in order to acquire a language, two conditions are necessary: Comprehensible input must be available to the learner. and a low affective filter should allow input in. A low affective filter refers to low anxiety, high motivation, and greater confidence which, according to Krashen, are the conditions for success in acquiring a non-native language. The implications of this principle suggest that learners should have the opportunity to comprehend language before they are asked to produce it, shifting the emphasis from output to input. In order that the input be meaningful, it needs to be comprehensible. In order that input be meaningful, comprehensible, and challenging, it must appear in a meaningful context and in quantity. The implications of the L2 acquisition theory for CALL are not drill and practice of discrete grammatical structures or vocabulary learning in isolation but, rather, the integration of language elements in meaningful context for real purposes.

Based upon this theory, different ways of teaching communicative skills have been suggested and implemented, such as using simulations and games, word processing, and electronic mail. The potential of hypermedia technology also seems to be appropriate for promoting communicative CALL.

Communicative CALL and Hypermedia Assisted Instruction. Underwood (1984) has discussed the premises for communicative and noncommunicative CALL in his book *Linguistics, Computers and the Language Teacher: A Communicative Approach.* Table 1 and Table 2 explain the comparison of these features with the characteristics of hypermedia. It seems that the capabilities of hypermedia could match each of the communicative CALL parameters. Research has shown that an optimal language learning environment is crucial to any successful language learning and teaching. Teaching methods such as stressing the role of context and providing realistic environments for language learning are often used to help learners acquire effective communicative skills (Bransford, Sherwood, & Hasselbring, 1988; Omaggio, 1986; Walker de Felix, Johnson, & Schick, 1990). A hypermedia-based CALL can make good use of graphics, text, sound, and animation, in order to present a target language as naturally as possible in "real" and varied communicative situations. By immersing students in the "natural" and enriched environment created by the computer, students are exposed to the target language with high frequency and efficiency. Moreover, because hypermedia assisted instruction is capable of meeting learners' different needs and varying abilities, such instruction should be highly motivating and stimulating. Therefore, the technology of hypermedia should be a good tool for promoting learners' communicative skills.

TABLE 1. Linguistic Parameters for CALL–Noncommunicative and Communicative

Linguistic Parameters
Noncommunicative CALL
• Program incorporates grammatical sequencing
• Program judges to inform students of their errors
• Program is in control
• Subject matter is irrelevant to student
• Lesson is predetermined
• Student perceives task as a required lesson
• Student views task as identical to classroom activities
Communicative CALL
• Program does not impose grammatical sequencing
• Program judges more to provide helpful hints
• Student is in control
• Student relates to subject matter in a personal way
• Student creates own learning experience
• Student perceives task as motivating supplement
• Student views task as a novel activity

Note. Underwood's premises presented here are based upon a summary by Chapelle (1990, p. 202)

Semantic-Network-Based Hypermedia Learning Environment for Second Language Learning

From the memory structure theory and levels of processing theory, we know that information stored in short-term memory is likely to be lost; whereas, information in long-term memory, usually processed at a deeper level, will be retained. Semantic network theory tells us that information in memory exists in an interconnected network. To process information at a

TABLE 2. Parallel Features Between Communicative CALL and Hypermedia

Communicative CALL	Hypermedia
• Program does not impose grammatical sequencing	• Nonsequential and nonlinear
• Program judges more to provide helpful hints	• Contextual
• Student is in control	• High level of learner control
• Student relates to subject matter in a personal way	• Learners can construct their own knowledge structure
• Student creates own learning experience	• Better accommodate learners with different styles
• Student perceives task as motivating supplement	• Multimedia aspect is a source for motivation
• Student views task as a novel activity	• Provide new experience

deeper level often requires building connections between the new piece of information and the existing network of information. In learning a concept, establishing semantic ties between this new concept with existing ones can promote understanding and retention of a concept. The more semantic ties this new concept has with the existing concepts, the more stable it will become. If this new concept has only one or two ties with others, it is likely to swing around and become disconnected; whereas, if it has many semantic ties with others, its movement within a semantic network is confined and therefore very stable (Davidian, 1982). The more stable the concept, the firmer the relationship this concept has with the existing network of information, and the more meaningful and better integrated this concept becomes (Norman, 1976b) (Figure 1). Such concepts are then likely to be retained. Semantic-network-based hypermedia provides a computerized technology to facilitate this integration of new information to the existing knowledge structure in human memory.

Second language learning, like a child learning his or her mother tongue, is a continuous and lifelong process of being exposed to various aspects of the target language (Brown, 1987; Foelsche, 1990; Omaggio, 1986). In a semantic-network-based hypermedia learning environment for second language learning, the integration of knowledge is assisted, on the one hand, by the multimedia materials to provide a multidimensional perspective of the target language. Listening, speaking, reading, and writing–

FIGURE 1. An illustration of knowledge acquisition in a semantic-network context

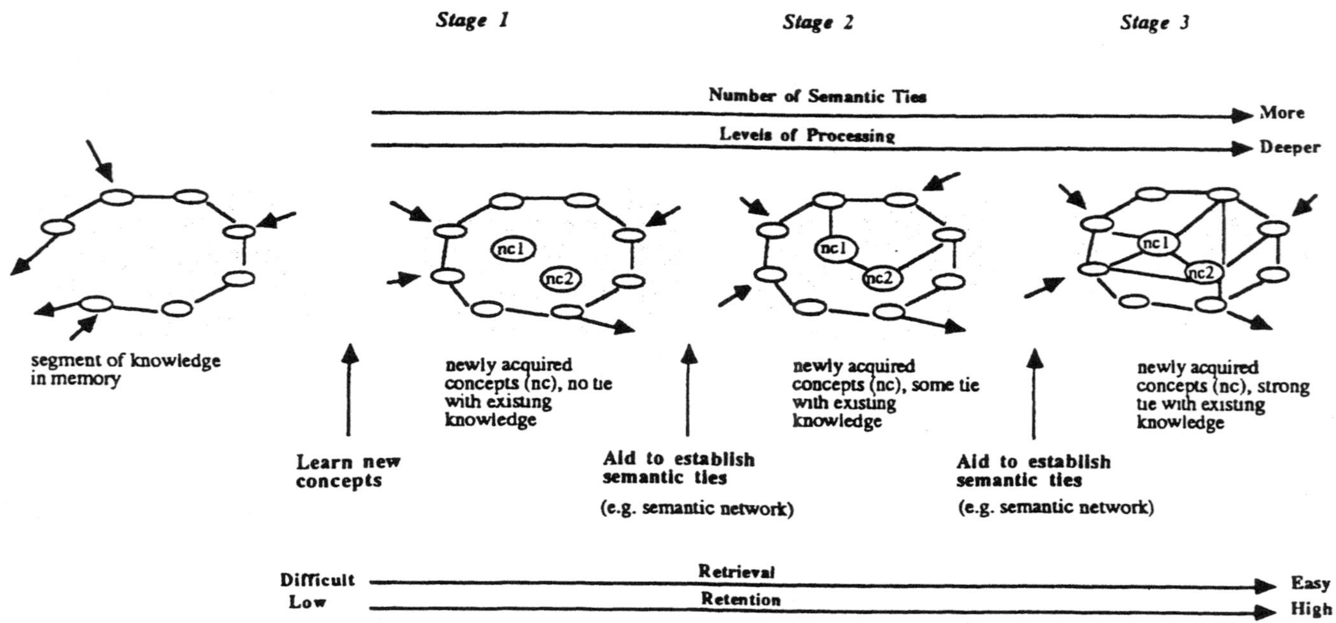

four equally critical skills to a second language learner–are all emphasized and can be integrated through sound, graphics, texts, and video; that is, in such an environment, learners are presented with a holistic picture of the target language. On the other hand, for an adult learner, language learning is often a conscious and goal-directed process of participating, interacting, imitating, and synthesizing. The emphasis on the interrelatedness among concepts in a semantic-network-based hypermedia learning environment and the high level interaction between learners and computers provides a much more meaningful context for learning. Take learning vocabulary, for example. In a semantic-network-based hypermedia learning environment, a learner can be flooded (immersed) in an enriched multidimensional cultural context, connecting history, geography, art, cultural customs, and social factors of a target country with the linguistic aspects of the target language. The words to be learned are no longer isolated by themselves but, instead, are meaningfully linked to a much larger context. While flooding learners in a target language, different linguistic features of a word can be more easily focused (conscious learning) through a semantic network. Features such as the definition, pronunciation, part of speech, and synonyms and antonyms of a word can be brought together in a networking structure and studied in relation with other words (Figure 2).

Focusing is objective when all the important aspects of a word are mapped out efficiently through a networking structure to assist learning; focusing is, at the same time, subjective when a learner is motivated by the high level interaction and multimedia materials of the hypermedia technology. This approach of providing a much broader view of the language while enabling a learner to focus on particular linguistic items is more comprehensible and significant for the purpose of communication, as not only the pronunciation, intonation, and syntax come into play, but also, and perhaps more importantly, the meaning. The retention of words learned in such an environment should be high, as the semantic ties with the existing knowledge are strong and stable. The transfer of proper word use to other situations should occur more likely, as learners are embedded in a "realistic" communicative situation made possible only through computer technology. Therefore, such a learning environment should promote deep processing of information and thus facilitate language learning. In short, the integration of hypermedia assisted instruction into second language learning (vocabulary learning in particular), based upon levels of processing theory and modes of learning theory, can be summarized as follows (Figure 3).

FIGURE 2. Flooding in larger cultural context while focusing on specific linguistic items (R = relationship, W = word)

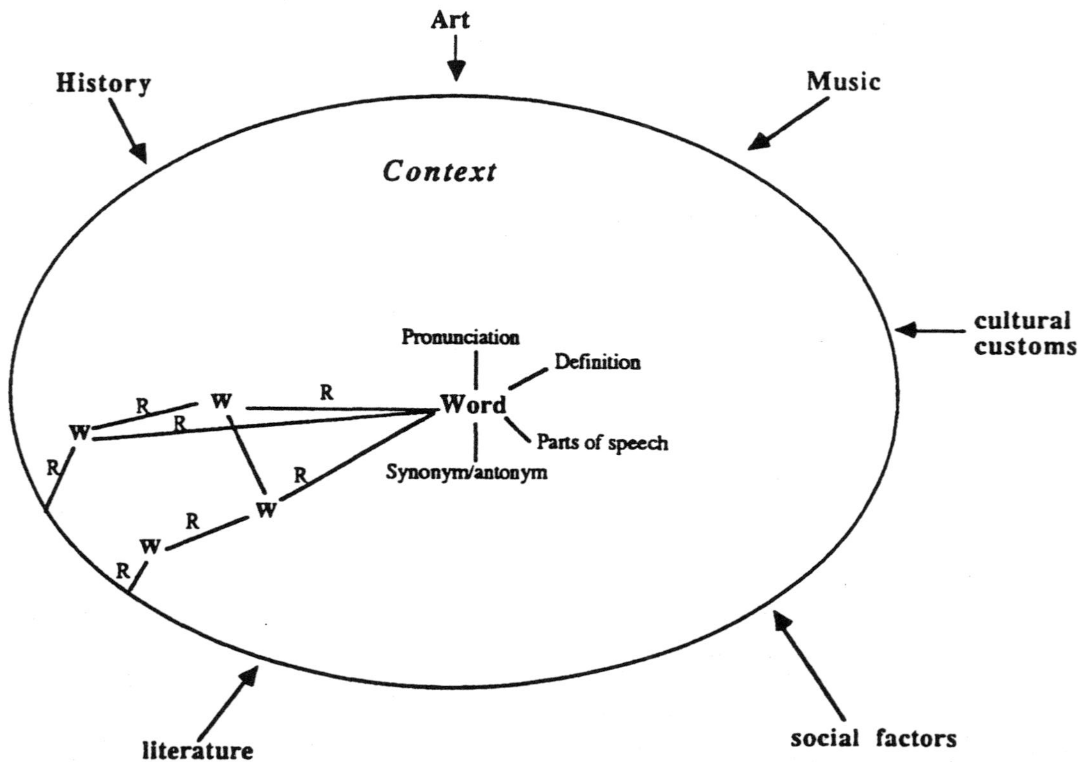

FIGURE 3. Integrating hypermedia assisted instruction into vocabulary learning, based upon levels of processing theory by F.I.M. Craik, R.S. Lockhart, 1972, and modes (accretion, restructuring, and tuning) of learning theory by D.A. Norman, 1978 and D.E. Rumelhart and D.A. Norman, 1978

Levels of Processing (→ Deeper) / Time (→ More)	Mode of Learning	Content of Learning: Second Language Learning (Vocabulary)	Content of Learning: Characteristics	Technology of Learning: Hypermedia	Technology of Learning: Characteristics
	Accretion	Learning -definition -pronunciation -parts of speech -synonyms/antonyms - relationship with other words -sentence	Learning bits and pieces	Presentation /Representation capabilities	Present expert's knowledge /learner-characteristics tailored-model through nodes, links and semantic networks
	Restructuring	Learning in context Learning to use words appropriately in similar or different contexts	Bits and pieces brought together in context to make more sense	Construction capability	Create and reorganize links, create one's own knowledge structure or learning model through links, dynamic learner control and semantic networks
	Tuning	Continuous practice to build up a language feel	The appropriate use of words become automatic (Transfer knowledge of using a word from one situation to other situations)	Collaborating /Sharing capability	Make one's knowledge structure more accurate, efficient through sharing on a network

CONCLUSION

The multimedia capabilities, the high level interactivity, and the power of association have aroused much excitement about the technology of hypermedia. Its parallel features to those of the human memory system are especially attractive. A semantic-network-based hypermedia learning environment, grounded in levels of processing theory and modes of learning theory, seems to be particularly appropriate for second language learning, as it provides not only a vivid and natural environment for the accumulation of the facts of a second/foreign language but also tools to synthesize and integrate the new knowledge, and reconstruct the existing knowledge. As a new tool for learning and teaching, the potential of hypermedia is being explored, and its promises are yet to be fully realized.

REFERENCES

Anderson, J. R. & Bower, B. H. (1973). *Human associative memory.* Washington, DC: Winston.

Bransford, J. D., Sherwood, R. S., & Hasselbring, T. S. (1988). Effects of the video revolution on development: Some initial thoughts. In: G. Forman & P. B. Pufall (Eds.), *Constructivism in the computer age* (pp. 173-201). Hillsdale, NJ: Lawrence Erlbaum.

Brown, H. D. (1987). *Principles of language learning and teaching* (2nd ed.). Englewood Cliffs, NJ: Prentice-Hall.

Chapelle, C. (1990). The discourse of computer-assisted language learning: Toward a context for descriptive research. *TESOL Quarterly, 24*(2), 199-225.

Chapelle, C. & Jamieson, J. (1986). Computer-assisted language learning as a predictor of success in acquiring English as a second language. *TESOL Quarterly, 20* (1), 27-46.

Conklin, J. (1987). Hypertext: An introduction and survey. *Computer,* pp. 17-41.

Craik, F. I. M. & Lockhart, R. S. (1972). Levels of processing: A framework for memory research. *Journal of Verbal Learning and Verbal Behavior, 11*, 671-684.

Davidian, R. D. (1982). *Semantic network model for language learning.* Chicago, IL: The 10th Illinois TESOL/Biannual convention. (ERIC Document Reproduction Service No. ED 225 363).

Dede, C. J. & Palumbo, D. (1991). Implications of hypermedia for human thoughts and communication. *International Association for Impact Assessment Bulletin, 9* (1/2), 15-28.

Dewey, J. (1966). *Democracy and education: An introduction to Philosophy of Education.* New York: The Free Press.

Duchastel, P. C. (1990). Discussion: Formal and informal learning with hypermedia. In: D.H. Jonassen & H. Mandle (Eds.), *Designing hypermedia for learning* (pp. 135-143). Published in cooperation with NATO Scientific Affairs Division.

Foelsche, O. (1990). Hypertext/hypermedia-like environments and language learning. In: D.H. Jonassen & H. Mandle (Eds.), *Designing hypermedia for learning* (pp. 291-310). Published in cooperation with NATO Scientific Affairs Division.

Hammond, N. (1989). Hypermedia and learning: Who guides whom? In: H. Maurer (Ed.), *Computer assisted learning* (pp. 167-181). New York: Springler-Verlag.

Heller, R. S. (1990). The role of hypermedia in education: A look at the research issues. *Journal of Research on Computing in Education*, 22, 431-441.

Hope, G. (1982): Elementary French computer-assisted instruction. *Foreign Language Annals, 15* (5), 347-353.

Hymes, D. H. (1971). *On communicative competence*. Philadelphia, PA: University of Pennsylvania.

Jonassen, D. H. (1989). *Hypertext/hypermedia*. Englewood Cliffs, NJ: Educational Technology Publications.

Jonassen, D. H. (1990). Semantic network elicitation: Tools for structuring hypertext. In: R. McAleese & C. Green (Eds.), *Hypertext: State of the art* (pp. 142-154). Oxford, England: Intellect.

Jones, G. (1986). Computers simulations in language teaching–The Kingdom experiment. *System, 14* (2), 179-186.

Krashen, S. (1982). *Principles and practice in second language acquisition*. New York: Pergamon.

Lindsay, P. H. & Norman, D.A. (1972). *Human information processing*. New York: Academic.

Marchionini, G. (1988). Introduction to special issue on hypermedia. *Educational Technology, 28* (11), 7-12.

Mayes, T., Kibby, M., & Anderson, T. (1990). Learning about learning from hypertext. In: D. H. Jonassen & H. Mandle (Eds.), *Designing hypermedia for learning* (pp. 227-250), Published in cooperation with NATO Scientific Affairs Division.

Miller, George. (1956). The magic number seven, plus or minus two: Some limits on our capacity for processing information, *Psychology Review, 63*, 81-97.

Morgan, L. Z. (1986). Computer-assisted instruction-how, when and why. *Foreign Language Annals, 19* (6), 515-517.

Norman, D. A. (1976a). *Memory and attention* (2nd ed.). New York: John Wiley & Sons.

Norman, D. A. (1976b). *Studies of learning and self-contained educational systems* (Technical Report Number 7601). Washington, DC: Office of Naval Research, Advanced Research Project Agency. (ERIC Document Reproduction Service ED 121 786).

Norman, D. A. (1978). Notes toward a theory of complex learning. In: A. M. Lesgold, J. W. Pellegrino, S. D. Fokkema, & R. Glaser (Eds.), *Cognitive psychology and instruction* (pp. 39-48). New York: Plenum.

Norman, D. A. (1983). Some observations on mental models. In: D. Grentner & A. Stevens (Eds.), *Mental models* (pp. 6-14). Hillsdale, NJ: Lawrence Erlbaum.

Norman, D. A., Rumelhart, D. E., & the LNR Research Group. (1975). *Explorations in cognition.* San Francisco: W. H. Freeman.

Norman, D. A., Gentner, D. R., & Stevens, A.L. (1976). Comments on learning: Schemata and memory representation. In: D. Klahr (Ed.), *Cognition and instruction* (pp. 177-196). Hillsdale, NJ: Lawrence Erlbaum Associates.

Omaggio, A. C. (1986). *Teaching language in context.* Boston, MA: Heinle & Heinle.

Rumelhart, D. E. & Norman D. A. (1978). Accretion, tuning, and restructuring: Three modes of learning. In: J. W. Cotton & R. L. Klatzsy (Eds.), *Semantic factors in cognition* (pp. 37-53). Hillsdale, NJ: Lawrence Erlbaum.

Schaeffer, R. H. (1981). Meaningful practice on the computer: Is it possible? *Foreign Language Annals, 14* (2), 133-137.

Taylor, H. F. (1979). Students' reactions to computer assisted instruction in German. *Foreign Language Annals, 12* (4), 289-291.

Underwood, J. (1984). *Linguistics, computers, and the language teacher: A communicative approach.* Rowley, MA: Newbury House.

Walker de Felix, J., Johnson, R. T., & Schick, J. E. (1990). Socio-and psycholinguistic considerations in interactive video instruction for limited English proficient students. *Computers in the Schools, 7* (1/2), 173-190.

Widdowson, H. G. (1979). The teaching of English as communication. In: C. J. Brumfit & K. Johnson (Eds.), *The communicative approach to language teaching* (pp.117-121). London: Oxford University Press.

Richard C. Overbaugh

An Example of Software Development and Authoring with *HyperCard*: Creating an Interactive Video Simulation for Teaching Basic Principles of Classroom Management to Pre-Service Teachers

INTERACTIVE VIDEO COURSEWARE DEVELOPMENT

Laserdiscs are a relatively recent technological development that code video and audio as digital data, portions of which can be accessed in .5 seconds or less. This quick access provides the opportunity to add video to branching computer-based programs resulting in simulated experiences that are relatively realistic. This article describes, in two distinct sections, the development of an interactive video simulation, the *Classroom Management Simulation*, that teaches eight basic principles of classroom management to pre-service teachers. The first section focuses on the time-consuming planning of the simulation, based on instructional design theory and empirical research. The second section describes how *HyperCard* was

RICHARD C. OVERBAUGH is Assistant Professor of Instructional Computing, Darden College of Education, Old Dominion University, Norfolk, VA 23529.

[Haworth co-indexing entry note]: "An Example of Software Development and Authoring with *HyperCard*: Creating an Interactive Video Simulation for Teaching Basic Principles of Classroom Management to Pre-Service Teachers." Overbaugh, Richard C. Co-published simultaneously in *Computers in the Schools* (The Haworth Press, Inc.) Vol. 10, No. 3/4, 1994, pp. 313-338; and: *Multimedia and Megachange: New Roles for Educational Computing* (eds: W. Michael Reed, John K. Burton, and Min Liu) The Haworth Press, Inc., 1994, pp. 313-338. Multiple copies of this article/chapter may be purchased from The Haworth Document Delivery Center [1-800-3-HAWORTH; 9:00 a.m. - 5:00 p.m. (EST)].

used to program the simulation, which utilizes a commercially available videodisc, in order to provide prospective interactive video courseware developers with a complete development model. A final section briefly reports on results of field testing the *Classroom Management Simulation*.

INSTRUCTIONAL DESIGN

The instructional design process was broken into two phases: General Course Specifications and Lesson Design. Lesson Design is further broken into four distinct but related domains: Instructional Set, Teaching Strategies, Student Performance, and Issues Unique to Computer-based Instruction.

Phase I: General Course Specifications

Identifying the Overall Instructional Content, Objectives, and Conditions

The purpose of the simulation is to teach pre-service education students about basic classroom management principles and to facilitate the development of skills to solve similar problems in a typical classroom. The simulation places users in the role of a typical ninth-grade classroom teacher to help them develop and apply eight basic principles of effective classroom management: (a) fairness, (b) consistency, (c) firmness, (d) courtesy, (e) flexibility, (f) humor, (g) respect, and (h) trust. Four scenarios are supplied: (a) a student comes into class late without offering a late slip; (b) a student refuses to pick up some paper he has thrown on the floor around his desk; (c) a student is doing work for another class; and (d) a class is noisy and rowdy at the start of the period. Each situation is presented by a brief film clip, after which the user is asked to assess the problem and determine a strategy for solution. The simulation then plays a possible result of the user's choice of action and stops again for another assessment and choice of action. The number of steps required to reach a conclusion vary according to the scenario complexity and the choices made by the user.

The original videodisc simulation, *Classroom Discipline: A Simulation Approach* (1987), is a level two interactive video program for a now defunct Sony videodisc player and was rewritten by the author with *HyperCard* to be a level three application. The new program generally follows the original course structure but demands a higher level of user interaction and cognitive engagement via questions requiring learner-generated text responses. The original program simply presented multiple choices selected through a keypad but, to avoid influencing users' choices, the *HyperCard*-based program does not present a menu of available choices until after users have entered their own assessments and strategies.

Task Analysis

Now that the general content, broad objectives, and target audience have been identified, the next step is to apply five interrelated task analyses to the general course specifications in order to provide sufficient detail for lesson design. The five analyses are: (a) defining an appropriate learning hierarchy, (b) describing the student model and identifying the proposed learner starting point, (c) specifying the minimum requirements of the learning environment, (d) writing detailed objectives, and (e) examining the performance/content specifications (Aronson & Briggs, 1983; Carrier & Jonassen, 1988; Landa, 1983; Roblyer, 1988).

Learning Hierarchy. Because a learning hierarchy is only appropriate for learning tasks that need to be taught via a progressive presentation of their prerequisite parts (Gropper, 1983; Hannum, 1988; Landa, 1983), none was developed for the *Classroom Management Simulation.*

Prerequisite Skills. Prerequisite skills were examined by specifying (a) the student model including the students' present knowledge state and motivational interests, (b) the instructional environment, and (c) the learner starting point.

The simulation was designed to be used by pre-service education majors whose knowledge relevant to classroom management is based primarily on their previous schooling. The students' motivation to use this program has two perspectives. First, because of their chosen profession, the students should be self-motivated to learn to assess and handle common management problems. Second, the use of a laserdisc to simulate a classroom provides a near-to-real learning environment which, coupled with the freedom to try different–both good and bad–techniques should motivate learners to experiment with various management strategies. The use of a computer simulation also takes away inherent risks associated with real subjects (Gropper, 1983) and encourages experimentation.

Although designed to be used by individuals, the simulation can easily be used by small groups or an entire class. Since each step of a scenario requires users to assess the situation, devise a plan and, usually, predict the effects of the plan, small groups can easily engage in discussions about their ideas, arrive at a consensus, and enter their joint decision. Similarly, an entire class can discuss various options and select one. Therefore, the minimum requirements are (a) a Macintosh computer with two disk drives (although a hard drive is preferable to avoid disk swapping), (b) a videodisc player, and (c) a monitor.

Detailed Objectives and Level of Cognitive Engagement Specification. Three objectives adequately delineate the program's content:

1. Users will learn eight basic principles of good management: (a) fairness, (b) consistency, (c) firmness, (d) courtesy, (e) flexibility, (f) trust, (g) respect, and (h) humor.
2. Users will improve their ability to assess the management problem situation, taking into account the problem students' demeanor, mental state, and the classroom climate.
3. Users will improve their ability to assess the effects a teacher's disciplinary actions might have on target students.

The learning task, therefore, involves both learning to follow rules and learning to derive rules (Landa, 1983). The task also encompasses all three types of performance–(a) remember, (b) use, and (c) find–and the last three (of four) content types–(a) concepts, (b) procedures, and (c) principles as specified by Merrill (1983) (Figure 1). The eight classroom management principles must be *remembered* in order to *use* them with the management problems presented by the simulation. The purpose of the program is to help pre-service teachers become aware of management strategies and *find* their own methods of assessing classroom situations and devise techniques with which to solve them. The simulation content involves the *concepts* of the eight management heuristics, their application *procedures*, and *principles* governing their use and development.

Phase II: Lesson Design

The second phase of Instructional Design is the development of the actual lessons based on the General Course Specifications. The lesson design phase is broken into four domains: (I) instructional set, (II) teaching strategies, (III) student performance, and (IV) other design issues. The first three domains are based on Gagne's (Gagne & Briggs, 1979) nine events of learning and the final domain addresses issues that are unique to computer-based learning.

FIGURE 1. Merrill's performance-content matrix

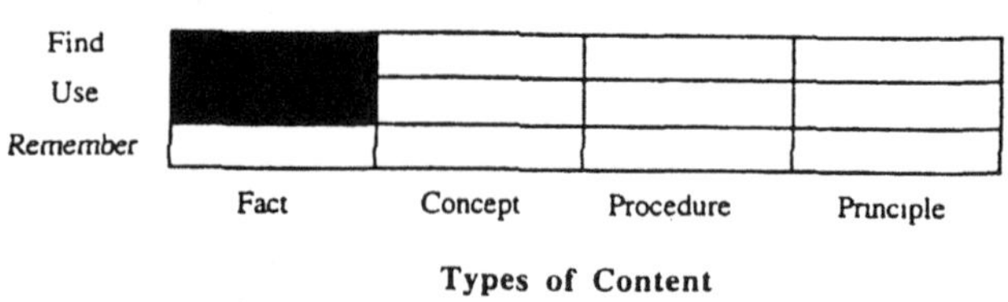

Lesson Design Domain I: Instructional Set–Gaining Attention

Importance. The target audience–pre-service teachers–needs to know how to handle classroom management problems as part of their classroom skills repertoire to be successful in their chosen profession. Therefore, these students should already understand the importance of gaining whatever management skills they can before entering the field and facing a real classroom.

Directions. The users' attention is gained through hardware and software directions which allows them to focus on the content rather than on program operation (Jonassen & Hannum, 1987). The technical skills needed are extremely basic: (a) turning on the computer, (b) inserting program disks or accessing the program on a hard drive, (c) moving the mouse pointer around the screen, and (d) clicking with a mouse on *HyperCard* "buttons" and "fields." When keyboard input is required, the cursor is automatically placed in the appropriate window (field) so the users need only enter text and click on a DONE button when finished.

Orienting Devices (Informing Learner of Objectives). Three orienting devices are presented in the introductory program segment: Pre-questions, Learner Expectations, and Objectives which are designed to pre-structure users' existing knowledge bases, enhance cognitive readiness, provide motivation, and reduce anxiety.

Pre-Questions. The pre-questions are designed to raise the users' awareness of their knowledge of what they do or do not know about management techniques (Anderson, Spiro, & Anderson, 1978; Hamilton, 1985) (e.g., What would you do if a student replies, to your request that he clean up a mess he created, with an insolent "NO!"?). The user will not be expected to answer the questions, but, instead, reflect for a moment about each.

Learner Expectations. After the pre-questions, users are presented with a list of expectations–the skills they are expected to develop as a result of using the program (Aronson & Briggs, 1983; Hannafin & Hooper, 1988). These expectations include developing situational assessment skills, learning to take other students' possible reactions into account when disciplining one or more students, and learning to think ahead to predict the effects management strategies might have on target students and their classmates.

Objectives. Users are further prepared to assimilate the program content by reading the specific objectives (Ho, Savenye, & Haas, 1986):

1. Upon completion of the program, you will know and understand eight principles of good management: (a) fairness, (b) consistency,

(c) firmness, (d) courtesy and dignity, (e) flexibility, (f) trust, (g) respect, and (h) humor.
2. You will learn to assess management problem situations, taking into account the problem student's demeanor, mental state, and the classroom climate.
3. You will learn to assess the effects your management strategies might have on students.

The above orienting devices also provide motivation and reduce anxiety because users will know what to expect when they engage the simulation and what the simulation will expect from them (Keller, 1983; Keller & Suzuki, 1988).

Stimulating Recall of Prior Learning and Supplying Missing Prerequisites

Although stimulating students' recall of previous learning before new learning can take place is often necessary (Aronson & Briggs, 1983; Reigeluth & Stein, 1983; Wager & Gagne, 1988), no prerequisites are required to successfully use the *Classroom Management Simulation*. Clearly, however, users of the simulation will have previously established ideas about the management principles based on their experiences as students. These ideas are addressed, utilized, and modified by the program, but, in a traditional sense, are not required.

Lesson Design Domain II: Teaching Strategies–Presenting Stimuli with Distinctive Features

Pedagogical Perspective. Because this subject matter is effectively presented in a realistic manner, the simulation utilizes video to present the four scenarios (Aronson & Briggs, 1983; Collins & Stevens, 1983; Gropper, 1983; Reigeluth & Stein, 1983; Scandura, 1983) which should cause it to be more meaningful to the intended audience (Keller, 1983; Keller & Suzuki, 1988). Also, the initial film segments are limited in length to 90 seconds to ensure that attention will not wander.

Technical Perspective. The screens were kept simple and uncluttered to avoid overload and confusion (Jonassen & Hannum, 1987). The screen format, including attention-focusing devices (e.g., highlighting and boldfacing), is consistent throughout the program to create continuity and maintain flow. Menus, buttons, and text styles are also constant. Scrolling text fields are utilized only when users are required to enter text, to permit unlimited text generation.

Providing Learning Guidance. The overall learning process in the management simulation is classified as inquiry learning because users are actually forming hypotheses and following through to determine whether or not the hypotheses are efficacious for solving that particular problem (Collins & Stevens, 1983). Learners are guided to each scenario's conclusion and are then asked to evaluate their chosen strategies before program feedback is provided.

Counter Examples. The *Classroom Management Simulation* utilizes the notion of counter examples (Aronson & Briggs, 1983; Collins & Stevens, 1983; Jonassen & Hannum, 1987; Merrill, 1983) to help learners better understand favorable management techniques. Inducing inexperienced users to question their ideas is important. To facilitate this, the simulation permits users to make choices that are undesirable in practice but are ones that might be chosen by an inexperienced practitioner. The purpose is to cause users to confront and modify their existing beliefs about classroom management techniques by showing them what is not effective as well as what is effective.

Enhancing Retention and Learning Transfer. The primary purpose of the simulation is to help pre-service education students develop skills to solve typical classroom management problems. Varied practice and review are provided to help learners retain newly acquired management knowledge.

Varied Practice. Learners need the opportunity, through practice, to create new solutions in varied situations to develop, generalize, and transfer problem-solving skills (Aronson & Briggs, 1983; Gropper, 1983). The management simulation's multiple solutions to each problem provides learners with varied practice. Each time a scenario is engaged, learners assess and reassess the problem, then develop and try new strategies. Therefore, even though there are only four base scenarios, the numerous possible solutions result in many different problem situations. By reacting to these different situations and devising new plans, users should develop effective strategies for management problem assessment and solution.

Review. Review is an effective device to enhance retention (Jonassen & Hannum, 1987; Reigeluth & Stein, 1983) and is provided in three different forms at the end of each scenario. First, each choice made and the responses entered by learners during the course of the simulation are presented in paragraph form for the user to read. Even though this combination of program-supplied and user-generated text often suffers from syntactic mismatch, the paragraph is usually readable and provides a meaningful summary. Second, users are asked to evaluate their solution with regard to the management principles, which requires them to think about their strategies. Third, the program provides feedback that includes a discussion of the chosen strategies.

Lesson Design Domain III: Student Performance–Eliciting Performance and Assessing Performance

Eliciting performance, which refers to techniques that cause user response (Wager & Gagne, 1988) which is subject to criterion-based assessment (Jonassen & Hannum, 1987), is guided by several principles: (a) objective-performance continuity, (b) active participation, (c) performance realism, (d) time allocation, and (e) acceptable standards.

Objective-Performance/Content Match and Active Participation. The level of cognitive engagement required to develop the problem-solving strategies specified by the objectives is high. Students are required to make assessments, devise plans, and predict results, thus creating an objective-performance/content match (Gropper, 1983; Jonassen & Hannum, 1987; Merrill, 1983). The interactive nature of the simulation also fulfills the second major requirement for performance elicitation–active participation (Jonassen & Hannum). While a user could get through the program by simply clicking on choices or DONE buttons, most screens present a blank script box with the ready cursor blinking to encourage text entry.

Performance Realism, Time Allocation, and Acceptable Standards. For the most effective instruction, students should perform in conditions the same as or similar to the "real life" situation in which the skill is normally required (Gropper, 1983; Montague, 1988; Salisbury, 1988). Again, a laserdisc was chosen to present the scenarios because film clips are the most effective way to present real-life situations in artificial settings.

Merrill (1983) recommends that user response time should be unlimited for tasks which include synthesis. The *Classroom Management Simulation* has no time limits and users can take as much time as they wish to enter text. The program also does not impose minimum quality requirements so users are able to respond at their present level to promote achievement-striving behavior and boost user satisfaction (Gropper, 1983; Hannafin & Peck, 1988; Keller, 1983).

Providing Feedback

Because the simulation is designed to foster the development of techniques to help in situational assessment and plan development, the simulation provides two types of feedback. First, after the end of each scenario, users are asked to consider the management principles they used and to evaluate their performance. Second, following the self-evaluation, the program provides explanatory feedback based on the choices made.

Lesson Design Domain IV: Other Design Issues

Learner Control. During computer-based instruction, learners should not have complete control over specific instructional events or instructional sequence (Jonassen & Hannum, 1987), but student attitudes toward the learning task are usually poor when the computer maintains complete control (Milheim, 1989). Therefore, user control through program-generated advisement gives users a sense of control that nurtures better attitudes and enhances expectations for success (Jonassen & Hannum; Keller, 1983). The simulation ultimately leaves program control to the user's discretion, but offers advisement regarding scenario sequence and repetition. The program suggests that users begin with the first scenario and work through it several times until various effective and non-effective strategies have been explored before going on to the second scenario. At the conclusion of individual scenarios, the program recommends that the scenario be repeated to either look for a better solution if the strategy chosen was less than desirable or to explore different strategies if the one chosen was effective.

During each scenario, users are intentionally not permitted to go back and modify their strategies because the program was designed to simulate a real classroom in which the consequences resulting from a chosen action are not easily reversible. If users make a poor choice, they must follow through to discover what consequences will occur. Also, once an initially poor choice is made, certain situations can be salvaged by subsequent strategy selections.

PROGRAM CONSTRUCTION

The next section of this paper describes how the *HyperCard* authoring package was used to create the *Classroom Management Simulation* based on the instructional design section. This information will hopefully serve as a resource for anyone considering tackling a similar project. Included in the discussion is: (a) why *HyperCard* and *The Voyager VideoStack 2.0* interface software were selected, (b) how certain cards were designed and why, (d) examples of scripts to perform useful functions such as data file creation, and (e) some limitations of *HyperCard* that were discovered during software development.

Why *Hypercard* and *The Voyager Video Stack*?

HyperCard

Several authoring packages, including some based on the IBM platform, were investigated before *HyperCard* was chosen. Since most of the packages would have been technically adequate for this project, other factors were considered. The decision was made to choose the one that was able to meet the minimum technical requirements, was priced reasonably, and was easy to use. *HyperCard* is one of the most basic authoring languages, and although some limitations were found, it appeared to be adequate for this program and it was quite easy to learn. Using *HyperCard* is very similar to using any Macintosh application. Text generation has the same font and style selection procedures, and the graphics features are nearly identical to other Macintosh graphics programs. Finally, even though funding was available for most any package desired, *HyperCard* was free (supplied by Apple and bundled with Macintosh computers), which makes it extremely attractive.

Why The Voyager VideoStack 2.0?

The Voyager VideoStack 2.0 is an inexpensive program that installs video resources in any *HyperCard* stack to enable users to control laserdisc players with simple commands. For example, to play a segment on a CAV laserdisc the command is simply:

Video Play, [*firstframe, lastframe*]

This command, when inserted in the script of a card or button, plays the video segment specified in the brackets. The program is also invaluable if different laserdisc players might be used. By pasting a laserdisc player selection button into a stack (from *The VoyagerVideoStack*), nearly any player can be used by clicking on the name of the player.

The Voyager VideoStack 2.0 (Riggins, Wheeler, & Henderson, 1989) has two other features that are extremely useful. First, among the program-supplied controller cards, one looks like a standard remote control with functions such as play, fast forward, reverse, step, still, and search. Using this onscreen controller makes searching through videodiscs quick and easy. The second useful feature, although it wasn't used for the *Classroom Management Simulation*, is the *Event Maker* which makes a list of all the video sequences needed for a stack and automatically makes buttons to play selected video segments that can then be copied into the user stack.

The Voyager Company permits non-profit organizations to distribute stacks that use their video resources as long as the stacks contain a specified acknowledgement. If the stacks are to be sold, a one-time licensing fee must be paid.

Programming the Simulation

Launch Stack

HyperCard stacks occupy large amounts of disk space, so the scenarios had to be created as separate stacks and be accessible from each other or from a stack created specifically for that purpose. Since the program includes optional segments such as an introduction, directions, and help screens, a fifth stack was created to house these segments and provide a home base for the scenario stacks. A data collection function was also planned to keep records of users' responses when interacting with the program, how many times they completed a scenario, and what conclusions they reached. Therefore, user names had to be input and data files created before the scenarios themselves were engaged. Finally, the laserdisc player had to be initialized. These functions all became part of the "Scenario Launch Stack," which is discussed in the next section.

Laserdisc Player Initialization. Laserdisc initialization was made as foolproof and user friendly as possible to decrease technical problems. An "Initialize Laserdisc Player" button is provided on the card in which user information is gathered, but when this card is closed, the program automatically checks to see if the player has been initialized via a *video getstatus* command. If not, a card appears instructing the user to check to make sure the player is on and to then click an "Initialize Laserdisc Player" button (Figure 2). This "Initialize Laserdisc Player" button contains another *video getstatus* command to see if the player is now ready and, if so, the program proceeds. If the player is still not ready, a warning is displayed, the user is advised again to make sure the power is on and the cables are secure and then to try to initialize the player again. The program will not proceed without the laserdisc player in the ready mode.

Orienting Devices. Three types of orienting devices are provided: (a) prequestions, (b) a list of expectations, and (c) the program objectives. Each device is presented in the introductory program segment which is accessible from the main menu.

Main Menu. The primary purpose of the Scenario Launch Stack is to serve as home base for everything included in the simulation, the center of which is the main menu. Besides the four scenarios, all other functions are

FIGURE 2. Script to verify laserdisc player readiness

```
On opencard
   set lockmessages to true
   vidcontrol player
   if the result contains "playerset" then
      Answer "Not available for this player!"
      exit mouseup
   end if
   video getstatus
   put the result into lazergo
   set lockmessages to false
   if lazergo contains "Still" then          Program automatically proceeds if
      go next                                laserdisc player is ready.
   else                                      Else warning and directions are shown if
      Put return&¬                           laserdisc player is not ready.
      "The laserdisc player is not ready."&return&return&¬
      "Make sure the player is ON" &return &"and"&Return&¬
      "the laserdisc is ready to play the correct side."&¬
      Return&Return&¬
      "If this is the first time you have used this program,"&¬
      &Return& "put 'Side 1' up."&return & return&¬
      "Now click 'Initialize Videodisc Player'."into card field 1
   end if
   end opencard
```

accessible from the main menu. The buttons are linked to the appropriate card within the launch stack or to another specified stack. The options are:

1. What is the purpose of this program?
2. 8 Principles of classroom management
3. Scenario 1. A student is late for class.
4. Scenario 2. A student refuses to pick up his mess.
5. Scenario 3. A student is off task.
6. Scenario 4. The noisy class.
7. Initialize laserdisc player.
8. Quit.

The menu card is an ideal place to check "automatically" to see if the correct side of the disc is ready to play, and whether or not the laserdisc player is in ready mode. The command *video getstatus* returns six items, three of which can be used to determine the laserdisc player's readiness. The first item indicates the player's status–Door Open, Park, Spinning Up . . . , Play, Still, Pause, Multi Speed. The second item indicates the disc loaded condition–Disc Loaded, Disc Not Loaded. The fifth item indicates which side is ready to play–Side 1, Side 2. Unfortunately, the *Classroom Discipline* disc was incorrectly coded "Side 1" on both sides, so it was not possible to program the simulation to make sure the correct side is loaded.

However, a pop-up field was added that asks users to verify that the correct videodisc side is ready to play.

Scenario Stacks

Title Cards. Each scenario begins with a title card that gives enough information to set the stage for forthcoming events (Figure 3). Two buttons are present: (a) Play Video and (b) Skip Video. The Play Video button plays the opening video segment, and the Skip Video button provides the option to bypass the initial segment on subsequent limes through the scenario. This is often desirable because the first film clip is the longest, and users often do not want to wait for it to finish to begin working on a new solution.

Response Cards. After the initial film clip, users are asked to describe specifically what the problem is. They may replay the film clip if desired by clicking on a "Replay Video" button. Then users are asked how they are going to solve the problem and why. Only after a problem description and a solution strategy have been generated by the user does the program supply a list of the options provided by the laserdisc. The best match for the user's strategy is selected, and a possible outcome is played on the

FIGURE 3. Typical title card with PLAYVIDEO and Skip Video buttons

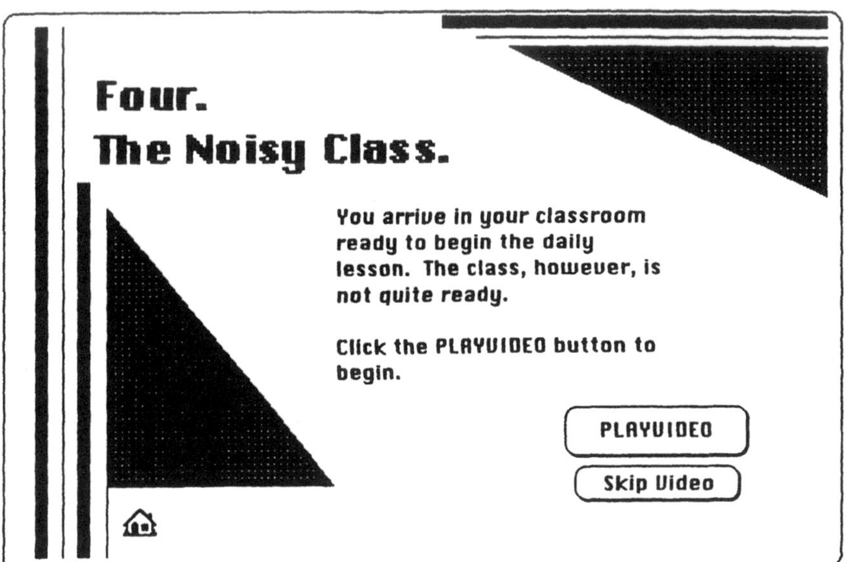

monitor. A "None of the above" button is provided for those occasions when the user's solution does not match any supplied by the program (Figure 4). When selected, the "None of the above" button links to a screen that explains that the program has a finite number of solutions. However, a short summary of the user's unique solution is presented, and they are asked questions designed to help them develop the idea, such as "What management principles are you using?" and "What effect do you think this strategy will have on the rest of the students?" When finished, the program returns to the previous menu and the user selects one of the programmed solutions. When the scenario reaches its conclusion, a button appears that links to a display of the unique solution and users are asked to make any changes in their strategy and provide self-evaluation.

The fields provided for user input are scrolling fields, so no limits are placed on text generation (though few students fill the visible portion of the field). Another useful feature of the response fields is that the cursor is automatically placed in the upper left hand corner of the field, eliminating the need to move the mouse pointer to the field and click the button (Figure 5).

FIGURE 4. Typical response card. The menu of available strategies does not appear until the DONE button is clicked

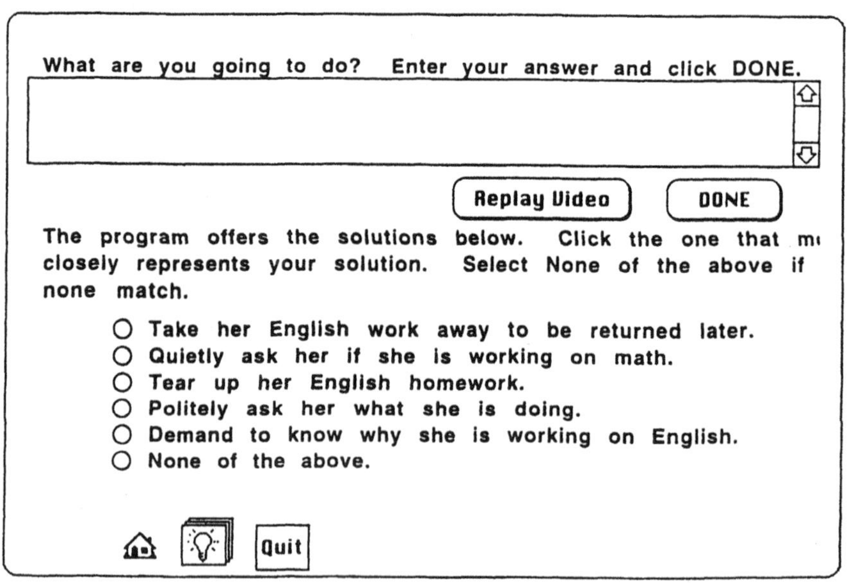

FIGURE 5. Steps to automatically place cursor in response field

Enter the following commands in the message box, after the field in which the cursor is to be placed has been created and positioned:

`Get Rect of Card Field 2`	Gets the coordinates of the field
`it`	Puts the coordinates of the upper left and lower right corners in the message box.

The following commands are then placed in the card script:

`On Opencard`	
`Put Empty into Card Field 2`	Clears text from previous use
`Click at X,Y`	Where X and Y are coordinates of the upper left corner of field.
`End Opencard`	

Summary Cards. Immediately following the end of each scenario, the user's text input, the program choices made, and the results of those choices are summarized in paragraph form on a summary card. The purpose is to provide users with a review of the problem solution strategies they identified, their reasons for selecting the strategies, and the results of their choices. The combination of program-generated text and user-generated text often results in syntactic mismatches, but the paragraph is usually very readable and effectively summarizes everything that occurred during the simulation (Figure 6).

To create the summary card, as users work through the scenario, each response is placed in a global variable before leaving the response card. The variable names Sum1, Sum2, Sum3, and so forth were used to represent the first response field for the summary card, second response field for the summary card, and so on, to reflect the stage of the scenarios and the user entered text. The summary card simply recaps the program choices selected and the results of those choices, interspersed with the user's text (Figure 7).

Self-Evaluation Cards. After the summary card, users are asked to evaluate their performance based on the management principles they employed. The purpose is to require evaluation and synthesis, which are levels of review higher than the summary.

Feedback Cards. The final card in each scenario is a feedback card, which provides a third review of the user's problem solution and also identifies the use, or lack of use, of applicable management principles. Management principle names are used in the text and are highlighted for emphasis. The *HyperCard* version used does not permit font changes within a field (although *HyperCard 2.0* does), so boxes are drawn around the key words (Figure 8).

FIGURE 6. Typical summary card with user generated text included

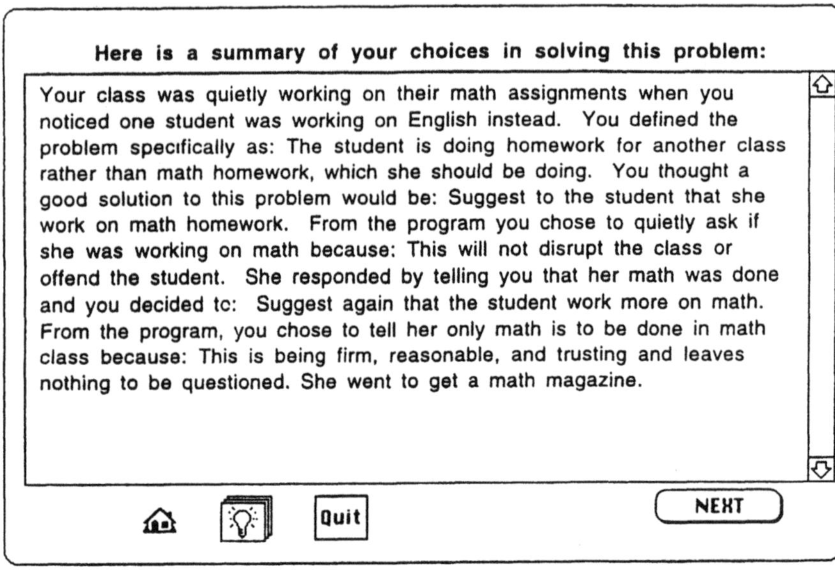

FIGURE 7. Script for typical summary card

```
on opencard
   global sum1, sum2, sum3, sum4, sum5, sum6, sum7, ShowUnique, summary
   set scroll of card field 2 to 0
   put "Your class was working quietly on their assignments when "&¬
   "you noticed one student had made quite a mess with "&¬
   "crumpled paper.  You defined the problem as:"¬
   && sum1 && "You decided to solve the problem by:"¬
   && sum2 && "From the program you chose to send the student " &¬
   "to the office because:" && sum3 && ¬
   "However, he refused to leave "&¬
   "and you decided your "¬
   &"next move would be:" ¬
   && sum4 && "From the program, you chose to tell him that the "&¬
   "whole class would wait until he left because:"¬
   && sum5 && "He continued to defy you by simply sitting there and"¬
   && "trying to stare you down."&&¬
   "You then thought you should: " && sum6 && ".  From the program"¬
   && "you chose to ask him if was being fair"  ¬
   &&"to the others because: " && sum7 &&¬
   " He continued to defy you by simply sitting there. "¬
   into card field 2
   put card field 2 into summary
end opencard
```

FIGURE 8. Typical feedback card with user's self-evaluation (from previous card)

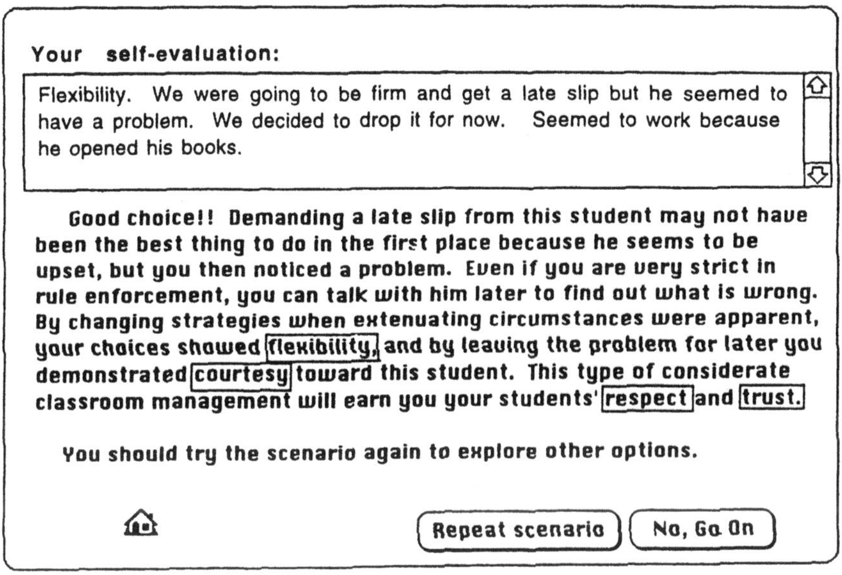

User Data Files

After the opening screen of the simulation, users are asked their name, student number, and whether or not they have used the program before. Dialog boxes are used to input the name and student number, and regular buttons are used to verify previous program use.

As mentioned earlier, for research purposes, records were kept of how many times students engaged the scenarios, what text they entered in response to questions, and what conclusions they reached. Although *HyperCard* does permit file creation, and writes and reads data, it is quite limited in how the files can be structured. In many other programming languages, a text file can be created on a separate data disk with the user's name as the file name into which the aforementioned data could be placed. This achieved, it would be a simple matter to use a word processor to print it out for later analysis. However, two problems in *HyperCard* made this process less straightforward: (a) a data file with the same name as the user could not be opened on a separate data disk and (b) there is no function to append files in *HyperCard*.

Data File Destination Problems. A file name that is also a variable name cannot have a destination other than the location of the *HyperCard* application because the destination (i.e., student data disk) must be named which *HyperCard* interprets as a constant, thus mixing a constant and a variable in the same file specification. For example, if one wishes to write a data file called Student1 on a data disk named "Data Disk" in the external drive, the command to open this file is:

open file ":DataDisk:Student1"

The problem arises when one tries to find a way to use the user's name as the file name. This was important because many students used the program and, if limited to the above command, each application would have needed to be customized for each user. A logical, but unworkable, solution was to put the user's name, obtained earlier, into a local variable for the file specification. However, when *HyperCard* encounters a variable name after a constant name in a file destination specification, the variable name is interpreted as a constant. So if the following command is used:

open file ":DataDisk:Lastname"

where Lastname is a variable containing the user's name, *HyperCard* will open a file on the external drive disk (named "DataDisk") called "Lastname," not the user name residing in the variable "Lastname." The only apparent way around this problem is to put the data files in the same location as the *HyperCard* application. When the following command is used:

open file Lastname

where Lastname is a variable containing the user's last name, a file with the user's last name will be opened in the same location as the *HyperCard* application. Quotes are not needed when the file name is a local variable and *HyperCard* requires that variable file names be local variables (Goodman, 1987).

Creating Multiple Data Files for the Same User. The second problem was that there is no straightforward way to append data files written by *HyperCard* (this problem is discussed more later). For example, if the command "open file Lastname" is used, the existing file (from the first or previous program use) will be overwritten with each subsequent program use. Therefore, in order to gather the data each time users complete a scenario, a new data file had to be created. With this method, since the data files were to be identified by the user's last name, it was necessary to use a different file name each time a scenario conclusion was reached, so that the same data file would not be overwritten. The solution was to include a counter variable, incremented each time through the program, that was added to the user's last name:

put counter + 1 into counter
put lastname + counter into filename
open file filename

where lastname is the user's last name, counter is the counter variable, and filename is a local variable. So, the third time through the program, the filename might be Smith3 (Figure 9).

Scripting Data Files. The data files were designed to contain the following information: (a) user name, (b) student number, (c) how many times the scenario was engaged, (d) the choices made, (e) the text generated by users in response to embedded questions, and (f) the conclusion

FIGURE 9. Script to create user data files

```
on opencard
  global userfeedback, showunique, showunique2, summary,¬
  firstname, lastname, studentnumber, numx, noneofabovel, noneofabove2
  if showunique = "Yes" or showunique2 = "Yes" then
    show card button 3                  This conditional shows a button if the user
  else                                  selected "None of the above" at any point which
    hide card button 3                  links to the unique solution screen for user
  end if                                self-evaluation.
  set scroll of card field 2 to 0
  put userfeedback into card field 2     Shows self-evaluation in field at top of screen.
  put numx + 1 into numx                Scenario repetition counter.
  put lastname into filename            Converts global variable to local variable.
  open file filename
  write numx to file filename           File for keeping track of how may times user
  close file filename                   engaged the scenario.
```

The next eight lines put all necessary data file information into the local variable "UserRecord." The data are also formatted with "returns" to make the file easy to read when imported into a word processor. The final four lines specify the data file name and write "userRecord" to disk.

```
  put Return & "_____________________________________________"&¬
  return & "User name:  "& firstname && Lastname & "        "&¬
  studentnumber & return &¬
  return & "Scenario conclusion 3.27" & return & return &¬
  "Number of conclusions reached:" && Numx & Return & Return &¬
  "Summary of user choices:" & return &¬
  Summary & return & return & "User's self evaluation:"& Return &¬
  Userfeedback & firstunique & secondunique into userrecord
  put lastname && "scen3-conc "& numx into filename
  open file filename
  write userrecord to file filename
  close file filename
end opencard
```

reached. All these data items were already contained in global variables, except the choices made and the user-generated text. However, these later two data items were already grouped together on the summary card, so the data from the summary card were simply put into another global variable. Then, all the global variables were combined into a single variable which was automatically written to a disk file when the final scenario card, the feedback card, was reached (Figure 9).

Error Trapping Multiple Use. Because student data files are kept, the program had to be able to (a) verify whether or not someone has used the program before and (b) know how many times a conclusion has been reached (in order for the data files to maintain sequential numbers and to prevent overwriting). Therefore, the counter variable is written to its own file along with the name of the user minus a numeric extension:

```
open file lastname
write counter to file lastname
close file lastname
```

By placing the counter in a separate file, rather than as a part of the user data files, the program can determine whether or not the user, or someone with the same last name, has previously used that particular program. When beginning the program, users are asked whether or not they have used the program before. If the response is "Yes," their file is opened and the counter variable is read, after which the counter number is used to continue numbering the data files. If the response is "Yes" and the users have not used the program before, they are warned that there are no data on record for them, to verify that their last name is spelled correctly, and to make sure they used this particular workstation the last time. If the response is "No," the program opens a new counter file and enters 0 into the variable "counter" (counter is incremented at the conclusion, not the beginning of each scenario). If the response is "No," and the users have used the program before, or someone with the same last name is on file, the current users are advised to use a variation of their last name or verify that they clicked "No" by mistake (Figure 10). With other programming languages, a file cannot be read if no file exists. However, when instructed to open a file, *HyperCard* looks to see if the file specified exists; if it doesn't, one is created with the name specified. Then, even though the file is empty, the read statement functions correctly and simply returns the value "empty" which is what can be used to verify previous program use.

Append File Follies

As mentioned earlier, there is no apparent append file function in *HyperCard*. However, in the quest to overcome this problem, two items were

FIGURE 10. Script from the "Yes" button after the user is asked whether or not they have used the program before

```
on mouseUp
  global firstname, lastname, numx
  put lastname into studentfile
  open file studentfile
  read from file studentfile until tab
  put it into numx
  close file studentfile
  if numx is empty then                  If empty, the user has not used the program
    put 0 into numx                      before and 0 is placed in file.
    open file studentfile
    write numx to file studentfile
    close file studentfile
    go to card id 5216
  else                                   The "else" warns user's name is on file and
                                         provides options.
    Put firstname && lastname & "," & return &¬
    "My records indicate you have used this program before.  If "&¬
    "you clicked Yes by mistake, click OK now. If you did not click"&¬
    " Yes by mistake, please quit the program, restart, and use a "&¬
    "slight variation of your last name" & return&¬
    "(i.e.: IMSmith instead of"¬
    &" Smith)." into card field 2
    show card field 2                    Shows above warning.
    show card button 3                   Shows 'OK' button.
    show card button 4                   Shows 'Quit' button.
  end if
```

discovered that may be of interest to others attempting to do the same. These comments are not intended to be any sort of final word on the subject as a possible append files function may have been overlooked. The following comments are intended to serve only as useful information about one person's observations.

HyperCard places information read from a data file in a local variable. A logical way, then, to append a file would be to read the existing data from the file and place it in a local variable such as stuph1. If the new information to be appended is contained in another variable, say newStuph, combining the contents of both variables within a third variable and writing it back to the same file makes sense:

```
open file studentRecord
read from file studentRecord
close file studentRecord
put it into stuph1
put stuph1 & newStuph into allStuph
open file studentRecord
```

```
write allStuph to file studentRecord
Close file studentRecord
```

What actually occurs is that the data contained in allStuph is appended to the data already existing in the file studentRecord so that there are now two copies of the original data plus the data contained in newStuph. There seemed to be an append function after all. However, it is necessary to avoid repeating the original data. Apparently *HyperCard* automatically goes to the end of the existing file and writes whatever has been specified in the variable allStuph, after the existing data are simply written to the file:

```
open file studentRecord
write newStuph to file studentRecord
Close file studentRecord
```

This seemed to work very well. *HyperCard* does, after all, seem to have a simple append file function. However, repeated testing of this function revealed that when the data file reaches approximately 10k, data are continually deleted from the middle of the file in a seemingly random manner to keep the file size at approximately 10k.

Software Development Summary

Many educators who have not been involved with software development are unaware of the opportunities to create effective educational software that are provided by easy-to-use authoring packages such as *HyperCard*. Other educators, who are familiar with software development, programming languages, and so-called "professional," full-featured (and expensive) software development packages, are suspicious of *HyperCard's* efficacy because of limitations imposed by its fairly rigid structure and lack of features. This article is intended to illustrate the usefulness of *HyperCard* to both groups by describing how an effective piece of software, *The Classroom Management Simulation*, was developed. The first section describes the necessary planning stages, which were based on a software development prescription derived from instructional design theory and empirical research. Only through careful and thorough planning, completed before programming begins, will educationally sound software applications result.

The second section was designed to illustrate how various software features can be written with *HyperCard*. Educators, who are interested in the language examples, may use them as templates for their own software development or as a resource for developing other features. The examples are not intended to be inclusive as there are many ways to solve programming problems. Other educators may only be interested in learning how useful *HyperCard* can be.

In conclusion, software development is a long and arduous task that requires careful planning. However, those educators who wish to pursue software development and who do not have programming expertise will find that *HyperCard* (or a similar authoring package) is an easy-to-use tool that may well fulfill their needs.

FIELD TESTING THE SIMULATION

The completed *Classroom Management Simulation* was field tested with 88 Curriculum and Instruction students (59 first-year and 29 final-year) at West Virginia University. Students worked in small groups of two to four, at one of 10 interactive video workstations, for three total hours over two weeks. Both the first-year and final-year groups improved their achievement scores.

The simulation was also successful from a non-quantitative point of view. The sample unanimously indicated they enjoyed using the program, particularly because the video made it seem realistic. This positive attitude is similar to attitudes found in other studies involving interactive video courseware (Abrams & Streit, 1986; Branch et al., 1987; Milheim, 1989). Many also said the program was self-explanatory and easy to use. It should be noted that very few final-year students and almost no first-year students had Macintosh experience, yet none had any trouble using the program because the only skill needed to successfully engage the program was to move the mouse and click on *HyperCard* "buttons."

Most students wanted more solution choices for each scenario which can easily be added. As discussed in the Program Construction section, if a response is entered that is not one of the program choices, users are directed to develop their unique responses that are then saved in the user data files along with all other responses. If the same unique solutions appear an adequate number of times, they can be added to the simulation. If appropriate video segments cannot be found to accompany the added solutions, conclusions can be text-based only, instead of text and video. Also, most students indicated they would like more scenarios.

Nearly every student enjoyed using the simulation, indicating that the experience was as close to reality as possible given the instructional medium. In actual use, most students were very conscientious about responding to the program's questions the first several times through each scenario, particularly the final-year group. After five or six times through each scenario, however, most began to simply click DONE buttons and choose a strategy to see what would happen. When questioned, they indicated that they had tried out the strategies they thought were appropriate and were just "playing around" to see what might happen in other solution paths.

CONCLUSION

In conclusion, interactive video computer-based simulations are useful tools for introducing pre-service teachers to classroom situations. Simulations such as the *Classroom Management Simulation*, although not the "real thing," can potentially be more useful for initial classroom interaction because they are dependable, consistent, and easily accessible. Curriculum and instruction faculty often have difficulty finding and coordinating quality initial field experiences for their students. If such experiences can be effectively simulated with laserdisc technology and computer-based simulations, initial field work can be pursued at any time, therefore making those experiences dependable and easily accessible. Easy accessibility, combined with the time compression inherent in practicing management strategies with a simulation, will also result in time and cost savings. That is, simulated field experiences are available at any time, saving the time and travel costs associated with actual field experience. Also, because the experiences will be the same, or similar (depending on the nature of the simulation and what choices students make within the programs), the pre-service teachers will have common experiences that lend themselves more easily to classroom discussion. Simulated field work may reduce anxiety because users know they can try ideas without risking failure with "real" students or worrying about possible negative effects from unacceptable courses of action. Therefore, interactive video simulations potentially provide an important, "risk free" stepping stone from non-experienced student to classroom professional. With these advantages, interactive video computer-based simulations are promising tools to help prepare educators.

REFERENCES

Abrams, A. & Streit, L. (1986). Effectiveness of interactive video in teaching basic photography. *T.H.E. Journal*, 12(2), 92-96.

Anderson, R.C., Spiro, R.I., & Anderson, M.C. (1978). Schemata as scaffolding for the representation of information in connected discourse. *American Educational Research Journal, 15*, 433-440.

Aronson, D.T. & Briggs, L.J. (1983). Contributions of Gagne and Briggs to a prescriptive model of instruction. In: C.M. Reigeluth (Ed.), *Instructional-design theories and models* (pp. 75-100). Hillsdale, NJ: Lawrence Erlbaum Associates.

Carrier, C.A. & Jonassen, D.H. (1988). Adapting courseware to accommodate individual differences. In: D. H. Jonassen (Ed.), *Instructional designs for microcomputer courseware* (pp. 203-26). Hillsdale, NJ: Lawrence Erlbaum Associates.

Classroom discipline: A simulation approach [Computer Program Documentation]. (1987). Alberta, Canada: University of Alberta, The Instructional Technology Centre.

Collins, A. & Stevens, A.L. (1983). A cognitive theory of inquiry teaching. In: C.M. Reigeluth (Ed.), *Instructional-design theories and models* (pp. 247-278). Hillsdale, NJ: Lawrence Erlbaum Associates.

Gagne, R.M. & Briggs, L.J. (1979). *Principles of instructional design* (2nd ed.). New York, NY: Holt, Rinehart and Winston.

Goodman, D. (1987). *The complete HyperCard handbook.* New York: Bantam Books.

Gropper, G.L. (1983). A behavioral approach to instructional prescription. In: C.M. Reigeluth (Ed.), *Instructional-design theories and models* (pp. 37-54). Hillsdale, NJ: Lawrence Erlbaum Associates.

Hamilton, R.I. (1985). A framework for the evaluation of the effectiveness of adjunct questions and objectives. *Review of Educational Research, 55*(1), 47-85.

Hannafin, M.J. & Hooper, S. (1988). *Empirically-based guidelines for designing interactive video.* Paper presented at the 1988 meeting of the American Educational Research Association, New Orleans, LA.

Hannafin, M.J. & Peck, K.L. (1988). *The design, development and evaluation of instructional software.* New York: Macmillan.

Hannum, W. (1988). Designing courseware to fit subject matter structure. In: D. H. Jonassen (Ed.), *Instructional designs for microcomputer courseware* (pp. 275-296). Hillsdale, NJ: Lawrence Erlbaum Associates.

Ho, C.P., Savenye, W., & Haas, N. (1986). The effects of orienting objectives and review on learning from interactive video. *Journal of Computer-Based Instruction, 13*(4), 126-129.

Jonassen, D.H. & Hannum, W.C. (1987, December). Research-based principles for designing computer software. *Instructional Technology*, pp. 7-14.

Keller, J.M. (1983). Motivational design of instruction. In: C.M. Reigeluth (Ed.), *Instructional-design theories and models* (pp. 383-436). Hillsdale, NJ: Lawrence Erlbaum Associates.

Keller, J.M. & Suzuki, K. (1988). Use of the ARCS motivation model in courseware design. In: D. H. Jonassen (Ed.), *Instructional designs for microcomputer courseware* (pp. 401-434). Hillsdale, NJ: Lawrence Erlbaum Associates.

Landa, L.N. (1983). The algo-heuristic theory of instruction. In: C.M. Reigeluth (Ed.), *Instructional-design theories and models* (pp. 55-73). Hillsdale, NJ: Lawrence Erlbaum Associates.

Merrill, M.D. (1983). Component display theory. In: C.M. Reigeluth (Ed.), *Instructional-design theories and models* (pp. 279-334). Hillsdale, NJ: Lawrence Erlbaum Associates.

Milheim, W.D. (1989). *Perceived attitudinal effects of various types of learner control in an interactive video lesson.* Paper presented at the 1989 meeting of the Association for Educational Communications and Technology, Dallas, TX. (ERIC Document Reproduction Service No. 308-828)

Montague, W.E. (1988). Promoting cognitive processing and learning by designing the learning environment. In: D. H. Jonassen (Ed.), *Instructional designs for microcomputer courseware* (pp. 125-150). Hillsdale, NJ: Lawrence Erlbaum Associates.

Reigeluth, C.M. & Stein, F. S. (1983). The elaboration theory of instruction. In: C.M. Reigeluth (Ed.), *Instructional-design theories and models* (pp. 335-82). Hillsdale, NJ: Lawrence Erlbaum Associates.

Riggins, S., Wheeler, J., & Henderson, M. (1989). *The Voyager VideoStack 2.0* [Computer program]. The Voyager Company, 1351 Pacific Coast Highway, Santa Monica, California 90401.

Roblyer, M.D. (1988). Fundamental problems and principles of designing effective courseware. In: D. H. Jonassen (Ed.), *Instructional designs for microcomputer courseware* (pp. 7-34). Hillsdale, NJ: Lawrence Erlbaum Associates.

Salisbury, D. (1988). Effective drill and practice strategies. In: D. H. Jonassen (Ed.), *Instructional designs for microcomputer courseware* (pp. 103-124). Hillsdale, NJ: Lawrence Erlbaum Associates.

Scandura, J. M. (1983). Instructional strategies based on the structural learning theory. In: C.M. Reigeluth (Ed.), *Instructional-design theories and models* (pp. 213-78). Hillsdale, NJ: Lawrence Erlbaum Associates.

Wager, W. & Gagne, R.M. (1988). Designing computer-aided instruction. In: D. H. Jonassen (Ed.), *Instructional designs for microcomputer courseware* (pp. 35-60). Hillsdale, NJ: Lawrence Erlbaum Associates.

Robert Perkins

Integrating Alternative Input Devices and Hypermedia for Use by Exceptional Individuals

INTRODUCTION

Hypermedia programs are being used with computers in many new and innovative ways. Stacks, or files created by hypermedia programs, are used as application programs (Venezky & Osin, 1991), tutorials for other software applications (*Microsoft Works* for the Macintosh), as interactive instructional programs with videodiscs (*Hurricane Hugo* from CNN News and IBM), and even as database managers (Church & Bender, 1989). There are many different hypermedia programs available, each program compatible with a specific computer. *HyperCard* was created for the Macintosh, *LinkWay* was created for IBM, *HyperScreen* and *Tutor-Tech* are available for the Apple II series (IIe, IIc, IIgs), and *HyperStudio* for the Apple IIgs. Each hypermedia program has its own unique features, but the basic concept of stacks with cards (or pages) is generally the same for all of them.

Hypermedia programs can be used as a tool to provide teachers with the ability to create educational software. "New trends in software that embody the 'hypermedia' concept . . . can be defined as interactive informa-

ROBERT PERKINS is Associate Professor and Project Coordinator, Demonstration Microcomputer Laboratory for the Handicapped, School of Education, College of Charleston, Charleston, SC 29424.

[Haworth co-indexing entry note]: "Integrating Alternative Input Devices and Hypermedia for Use by Exceptional Individuals." Perkins, Robert. Co-published simultaneously in *Computers in the Schools* (The Haworth Press, Inc.) Vol. 10, No. 3/4, 1994, pp. 339-351; and: *Multimedia and Megachange: New Roles for Educational Computing* (eds: W. Michael Reed, John K. Burton, and Min Liu) The Haworth Press, Inc., 1994, pp. 339-351. Multiple copies of this article/chapter may be purchased from The Haworth Document Delivery Center [1-800-3-HAWORTH; 9:00 a.m. - 5:00 p.m. (EST)].

tion systems by which non-programmers can create and organize text, data, pictures, music, sound, voice, video, and animation through easy-to-use nontechnical procedures" (Church & Bender, 1989, p. 34). Hypermedia is appropriate for teaching specific learners and specific skills (Locatis, Letourneau, & Banvard, 1989). Because of the lack of available software for exceptional individuals, this is especially appropriate in special education (Church & Bender). Teachers can create the Computer-Aided Instruction (CAI) necessary to teach the specific objectives that they need and not have to learn how to program a computer to do it.

Exceptional individuals can benefit from CAI created by hypermedia programs, but they may have difficulty operating these CAI programs because of the restrictiveness of some input devices. Alternative means of computer input must be provided to make computer access possible. The simplest method of input that deviates the least from normal input methods will allow the fastest and most accurate control of the computer by exceptional individuals (Lahm & Greszco, 1988). If the mouse or the *TouchWindow* can be manipulated, they would be the best choice of input devices. However, for some individuals, specialized switches are the only means of computer input.

The various hypermedia programs use standard input devices such as the mouse and the keyboard. Some programs recognize other types of devices such as the *TouchWindow,* graphics tablets, or joysticks. These hypermedia programs can also be combined with other interfaces that allow other types of input devices such as switches. These input devices will be discussed along with ways that they can be integrated with hypermedia programs.

Hypermedia

Some hypermedia authoring programs contain pages or cards (each page or card is a new computer screen) with a minimum of three features: text, graphics, and buttons. Text (words) and graphics (pictures) are common in computer software, but buttons are the feature that adds power to hypermedia programs. Buttons are areas on the computer screen that are sensitive to mouse presses (clicks). For the user, pressing a button can make things happen. At the press of a button, the computer may take the user to another card and present new text or graphics; it might register a choice made by the user, and react to the choice the user made; it might use speech to provide instructions or feedback; or, other devices may be operated by the buttons such as CD-ROM players and laser videodisc players (Van Horn, 1991).

Because of the uniqueness of special populations, obtaining programs that teach specific objectives needed by exceptional individuals may be difficult (Church & Bender, 1989). Hypermedia programs may be operated by individuals with cognitive disabilities, those individuals who are unable to read, those individuals with communication disorders, and those individuals with physical disabilities, to name a few (Perkins, 1991). Hypermedia programs can provide power for educators or parents to tailor specific lessons for individuals by using these programs as authoring languages. Authoring languages allow noncomputer programmers to write computer programs without learning computer languages (Church & Bender, 1989; Van Horn, 1991). What makes hypermedia programs important to teachers and parents of exceptional individuals is that the exact objectives necessary to teach an individual a specific skill can be included in programs created by subject matter experts without much programming background (Church & Bender, 1989). This could alleviate the shortage of appropriate instructional programs for exceptional individuals.

Speech

One of the potential actions that a button can perform when it is pressed is to reproduce speech. Speech can be used to provide instructions or prompts for nonreaders, as well as reinforcement and feedback while stacks are being used by exceptional individuals. Speech has been found to be effective in teaching sight word acquisition to learning disabled students (Weiner, 1991). Developing prereading skills is another area where CAI with added speech is useful (Bullough & Beatty, 1991).

Current computerized speech technology falls into three categories: text-to-speech synthesis, linear predictive coding, and digitized speech (Church & Bender, 1989; Weiner, 1991). Hypermedia programs handle speech differently depending on the hardware available and the capability of the programs (Church & Bender, 1989).

Text-to-speech synthesis allows text within a computer program to be "spoken" by the computer. Text-to-speech synthesis has two advantages: (a) It has many phoneme codes to do the synthesizing, making it very flexible, and (b) the amount of computer memory necessary is small. The quality of the speech is the disadvantage of synthesized speech because it sounds robotic (Church & Bender, 1989; Weiner, 1991).

The advantage of linear predictive coding, which uses speech digitizing and mathematical modeling to reproduce speech, is the improved speech quality with a minimal amount of memory. Tables of words and phrases are available that use much less memory than digitized speech, and the quality is better than text-to-speech. The disadvantage of this type of speech is that the user is confined to tables of preselected words (Church & Bender, 1989; Weiner, 1991).

Digitized sound is more realistic than synthesized sound because it is an actual recording. However, one consideration to keep in mind is that digitized sound requires a large amount of computer memory (Alessi & Trollip, 1991; Church & Bender, 1989; Weiner, 1991), both in the computer's RAM and on the disks. A hard drive is a necessity if a large amount of digitized sound is to be used in stacks. Sound files are excellent use for CD-ROM, with its large storage capacity.

Hardware is required to do the actual digitizing of the speech (Church & Bender, 1989). Depending on which computer is used, additional hardware to reproduce speech may also be needed. Some computers come with built in sound chips (Macintosh, Apple IIgs, and Tandy 1000 computers) and some require additional hardware (all other Apple II series and MS-DOS computers). There are a number of third-party manufacturers that make speech synthesizers and digitizers for these machines (Church & Bender, 1989; Weiner, 1991).

Video

All of the hypermedia programs are able to either create or import computer graphics. Due to limitations of the computer, it may not be able to provide recognizable pictorial representations of concepts necessary using its own graphics capability (Venezky & Osin, 1991). Laser videodiscs can provide both high quality sound and video using minimal computer memory (Alessi & Trollip, 1991; Venezky & Osin, 1991). The video and sound that is played can be randomly accessed by the computer (Bullough & Beatty, 1991). Any audio or video (segment or still frame) can be accessed in any order within seconds (Alessi & Trollip, 1991; Venezky & Osin, 1991).

Most hypermedia programs have the capability to control videodisc players, thus allowing authors to create interactive lessons with video and sound (Bullough & Beatty, 1991). The way that this interaction is accomplished varies. Some hypermedia programs require the codes to be sent to the player to be embedded in a stack's cards. Others provide tools within a hypermedia program that will create the video selection to be played. Some hypermedia programs require other applications to create video segments that will play within stacks.

ALTERNATIVE INPUT DEVICES

Even though some hypermedia programs will work with keypress or joysticks, the primary input device for most hypermedia programs is a mouse. A mouse provides accurate and reliable pointing, but many disabled individuals are unable to use it. For most people using a mouse for the first time, a certain amount of manual dexterity, eye-hand coordination, and much practice is required (Lahm & Greszco, 1988). Because a mouse is also an indirect pointing device, those using it must realize the connection between moving the mouse on the desk and the arrow moving on the computer screen (Alessi & Trollip, 1991; Lahm & Greszco, 1988). Stack access is limited to only those who can physically manipulate the mouse or keyboard and can also cognitively make this abstract connection between mouse and screen.

Users who do not have fine motor control may not be able to move the mouse or click the mouse and may need an alternative to the keyboard or mouse. There are two groups of alternative input devices for computers: those that require special programs that recognize the device (e.g., the *TouchWindow*) and those in which the input is translated by an emulator, making input transparent to the program that it is operating (Church & Bender, 1989).

Devices Requiring Special Programs

There are many devices that can be used as input devices, but require programs that recognize their presence. Some are common devices such as joysticks or graphics tablets. Two commercial alternatives available are the *Muppet Learning Keys* and the *Power Pad.* Both connect through a computer I/O port. Presently, some hypermedia programs recognize joysticks and graphics tablets but do not recognize the *Muppet Learning Keys* or *Power Pad.*

The *TouchWindow* is another device that must be used with programs that recognize its presence. Both *Tutor-Tech* and *HyperStudio* can work with the *TouchWindow.* A *TouchWindow* is a clear plastic membrane that can be attached over the computer monitor and plugged into the computer's game port. The user simply presses the computer monitor to respond within the program.

There are two reasons for using a *TouchWindow* rather than the mouse or keyboard in CAI. First, for some individuals, there may be less fine motor control required in pointing at the monitor versus moving a mouse and clicking it. Second, some individuals cannot make the connection between the mouse on the table and the arrow on the computer screen (Church & Bender, 1989). With the *TouchWindow,* there is a direct connection between pointing on the screen and interacting with the CAI program.

For individuals with fine motor control problems and those not associating the mouse and arrow relationship using hypermedia stacks, the *Touch-*

Window is an excellent solution. Users press the *TouchWindow* where buttons appear on the computer monitor. The computer reacts as if the mouse had been moved to that position and the mouse button clicked. This allows users to easily operate stacks, because of the direct interaction between the user, the computer monitor, and the stack. This does require that the user be able to move a finger or other pointing device across the computer monitor and lightly press the *TouchWindow*. It provides a direct connection between the computer screen and events within the stack (Alessi & Trollip, 1991; Male, 1988) with less eye-hand coordination than moving and clicking a mouse requires.

Transparent Input Devices

Transparent input devices work with almost all programs, because the program does not need to know whether the device is there (Lahm & Greszco, 1988), but the computer does require an emulator to translate the input into information that the computer can recognize. The input devices are plugged into the emulator and the device's input is translated into information that the respective programs require without concern about how it was input. The device emulates the computer's keyboard or mouse (Church & Bender, 1989).

There are many alternative input devices available that capitalize on an individual's strengths. They range from switches (which can be anything that can register on/off status) that are operated by using specific muscles, eye blinks, or blowing to alternative keyboards such as the *Unicorn Keyboard* and the *TASH Mini Keyboard* that can be altered to suit the individual's needs.

Emulators that are available to do the translating are specific to the computer that they are attached to. Some examples are the *Adaptive Firmware Card* (AFC), which is available for Apple II computers; *Aid Plus Me*, which is available for Apple II, PC compatibles, and Macintosh computers; *PC-A.i.d.*, which is used with PC compatibles; and *Ke:nx* which is used with the Macintosh. These emulators can accept input from any switch with a 9 mm jack, a mini keyboard, a *Unicorn Keyboard*, and many other ASCII devices and alternative keyboards. Since the emulator is transparent to programs and stacks, no special instructions need to be given to the hypermedia programs to recognize the alternative input devices. The emulator does need to be set up to provide input to the computer by specifying the method and device to be used, however.

Emulators can substitute mouse input, using mouse emulation for the mouse input methods. In the case of the *Adaptive Firmware Card*'s switch input method, a switch press is required for each of the following steps to make a choice: aim the mouse, move the mouse, stop the mouse, and click the mouse button. Because of the complication of using a switch as an input device for mouse activities, the AFC manual states "Avoid mouse emulation . . . Look for keyboard equivalents" (*Adaptive Firmware Card* Operator's Manual and Application Guide, 1988, 18-3). In some hypermedia programs, there are no keyboard equivalents to use.

Rather than having the switch control mouse movement, hypermedia stacks can eliminate the need for mouse movement by capitalizing on their own features or using the emulator's capabilities. An alternative to pressing the mouse (clicking) is all that needs to be addressed. A solution is available because emulators are able to convert a switch press into a mouse click.

Sometimes a little creativity is necessary to minimize the amount of effort required by the individual using an input method. In the case of the *Adaptive Firmware Card,* using its own switch-input scanning method of emulating a mouse still requires two switch presses to make a choice, one to have the AFC expect mouse input and one to click the mouse. Eliminating the need for one of these switch presses (activating mouse input) is necessary to make this process more efficient. The AFC has the capability to use Morse Code as an input method. By designating an "E" (a short press or "dit") and a "T" (a long press or "dah") in Morse Code as a mouse click, a single switch input can do both of these steps no matter how long the switch is pressed (Perkins, 1991).

Scanning

Basic cause and effect skills should be taught initially as a prerequisite to using other CAI programs (Esposito & Campbell, 1987). The individual will have to see a relationship between computer input and something happening within the program that he or she is operating. There are commercial programs available to do this, but teachers and parents can also create stacks that teach cause and effect. Each card will have a full screen button that goes to the next page (with any desired special effects). By pressing the switch, the stack will proceed to the next card and present a graphic or sound or a combination of both to reinforce the pressing of the switch.

Eventually, this linear process will not be adequate to develop CAI. Users will need to be provided with a choice, or branching within the stack. Individuals using emulators who are ready to move to stacks that include branching need a way to make choices. Scanning is a process that many physically impaired individuals use to operate computers. Scanning displays the possible choices available to a user on the computer screen with a cursor or other method of highlighting each choice in turn. When the preferred choice is highlighted, it is selected by a switch press (Green & Brightman, 1990). Users do not have to move a mouse or type in their responses. The computer automatically provides the choices and waits for the user to respond when the selection is highlighted.

Scanning within stacks can be accomplished in one of three ways, depending on the hypermedia program capabilities: (a) If scanning through buttons is a built in feature, (b) if self-activating buttons are a feature, and (c) if neither of the other features is available. This is a hierarchy of efficiency for the individual's computer input. The first feature available within the hypermedia program used is the best.

For those hypermedia programs that already have the built-in capability to scan buttons, having more than one button on a page and activating its scanning capability are all that is required. Each button will be highlighted in turn (usually the delay between buttons can be specified). If the mouse is clicked, the stack moves on; if not, the next button is highlighted. This cycle continues until the mouse (switch) is clicked.

For those hypermedia programs that can create buttons that will activate themselves after a delay, then scanning is done by creating a series of cards, all identical with the same choices on them, but with one of the choices highlighted to make it different from the others. On each of the cards in the cycle there are two buttons, one to register a mouse click and one to automatically go to the next card if there is no activity in a specified amount of time. The user sees the highlighting go from one choice on the card to the next as the cards automatically change (due to the self-activating button). The scanning allows the user to click when the choice that he/she wants is highlighted, thus activating the second button. If no item is selected in the series, the process goes back to the first card in the series. This minimizes the amount of input activity required from the user to simply a mouse click.

Hypermedia programs that can not make use of the first two methods must rely on the emulator to do the scanning. Some hypermedia programs allow keyboard entries to control movement from button to button (i.e., *Tutor-Tech*). By setting up the emulator to recognize the difference between a mouse movement (TAB) and mouse click (RETURN) using two different Morse code signals, scanning can be accomplished. The individual might use a short switch press to TAB and a long switch press to RETURN.

HYPERMEDIA PROGRAM FEATURES

The following information is provided as a guide to some of the available features in specific hypermedia programs. The information is not a complete description of the programs, but does relate to some devices and emulators already mentioned. Deciding which program to use will also depend on whether computer hardware is already in place or is to be purchased at the same time as the software and emulators.

HyperCard

As mentioned previously, *HyperCard* is a hypermedia program created for the Macintosh computer. It is credited with starting the hypermedia trend in database creation (Church & Bender, 1989). *HyperCard* is also "considered by many to be the most revolutionary educational development since the introduction of microcomputers in the late seventies" (Van Horn, 1991, p. 195). Many application programs for the Macintosh use *HyperCard* stacks as tutorials. There are also many educational public domain and *HyperCard* stackware available. One feature that has made this a very popular program is that it is shipped with every Macintosh computer sold, making it available to all Macintosh users.

HyperCard can use pictures from any Macintosh paint or drawing programs for graphics and can import text from most word processors. Digitized sound can be added to *HyperCard* stacks by using a device and program called *Mac Recorder* to create the sound files. *HyperCard* also uses a program *(Voyager Video Stack)* to save videodisc segments to use with stacks.

HyperCard can use the keyboard as well as a mouse for input by the user. The Macintosh has one feature that is included with the system software, called *CloseView*, that allows the Macintosh screen to be magnified (up to 16 times), allowing the computer to be used by those with vision problems. *CloseView* is also shipped with all Macintosh computers and is transparent to any Macintosh program.

For those capabilities that are not built into *HyperCard*, the user can "program" using HyperTalk, a scripting language similar to Pascal, to create the additional features necessary.

LinkWay

LinkWay is the hypermedia program available from IBM for MS-DOS microcomputers. *LinkWay* facilitates mouse and keyboard input; however, an additional speech board is necessary for most MS-DOS computers. As with other hypermedia programs, *LinkWay* includes its own painting tools to create graphics, or it can also access a videodisc player. A scripting language is included so that *LinkWay* can be "programmed" for additional capabilities. This scripting language is used to control speech and optical discs (Hertzberg, 1991).

HyperStudio

HyperStudio is an appropriate hypermedia program for use with alternative input devices; it has features built-in that increase the accessibility of stacks to individuals who have special needs (Perkins, 1991). One feature is that *HyperStudio* has the built in capability to recognize the presence of a *TouchWindow.* Another feature that *HyperStudio* has built-in is a feature called auto-activated buttons. These buttons are programmed to activate themselves after a specified period of time. Additional features include the ability to record digitized sound, create animation, and operate a videodisc player (using a built-in interface with videodisc controls to save the segments).

Sound digitizing in *HyperStudio* can be accomplished from two audio sources, a recording from a tape recorder or other audio source, or through its own microphone. Sounds can be recorded as the lesson is being created, or through a separate application (the *Sound Shop,* which comes with *HyperStudio*) that provides extensive sound editing capabilities. Since the sound is digitized rather than synthesized, the quality is nearly as good as the original source. It does not require an additional speech synthesizer because it is using digitized sound and the computer's own sound chip. By recording the teacher's or parents' voice using the microphone that comes with the program, the individual will hear voices that are familiar. The digitized sound is controlled by buttons within the *HyperStudio* stack.

HyperStudio also has available what are called "extended commands" (XCMDs). These are program codes that can be added to do specific things. Available from the publisher are XCMDs that allow keyboard input, but more importantly, there are XCMDs that can control scanning buttons. Other XCMDs are available, or they can be created in programming languages such as Pascal, and added to stacks.

HyperScreen

The biggest advantage that *HyperScreen* has is that it will run on an Apple II computer with 128K of memory. *HyperScreen* also recognizes the *Echo Speech Synthesizer*, and allows words to be typed in (phonetically) while the stack is being created (text-to-speech synthesis). *HyperScreen* also can create scanning buttons. *HyperScreen* uses embedded videodisc codes created by the stack's author to control the player.

Tutor-Tech

Tutor-Tech will also run on an Apple II computer with 128K of memory. *Tutor-Tech* can utilize the mouse, keyboard, and joystick as input devices. *Tutor-Tech* also has the capability of working with the *TouchWindow*, but it takes two hands to use it, one to interact with the screen and the other to click using one of its buttons at the bottom of the *TouchWindow*. *Tutor-Tech* recognizes the *Echo Speech Synthesizer*. It requires the words that are to be spoken to be part of a fixed table of words and phrases (linear predictive code). *Tutor-Tech* also uses embedded codes to control a videodisc player.

CONCLUSION

Hypermedia programs can be used by parents and teachers to create CAI stacks for exceptional individuals. These stacks can be used with a variety of alternative input devices to make the stacks more accessible to exceptional individuals. Integrating hypermedia and alternative input devices can teach exceptional individuals objectives that they need, since no CAI programs are currently available to do that.

Hypermedia programs can empower handicapped individuals by providing automation to tasks that hinder the individuals. Hypermedia programs can also provide the capability to both teachers and parents to create the stacks necessary for exceptional individuals to use. There are many features that are available within hypermedia programs that make hypermedia stacks more easily accessible to exceptional individuals. Hypermedia, the combination of information sources such as video, text, speech, and graphics, makes CAI creation possible for those who need it the most. Just as importantly, these stacks can be authored without learning a programming language.

With a little creativity, any hypermedia program can be combined with the necessary alternative input devices to make the stacks available to be operated by exceptional individuals, whether they are visually impaired, cognitively impaired, or physically impaired. Special input devices or emulators may be necessary to take advantage of the strengths of a particular individual, but the capability is there.

A description of some of the available hypermedia programs and their features was discussed as a starting point in assessing how these programs may meet specific needs. Needs are as different as the exceptional individuals that will be served. Decisions regarding which hypermedia program to use may be determined by the equipment already in place, since the programs are machine specific. When initial machine purchases are being considered, the information provided is a guide, but comparisons should still be made before purchasing equipment.

Integration of hypermedia and alternative input devices is very exciting since there are many different technologies that can be incorporated, such as video and speech. The fact that one does not have to be a programmer to create computer programs, and that software can be operated by exceptional individuals, is worth investigating, both for the practitioner in the classroom and those researching educational technology.

REFERENCES

Adaptive Firmware Card operator's manual and application guide, (1988). Wauconda, IL: Don Johnston Developmental Equipment, Inc.

Alessi, S. M. & Trollip, S. R. (1991). *Computer-based instruction: Methods and development*, Englewood Cliffs, NJ: Prentice Hall.

Bullough, R. V. & Beatty, L. F. (1991). *Classroom applications of microcomputers*, New York, NY: Macmillan.

Church, G. & Bender, M. (1989). *Teaching with computers: A curriculum for special educators*, Boston, MA: A College-Hill Publication.

Esposito, L. & Campbell, P. H. (1987). Computers and severely and physically handicapped individuals. In: Lindsey, J. D. (Ed.), *Computers and Exceptional Individuals*, (pp. 105-124), Columbus: Merrill Publishing Company.

Green, P. & Brightman, A. J. (1990). *Independence day: Designing computer solutions for individuals with disability*, Allen TX: Developmental Learning Materials.

Hertzberg, L. (1991). Multimedia authoring languages. *Electronic Learning 11*(3), 30-32.

Lahm, E. A. & Greszco, K. (1988). Therapeutic applications and adaptive devices. In: Behrmann, M. M. (Ed.), *Integrating computers into the curriculum: A handbook for special educators*, (pp. 29-58). Boston: Little, Brown and Co.

Locatis, C, Letourneau, G., & Banvard, R. (1989). Hypermedia and instruction. *Educational Research and Development 37*(4), 65-77.

Male, M. (1988). *Special magic: Computers, classroom strategies, and exceptional users*, Mountain View, CA: Mayfield.

Perkins, R. (1991). Using *HyperStudio* to create lessons that use alternative input devices. *Technology and Teacher Education Annual* (pp. 80-83), Society for Technology and Teacher Education.

Van Horn, R. (1991). *Advanced technology in education*, Pacific Grove, CA: Brooks/Cole.

Venezky, R. & Osin, L. (1991). *The intelligent design of computer-assisted instruction*, White Plains, NY: Longman.

Weiner, R. (1991). Computerized Speech: A study of its effect on learning. *Technical Horizons in Education Journal 18*(7), 100-102.

Zhengmai Zhao
Tim O'Shea
Pat Fung

The Effects of Visible Link-Types on Learning in the Hypertext Environment: An Empirical Study

INTRODUCTION

This study examines the effects of a proposed approach to promoting the use of hypertext for learning. Two homogeneous groups were involved in the investigation. The two groups used different versions of a hypertext learning system. One version with visible link-types, the other without. We compare both the learning outcomes and learning processes of the two groups. The results indicate that labelling links explicitly with the semantic relations has a positive influence on learning outcomes. However, it has also raised other issues which merit further investigation.

The higher degree of learner control supported in hypertext has two sides. On the plus side, allowing learners to decide the pace and sequencing of navigation offers them opportunities to accommodate their individual differences and not only learn course content but also even, according to Marchionini (1988), to learn how to learn. On the minus side, it introduces

ZHENGMAI ZHAO is a research student, TIM O'SHEA is Professor, and PAT FUNG is Research Fellow, Institute of Educational Technology, The Open University, Walton Hall, Milton Keynes, MK7 6AA, UK.

[Haworth co-indexing entry note]: "The Effects of Visible Link-Types on Learning in the Hypertext Environment: An Empirical Study." Zhao, Zhengmai, Tim O'Shea, and Pat Fung. Co-published simultaneously in *Computers in the Schools* (The Haworth Press, Inc.) Vol. 10, No. 3/4, 1994, pp. 353-370; and: *Multimedia and Megachange: New Roles for Educational Computing* (eds: W. Michael Reed, John K. Burton, and Min Liu) The Haworth Press, Inc., 1994, pp. 353-370. Multiple copies of this article/chapter may be purchased from The Haworth Document Delivery Center [1-800-3-HAWORTH; 9:00 a.m. - 5:00 p.m. (EST)].

the problem of cognitive overload (Conklin, 1987). Without sufficient guidance, learners, particularly novice learners, facing a number of choices about which links to follow and which to leave alone, experience a definite distraction that degrades the effectiveness of learning. This might account for the fact that few evaluations of hypertext in education have shown the strength of hypertext over other media in terms of overall learning outcomes (Jonassen & Grabinger, 1990). We believe that achieving a balance between the two sides of learner control may be the key to enhancing the use of hypertext for learning. Hypertext researchers and designers have been developing approaches to mitigate the problem of cognitive overload. Some approaches include, among others, guided tours (Allinson & Hammond, 1989), graphical browsers (Nielson, 1990), computed links (Kibby & Mayes, 1989), and museum layouts (Travers, 1989). In this paper, we propose an approach to easing the problem of cognitive overload through attention to the basic design of hypertext learning systems.

Hypertext researchers and designers have noticed the analogy of hypertext structures to semantic networks (Conklin, 1987). Many of them believe that the characteristics of nodes and links offer hypertext the ability to mimic the semantic network (Jonassen, 1990). "When what people have in their mind is elicited and compared to various computer representations for hypertext, the semantic net representation often proves particularly convenient" (Rada, 1991, p. 34). As a form of knowledge representation, semantic networks have been incorporated in a number of experimental hypertext systems, such as *Thoth-II* (Collier, 1987), *Textnet* (Trigg, 1983), and *SemNet* (Fairchild, Poltrock, & Furnas, 1988).

A semantic network is composed of nodes and links that represent, respectively, concepts and relations between concepts. The links in a semantic network are necessarily labelled explicitly to indicate such relations. A network without such labelling is a network, but not a semantic network. Research in the area of semantic networks is well documented (Quillian, 1968; Woods, 1975). Setting this in the context of hypertext learning systems, we hypothesize that in a hypertext learning system, typing links according to the semantic relations between nodes, and labelling links explicitly with such link-types, might improve learning results. Furthermore, we believe that this kind of labelling can lower the learner's cognitive overload in making decisions about which links to follow and which to leave alone. This is because such labelling can serve as a guide to the learner by providing more specific reasons for the connections among nodes in the local hyperspace, or even in the global space. It is also because the provision of such labelling can make the conceptual model of the knowledge domain intuitively clearer to the learner.

The empirical study described in this paper was undertaken to test this hypothesis by comparing the learning results and learning processes of two experimental groups. The two groups involved in the investigation used different versions of a hypertext learning system. One version was with visible link-types, one without. In the following description, the version with visible link-types will be called Version A, and the version without visible link-types will be called Version B. Similarly, the group using Version A will be referred to as Group A, and the group using Version B referred to as Group B.

METHOD

Subjects

Twenty adult volunteer subjects, who were staff or students of the Open University, took part in the study. They were randomly divided into two groups without regard to gender.

Hypertext System

In this section, we first describe the general features of the hypertext system used in the experiment, then explain the specific features of its two versions.

The domain of the experimental hypertext system is the search tree of data structures in computing. It was developed using *HyperCard,*™ and was composed of 37 nodes (cards) and about 200 links, containing about 2000 words, and a dozen graphics and animation. Links in our system are of two basic sorts: organizational and referential. The primary function of the organizational link is to build the hierarchical structure for the hypertext knowledge base. In our system, such links as "Start from the Beginning," "Go to the Content Table," and links from entries of a content table to their sections fall into this category. In general, the referential link is the kind of link that most clearly distinguishes hypertext from conventional text. Two nodes are associated with each other by a referential link based on their semantic relationships. In our hypertext system, the referential links can be further divided into lexical links and textual links. The former connect regions of nodes to nodes, and the latter connect nodes to nodes.

In Figure 1, the organizational links, and textual and lexical referential links used in our system, are represented using thin, thick, and bidirectional arrow lines respectively. Although we do not use bidirectional arrow lines for organizational and textual referential links, most of them are also bidirectional.

The two experimental groups used two different versions of the system. The two versions have the same contents, same structures, and same organizational links. In both versions, textual links are represented by buttons placed outside the main information space and lexical links are represented by the "hotpoint," a textual string with an underline. However, in

FIGURE 1. Simplified View of the Experimental Hypertext Structure

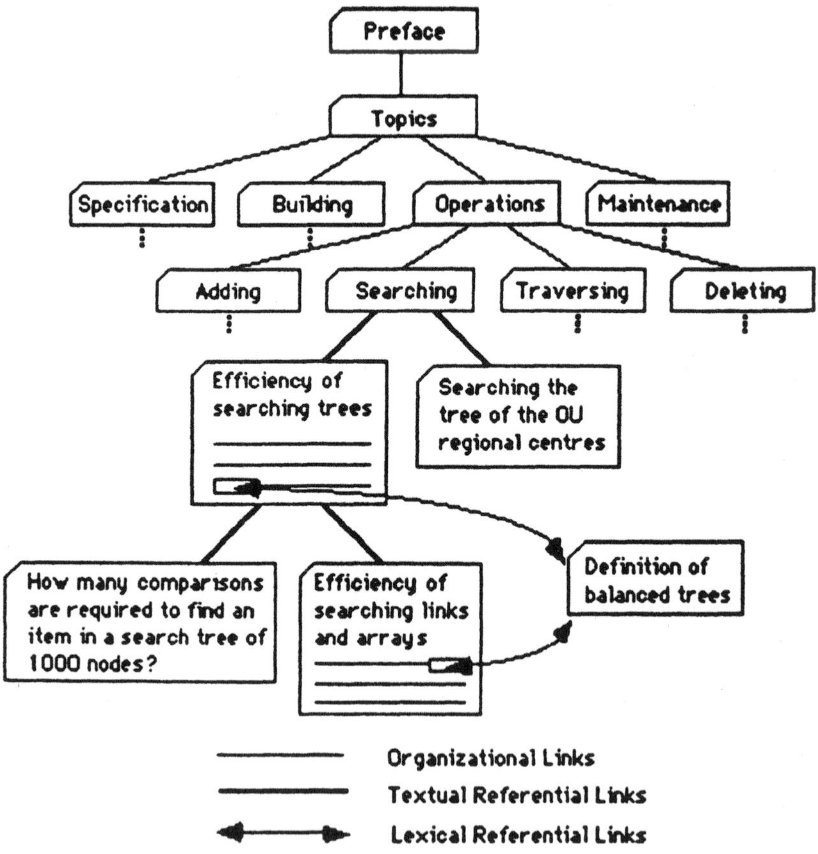

each version, the referential links, both textual and lexical, are labelled in different ways.

In Version A, the textual referential link is labelled explicitly by using the semantic relation (i.e., the link-type) between the two nodes it connects such as "has an example," "is an example of," "has contrast with," "has an analysis," "is an analysis of," and so forth (Figure 2). In the case of the lexical referential link, since the link source is part of the text, its denotation is totally dependent on the context. To let the learner view the link-type, every "hotpoint" is attached with a small information palette. Once the learner moves the cursor over a "hotpoint," it is highlighted and its palette, with the link-type information, appears at the bottom of the window (Figure 2). When the cursor is moved out of the "hotpoint," it is restored and its palette disappears simultaneously.

In contrast to this, in Version B, all textual referential links are labelled as "related content." In the lexical referential link, no palette with the link-type information is attached to the "hotpoint." Figure 3 shows an example of the labelling in Version B.

FIGURE 2. An Example of Labelling the Referential Links in Version A

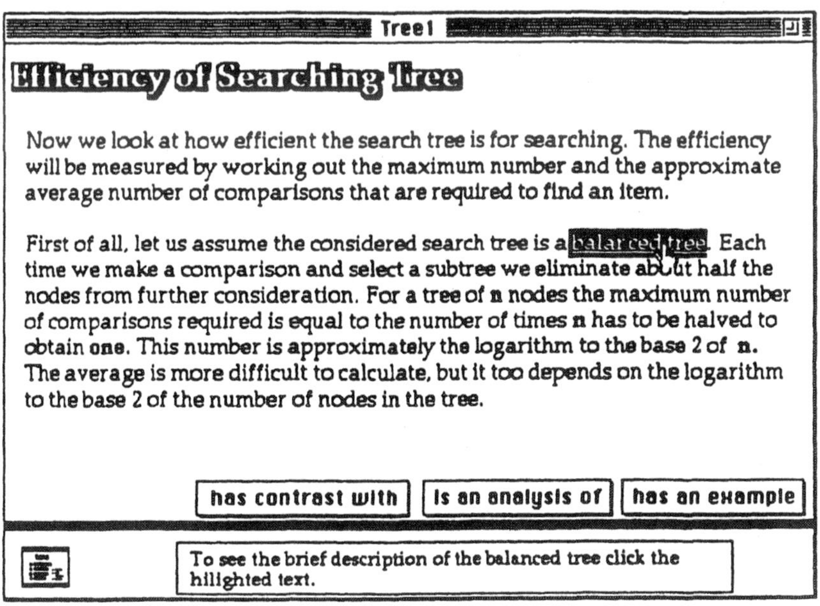

FIGURE 3. An Example of Labelling the Referential Links in Version B

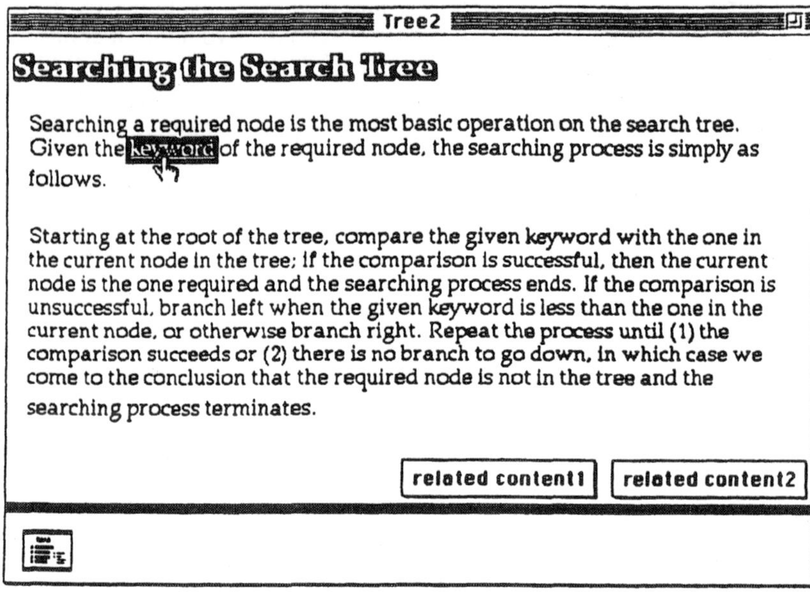

Procedure

The procedure included three steps. The first step asked the subject to do a pre-test, which consisted of two tasks:

Task 1: filling in a printed form designed to investigate the subject's prior experience of using a Macintosh machine and prior knowledge of hypertext and data structures in computing;
Task 2: completing a hypertext questionnaire.

The questionnaire used for Task 2 involved 10 multiple-choice questions, and each question was assigned one point (Appendix). In the next step, the subject was exposed to a specific version of the experimental hypertext system according to which group he or she had been assigned. After sufficient browsing, the subject was in the final step of completing the post-test. The post-test was comprised of two parts: the same hypertext questionnaire used in the pre-test, and a printed attitude questionnaire. The subject's scores on the hypertext questionnaire for both pre- and post-test were recorded automatically by the system. The system also recorded behavioral traces of learner performances, including the sequence of the cards browsed, the time spent reading each card, as well as the activation of referential links. These data were intended for subsequent analysis of subjects' learning processes.

RESULTS

Improvement Scores

The improvement score is the difference between subject's pre- and post-test scores on the hypertext questionnaire. The mean improvement scores were 5.6 for Group A and 3.8 for Group B. The difference between the mean improvement scores for the two groups was 1.8. By applying the Mann-Whitney test to the individual improvement scores for the two groups, the result showed that the difference was significant ($p < .05$). Table 1 gives the mean scores achieved in answering the hypertext questionnaire for the two groups.

Attitude Toward the System

A printed attitude questionnaire was used as part of the post-test to probe the subject's attitude toward the system. The questionnaire consisted of four scaled questions as well as an open question:

1. How did you enjoy using this hypertext system?
2. How easy did you find it to browse through this hypertext system?
3. Did you find the labels on the buttons helpful in finding the information you wanted?
4. What do you think of the way a "hotpoint" (a textual string with an underline) was represented in the hypertext system?

Subjects' answers to these questions are shown in Table 2.

TABLE 1. Mean Scores of the Hypertext Questionnaire

Group	Pre-test	Post-test	Improvement
A	1.9	7.5	5.6
B	2.3	6.1	3.8

TABLE 2. Subjects' Responses to the Scaled Questions

Q1	Very Much	Fairly	Not Very	Not at All	
Group A	4	6	0	0	
Group B	3	5	2	0	
Q2	Very Easy	Easy	Average	Difficult	Very Difficult
Group A	5	3	2	0	0
Group B	0	4	5	1	0
Q3	Very Helpful	Helpful	Not Very Helpful		Very Difficult
Group A	2	8	0		0
Group B	0	7	3		0
Q4	Very Good	Good	Average	Poor	Very Poor
Group A	4	5	1	0	0
Group B	1	2	5	1	0

Subjects' responses to the open prompt ("Please write any other comments you may wish to make about the hypertext system.") are summarized as follows:

1. Lack of a complete overview of the net structure was a hindrance; I wanted an overview diagram.
2. I sometimes forgot which parts of the system I had already explored; perhaps there could be a dynamic "where you've already been" page (presumably with a map of the hyperspace).
3. The visual demonstrations of examples were very helpful, but I'd rather be able to manipulate the examples by myself to test my understanding than watch the system doing it.
4. Information contained in most cards was too dense.

Dislike of the "related content" button is the specific complaint from the Group B.

Learning Processes

Table 3 shows the mean average of the sets of figures that were recorded automatically by the system to reveal subjects' learning processes. They indicate the whole browsing time, the total number of cards browsed, the sum of different cards browsed, the number of times textual referential links were activated, and the number of times lexical referential links were activated.

TABLE 3. Mean Averages of Subjects' Browsing Processes

Group	Browsing Time (mins)	Cards Browsed	Different Cards Browsed	Textual Referential Links Activated	Lexical Referential Links Activated
A	21.9	89.3	27.7	25.1	10.2
B	21.1	81.6	26.6	31.8	9.6

CONCLUSION AND DISCUSSION

In this experiment, the result concerning subjects' improvement scores confirmed the kernel of our hypothesis that labelling links with the semantic relations in a hypertext learning system has a positive influence on learning results. However, our belief about how and why this labelling can foster the learning (i.e., that the proposed method of labelling links with link-types can lower the learner's cognitive overhead by providing a guide and by making the conceptual model of the knowledge domain clearer) was not supported convincingly from the viewpoint of learning processes.

On the one hand, our subjects' answers to the attitude questionnaire (Table 2) did confirm our belief. Half the subjects from Group A but none from Group B found it very easy to browse through the hypertext. To the question "Did you find the labels on the buttons helpful in finding the information you wanted?" in Group A, two answered "very helpful" and eight said "helpful"; while in Group B, none answered "very helpful," seven said "helpful," and three said "not very helpful." Almost all subjects from Group A felt that the way the "hotpoint" was represented was very good or good, while most participants from Group B thought the way of representing the "hotpoint" in their version was just average.

On the other hand, however, we could not derive any evidence of how learning was facilitated by the visible link-types from the analysis of our subjects' learning processes (Table 3). Apart from the number of times textual referential links were activated, the differences between two groups were trivial with regard to subjects' behavioral traces. Although the difference of the mean times of activating textual referential links between two groups might suggest that the subjects viewing visible link-types in Group A were probably more confident in finding the information they wanted than their counterparts in Group B, this difference was not statistically significant. This lack of difference might be due to the modest scale of the experimental system or less sensitive measures for observing our subjects' performances, or both.

In our study, it was shown that subjects with visible link-types gained better learning outcomes than those without. This fact may be interpreted by using Jonassen's assumption about the potential of hypertext for learning (Jonassen, 1990). His assumption is based on current conceptions of learning developed from principles of cognitive psychology: Learning is a reorganization of knowledge structures by constructing new nodes and interrelating them with existing nodes and with each other (Norman, 1976). The more links that can be formed between existing knowledge and new knowledge, the better the information will be comprehended and the easier learning will be. During the process of learning, the learner's knowledge structure begins to resemble the instructor's. Jonassen's assumption consists of three points. Firstly, he presumes that learning may be conceived of as the mapping of subject matter knowledge (usually that possessed by the teacher or expert) onto the learner's knowledge structure. Secondly, he hypothesizes that hypertext structures can be designed to reflect the semantic structure of a domain expert. Finally, he infers that, if these two points are true, " . . . there is good reason to believe that (using hypertext) the expert's logic may be mapped directly onto the novice browser" (p. 144). A hypertext learning system that labels its links in our proposed way does more closely resemble a semantic network, so it could facilitate mapping of the subject matter knowledge structure onto the learner's knowledge structure according to Jonassen's theory. But as Jonassen himself pointed out, this hypothesis obviously demands empirical verification.

In our experiment, we also examined more closely relationships among the learning outcomes, the kinds of subjects, and the types of hypertext versions used. To do that, each group was further divided into two parts according to achievement on the pre-test (both the printed and the hypertextual questionnaire); i.e., subjects' prior knowledge of the experimental domain (search trees of data structures), use of a Macintosh machine as well as hypertext systems. The subject who achieved more was recognized as the learner with higher individual learning prerequisites, and the subject who achieved less was considered as the learner with lower individual learning prerequisites. We found that in Group B the subjects with lower learning prerequisites performed slightly worse than those with higher learning prerequisites. Conversely in Group A the subjects with lower learning prerequisites did a little better than those with higher learning prerequisites (Table 4). Although not significant, it seems to suggest the learners with lower learning prerequisites could benefit more from the visible link-types than the learners with higher learning prerequisites.

TABLE 4. Mean Improvement Scores of Subjects with Different Learning Prerequisites

Group	Higher Prerequisites	Lower Prerequisites
A	5.2	6.3
B	4.4	3.2

FURTHER WORK

The results of the current study prompted us to look further into the effects of visible link-types on learning in hypertext environment.

In the hypertext system used for our current study, the semantic network is embedded within the document. That means no diagram that represents a part or whole of the underlying semantic net is explicitly displayed to the user. In the system, links are implemented by using either buttons generally placed in a specific area of the document window or "hotpoints" embedded within text. The method of representing visible link-types is by labelling buttons, and attaching "hotpoints," to information that reflects semantic relations. In this case, the user can only "see" a very small part of the underlying semantic net that formed by the current node in the center and those which immediately connect to it. Figure 4 shows such a small piece of embedded semantic net. Users at the current node, "Efficiency of Searching Tree," can only know that there exist three nodes connected to it directly and their conceptual relations with the current node. The users have no indication of the contents of these nodes, even their names, until they eventually jump to these nodes.

The semantic network can be independent of the document. A diagram showing a part or whole of the underlying semantic network could be viewed by the user in an independent semantic net hypertext. In such a system, edges (connecting lines) in the diagram could be another way to represent links. Figure 5 illustrates the basic concept of the independent semantic network. Each node in this diagram represents a text block. In contrast to the embedded case, the user here would be able to explicitly view a wider area of the underlying semantic net. What interests us in the independent semantic net hypertext is the edges in its structure diagram, which are an alternative implementation of links.

Our further work is concentrating on an investigation of whether our proposed approach of visible link-types still has positive effects on learning in an independent semantic net hypertext. A new empirical study has been started. Subjects in this study will be presented with an independent

FIGURE 4. A Piece of the Embedded Semantic Network

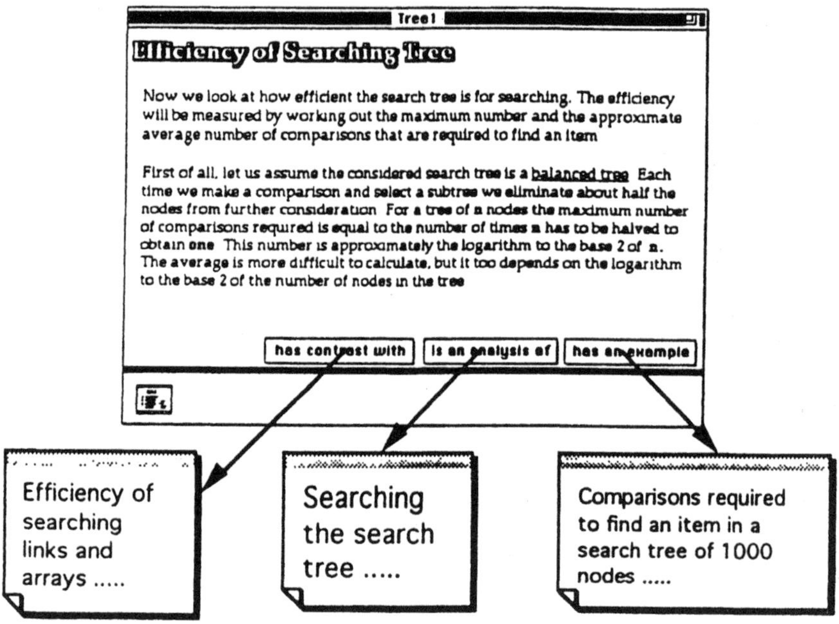

semantic net hypertext where an overview diagram, together with a local diagram, will be used to display the hypertext structure. The edges, which represent links in the local diagram, will consist of either plain lines or will contain the additional semantic information (i.e., labels and directions). Both learning outcomes and learning processes will be examined, and possibly different learning tasks will also be considered.

In summary, we have established that labelling links explicitly with semantic information can have a positive influence on learning outcomes. We are now trying to generalize this finding to independent semantic net hypertexts and to different learning tasks. Our methodology remains one of controlled comparative studies with detailed analysis of both learning outcomes and learning processes.

FIGURE 5. A Simplified View of the Proposed Independent Semantic Net Hypertext. The Current Position of the User Is Represented by the Shaded Dot

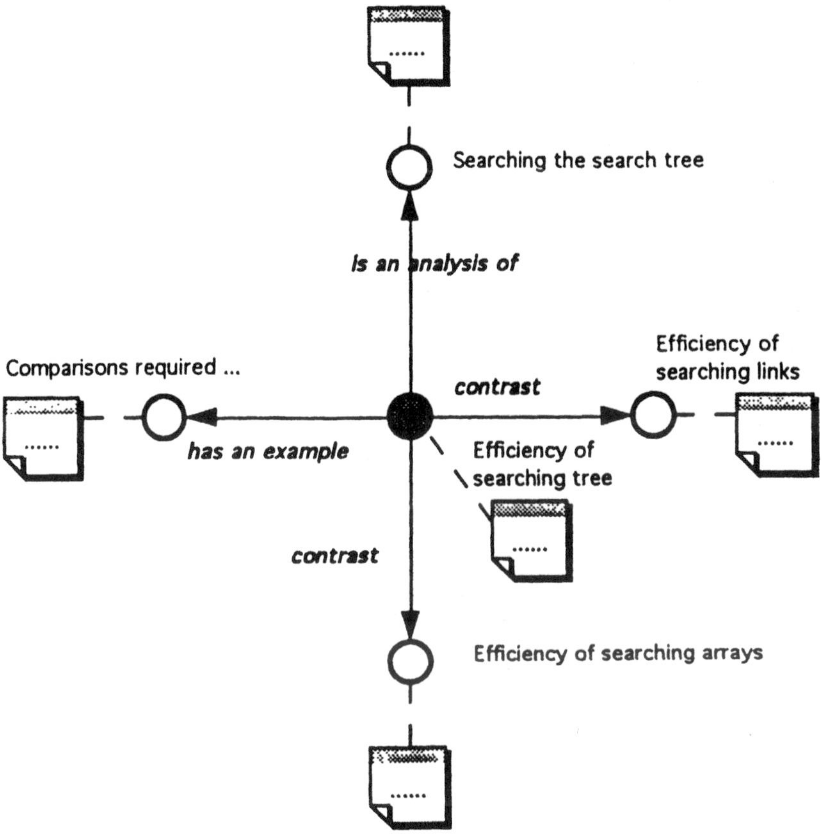

REFERENCES

Allinson, L. & Hammond, N. (1989). A learning support environment: The Hitch-Hiker's Guide. In: R. McAleece (Eds.), *Hypertext: From theory to practice* (pp.62-74). Norwood, NJ: Ablex.

Collier, G. (1987). Thoth-II: Hypertext with explicit semantics. *Hypertext '87* (pp. 269-289). Chapel Hill, NC: University of North Carolina.

Conklin, J. (1987). Hypertext: An introduction and survey. *Computer, 20*(9), 17-41.

Fairchild, K., Poltrock, S., & Furnas, G. (1988). SemNet: Three dimensional graphic representations of large knowledge bases. In: R. Guideon (Eds.), *Cog-*

nitive science and its application for human computer interaction (pp. 201-233). Hinsdale, IL: LEA.

Jonassen, D. (1990). Semantic network elicitation: Tools for structuring hypertext. In: R. McAleece (Eds.), *Hypertext: State of the art* (pp. 142-152). Oxford: Intellect Books.

Jonassen, D. H. & Grabinger, R. S. (1990). Problems and issues in designing hypertext/hypermedia for learning. In: D. H. Jonassen, & H. Mandl (Eds.), *Designing hypermedia for learning* (pp. 3-25). Heidelberg: Springer-Verlag.

Kibby, M. R. & Mayes, J. T. (1989). Towards intelligent hypertext. In: R. McAleese (Eds.), *Hypertext: from theory to practice* (pp. 164-171). Norwood, NJ: Ablex.

Marchionini, G. (1988). Hypermedia and learning: freedom and chaos. *Educational Technology, 28*(11), 8-12.

Nielsen, J. (1990). The art of navigation through hypertext. *Communications of the Association of Computing Machinery, 33*(3), 296-310.

Norman, D. (1976). *Studies in learning and self-contained education systems, 1973-1976.* (Technical Report No 7601). Washington, DC: Office of Naval Research, Advanced Research Projects Agency. (ED 121 786).

Quillian, M. R. (1968). Semantic memory. In: M. Minsky (Eds.), *Semantic Information Processing*. Cambridge, MA: MIT Press.

Rada, R. (1991). *Hypertext: from text to expertext.* London: McGraw-Hill.

Travers, M. (1989). A visual representation for knowledge structures. *Proceedings Hypertext '89* (pp. 147-158). New York: ACM.

Trigg, R. H. (1983). A network-based approach to text handling for the online scientific community. *Ph.D thesis.* Department of Computer Science, University of Maryland (University Microfilms *8429934).

Woods, W. A. (1975). What's in a link? In: D. Bobrow & A. Collins (Eds.), *Representation and understanding: studies in cognitive science* (pp. 35-82). New York: Academic Press.

APPENDIX: The hypertextual questionnaire

1. Which of the trees below is a search tree (The number in each node represents that node's keyword)?

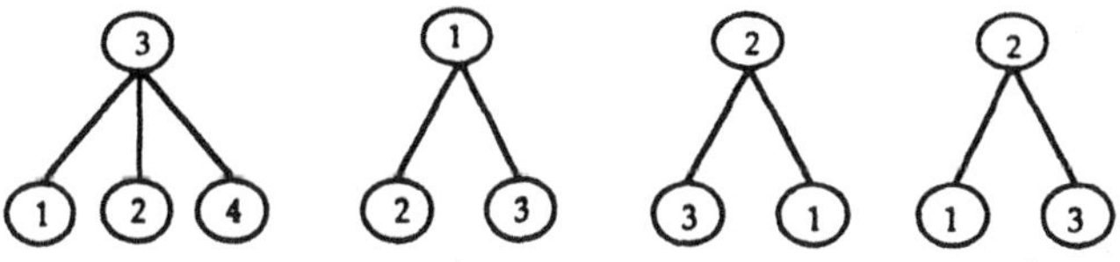

a. b. c. d.

2. Which of the trees below is the result of using the following data items to construct a search tree in this order: 3,1,2,4?

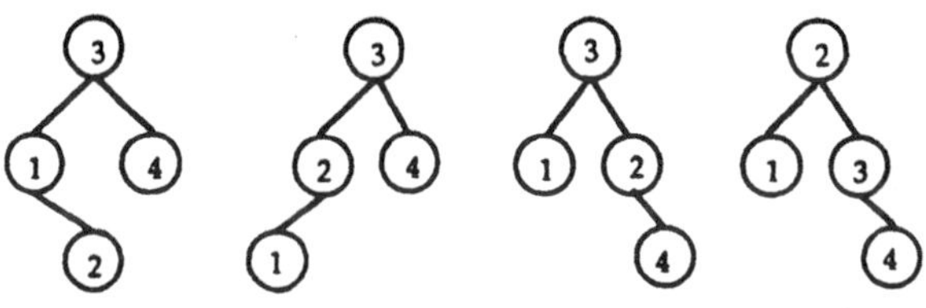

a. b. c. d.

3. According to the method introduced in our hypertext, which of the trees below is the result of adding a node with keyword "5" to the tree on the right?

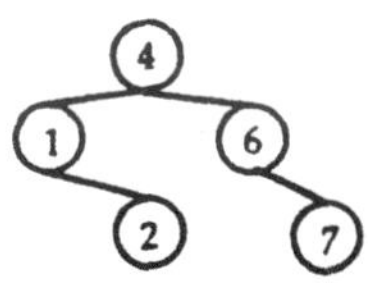

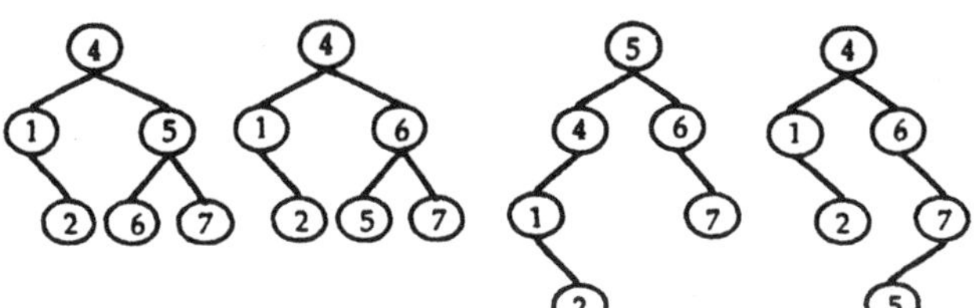

a. b. c. d.

APPENDIX (continued)

4. According to the method of deletion introduced in our hypertext, which of the trees below is the result of deleting a node with keyword "5" from the tree on the right?

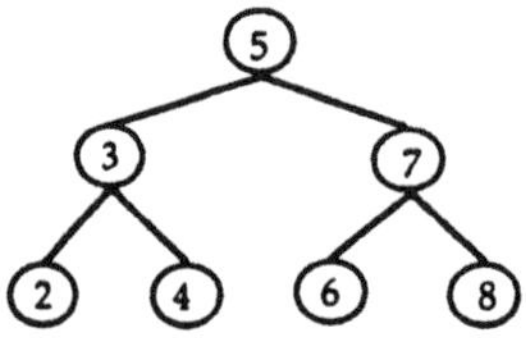

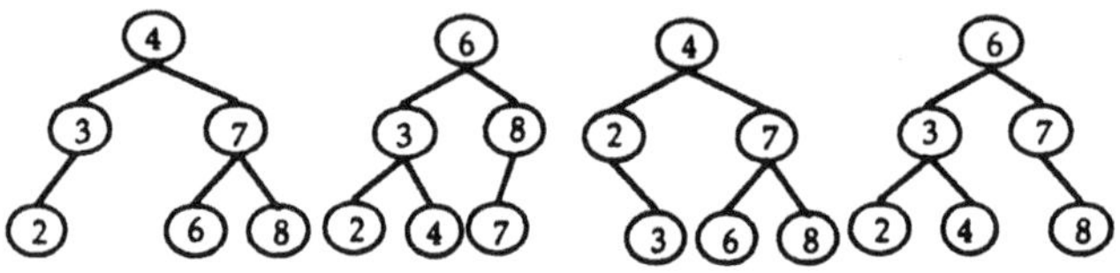

a. b. c. d.

5. Which one of the statements below is correct?

   (a) The operations of addition and deletion are usually allowed to be performed on an array.

   (b) The effectiveness of the adding operation on a search tree and on links is about the same level.

   (c) The operation of deletion is usually not allowed to be performed on links.

   (d) The effectiveness of the adding operation on a search tree is higher than on links.

6. If you use the search tree.on the right to find the node with keyword "4", which of the following sequences of nodes would be the correct one to follow?

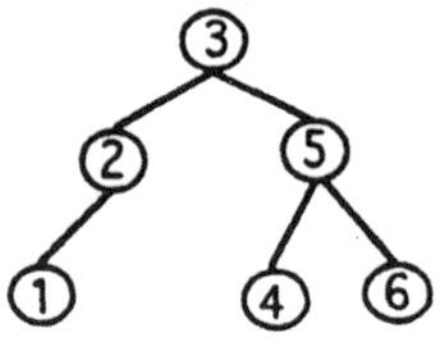

   (a) 5,3,4.

   (b) 5,6,4.

(c) 3,5,4.

(d) 2,3,4.

7. In terms of the effectiveness of searching, the balanced search tree performs

   (a) better than both links and the array.

   (b) better than links, but not as well as the array.

   (c) as well as the array, but better than links.

   (d) as well as links, but not as well as the array.

8. In order to traverse a search tree in ascending order, we must visit

   (a) all nodes in the right subtree of the root node first, then the root, and nodes in the left subtree of the root last.

   (b) all nodes in the left subtree of the root first, then the root node, and nodes in the right subtree of the root last.

   (c) the root first, then all nodes in the left subtree of the root, and all nodes in the right subtree of the root last.

   (d) all nodes in the right subtree of the root first, then all nodes in the left subtree, and the root node last.

9. According to the description of traversing given in our hypertext, traversing a search tree is

   (a) easier than traversing an array.

   (b) less easy than traversing an array and links.

APPENDIX (continued)

(c) as easy as traversing links.

(d) easier than traversing links.

10. The purpose of maintenance of the search tree is to promote the searching effectiveness

(a) by keeping the tree unbalanced.

(b) by keeping the tree as a binary tree.

(c) by keeping the tree balanced.

(d) by keeping the tree as a search tree.

DESIGN

Wayne A. Nelson

Efforts to Improve Computer-Based Instruction: The Role of Knowledge Representation and Knowledge Construction in Hypermedia Systems

Some people believe that hypermedia systems hold great promise for improving education. Predictions that hypermedia will significantly change the ways people read, write and think have spawned considerable research (Beeman, Anderson, Bader, Larkin, McClard, McQuillian, & Shields, 1987; Kerr, 1986). Some writers envision a future where intelligent electronic books will replace libraries and student notebooks (Barker, 1990). Others hold more cautious opinions, noting that hypermedia is just another technology of little value to education without strong grounding in

WAYNE A. NELSON is Associate Professor, Department of Educational Leadership, Southern Illinois University at Edwardsville, Edwardsville, IL 62026-1125.

[Haworth co-indexing entry note]: "Efforts to Improve Computer-Based Instruction: The Role of Knowledge Representation and Knowledge Construction in Hypermedia Systems." Nelson, Wayne A. Co-published simultaneously in *Computers in the Schools* (The Haworth Press, Inc.) Vol. 10, No. 3/4, 1994, pp. 371-399; and: *Multimedia and Megachange: New Roles for Educational Computing* (eds: W. Michael Reed, John K. Burton, and Min Liu) The Haworth Press, Inc., 1994, pp. 371-399. Multiple copies of this article/chapter may be purchased from The Haworth Document Delivery Center [1-800-3-HAWORTH; 9:00 a.m. - 5:00 p.m. (EST)].

instructional theory (Duffy & Knuth, 1990). Of course, some compromise between these two views will likely be the ultimate role for hypermedia in education. While the technology can provide powerful tools for organizing information and presenting it to students, hypermedia is not inherently instructional (Nelson & Palumbo, 1992). The ways that hypermedia systems can best support learning and instruction have yet to be determined, but the research to date is encouraging.

Hypermedia systems are based on conceptual foundations first proposed by Vannevar Bush in 1945. He was interested in developing a mechanized system, called a *memex*, that could make the job of finding and reading scientific literature more efficient. The solution was a two-screen system that linked information stored on microfilm in a special kind of indexing strategy that featured massive, personally constructed cross-references. Readers could link two items together, naming the link by typing a code that was stored on the microfilm. Thereafter, whenever the reader viewed a document on one screen, any related document that had been previously linked would appear on the second screen. Bush's ideas were expanded by Ted Nelson, who first coined the term *hypertext*. Nelson was interested in designing a literary system that could provide rapid and efficient access to large amounts of information. His system, called *Xanadu*, was designed to store information in an environment that linked multiple windows of information in ever expanding webs. He was especially motivated by the desire to allow people from all walks of life access to the power of personal computers, and true to the hacker ethic, that this information should be widely distributed (Levy, 1984). Nelson's ongoing project has the ultimate goal of developing on-line libraries which will greatly increase access to information on a global scale (Nelson, 1981).

Bush created his system with the belief that human memory was associative, an idea that can be traced to the sixteenth century philosopher Hobbes (Schwartz & Reisberg, 1991). Subsequent efforts to develop hypermedia systems have largely maintained this associative characteristic, storing information in small units called nodes (usually a screen of information or less) that are bound together by links (Conklin, 1987). A reader progresses through a hypermedia document by selecting links between ideas, causing the related information to be displayed. This architecture gives readers unprecedented control over the scope and sequence of what is read, as long as the author provides enough links, and as long as the links make sense to the reader.

Therein lies the problem for hypermedia in education: Each reader's prior knowledge will be unique (as will the author's), making the design of hypermedia databases for instruction very difficult. An association that seems obvious to one person may be very confusing to another. As educators design hypermedia materials, concerns for user disorientation and motivation that have been addressed elsewhere continue to be appropriate (Hammond, 1989; Heller, 1990; Oren, Salomen, Kreitman, & Don, 1990), but additional considerations need to include how knowledge is represented and communicated to learners. This article suggests that to improve the instructional capabilities of hypermedia systems for education, designers need to go beyond the common approach of using the technology to author and deliver associatively linked knowledge bases to learners. Instead, hypermedia systems must reflect the characteristics of current theories of knowledge representation and knowledge construction to better promote learning. The remainder of this article reviews current theories of learning and knowledge representation drawn from cognitive science, suggesting ways to incorporate notions of knowledge representation within hypermedia systems, and describing current research projects that employ hypermedia systems as effective instructional environments.

KNOWLEDGE REPRESENTATION IN HUMAN MEMORY

The parallels between human memory and the architecture of hypermedia systems have been emphasized by many authors. Indeed, the computer has provided a strong metaphor for theorizing about human memory for the last 20 years or more (Atkinson & Schiffrin, 1968); therefore, the vocabulary used by cognitive psychologists and hypermedia developers is similar. As mentioned above, early hypermedia systems were designed to reflect the associative nature of human memory and were influenced by the traditional stimulus-response explanations prominent in behavioral psychology at the time (Klatzky, 1980). For behaviorists, explanations of mental activity were necessary only as internal "intervening variables" mediating complex responses that could not be explained in terms of stimuli (Martindale, 1991). Cognitive psychology has become widely accepted since the time of Bush's *memex*, resulting in more explicit descriptions of the processes and organization of human memory. Now the emphasis is inverted, focusing on internal mental processes that influence observable behavior.

Networks in Semantic Memory

While a variety of theories explaining the nature and organization of information stored in semantic memory continue to emerge within cognitive psychology, the dominant class of theories views memory as a neo-associational network (Anderson & Bower, 1973). Such networks are composed of stored information (nodes) and relational links that interconnect the information. Original proposals described semantic memory as a hierarchical network (Figure 1a), with general concepts stored at the "top" and more specific concepts stored below (Collins & Quillian, 1969). Associations are represented by "pointers" connecting ideas, and indicating the type of relationship, such as property, attribute, or value.

Later, the model was revised to remove the strict hierarchy and incorporate a retrieval mechanism that emphasized spreading activation, where the search of the network spreads out from an initial concept following the links between concepts (Collins & Loftus, 1975). More recently, propositional networks that store information in units larger than a single concept have been investigated (Anderson, 1983). Propositions are formed by connecting two or more concepts with an explicit relation, allowing for various types of associations. More complex higher order relationships can also be formed by combining propositions (Figure lb).

Higher Order Knowledge Structures

The power of human memory, however, lies not only in the storage and retrieval of individual knowledge units, but in the larger organizational schemes by which knowledge is interrelated (Rumelhart, 1977). There is convincing evidence that higher order knowledge structures, usually referred to as schemata, but also as frames, scripts and mental models, facilitate the psychological processes that allow us to perceive relationships, combine ideas, extrapolate, and infer. The notion that schemata are prototypical knowledge structures that are instantiated with the details of a particular situation was first proposed by Bartlett (1932). Minsky (1986) has suggested that general knowledge structures called frames exist, acting like "a skeleton, somewhat like an application form with many blanks or slots to be filled" (Minsky, 1986, p. 245). He proposes that both language and vision employ default assumptions that fill frames with the details of the current situation. For example, when you see a person standing in a floor-length robe, you assume that inside the robe are legs. In a related theory, scripts that represent prototypical events such as eating at a restaurant or going to a movie are employed to guide us in perceiving, comprehending, and acting (Schank & Abelson, 1977). Scripts store general characters, props, and even scenes, in the form of variables that are given specific values when we encounter the situation represented in the script. For example, scripts help us to predict what will happen next at a restaurant, and also provide some basis for the surprise we might feel when a waitress asks for the dessert order before asking for the cocktail order.

FIGURE 1. Network theories of long-term memory

a. Semantic network

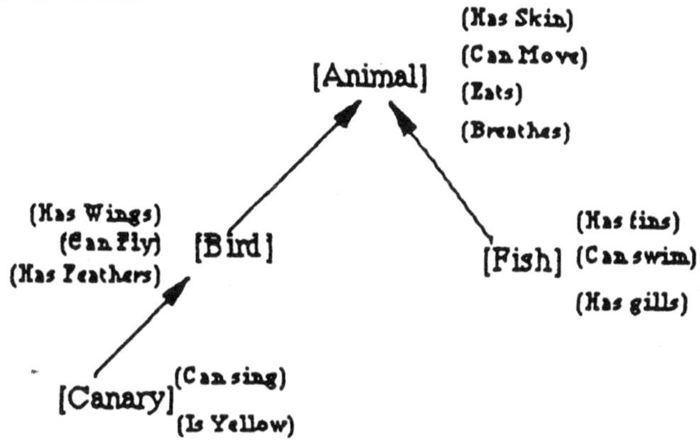

b. Propositional network

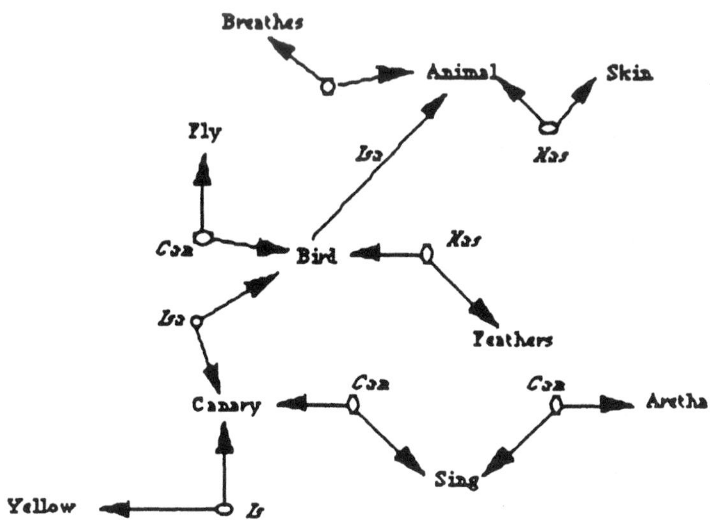

More recently, the differences in understanding and performance exhibited by novices and experts in various physical and conceptual domains have been attributed to knowledge structures called mental models (Gentner & Stevens, 1983). These models embody a set of beliefs that provides an account of cause-and-effect relationships, including the terminology and concepts involved in the phenomena. Finally, others believe that the knowledge represented in networks and schemata results from the blurting together of many similar episodes or "cases" that are encountered during a lifetime (Neisser, 1981). Research examining the possibilities of representing knowledge in the form of cross-referenced cases, and then reasoning with such a database, is now being completed (Schank & Riesbeck, 1989). This work may help to explain how knowledge is acquired and developed from specific situations (Brown, Collins, & Duguid, 1989; Greeno, 1989).

Other Forms of Knowledge Representation

Many theorists in cognitive science recognize that another type of information, procedural knowledge, facilitates the performance of various mental and physical tasks. Researchers generally agree that procedural knowledge can be represented as a set of rules, also called productions, that are stored as IF . . . THEN statements (Figure 2). Of course, complex conditions for applying a rule (the "if") can exist, as well as for performing the task(s) if conditions are judged to be true. Rules can also be nested within other rules, forming complex knowledge structures that are stored in efficient representations, and that can "automatically" control performance without significant mental effort (Norman, 1982).

Human memory can also store and process information in the form of pictures and images. While there is still considerable debate regarding the mechanisms supporting this capability (Kosslyn, 1981; Pylyshyn, 1981), evidence suggests that the characteristics of memory for pictures and images are similar to those for verbal information. For example, people are able to process images in working memory as shown in mental rotation experiments (Shepard & Metzler, 1971), and there is some indication that pictures activate schema (Friedman, 1979). Paivio (1986) has suggested that human memory works as a dual-coding system, where information is stored in separate verbal and imaginal systems, with connections between the two systems allowing us to label pictures with names and embellish names with pictures.

Alternate Perspectives on Learning

From the perspectives provided by cognitive science discussed above, learning can be described as the reorganization of knowledge within a

FIGURE 2. Procedural knowledge stored as productions in nested IF . . . THEN structures

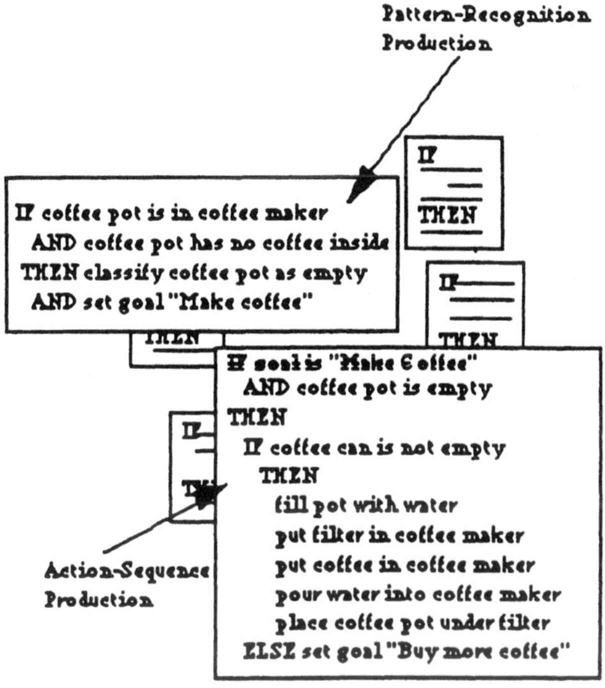

structured associative network of memories. More precisely, learning involves building new knowledge nodes, and connecting them to existing knowledge nodes and to each other (Norman, 1976). As connections between existing knowledge and newly acquired knowledge become more numerous, the likelihood increases that additional related information will be learned. Learning becomes a function of a person's ability to connect new material within existing knowledge structures. The effectiveness of learning is determined by both the comprehensiveness of new knowledge nodes and the appropriate and effective number of links established between nodes.

This description of learning assumes an objective, realistic interpretation of the nature of knowledge–that knowledge is external to the individual and can be transferred from the world to the mind of the learner. The realist philosophy holds that the knowledge structures acquired through learning will be similar for individuals who receive the same instruction, read the same books, view the same films, etc.; and there is evidence that over time, students' knowledge structures begin to resemble the structure of the content (Shavelson, 1972). However, an alternative view of learning, constructivism, is receiving increasing attention within cognitive science and education. This philosophy asserts that knowledge is internal to the individual, constructed through interactions with the environment and through negotiations of meaning with other individuals. The constructivist perspective describes learning as a process of sense-making and building internal knowledge structures based on interpretations of personal experience (Bednar, Cunningham, Duffy, & Perry, 1990). The development of a learner's knowledge base comes from experiencing problems in diverse contexts, sharing multiple perspectives, scaffolding, and cognitive apprenticeships (Brown, Collins, & Duguid, 1989; Vygotsky, 1962).

While these two views of learning may seem disparate, it is possible to design hypermedia systems that better reflect current conceptions of learning from either perspective. The associativity that is central to hypermedia systems can be extended by using the technology to more explicitly represent knowledge and convey this knowledge to learners. It is not sufficient simply to present an associatively linked database to learners and expect that browsing or searching will result in effective learning. Hypermedia systems should help learners to engage in the types of processing necessary to relate new information to existing knowledge. Similarly, the multimedia capabilities of hypermedia environments allow the development of systems that can provide experiences in multiple contexts, encourage sharing of information, and make available appropriate tools so that learners can construct personal knowledge structures through interaction with hypermedia systems, teachers, and other learners.

HYPERMEDIA SYSTEMS AND KNOWLEDGE REPRESENTATION

Hypermedia systems extend conventional database design principles by allowing the specification of a wider range of relationships between items of information stored in the system. The associative nature of hypermedia potentially enables the technology to achieve organizational structures similar to human memory. Unfortunately, few of the currently available hypermedia development systems readily support explicit knowledge representation schemes that can promote effective learning. In order for hypermedia systems to represent knowledge in formats similar to human memory, such limitations have to be overcome (Collier, 1987). When this is achieved, we should be able to design hypermedia systems for learning that more readily convey knowledge in ways that are parallel to knowledge representation in human memory. What follows is a discussion of how systems currently under development are moving in this direction.

Semantic Networks

One of the major characteristics of the network view of knowledge representation is the specification of relationships between information. Links do not simply connect information nodes, they also indicate the nature and strength of the relationship between nodes. This capability is not currently available in most hypermedia development environments. In particular, none of the authoring environments such as *HyperCard,*™ *SuperCard,*™ *Hyperties,*™ or *Toolbook*™ allow the author to define links with "values" that explicitly communicate the type and strength of relationships between nodes. Instead, authors of hypermedia documents must take the steps necessary to design systems that explicitly communicate the relationships between nodes of information, even if the development environment does not readily support this feature.

One way to convey the nature of relationships between nodes is to include labels in the text that indicate the type of relationship for each link. Duncan and McAleese (1982) have developed a qualified citation index that indicates the kind of information that each citation provides. The author simply attaches a label such as "background," "definition," or "expansion" to each citation. The reader then has some idea of which citations to follow for a particular interest. In one study, hypertext documents were constructed in a similar fashion by indicating the type of information each link would provide (Nelson, 1991a). Learners with high and low prior knowledge read the hypertext documents while completing different tasks (study, browse, search). Results indicated that readers who were "studying" generally accessed more definition and example links, while readers who were "searching" or "browsing" accessed more links for related information and elaborations. Regardless of prior knowledge and task, readers tended to choose links providing basic information (definitions and examples) early in their reading, and focused on elaborations and related ideas later in their reading.

One problem with labeling links in a hypermedia system is the selection of terms for the labels. Linguistic studies suggest that there can be as many as 25 categories of relationships (Evanechko & Maguire, 1972). Readers may only be able to distinguish between a limited number of relationships, so it is necessary to reduce the number of categories where possible. Duncan (1989) has suggested seven link categories: being, showing, causing, using, having, including, and similarity. In part, the choice of link categories will be dictated by the content domain. Further research is needed to determine appropriate link categories that are useful within and across subject domains.

Frames can be used to provide a more consistent organizational structure for knowledge than the strategies for labeling links discussed above, and may be effectively employed in hypermedia systems. Frames are probably most appropriate for domains where "parts" or "kinds" are consistent for each concept (Hannum, 1988), because frames typically maintain the same structural relationships across instances. Take as an example biology, where fish, animals, and birds have similar parts (circulatory systems, respiratory systems, nervous systems, etc.), or there are similar kinds of needs and influences (food, habitat, population, predators, etc.). Learners can see the relationships between the parts and kinds when the knowledge is represented in frames because the consistency across categories is maintained by the frame structure. Frames can also be embedded within other frames to form hierarchies, or presented as empty or partially empty "skeletons" so that learners can enter the information themselves. Many other interesting and effective uses of frames for knowledge representation and instruction are summarized by West, Farmer, and Wolff (1990).

A problem with labeling links in hypermedia text or using frames to represent knowledge is that more complex relationships between nodes are difficult to convey, especially for large knowledge bases. A more effective strategy is to portray the network in some visual manner, activating both the learner's visual and verbal systems (Paivio, 1986). At least one hypermedia system (*Notecards*™ from Xerox) employs a graphical browser as an integral component of the system. With other environments, the designer must construct the browser, such as the map included in the *HyperCard* "Help" stack. A graphical browser, also known as a concept map, knowledge map, or semantic map, consists of nodes labeled with short, descriptive titles. The links between nodes are indicated by lines that can be labeled to denote the nature of the relationships (Figure 3). Learners can select any node or link by clicking the mouse, causing more information to be displayed (either on the map in a pop-up window, or on another screen).

Several studies have examined the effectiveness of various concept mapping strategies for learning (Bean, Sorter, Singer, & Frazee, 1986; Davidson, 1982; Diekhoff, 1982; Novak, 1990). With the advent of hypermedia, these techniques have been adapted to the computer medium. In one study, knowledge maps were shown to be more effective than traditional text for learning technical material (Rewey, Dansereau, Skaggs,

FIGURE 3. A graphical browser can be used to visually indicate the relationships between concepts

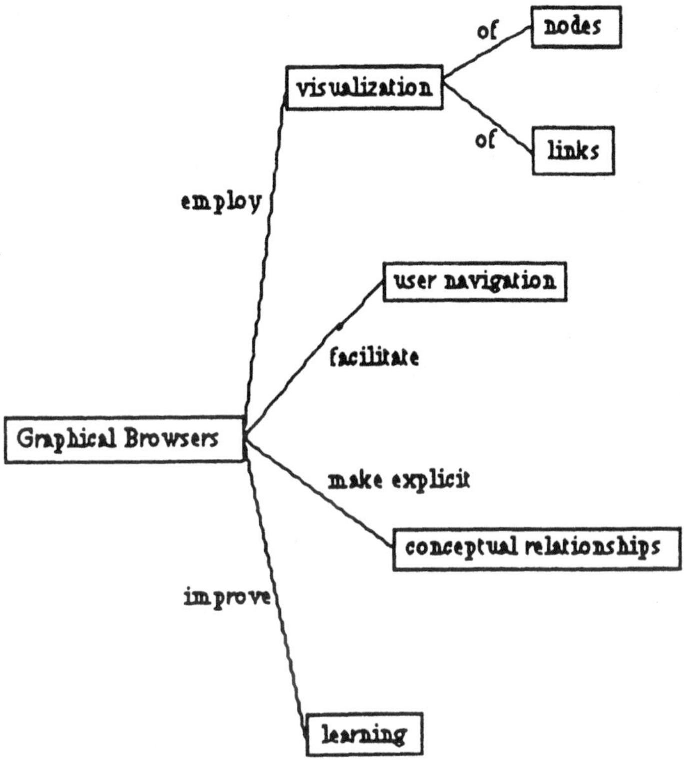

Hall, Pitre, 1989). Effects on recall have not been replicated when comparing knowledge maps to hypermedia documents, however (Hall, Dansereau, & Pitre, 1989). Another study investigated whether learners using graphical browsers acquired the specific structural relationships embodied in the material (Jonassen & Wang, 1991). No differences were found in comparisons between graphical browsers and conventional hypertext, but problems with dependent measures and time of treatment may have contributed to the lack of differences in the experiment.

When employing graphical browsers, it is important to remember that learners need to be actively involved in processing information. Passive viewing of a knowledge map may not be as effective as having the learners identify the relationships between nodes in a hypermedia database. For example, the HAKCS hypermedia system for physics instruction (Lidwell,

Palumbo, Troutman, & Hobbins, 1991) organizes the physical domain into concepts defined by experts which are then further subdivided into specific units of information. Learners demonstrate mastery of prespecified sub-domains by identifying appropriate associations between nodes. An interesting feature of the HAKCS system is that information is represented in a three-dimensional space, allowing complex relationships to be communicated to the learner. However, learners may unconsciously perceive the distance between nodes in hyperspace as directly related to the strength of their association (Locatis, Letourneau, & Banvard, 1989). Such a physical metaphor may limit the types of relationships that can be represented, but work involving scientific visualization techniques may ultimately result in three-dimensional representations for hypermedia systems that are effective interfaces for learning (Dede, 1991).

Another technique for increasing learner activity with hypermedia systems that feature graphical browsing interfaces is to allow the learners to construct concept maps based on information provided by the hypermedia system. Nelson (1991b) has developed a Knowledge Mapping system where a teacher can use a Knowledge Editor to specify concepts and relations in a domain (Figure 4). After the teacher identifies the concepts and relations, the system provides tools to assist the learner in constructing a map of the conceptual domain (Figure 4). Learners can view the concept descriptions and relations specified by the teacher, and construct a map reflecting the organization of the concepts. Previous research has found that maps constructed by learners are an accurate measure of cognitive structure, equivalent to other methods of eliciting conceptual organization (Jonassen, 1987). If this is the case, then the maps constructed by learners may also be used as a form of learner modeling (Nelson, 1991b) in order to implement aspects of intelligent tutoring within hypermedia systems (Barker, 1990; Canter, Rivers, & Storrs, 1985).

Rule-Based Hypermedia Systems

Rule-based knowledge representation schemes are usually associated with expert systems and intelligent tutoring systems that typically do not incorporate hypermedia to any great extent. However, object-oriented systems such as *HyperCard*™ and *Toolbook*™ can integrate rule-based and hypermedia technologies. Hypermedia systems can serve as effective "front-ends" to rule-based systems, interacting with the user to gather information about the problem, then passing the information to an expert system for possible solution. At least one expert system shell, *HyperX,*™ makes extensive use of *HyperCard* as an interface between the knowledge base, inference engine, and user (Millennium Software, 1989). Hypermedia systems have been used to augment consultation sessions with expert systems, providing elaborations of symptoms, reasoning, and conclusions (Raybould, 1990).

Another interesting combination of rule-based systems and hypermedia has been described by Fischer and his associates (Fischer, 1991; Fischer, McCall, & Morch, 1989). A learning-on-demand system to support design activity has been developed, featuring rule-based "demons" that lie in the background of the software, interrupting the user when errors are made. Essentially, the demons deliver a critique of the design in its current state, identifying potential problems and suggesting ways that the design might be improved. Hypermedia is incorporated through a "catalog explorer" (Fischer & Nakakoji, in press) that contains a library of design components relevant to the domain. The user can explore the design catalog in order to find possible solutions to the problem identified in the demon's critique. For example, in a system for designing automobiles, a user places the rear wheel assembly too close to the front wheels. A demon then interrupts, informing the user that the center of gravity of the car would be affected by the current placement of the wheels. A window showing information about weight displacement in automobiles is displayed, with hypermedia links to other topics such as aerodynamics, passenger compartments, or the effects of drive shaft length on horsepower. The learning-on-demand and design catalog approaches work well in design domains, where much of the work on a new design involves reworking previous designs. It remains to be seen whether these techniques can be applied to domains other than design.

It has been suggested that encouraging students to organize the knowledge and identify the rules necessary for an expert system may facilitate learning in domains where expert systems can be constructed (Trollip & Lippert, 1987). Hypermedia systems may serve as effective tools for such activities. The database capabilities of hypermedia might be used to store and organize the domain knowledge collected through interviews or literature reviews, while search and parsing mechanisms could be constructed to better organize the database. Sophisticated machine learning algorithms (Thompson & Thompson, 1986) might even be employed to identify consistent patterns in the database that may be used to construct the rules necessary for reasoning and explaining conclusions.

Hypermedia systems can also convey the procedural information embodied in rules in much the same way that concept maps visually represent the conceptual relationships of semantic networks. For example, decision processes commonly represented by rules in expert systems can be presented to learners as flow charts (Harbour, Byers, & Wilhelmsen, 1991).

FIGURE 4. The Knowledge Editor and Knowledge Map tools (Nelson, 1991b)

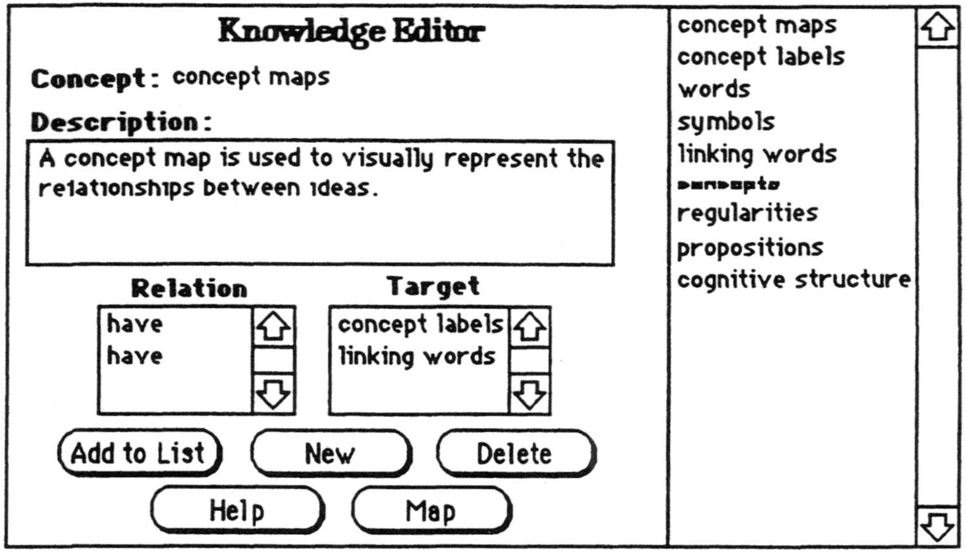

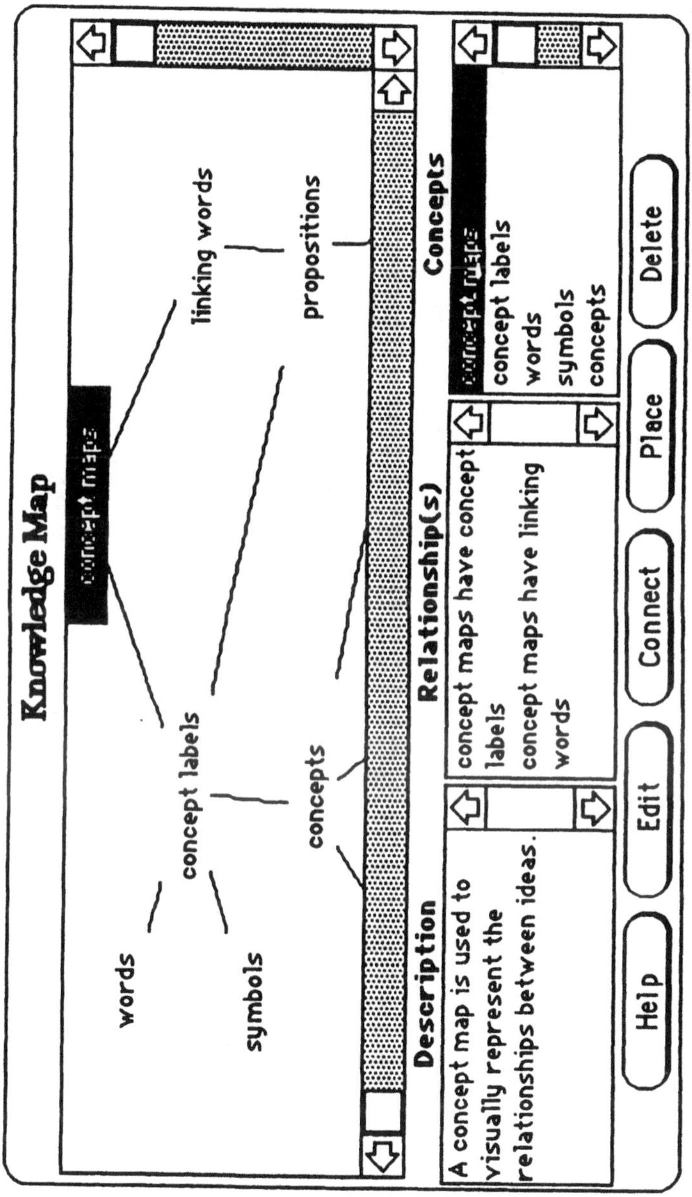
Knowledge Map
concept maps
linking words
propositions
concept labels
words
symbols
concepts
Description
A concept map is used to visually represent the relationships between ideas.
Relationship(s)
concept maps have concept labels
concept maps have linking words
Concepts
concept maps
concept labels
words
symbols
concepts
Help
Edit
Connect
Place
Delete

Learners can follow the visual representation of the decision-making process, selecting various components for elaboration. In essence, the flowchart becomes a graphical browser for the procedure. In addition, details of the procedure can be modeled using video presentation, and learners can "practice" or simulate performance of the procedure. This technique is especially effective when coupled with performance assessment techniques that utilize touch screen input devices or other pointing devices (Iuppa, 1988).

HYPERMEDIA SYSTEMS AND KNOWLEDGE CONSTRUCTION

Theories of learning and instruction influenced by constructivism maintain that learners should be provided with a variety of experiences and multiple perspectives in order to embellish personal cognitive structures. This view has resulted in a number of new approaches to teaching in the public schools, including cooperative learning, the whole language movement, and hands-on science. Similar shifts are occurring within computer-based instruction as designers struggle to incorporate these new ideas. Hypermedia will continue to play an important role in these efforts because of the capabilities of the medium to integrate multiple information formats (text, graphics, and video) and because of the relative ease in authoring provided by object-oriented development systems. The following discussion of case-based, exploratory, and cooperative learning environments focuses on ways to implement hypermedia-based instruction that reflects constructivist principles.

Case-Based Hypermedia Systems

Case-based knowledge representation has recently emerged within artificial intelligence research as a method for using past experiences to solve current problems (Schank & Riesbeck, 1989). The techniques of case-based reasoning have been implemented in many expert systems (Barletta, 1991), and are beginning to be employed for instruction in hypermedia systems (Spiro, Coulson, Feltovich, & Anderson, 1988). Instead of rules, case-based systems reason with cases that contain descriptions of features from various situations. Cases represent examples that lead to particular outcomes, and are indexed in various ways so that the system can quickly identify and retrieve all cases relevant to a particular problem situation. If no case is an exact match, then the system adapts the most relevant cases to meet the needs of the current situation. In other words, the system can learn and generalize by extracting the most useful information from previous cases that may be applicable to the current problem. In fact, special analytical techniques can be applied to cases in order to extract prototypical cases and "build domain theories in areas where even the experts don't understand how the underlying processes in their domain work" (Barletta, 1991, p. 46).

An interesting application of case-based hypermedia systems for instruction has been demonstrated by Spiro and his colleagues. Cognitive flexibility theory (Spiro, Coulson, Feltovich, & Anderson, 1988) suggests that people acquire knowledge in ill-structured domains by constructing multiple representations and linkages among knowledge units. This can be achieved by designing hypermedia documents that present multiple cases where similar concepts are linked across cases (Spiro & Jehng, 1990). Learners visit, and more importantly revisit, the same case or concept information in a variety of contexts. The same material is thereby covered in different ways and at different times during the learner's exploration of the system, highlighting different aspects of the same case depending on the context.

While the case, mini-case, or scenario is central to cased based instruction using hypermedia, it is not always easy to acquire the information needed to develop cases. One method is to collect cases through interviews with experts, as is commonly done in many knowledge engineering projects. Terminology in the domain can be defined, and representative examples (cases) of problem solving by the expert can be collected and indexed. Another method, called facet analysis (Vickery, 1986), can also be used to construct the knowledge base necessary for a case-based instructional system. This theory recognizes that knowledge can be represented in different ways, depending on the point of view. For example, cars can be organized and classified by make, year of production, type of use, etc. Facet analysis may be useful in both eliciting and organizing cases because experts will view cases differently, depending on their orientation toward the case. A manager in a factory might have a completely different opinion about a case than a foreman or a laborer. It is important to assemble various perspectives on a problem for presentation to the learner, and facet analysis can help in the process of knowledge acquisition for case-based instructional systems.

Once the information for a case-based system is acquired, it is also necessary to design an effective interface for the hypermedia system that will engage the learner and support various learning activities. A promising approach involving mimetic interfaces has been suggested by Laurel (1991), and may be adapted for case-based hypermedia systems. A mimetic interface utilizes aspects of theater and drama as a metaphor for the interface. Agents and actors designed as dramatic characters communicate with users in various ways in order to perform tasks related to work, information, learning, and even entertainment (Laurel, 1990). Agents and actors can have different traits and must be given representations that embody the role of the character, so that users can predict what an agent is likely to do in a given situation. This can be accomplished with text in some situations, but may require graphics, animation, or video in more complex systems. Thankfully, the task of creating complex actors and agents is made easier with the availability of tools such as *MacRecorder*™ (Farallon, 1990a) and *Interface*™ (Bright Star, 1989).

Oren, Salomen, Kreitman, and Don (1990) have described an innovative mimetic interface for an encyclopedic hypermedia system that uses "guides" (a scout, an Indian, a rancher, a sea captain, etc.) to present information about the westward expansion period of American history. Each guide provides the reader with information based on his or her particular perspective of the events of the period. Users may explore based on their own interests, or follow paths suggested by a guide. In a video version of the software, users may view "stories" told by each guide in first-person narrative. Guides even act as agents in some situations, altering the learner's path through the database and offering alternative perspectives on the information included in the system.

Another hypermedia system incorporating case-based knowledge representation and a mimetic interface is currently being developed by the author. The system presents scenarios based on situations typically encountered by new teachers. The learner can view any scenario from multiple perspectives provided by a beginning teacher, an experienced teacher, an administrator, students in the classroom, parents, or an expert from a teacher education program (Figure 5). Various aspects of each scenario are linked to other similar scenarios so that learners can begin to understand the complexities of the classroom and develop personal theories about how to teach. The software will also provide tools to allow learners to personalize the database by adding and linking new scenarios, asking questions of other users, and commenting on particular issues.

Exploratory Hypermedia Environments

Some of the keys to learning emphasized by constructivism include a focus on personal experience, multiple perspectives, and learner exploration. Such views on learning and instruction have been advocated for many years (Dewey, 1933; Bruner, 1961), seemingly being rediscovered by each successive generation of teachers and learners. The emergence of

FIGURE 5. A prototype case-based system for learning about teaching

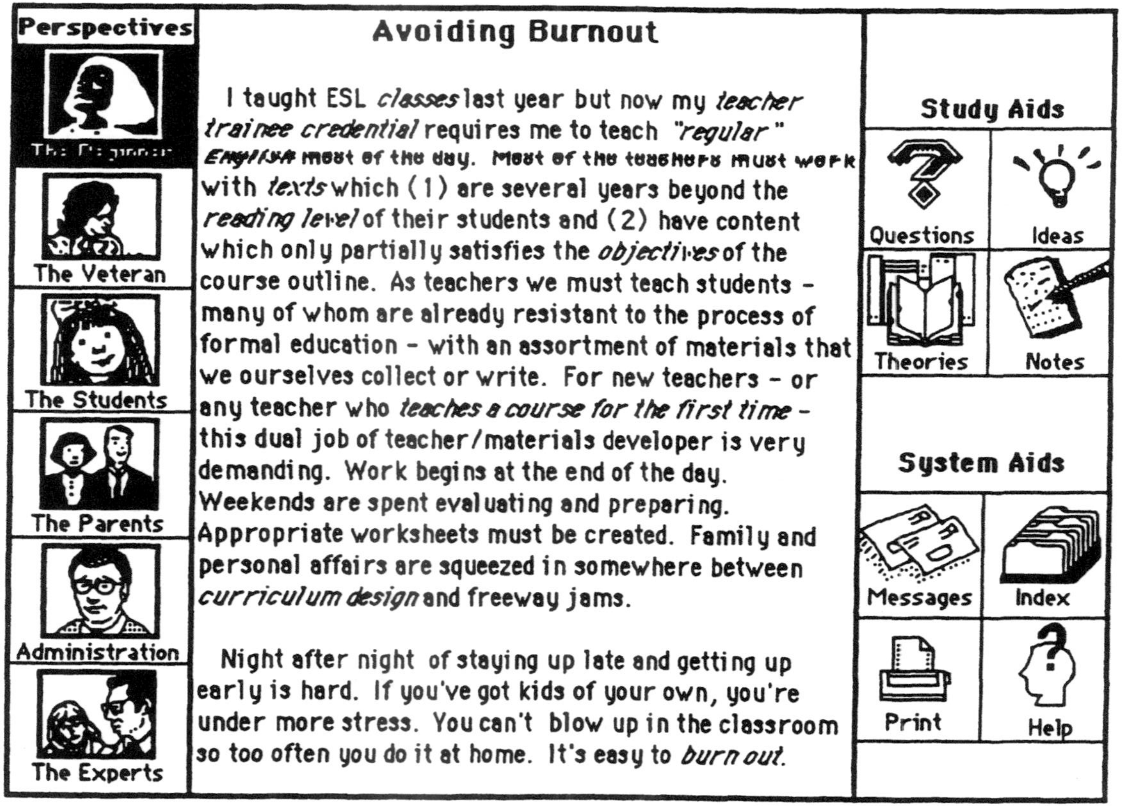

microcomputers in education facilitated the development of "microworlds" designed to encourage the exploration and discovery necessary for the construction of knowledge based on personal experience (Papert, 1980). Many exploratory microworld environments have already been developed (Lawler & Yazdani, 1987), but hypermedia systems have the capabilities to more easily develop realistic problem-solving environments that are situated in meaningful settings (Brown, Collins, & Duguid, 1989; Greeno, 1989).

In exploratory hypermedia systems the knowledge representation is embedded in the context of the situation, and learning involves the construction of personal knowledge through exploration and cooperative learning strategies that feature communication and collaboration. As an example of an exploratory hypermedia learning environment, consider *Salamanca* (Bueno & Nelson, 1993), which was designed to support natural language learning strategies (language play, semantic processing, and delayed oral practice) for Spanish language acquisition. The software simulates a visit to the Spanish city "Salamanca," utilizing pictures, drawings, sound, and text to illustrate key ideas, events, and stories that engage learners in listening for information and demonstrating understanding. The basic assumption made in the design of *Salamanca* was that communicative competence in a second language is not learned, but acquired through interaction with comprehensible input from the environment. The main goal of the software is to provide an electronic setting for receiving comprehensible input in spoken and written forms just beyond the student's present level of competence.

The software opens with a "tour" of Salamanca, providing numerous opportunities for the learner to obtain cultural information by clicking on objects within the city (buildings, bridges, a coat of arms, etc.). As the tour continues, Paloma, the protagonist in the electronic environment, is introduced, and presents a series of descriptions in Spanish that provide general information regarding the operation and content of the different areas of the software. Paloma also introduces the user to several settings in Salamanca where the students can hear authentic dialogues designed to provide both comprehensible input and a series of formulaic expressions needed for communication in certain settings. Learners can call Paloma on the phone, or go to the park to play the games "Hide and Seek" and "I Spy" with Paloma's cousin Manolo (Figure 6). Similar activities are provided if the learner visits Paloma's apartment, where "Veo Veo" (a Spanish guessing game) can be played, songs can be heard on the phonograph, or the learner can read Spanish comics. After completing the initial "tour," the learner is free to explore any component of the software. Both

FIGURE 6. Playing "I Spy" in the park with Manolo

Paloma's and Manolo's apartments can be visited, or the learner can call them on the phone. A dictionary of Spanish words and a "repeat" feature for some of the recorded dialogue is available at any time. The user also has the opportunity to visit the school, where several authentic activities are provided, including a recorded and illustrated "lesson" describing wine making, a language arts lesson featuring sentence completion and letter writing, and a "cultural safari" where users can respond to various situations requiring cultural knowledge.

Salamanca was pilot tested with 13 fifth and sixth grade students at a "magnet" school in a large midwestern city (Bueno, 1991). Students worked in groups of three at the computers for 14 sessions over the course of two months. As the students became more familiar with the software and gained more experience working together in groups, their initiations seemed to include more cooperative overtures and greater direction in regard to the activity in which they were involved. In early interactions, the students appeared to just be browsing, but during subsequent interactions the students began to respond directly to the lesson activities, actively seeking opportunities to recognize and remember familiar vocabulary. The students also engaged in practice activities that differed from the formal practice required of them in the traditional classroom. The activities can include making sense of the simulated target culture by creating conditions for their learning, and seeking opportunities to respond in the target language.

Whether exploratory environments like *Salamanca* should be structured to provide exposure to concepts appropriate to the intellectual development of learners or whether they should present simulated environments where students can expand their grasp of the task of learning a second language merits further research. It appears, however, that exploratory hypermedia environments have value for learners as resources for accessing target language meaning. In addition, *Salamanca* appeared to expand the learners' concept of learning Spanish. Finally, the students' interactions with Salamanca seemed to encourage participatory and cooperative learning behaviors. It is not clear, however, whether the characteristics of learning observed in this study resulted from the novelty of the computer in the classroom or from the exploratory nature of the hypermedia system. Further research is needed to determine the long-range effects of such systems on learning in a variety of disciplines.

Cooperative Hypermedia Environments

Some of the aspects of student exploration of Salamanca seem to be related to the cooperative environment in which the hypermedia system was tested. Although *Salamanca* was not specifically designed for cooperative learning, many interactions of a cooperative nature were observed between students, and seemed to be fostered by the software. Recently, many educators have begun to emphasize the computer as a medium for cooperative learning. Research has shown that student achievement is improved when computer-assisted instruction is implemented using a cooperative model (Johnson, Johnson, & Stanne, 1985). Principles for the design of instructional "groupware" have been suggested (Dodl, 1990), including the support of collaborative communication, organization of information, consensus building, and group inquiry. Hypermedia can play a central role in this new type of instructional software, especially with regard to the organization of ideas and collaborative communication.

The possibilities for cooperative learning will also be enhanced when the next generation of computer hardware and systems software becomes readily available. Already, the business community is experimenting with computer-supported collaborative work environments where group meetings and writing tasks can be enhanced with synchronous computer systems that allow multiple users to simultaneously edit a single file (Schrage, 1990; Stefik et al., 1987). Asynchronous communication across computer networks is also being used for collaborative work, and user interface guidelines for groupware are beginning to emerge (Grudin, 1990; Vertelney, 1990). System 7 for the Apple Macintosh™ allows many aspects of groupware to be more easily implemented. Files can be shared across networks, regardless of which machine they reside on, and products are already available to facilitate collaboration through synchronous editing of a shared file on a network (Farallon, 1990b).

Educators are making creative use of computer networks for cooperative learning (Davies, 1988), and the integration of hypermedia systems and computer networks should encourage others to become involved. One of the first projects to successfully incorporate hypermedia as a shared database for learning and instruction was the Intermedia project at Brown University (Yankelovich, Landow, & Heywood, 1987). Students in several different classes (English, Biology, etc.) have used the system to construct personal knowledge bases and share information with other students. The experiences with Intermedia suggest that the kinds of activities supported by hypermedia change not only the ways students learn, but the ways teachers teach (Beeman et al., 1987). The CSILE (Computer-Supported Intentional Learning Environments) project demonstrates other kinds of learning activities that are possible with hypermedia systems (Scardmalia, 1991). The software developed for this project provides knowledge-building environments for students to collaborate by sharing information through the system, commenting and elaborating on each other's ideas. Both external and student-generated databases are available, and students send "notes" to other students, teachers, and experts in the community. Additional tools include facilities for developing explanatory analogies (including graphics), publication, and database exploration. Both Intermedia and CSILE illustrate the possible uses of hypermedia to facilitate the social construction of knowledge in a collaborative learning environment, and the success of these projects can serve as models for the integration of hypermedia systems into the curriculum from early childhood through post-graduate education.

SUMMARY

This article has surveyed various theories of knowledge representation in human memory, including semantic networks, frames, rules, cases, and images. Examples of hypermedia systems that employ these representation schemes through the use of labeled links, graphical browsers, frames, and rules have been presented. The underlying assumption of this discussion has been that transfer of knowledge from the hypermedia system to the mind of the user (learning) can be facilitated when the system organizes information in ways that more closely parallel the organization of human memory. Hypermedia systems based on an alternative view of learning and instruction, where learners construct personal representations of reality through interaction and experience, have also been discussed. Case-based systems, exploratory environments, and cooperative learning systems represent examples of the use of hypermedia to support learning that is grounded in realistic situations and social interactions. It is evident that hypermedia systems possess the flexibility necessary to support learning and instruction from a wide variety of perspectives.

The excitement that surrounded the introduction of hypermedia systems in education has given way to caution and concern on the part of some (Raskin, 1987). While the technology provides new and interesting ways to present information to learners, there is nothing inherently instructional in associatively linked databases of information. The problem for educators is to find ways to use hypermedia to better facilitate learning and instruction. In order to realize the benefits of hypermedia in education, systems should be designed to more explicitly represent knowledge based on appropriate theories drawn from research in cognitive science. Concern for personal construction of knowledge through experiences in multiple contexts, coupled with learning activities emphasizing exploration and social interaction, will also assure that future hypermedia systems for education more effectively contribute to the processes of learning and instruction.

REFERENCES

Anderson, J. R. (1983). *The architecture of cognition.* Cambridge, MA: Harvard University Press.

Anderson, J. R. & Bower, G. H. (1973). *Human associative memory.* Washington, DC: Winston & Sons.

Atkinson, R. C. & Schiffrin, R. M. (1968). Human memory: A proposed system and its control processes. In: K. W. Spence & J. T. Spence (Eds.), *The psychology of learning and motivation: Advances in research and theory* (Vol. 2) (pp. 89-193). New York: Academic Press.

Barker, P. (1990). Intelligent electronic books. *Journal of Artificial Intelligence in Education, 2* (1), 7-13.

Barletta, R. (1991). An introduction to case-based reasoning. *AI Expert, 6*(8), 42-49.

Bartlett, F. C. (1932). *Remembering: A study in experimental and social psychology.* Cambridge: Cambridge University Press.

Bean, T. W., Sorter, J., Singer, H., & Frazee, C. (1986). Teaching students how to make predictions about events in history with a graphic organizer plus options guide. *Journal of Reading, 29*, 239-745.

Bednar, A. K., Cunningham, D., Duffy, T. M., & Perry, J. D. (1990). Theory into practice: How do we link: In: G. Anglin (Ed.), *Instructional technology: Past, present and future* (pp. 88-101). Englewood, CO: Libraries, Unlimited.

Beeman, W. O., Anderson, K. T., Bader, G., Larkin, J., McClard, A. P., McQuillian, P., & Shields, M. (1987). Hypertext and pluralism: From lineal to nonlineal thinking. *Hypertext '87 Proceedings* (pp. 1-20). New York: ACM Press.

Bright Star Technology, Inc. (1989). *Interface* [Computer program]. Bellevue, WA: Bright Star Technology.

Brown, J. S., Collins, A., & Duguid, P. (1989). Situated cognition and the culture of learning. *Educational Researcher, 19* (1), 32-42.

Bruner, J. (1961). The act of discovery. *Harvard Educational Review, 31*, 21-32.

Bueno, K. (1991). *An ethnographic study of the introduction of a contextualized computer environment in an elementary school Spanish classroom.* Unpublished doctoral dissertation, St. Louis University, St Louis.

Bueno, K. & Nelson, W. A. (1993). Collaborative second language learning with a contextualized computer environment. *Journal of Educational Multimedia and Hypermedia, 4*(2), 177-208.

Bush, V. (1945). As we may think. *Atlantic Monthly*, no. 176, pp. 101-108.

Canter, D., Rivers, R., & Storrs, G (1985). Characterizing user navigation through complex data structures. *Behavioral and Information Technology, 4*(2), 93-10

Collier, G. H. (1987). Thoth-II: Hypertext with explicit semantics. *Hypertext '87 Proceedings* (pp. 269-290). New York: ACM Press.

Collins, A. M. & Quillian, M. R. (1969). Retrieval time from semantic memory. *Journal of Verbal Learning and Verbal Behavior, 8*, 240-247.

Collins, A. M. & Loftus, E. F. (1975). A Spreading-activation theory of semantic memory. *Psychological Review, 82*, 407-428.

Conklin, J. (1987). Hypertext: An introduction and survey. *IEEE Computer, 20*(9), 17-41.

Davidson, J. L. (1982). The group mapping activity for instruction in reading and thinking. *Journal of Reading, 26*, 52-56.

Davies, D. (1988). Computer-supported cooperative learning systems: Interactive group technologies and open learning. *Programmed Learning and Educational Technology, 25*(3), 205-215.

Dede, C. (1991). Designing a tool for imaging mental models underlying training. In: L. Birnbaum (Ed.), *Proceedings of the International Conference on the Learning Sciences* (pp. 113-120). Charlottesville, VA: Association for the Advancement of Computers in Education.

Dewey, J. (1933). *How we think*. New York: Heath.

Diekhoff, G. M. (1982). Cognitive maps as a way of presenting the dimensions of comparison within the history of psychology. *Teaching of psychology, 9*, 115-116.

Dodl, N. R. (1990). Instructional groupware: Design considerations. In: D. Dalton (Ed.), *Proceedings of the 32nd International Association for the Development of Computer-Based Instructional Systems Conference* (pp. 344-352). Columbus, OH: ADCIS International.

Duffy, T. M. & Knuth, R. A. (1990). Hypermedia and instruction: Where is the match? In: D. Jonassen and H. Mandl (Eds.), *Designing hypermedia for learning*. Heidelberg, FRG: Springer-Verlag.

Duncan, E. (1989). Structuring knowledge bases for designers of learning materials. *Hypertext 1*(1), 20-33.

Duncan, E & McAleese, R. (1982). Qualified citation indexing online? In M. E. Williams & T. Hogan (Eds.), *National Online Meeting Proceedings* (pp. 77-85). Medford, NJ: Learned Information.

Evanechko, O. & Maguire, O. (1972). The dimensions of children's meaning space. *American Educational Research Journal, 9*(2), 507-523.

Farallon Computing, Inc. (1990a). *MacRecorder Sound System* [Computer program]. Emeryville, CA: Farallon Computing.

Farallon Computing, Inc. (1990b). *Timbuktu* (Computer program]. Emeryville, CA: Farallon Computing.

Fischer, G. (1991). Supporting learning on demand with design environments. In: L. Birnbaum (Ed.), *Proceedings of the 1991 International Conference on the Learning Sciences* (pp. 165-172). Charlottesville, VA: Association for the Advancement of Computing in Education.

Fischer, G. McCall, R., & Morch, A. (1989). JANUS: integrating hypertext with a knowledge-based design environment. *Proceedings of Hypertext '89* (pp. 105-117). New York: ACM Press.

Fischer, G. & Nakakoji, K. (in press). Making design objects relevant to the task at hand. *Proceedings of Association for the Advancement of Artificial Intelligence '91, Ninth National Conference on Artificial Intelligence*. Cambridge, MA: M. I. T. Press.

Friedman, A. (1979). Framing pictures: The role of knowledge in automatized encoding and memory for gist. *Journal of Experimental Psychology: General, 105*, 169-190.

Gentner, D. & Stevens, A. (Eds.). (1983). *Mental models*. Hillsdale, NJ: Erlbaum.
Greeno, J. G. (1989). Situations, mental models, and generative knowledge. In: D. Klahr & K. Kotovsky (Eds.), *Complex information processing: The Impact of Herbert A. Simon* (pp. 285-318). Hillsdale, NJ: Erlbaum.
Grudin, J. (1990). Groupware and cooperative work: Problems and perspectives. In: B. Laurel (Ed.), *The art of human-computer interface design* (pp. 161-170). Reading, MA: Addison-Wesley.
Hall, R. H., Dansereau, D. F., & Pitre, L. P. (1989, March). *Knowledge maps and the presentation of related information domains*. Paper presented at the annual meeting of the American Educational Research Association, San Francisco, CA.
Hammond, N. (1989). Hypermedia and learning: Who guides whom? In: H. Maurer (Ed.), *Computer Assisted Learning* (pp. 167-181). New York: Springer-Verlag.
Hannum, W. (1988). Designing courseware to fit subject matter structure. In: D. H. Jonassen (Ed.), *Instructional designs for microcomputer courseware* (pp. 275-296). Hillsdale, NJ: Erlbaum.
Harbour, J. L., Byers, J. C., & Wilhelmsen, C. (1991). Hypermedia approach to a multiple design and development need: A case study. *Performance and Instruction, 30*(4), 11-19.
Heller, R. S. (1990). The role of hypermedia in education: A look at the research issues. *Journal of Research on Computing in Education, 22*, 431-441.
Iuppa, N. (1988). *Advanced interactive video design*. White Plains, NY: Knowledge Industry Publ.
Johnson, R. T., Johnson, D. W., & Stanne, M. B. (1985). Effects of cooperative, competitive and individualistic goal structures on computer-assisted instruction. *Journal of Educational Psychology 77*(6), 668-677.
Jonassen, D. M. (1987). Assessing cognitive structure: Verifying a method using pattern notes. *Journal of Research and Development in Education, 20*(3), 1-13.
Jonassen, D. H. & Wang, S. (1991, February). *Conveying structural knowledge in hypertext knowledge bases*. Paper presented at the annual meeting of the Association for Educational Communications and Technology, Orlando, FL.
Kerr, S. T. (1986). Instructional text: The transition from page to screen. *Visible Language, 20*(4), 368-392.
Klatzky, R. L. (1980). *Human memory: Structure and processes* (2nd ed.). New York: W. H. Freeman.
Kosslyn, S. M. (1981). The medium and the message in mental imagery: A theory. *Psychological Review, 88*, 46-66.
Laurel, B. (1990). Interface agents: Metaphors with character. In: B. Laurel (Ed.), *The art of human-computer interface design* (pp. 355-365). Reading, MA: Addison-Wesley.
Laurel, B. (1991). *Computers as theater*. Reading, MA: Addison-Wesley.
Lawler, R. W. & Yazdani, M. (1987). *Artificial intelligence and education*. Norwood, NJ: Ablex.
Levy, S. (1984). *Hackers: Heroes of the computer revolution*. New York: Doubleday.
Lidwell, W., Palumbo, D., Troutman, T., &, Hobbins, W. (1991, August). *A new*

computer-based learning environment: The hypermedia-assisted knowledge construction system. Paper presented at the International Conference on the Learning Sciences, Chicago, IL.

Locatis, C., Letourneau, G., & Banvard, R. (1989). Hypermedia and instruction. *Educational Technology Research and Development, 37*(4), 65-77.

Martindale, C. (1991). *Cognitive psychology: A neural-network approach.* Pacific Grove, CA: Brooks/Cole.

Millennium Software (1989). *HyperX* [Computer program]. Laguna Beach, CA: Millennium Software.

Minsky, M. (1986). *The society of mind.* New York: Simon & Schuster.

Neisser, U. (1981). John Dean's memory: A case study. *Cognition, 9*,1-22.

Nelson, T. H. (1981). *Literary machines.* Swathmore, PA: Author.

Nelson, W. A. (1991a, April). *Effects of prior knowledge and task characteristics on information access in hypertext documents.* Paper presented at the annual meeting of the American Educational Research Association. Chicago, IL.

Nelson, W. A. (1991b, August). *Learner modeling for intelligent hypermedia environments.* Paper presented at the International Conference on the Learning Sciences, Evanston, IL.

Nelson, W. A. & Palumbo, D. B. (1992). Learning, instruction, and hypermedia. *Journal of Educational Multimedia and Hypermedia, 1*(3), 287-299.

Norman, D. A. (1976). *Studies in learning and self-contained education systems,* 1973-1976 (Technical Report Number 7601). Washington: Office of Naval Research, Advanced Research Project Agency.

Norman, D. A. (1982). *Learning and memory.* New York: W. H. Freeman.

Novak, J. D. (1990). Concept maps and Vee diagrams: Two metacognitive tools to facilitate meaningful learning. *Instructional Science, 19*, 1-25.

Oren, T., Salomen, G., Kreitman, K., & Don, A. (1990). Guides: Characterizing the interface. In: B. Laurel (Ed.), *The art of human-computer interface design* (pp. 367-381). Reading, MA: Addison-Wesley.

Paivio, A. (1986). *Mental representations: A dual coding approach.* Oxford: Oxford University Press.

Papert, S. (1980). *Mindstorms: Children, computers and powerful ideas.* New York: Basic Books.

Pylyshyn, Z. (1981). The imagery debate: Analogue media versus tacit knowledge. *Psychological Review, 88*,16-45.

Raskin, J. (1987). The hype in hypertext: A critique. *Hypertext '87 Proceedings* (pp. 325-330). New York: ACM Press.

Raybould, B. (1990). Solving human performance problems with computers. *Performance and Instruction, 29*(10), 4-14.

Rewey, K. L., Dansereau, D. F., Skaggs, L. P., Hall, R. H., & Pitre, U. (1989). Effects of scripted cooperation and knowledge maps on the processing of technical material. *Journal of Educational Psychology, 81*, 604-609.

Rumelhart, D. E. (1977). *Introduction to human information processing.* New York: John Wiley & Sons.

Scardmalia, M. (1991). An architecture for the social construction of knowledge.

In: L. Birnbaum (Ed.), *Proceedings of the International Conference on the Learning Sciences* (p. 397). Charlottesville, VA: Association for the Advancement of Computers in Education.

Schank, R. & Abelson, R. (1977). *Scripts, plans, goals and understanding*. Hillsdale, NJ: Erlbaum.

Schank, R. & Riesbeck, C. (1989). *Inside case-based reasoning*. Hillsdale, NJ: Erlbaum.

Schrage, M. (1990). *Shared minds*. New York: Random House.

Schwartz, R. & Reisberg, D. (1991). *Learning and memory*. New York: W. W. Norton.

Shavelson, R. J. (1972). Some aspects of the correspondence between content structure and cognitive structure in physics instruction. *Journal of Educational Psychology, 63*, 225-234.

Shepard, R. N. & Metzler, J. (1971). Mental rotation of three-dimensional objects. *Science*, 171, 701-703.

Spiro, R. J., Coulson, R. L., Feltovich, P. J. & Anderson, D. K. (1988). *Cognitive flexibility theory: Advanced knowledge acquisition in ill-structured domains* (Report No. 441). Champaign, IL: University of Illinois, Center for the Study of Reading.

Spiro, R. J. & Jehng, J. C. (1990). Cognitive flexibility and hypertext: Theory and technology for the nonlinear and multidimensional traversal of complex subject matter. In: D. Nix & R. J. Spiro (Eds.), *Cognition, education, and multimedia: Exploring ideas in high technology* (pp. 163-205). Hillsdale, NJ: Erlbaum.

Stefik, M., Foster, G., Bobrow, D. G., Kahn, K., Lanning, S., & Suchman, L. (1988). Beyond the chalkboard: Computer support for collaboration and problem solving in meetings. *Communications of the ACM, 30*(1), 32-47.

Thompson, B. & Thompson, W. (1986). Finding rules in data. *Byte, 12*(11), 149-158.

Trollip, S. R. & Lippert, R. C. (1987). Constructing knowledge bases: A promising instructional tool. *Journal of Computer-Based Instruction, 14*, 44-48.

Vertelney, H. (1990). An environment for collaboration. In: B. Laurel (Ed.), *The art of human-computer interface design* (pp. 161-170). Reading, MA: Addison-Wesley.

Vickery, B. C. (1986). Knowledge representation: a brief review. *Journal of Documentation, 42*(3), 145-159.

Vygotsky, L. (1962). *Thought and language*. Cambridge, MA: MIT Press.

West, C. K., Farmer, J. A., & Wolff, P. M. (1990). *Instructional design: Implications from cognitive science*. Englewood Cliffs, NJ: Prentice-Hall.

Yankelovich, N., Landow, G., & Heywood, P. (1987). *Designing hypermedia ideabases: The Intermedia experience* (IRIS Technical Report 87-4). Providence, RI: Brown University.

Herman G. Weller
Judi Repman
Gene E. Rooze

The Relationship of Learning, Behavior, and Cognitive Style in Hypermedia-Based Instruction: Implications for Design of HBI

INTRODUCTION

In the past two decades, developments in electronic technology have facilitated the production of several types of interactive teaching tools: computer-assisted instruction, interactive videotape/disc, simulations and microworlds, intelligent tutoring systems, multimedia, and hypermedia. However, in many instances, electronic technology has outdistanced instructional design processes to the extent that instructional designs and techniques have been mere reactions to the developing technology.

Proponents of the electronic teaching tools have hailed their interactivity as allowing the learner to become an active participant in learning, adjusting the instruction to conform to his or her needs and capabilities.

HERMAN G. WELLER is Assistant Professor, College of Education, University of Maine, Orono, ME 04469-5766.
JUDI REPMAN and GENE E. ROOZE are Assistant Professors, College of Education, Texas Tech University, Lubbock, TX 79409-1071.

[Haworth co-indexing entry note]: "The Relationship of Learning, Behavior, and Cognitive Style in Hypermedia-Based Instruction: Implications for Design of HBI." Weller, Herman G., Judi Repman, and Gene E. Rooze. Co-published simultaneously in *Computers in the Schools* (The Haworth Press, Inc.) Vol. 10, No. 3/4, 1994, pp. 401-420; and: *Multimedia and Megachange: New Roles for Educational Computing* (eds: W. Michael Reed, John K. Burton, and Min Liu) The Haworth Press, Inc., 1994, pp. 401-420. Multiple copies of this article/chapter may be purchased from The Haworth Document Delivery Center [1-800-3-HAWORTH; 9:00 a.m. - 5:00 p.m. (EST)].

The components of human-computer interactivity have been described (e.g., Weller, 1988) as the quantity and quality of the interactions; branching; learner control of display time, pausing and menu access, and sequencing of instructional events; action on the learner's responses; ease of operation; and readability. Three types of interactivity, *reactive, interactive*, and *proactive*, have been discussed by Lucas (1992) in terms of their appropriateness with regard to learner characteristics and instructional goals. With *reactive* interactivity, such as drill-and-practice programs, learners may be required simply to press the space bar to advance a computer program. With *interactive* interactivity, learners branch through a program based on their responses to questions posed by the computer. In *proactive* interactivity, learners function as decision-makers, constructing and deducing principles from their actions and experiences.

Upon close scrutiny the interactivity provided by modern electronic teaching tools appears to be a *generic* interactivity, providing a great deal of control and branching possibilities to all users, regardless of whether their cognitive styles make them more or less able to utilize and learn via this interactivity. Perhaps the potential mismatch between the user's cognitive style and the software's interactivity is best highlighted by a more recent electronic instructional tool, hypermedia. Hypermedia can represent knowledge in several different forms, and hypermedia-based instruction (HBI) apparently does not conform to any one informational and instructional model (Jonassen, 1991). Designers of (HBI) environments apparently "assume that users with abilities to select information, make connections with existing knowledge, organize their approach to accomplishing tasks, and monitor the process, will be those who can perform effectively in the type of self-regulated environment of a hypermedia system" (Gay, Trumbull, & Mazur, 1991, p. 190). However, very little investigation has been carried out on the interaction of various learner traits with aspects of the hypermedia environment.

The authors' research on learning in an HBI environment (Repman, Rooze, & Weller, 1991) indicates that students with different cognitive styles, specifically field dependence/field independence, are *served differently* by hypermedia-based instruction. In fact, the present study shows that the relation between the students' information-accessing behavior with HBI and their measured cognitive style tends to be the opposite for field independent students and field dependent students. In this paper, we will discuss our (a) development of HBI software that allows the student to study computer ethics in an interactive fashion, and (b) research on learning as a function of the student's cognitive style, with different versions of the software incorporating various instructional components.

Hypermedia-Based Instructional Environments

Hypermedia is a nonlinear informational database with tools for selecting information from the database for presentation to the user. The basic node and link structure of hypermedia allows users to access text, images, and sound in a way that differs greatly from software based on a linear, page-turning approach to information (Hooper, 1990). Kozma (1991, p. 204) notes that "Hypermedia environments are designed to help the reader build links among texts and other symbolic expressions and construct meaning based on these relationships."

Two important hypotheses have been posed concerning hypermedia-based learning environments. First, proponents claim that because these systems model the structure of human memory, they can serve as powerful cognitive amplifiers or cognition enhancers (Dede, 1987; Marchionini, 1988). Second, it has been suggested that hypermedia-based instructional systems promote a higher level of student involvement with instructional content. It has been postulated that students learning with HBI should be actively exploring knowledge-level and conceptual information in an environment that promotes the development of decision-making and problem-solving skills (Marchionini, 1988). It has been proposed that this kind of active involvement of students with a subject matter will lead learners to create their own relationships between ideas, thereby facilitating remembering, concept formation, and greater comprehension of subject matter (Kearsley, 1988). However, as Icarus is supposed to have discovered in his tragic mythological attempt at flight (Bulfinch, 1898, p. 199), to simply model natural phenomena does not guarantee that the model will be an effective tool.

Individual Learners and HBI

A variety of problems have been associated with students learning in HBI environments. Disorientation, or becoming lost, in a new and nonlinear learning environment appears to be a common phenomenon among novice users of HBI systems (Gay, Trumbull, & Mazur, 1991; Jonassen, 1991; Marchionini, 1988). Disorientation may result from the quantity of information available (information overload) or the design and structure of the database (Jonassen, 1991; Marchionini, 1988). Given the considerable amounts of both interactivity and information available with typical HBI, as well as the problems associated with this level of learner self-regulation and direction, it is apparent that research must be conducted to permit educators to make informed decisions concerning "whether it is possible or necessary to make HAI [hypermedia-assisted instruction] useful or available to all types of learners" (Heller, 1990, p. 437).

Ginsburg and Zelman (1988) have pointed out that the role of individual differences in technologically-based learning environments has often been overlooked. Research into the extreme example of individual differences, the novice-expert dichotomy, has indicated that, in a variety of subject areas, differences in performance are often the result of differences in factual as well as procedural knowledge (Shuell, 1986). HBI units can be structured to provide novice learners access to a variety of information falling within both realms of knowledge. For factual knowledge, definitions and more detailed explanations of terms might be obtained by clicking on terms that the student does not understand. For procedural knowledge, descriptions of certain procedures or processes could be obtained by clicking on mnemonic icons. Novice learners may also be assisted by employing such principles of instructional design as the provision of advance organizers and graphical organizers. These organizers could be in the form of maps in the HBI software (Heller, 1990; Jonassen, 1991; Kearsley, 1988). Unfortunately, there is very little research to date indicating whether all students are able to take advantage of such "special" features; notably lacking is research on learning as a function of such individual differences as cognitive style (Heller, 1990).

Teaching Computer Ethics via HBI

To investigate some of these questions raised in the literature concerning learning in hypermedia environments (outlined in the previous section), we decided to develop several versions of an HBI stack, each containing a different "special" feature as a possible learning enhancer. The topic of computer ethics was selected for the stack for several reasons (Weller, Repman, Rooze, & Parker, 1992). First, the necessity that students become aware of ethical issues associated with computing is being increasingly recognized. Second, little success in teaching computer ethics has been found for instructional approaches that revolve around the "preaching" of rules and regulations (Bear, 1986; Gilliland & Pollard, 1984; Hannah & Matus, 1984; Troutner, 1986). In contrast to a "preaching" (or lecturing) learning environment, HBI enables students to investigate complex ethical issues at a pace of their own choosing. Also, in the present case, HBI allowed the student to "experience" the consequences of his or her actions in an environment that was nonthreatening in the sense that the student was not required to speak up in class. Third, the complexity of computer ethics allowed us to develop a coherent, content-rich stack. Finally, there was an available pool of middle school students in our school district who were required to study computer ethics and who could help us with our research. Computer ethics is a required component of the district's eighth-grade computer literacy courses, and district computer education personnel graciously allowed us to try out our software with students in actual learning situations.

The *Computer Ethics Stack* includes several scenarios in which students are involved in making ethical decisions concerning computer use (see Hannah and Matus, 1984, and Gilliland and Pollard, 1984, for discussions of these, and similar, computer ethics scenarios). These scenarios involve decisions such as whether one should engage in computer crime, and whether one should allow unethical activities to continue after observing them. Each scenario includes several stories told from a different character's viewpoint. At any point during a scenario, students are able to access explanations of key terms (for example, see Figure 1). Several versions of this software were created to enable us to investigate the research questions described in the Method Section of this paper.

Field Dependent Learners versus Field Independent Learners

Field dependence/field independence, which has become one of the most commonly used measures of cognitive style, is a measure of how well a learner is able to restructure information based on the use of salient cues and field arrangement. Research results (Witkin, Moore, Goodenough, & Cox, 1977) have indicated that field dependent learners are less likely to impose a meaningful organization on a field that lacks structure and are less able to learn conceptual material when cues are not available. In an investigation of children's use of a computer-based concept lesson (Carrier, Davidson, Higson, & Williams, 1984), field dependent students frequently failed to take advantage of learner control in selecting options. Given the lack of structure, as well as the volume of information available in typical hypermedia-based learning environments, it is likely that field dependence/ field independence has an important relationship with student achievement in HBI.

RESEARCH QUESTIONS

The authors' research questions for this study were (a) Does cognitive style interact with the use of *advance organizers* in the hypermedia instruction to affect student learning? (b) Does cognitive style interact with the use of *structural organizers* in the hypermedia instruction to affect student

FIGURE 1. Ethical-decision scenario screen for the *theft of goods and services* type of computer crime. Students may access concept information by clicking on any of the buttons

Theft of goods & services: Story 1 **Message about Answer B**

Refusing to use **fraud** , as Mr. Bumstead has suggested, is really the only ethical thing for Margo to do. The consequences for her may be unpleasant, but that's what it is like in the real world. Just because you stand for what is right doesn't mean everybody will like it. That's just the price you must pay to maintain your **honesty**

The "real world" of business has many people who are willing to use **theft** or **embezzlement** or **sabotage** in order to get ahead. Also, it seems like someone is dumping a new computer **virus** onto society every day or so. Probably most of these lawbreakers will not ever be convicted of a **felony**, or even a **misdemeanor**. Even after a complete **audit** of a company's business the person who did wrong is not always discovered. For example, well over $100 million is stolen from financial institutions every year, but only about 15% of the cases are ever reported.

Click on the buttons to investigate each concept.

learning? (c) Does cognitive style interact with gender with the hypermedia instruction to affect student learning? and (d) Does cognitive style affect learner navigation through the hypermedia instruction?

METHOD

Sample

Thirty-three eighth-grade students enrolled in computer literacy courses at two public junior high schools in a medium-sized southwestern city were selected for the different versions of the computer ethics HBI software. Every student in the school district is required to take a semester-long course in computer literacy, including a unit on computer ethics. Students spend one class period daily in a computer room equipped with Apple Macintosh computers. At the time of the study, the students had not begun the study of computer ethics in their textbook. They were familiar with the operation of the Macintosh and with the creation of stacks with Apple *HyperCard*. Students were randomly assigned to one of four versions of the HBI software to control for differences between students in prior knowledge, as well as other history and maturation differences.

Instrumentation

As a measure of cognitive style, each student was administered, as a pretest, the Group Embedded Figures Test (GEFT) published by Consulting Psychologists Press, Palo Alto, California (1971). On the GEFT, each student is allowed a limited amount of time to locate and trace simple figures hidden within complex figures. The range of scores is 0-18, with higher scores indicating a greater degree of field independence. The GEFT has been used in a variety of research studies to assess field independence/dependence. A reliability coefficient of 0.82 has been computed for the GEFT, based on administration of parallel forms of the test (Witkin, Oltman, Raskin, & Karp, 1971). For purposes of the present study, students were classified into three groups based on their GEFT scores: field independent (GEFT > 12; $n = 8$), indeterminate (GEFT 9-12; $n = 5$), and field dependent (GEFT < 9; $n = 20$).

Development of the HBI Software, *Computer Ethics Stack*

Design of the HBI Software. In the development of instructional software, principles of instructional design dictate that one follow, as much as economic and political constraints will allow, the dictum that instructional goals should be specified before the software and hardware are chosen (Jonassen, 1985). In the present case, practical considerations decided the hardware and hypermedia software choices. The computer ethics topic was chosen for the authors' research unit in consultation with the city's computer coordinator and the computer teachers at two junior high schools with Macintosh microcomputer labs. Our hypermedia software was developed with Apple *HyperCard*, version 1.2, for the Macintosh computer.

Our design procedures were a combination of research considerations (r) and instructional software design considerations (i). These procedures were, in the approximate chronological order in which they occurred: specifying the research objectives (r), assessing our instructional intentions and the needs of the students (i), specifying the instructional content of the HBI software (i), determining the instructional actions of the software and the intended learning actions that the software would elicit from the students (i, r), deciding how we would evaluate the student learning and the HBI instruction (i, r), and determining how we would analyze the feedback on student use of the software and student learning (r).

Instructional Intentions. Our instructional intentions were to involve the students in the learning of computer ethics in a nonthreatening environment where they could examine ethically difficult situations from the viewpoint of different participants in each situation, make decisions as to the best action to be taken by each participant, and experience the consequences of each decision.

Needs of the Students. Because of the research nature of this study, all the students were presented with the same *core HBI*. All versions of the HBI contained the same basic instructions for program use and the same scenarios describing situations in which persons had to make ethical decisions concerning computer crime. Students could access the instructions at any point during the program. The language of the software was designed to be appropriate for the reading ability of an average eighth-grade student and the plots of the instructional scenarios were designed to interest this student.

Instructional Content of the HBI Software. The hypermedia instruction considered four types of computer crime: software piracy, invasion of privacy, theft of information, and theft of goods and services. Various concepts deemed important for understanding each type of crime were used in the text of screens that examined consequences for choices of alternative actions for each computer crime. These concepts were defined on concept clarification screens that the student could access. For example, the concepts for *piracy* were piracy, copyrights, patents, copy-protection, backup copy, public domain software, and shareware; and for *theft of goods and services* were theft, fraud, embezzlement, audit, sabotage, virus, misdemeanor, felony, and honesty.

Instructional Actions of the Software. The software presented scenarios in which characters had to react to computer crime by making ethical decisions: (a) whether to take part in computer crime, and (b) whether to allow the activity to continue after having observed it. For each of the four types of computer crime, there were two or three stories, each told from a different character's viewpoint. For each alternative decision that the student chose for a character, there followed a screen (*consequences screen*) that discussed the possible consequences, for the character, of making that choice. The student could click on any of several important computer-literacy terms in each consequences screen, to obtain a concept screen that explained that term.

Interactivity was varied through the use of HBI versions that contained or omitted features (advance and/or structural organizers) designed to facilitate the student's organization and branching capabilities. The *advance organizer* version of the software presented, in addition to the basic instructions: (a) a screen (*1-4 screen*) listing brief descriptions of the four types of computer crime (Figure 2), and (b) a map that showed schematically the branches of the entire program (Figure 3). The map could not be accessed again after the student had left the instructions for the first time. The core scenarios were included. At the top of each scenario, consequence discussion and concept definition screen, this HBI version exhibited a title (*location title*) that situated the screen with respect to scenario and type of computer crime.

The instructions of the *structural organizer* version of the HBI contained, in addition to the core instructions, a description and example of use of the map. The student could access the map from any screen. However, there was no *1-4 screen* in the instructions. The core scenarios were included, with *location titles*.

The *no advance organizer* version also included the core instructions, but the instructions contained no map or *1-4 screen*. This version contained the core scenarios, with *location titles*. The *no structural organizer* version included the core instructions, but the instructions contained no map or *1-4 screen*. The core scenarios were included, with no *location titles*.

Intended Student Learning Actions. The software was designed to provide the learner with many opportunities for branching to access more information. In all cases, branching was effected by the learner with a mouseclick on a *HyperCard* button. After reading the instructions and arriving at the menu (Figure 4), the student could quit the program, access the instructions again, or select one of four types of computer crime

FIGURE 2. The list in the instructions section of brief descriptions of the four types of computer crime dealt with by the program serves as an *advance organizer*

Four of the biggest ethical concerns for computer users:

1. **Making illegal copies of software--"software piracy."**

2. **Accessing private information about people, businesses and other organizations, without their permission--"privacy."**

3. **Using a computer to steal money, valuable items, or human services--"theft of goods and services."**

4. **Using a computer to gain access to individual or company secrets that cost them money and time to get--"theft of information."**

FIGURE 3. The map showing schematically the branches of the entire program and indicating the student's current location serves as a *structural organizer*

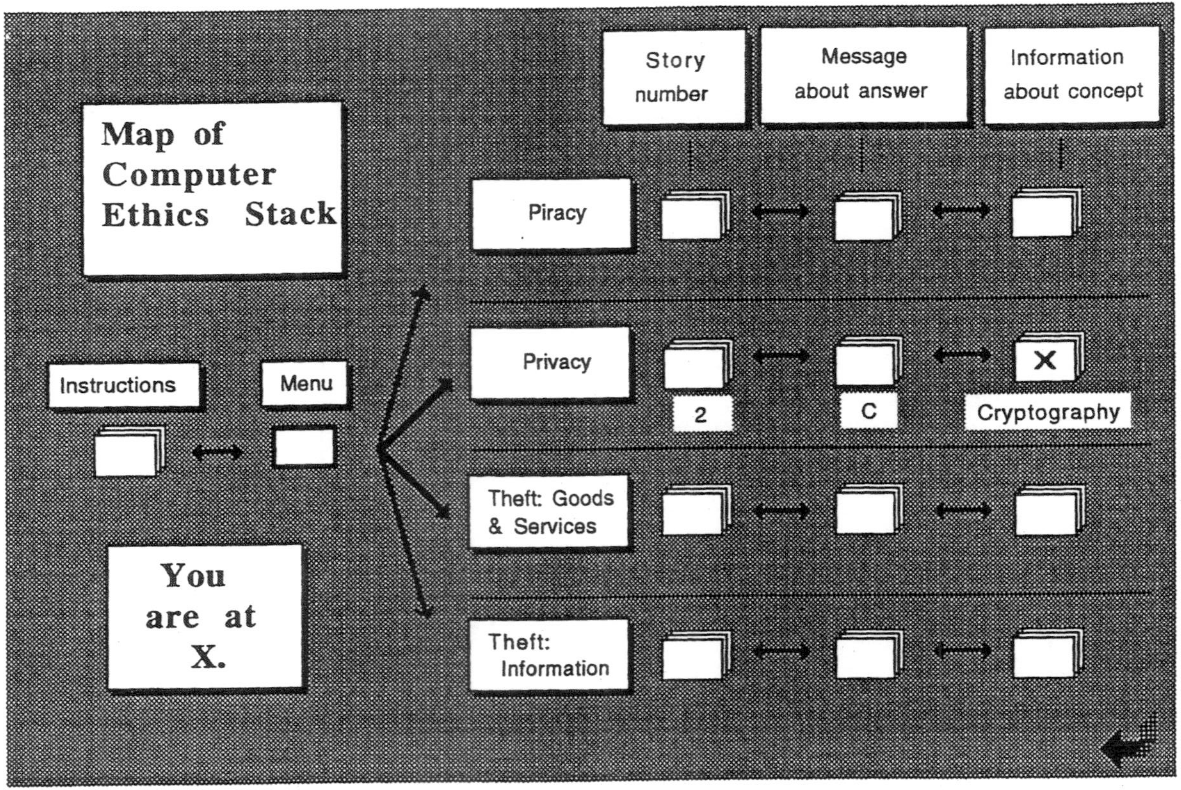

FIGURE 4. The menu for the hypermedia software shows the four types of computer ethics considerations dealt with by the program

(piracy, privacy, theft of goods and services, or theft of information). Selection of a crime type brought the student to story 1 for that type, in which a character was involved in a situation where he or she had to make a difficult ethical decision involving computer crime. The student could then return to the menu, access story 2 for that type of crime, or choose any one of three alternative actions for that character. Selection of an alternative action brought the student to a *consequences screen* concerning that character's action. While reading the consequences, the student could access the meaning of any of the important computer-literacy terms that were highlighted. The student had similar choices for story 2 and story 3.

Evaluation of Student Learning. As a measure of learning via the *Computer Ethics* HBI software, each student was administered a 20-item paper-and-pencil posttest on the lesson information, immediately following completion of the lesson. The posttest measured knowledge of computer ethics concepts and application of that knowledge.

Evaluation of HBI Instruction. A comparison was made of student learning (as demonstrated by the posttest) with both (a) the components of the student's HBI version, and (b) the student's cognitive style (as measured by the GEFT). This was to determine whether optimal learning occurred as a function of both field independence/field dependence and the presence/absence of a type of learning organizer. A determination was also made of the existence of any influence of gender on learning from the HBI.

Analysis of the Data

Computer audits of the pathways of the students through the software were compared with the students' cognitive styles and learning (posttest scores). Correlations were calculated between information-accessing frequency, cognitive style, and learning. Student pathways were analyzed for existence of patterns characteristic of field independent students or field dependent students.

Data Collection Function in the HBI Software. For each user, the HBI software recorded every mouseclick, calculated subtotals of mouseclicks for information categories, and displayed this information for the researcher on a data screen (Figure 5). No keystrokes were made. In a row in the upper left portion of the data screen, the total times that the student had accessed Instructions, the Map, and the Menu were shown.

Below these totals, an answer-frequency matrix appeared with the number of times the student had accessed each scenario (column *S*), and the access frequencies for answers A, B, or C for each scenario (columns *A*, *B*, and *C*). Each scenario was represented in the left column of the matrix by initials, e.g., PR1 is the first story for *computer piracy*, PV2 is the second

FIGURE 5. Blank data-collection screen used to tally and subtotal the user's mouseclicks

Record

Instructions 21 Map 1 Menu 2

Answers

	S	A	B	C	Total Answers
PR1	1	1	0	0	1
PR2	0	0	0	0	0
PR3	0	0	0	0	0
PV1	1	0	1	0	1
PV2	0	0	0	0	0
PV3	0	0	0	0	0
T$1	0	0	0	0	0
T$2	0	0	0	0	0
T$3	0	0	0	0	0
TI1	0	0	0	0	0
TI2	0	0	0	0	0
TI3	0	0	0	0	0
Total	2	1	0	0	2

	1	2	3	Total Answers
PR	1	0	0	1
PV	1	0	0	1
T$	0	0	0	0
TI	0	0	0	0
Total	2	0	0	2

Ethics Concepts:

Piracy 0
Copyrights 0
Patents 0
Copy-protection 1
Backup copy 0
Public domain software 0
Shareware 0
TOTAL PIRacy 1

Confidential records 0
Electronic mail 0
Password 0
Cryptography 0
Right to privacy 0
Right to know 0
and so forth

Path

White Card
Instructions 1
Instructions 2
Instructions 3
Instructions 4
and so forth

story for *computer privacy,* T$2 is the second story for *theft of goods and services,* and TI3 is the third story for *theft of information.* The *Total Answers* (*A* + *B* + *C*) for each scenario were shown in the right-hand column of the matrix. Along the bottom of this matrix, the total mouse-clicks for each column were shown.

In the lower left portion of the data screen, a concept-frequency matrix appeared with a summary of the number of times the student had accessed the first (column *1*), second (column *2*), or third (column *3*) scenario of type computer piracy (*PR*), computer privacy (*PV*), theft of goods and services (*T$*), and theft of information (*TI*). The *Total Answers* (*1* + *2* + *3*) for each type of scenario were shown in the right-hand column of the matrix. Along the bottom of this matrix, the total mouseclicks for each column were shown.

In the upper right portion of the data screen, the number of times that the student had accessed definitions of each ethics concept appeared. The researcher could scroll down to see the complete list. Subtotals were shown for the times that the student had accessed the piracy, privacy, theft of goods, and theft of information concepts. In the lower right portion of the data screen appeared the *audit* (every mouseclick) of the student's pathway through the software. Again, the researcher could scroll down to see the complete list.

RESULTS AND DISCUSSION

Interaction of Learner Cognitive Style and HBI Component

Field independent students learned computer ethics via the hypermedia software more effectively than did field dependent students. For the 28 students who could be classified as either field independent or field dependent, the Pearson *r* correlation between their posttest scores and their GEFT scores was moderately high ($r = 0.69$, $p < 0.01$). Inspection of the student groups and the HBI software versions they used (Table 1) showed that field independent students learned more effectively than did field dependent students (a) regardless of whether or not advance organizers were present and (b) regardless of whether or not structural organizers were present.

TABLE 1. Mean Posttest Results for Each Student Group

Cognitive Style	Software Version	Number in Group	Group Mean	Standard Deviation
field indep.	no structural organizer	4	13.5	2.6
field indep.	advance organizer	2	13.5	0.7
field indep.	no advance organizer	2	11.5	3.5
field dep.	no structural organizer	3	11.0	3.5
field dep.	advance organizer	5	9.0	2.7
field dep.	no advance organizer	6	7.5	2.5
field dep.	structural organizer	6	7.0	1.6

The groups of field dependent students learned with various effectiveness, as evidenced by their posttest means. The learning of the groups of field dependent students varied with the types of software enhancement included. However, the highest scores for field dependent students occurred when they used the software containing no structural organizer.

Gender, Achievement, and Learner Cognitive Style

For the 28 students who could be classified as either field independent or field dependent, there were (a) thirteen boys and seven girls in the field dependent group, and (b) six boys and two girls in the field independent group.

When all 28 students were considered together, there was no significant correlation (Pearson $r = 0.11, p = 0.56$) between gender and GEFT score. There was also no noticeable correlation ($r = 0.09$, $p = 0.64$) between gender and posttest score. When the field independent students were considered separately, there was no correlation between gender and GEFT score ($r = 0.00, p = 1.00$), and negligible correlation between gender and posttest score ($r = -0.10, p = 0.84$). Similarly, when the field dependent students were considered separately, there was no significant correlation between gender and GEFT score ($r = 0.09, p = 0.71$), and between gender and posttest score ($r = -0.06, p = 0.81$).

Learner Pathways Through the Software

Tracking the sequence of mouseclicks making up each student's pathway through the HBI software showed that the ways of seeking information (via question-answering and accessing of concept explanations) tended to be different for field dependent students than for field independent students. The manners of seeking information were dispersed in opposite fashion among field dependent students and among field independent students. Also, the relation of the student's cognitive style to the frequency at which he or she accessed information nodes during the hypermedia instruction tended to depend on whether the student could be classified as field independent or field dependent.

Information-Seeking Behaviors Are Dispersed Differently

The mouseclick audits showed that the ways that field independent students sought information were dispersed in an opposite manner than were the ways of field dependent students. The average number of times that a field dependent student answered questions (M = 14.3, SD = 5.3) was almost identical to the average number of questions for a field independent student (M = 14.0, SD = 4.3). The dispersion in the numbers of questions answered among field dependent students (variance = 27.6) was 1.5 times greater than the dispersion among field independent students (variance = 18.1). The average number of times that a field dependent student accessed concept explanations (M = 16.2, SD = 10.0) was nearly equal to the average number of concepts for a field independent student (M = 15.4, SD = 12.6). In contrast to the pattern for answers, the dispersion in the numbers of concepts accessed among field independent students (variance = 157.9) was 1.5 times greater than the dispersion among field dependent students (variance = 99.2).

It is illustrative to compare mouseclick audits for two students who typify the field independent group with those for two students who typify the field dependent group. Carla and Jerry had the second and third highest GEFT scores, respectively; Hal and Karen had the thirtieth and thirty-first highest GEFT scores [actual names are not used]. Carla and Jerry obtained the second and fifth highest scores, respectively, of all the students on the posttest. On the HBI software, they answered almost the average number of questions (16 and 13, respectively). However, Carla accessed over three times as many concept explanations (18) as did Jerry (5). Carla accessed the "deepest" information level several times while studying scenarios for each of the four types of computer crime (*piracy*, 8; *privacy*, 2; *theft of goods and services*, 4; and *theft of information*, 4). Jerry accessed the "deepest" information level sparingly and for only three types of computer crime (*piracy*, 2; *privacy*, 2; and *theft of goods and services*, 1).

Hal and Karen obtained the 14th and 17th highest scores, respectively, on the posttest. On the HBI software, Hal answered a below-average number of questions (10) and Karen answered a moderately above-average number of questions (18). They both accessed above-average numbers of concept explanations (22 and 21). Hal accessed the "deepest" information level several times, but only for three types of computer crime (*piracy*, 8; *privacy*, 8; *theft of goods and services*, 6). Karen accessed the "deepest" information level several times, but only for two types of computer crime (*theft of goods and services*, 4; *theft of information*, 17).

Relation of Cognitive Style to Information-Accessing Frequency

Although only one correlation between student cognitive style and frequency of accessing information was significant at $p \leq 0.10$, the trend of the correlations showed that this relation tended to depend on whether the student could be classified as field dependent or field independent.

When the field independent students were considered separately, there were moderately low positive correlations (a) between their GEFT scores and the total number of questions they answered (Pearson $r = 0.44$, $p = 0.28$), (b) between their GEFT scores and the total number of concept explanations they accessed ($r = 0.30$, $p = 0.46$), and (c) between their GEFT scores and the total number of answers plus concept explanations accessed ($r = 0.43$, $p = 0.29$). In contrast, when the field dependent students were considered separately, there were moderately low negative correlations (a) between their GEFT scores and the total number of questions they answered (Pearson $r = -0.31$, $p = 0.18$), (b) between their GEFT scores and the total number of concept explanations they accessed (Pearson $r = -0.31, p = 0.19$), and (c) between their GEFT scores and the total number of answers plus concept explanations accessed (Pearson $r = -0.38, p = 0.10$).

Thus, the higher the scores of the field independent students on the GEFT test, the more information nodes they tended to access in the HBI. In contrast, the higher the GEFT scores of the field dependent students, the smaller the number of information nodes they tended to access. These dissimilar relationships between cognitive style and HBI information-accessing behavior of the two groups of students suggest that the effectiveness of learning with HBI depends upon cognitive style. The low correlations between student cognitive style and frequency of accessing information suggest that other dimensions of cognitive style, perhaps impulsivity or risk-taking tendency, may be important as a function of the field independence/field dependence of the learner while he or she operates in a hypermedia environment. The limited numbers of students involved in the present study made significant correlations difficult to obtain and limited our focus on cognitive style to field independence/field dependence. To look more closely at the relationship between cognitive style and learning from HBI, we have initiated a follow-up study with a larger number of students.

CONCLUSIONS

The present study indicates that hypermedia-based instruction may not *serve* all learners equally well. Our investigation suggests that HBI may allow study of information in such a way that the effectiveness of learning depends upon a learner's cognitive style. Field dependent learners did not learn as effectively as did field independent learners. There were differences in the relations between the manners of accessing HBI information and the measures of the students' cognitive styles. Further research needs to be done to determine whether HBI that provides *proactive* interactivity, as did our *Computer Ethics* stack, may allow too much control and/or decision making for students with certain cognitive styles. Would it be more beneficial for all students for hypermedia software to diagnose the user's cognitive style, and then to provide *reactive* or *interactive* interactivity during instructional segments for learners whose cognitive styles may enable less effective learning with *proactive* interactivity?

This investigation also indicates that different organizing components of HBI may facilitate the learning of only those students with certain cognitive styles. When students studied with our *Computer Ethics* hypermedia stack, there was an interaction between cognitive style and HBI organizing component. Not only did field independent students learn more effectively than field dependent students, the learning of field dependent students varied with the types of software enhancement included. Similarly, the learning of field independent students varied with the types of software enhancement included. This finding leads to a question that is an extension of the one posed previously. When using hypermedia software, would it also be more beneficial to first diagnose the user's cognitive style and then to provide organizing components during instructional segments that are appropriate for that cognitive style?

Finally, other dimensions of cognitive style may operate in conjunction with the field independence/field dependence of the learner while he or she studies in a hypermedia environment. Further research needs to be done to determine the role of such factors as impulsivity or risk-taking tendency in learning via hypermedia.

REFERENCES

Bear, G. G. (1986). Teaching computer ethics: Why, what, who, when, and how. *Computers in the Schools, 3*(2), 113-118.

Bulfinch, T. (1898). *The age of fable.* (rev. ed.). Philadelphia: David McKay.

Carrier, C., Davidson, G., Higson, V., & Williams, M. (1984). Selection of options by field independent and dependent children in a computer-based concept lesson. *Journal of Computer-Based Instruction, 11*(2), 49-54.

Dede, C. J. (1987). Empowering environments, hypermedia and microworlds. *The Computing Teacher, 15*(3), 20-24.

Gay, G., Trumbull, D., & Mazur, J. (1991). Designing and testing navigational strategies and guidance tools for a hypermedia program. *Journal of Educational Computing Research, 7*, 189-202.

Gilliland, K. & Pollard, M. (1984). Ethics and computer use. *The Computing Teacher, 12*(1), 19-23.

Ginsburg, H. P. & Zelman, S. (1988). Understanding individual differences in the computer age. In: G. Forman & P. B. Pufall (Eds.), *Constructivism in the computer age* (pp. 151-170). Hillsdale, NJ: Lawrence Erlbaum.

Hannah, L. S. & Matus, C. B. (1984). A question of ethics. *The Computing Teacher, 12*(1), 11-14.

Heller, R. S. (1990). The role of hypermedia in education: A look at the research issues. *Journal of Research on Computing in Education, 22*, 431-441.

Hooper, K. (1990). HyperCard: A key to educational computing. In: S. Ambron & K. Hooper (Eds.), *Learning with interactive multimedia: Developing and using multimedia tools in education* (pp. 5-25). Redmond, WA: Microsoft Press.

Jonassen, D. H. (1985). Interactive lesson designs: A taxonomy. *Educational Technology, 25*(6), 7-17.

Jonassen, D. H. (1991). Hypertext as instructional design. *Educational Technology Research and Development, 39*(1), 83-92.

Kearsley, G. (1988). Authoring considerations for hypertext. *Educational Technology, 28*(11), 21-24.

Kozma, R. B. (1991). Learning with media. *Review of Educational Research, 61*, 179-211.

Lucas, L. (1992). Interactivity: What is it and how do you use it? *Journal of Educational Multimedia and Hypermedia, 1*, 7-10.

Marchionini, G. (1988). Hypermedia and learning: Freedom and chaos. *Educational Technology, 28*(11), 8-12.

Repman, J., Rooze, G. E., & Weller, H. G. (1991). Interaction of learner cognitive style with components of hypermedia-based instruction. *HyperNEXUS: Journal of Hypermedia and Multimedia Studies, 2*(1), 30-33.

Shuell, T. J. (1986). Individual differences: Changing conceptions in research and practice. *American Journal of Education, 94*, 356-377.

Troutner, J. (1986). Teaching computer ethics. *Journal of Computers in Mathematics and Science Teaching, 5*(3), 11-12.

Weller, H. G. (1988). Interactivity in microcomputer-based instruction: Its essential components and how it can be enhanced. *Educational Technology, 28*(2), 23-27.

Weller, H. G., Repman, J., Rooze, G. E., & Parker, R. D. (1992). Students and computer ethics: An alternative to preaching. *The Computing Teacher, 20*(1), 20-22.

Witkin, H. A., Moore, C. A., Goodenough, D. R., & Cox, P. W. (1977). Field-dependent and field-independent cognitive styles and their educational implications. *Review of Educational Research, 47*, 1-64.

Witkin, H. A., Oltman, P. K., Raskin, E., & Karp, S. A. (1971). *Manual*, Palo Alto, CA: Consulting Psychologists Press.

For Product Safety Concerns and Information please contact our EU representative GPSR@taylorandfrancis.com
Taylor & Francis Verlag GmbH, Kaufingerstraße 24, 80331 München, Germany

www.ingramcontent.com/pod-product-compliance
Ingram Content Group UK Ltd.
Pitfield, Milton Keynes, MK11 3LW, UK
UKHW022208190926
475702UK00003B/252

* 9 7 8 1 5 6 0 2 4 6 9 3 0 *